High Finance in the Sixties

BEING THREE "CHAPTERS OF ERIE"
AND OTHER PAPERS

HIGH FINANCE IN THE SIXTIES

CHAPTERS FROM THE EARLY HISTORY OF THE ERIE RAILWAY BY
CHARLES FRANCIS ADAMS, JR., HENRY ADAMS ALBERT STICKNEY, GEORGE TICKNOR CURTIS AND JEREMIAH S. BLACK

EDITED, WITH AN INTRODUCTION, BY

FREDERICK C. HICKS

PROFESSOR OF LAW AND LAW LIBRARIAN
IN THE YALE SCHOOL OF LAW

KENNIKAT PRESS, INC./PORT WASHINGTON, N. Y.

HIGH FINANCE IN THE SIXTIES

Copyright 1929 by Yale University Press
Reissued in 1966 by Kennikat Press

Library of Congress Catalog Card No. 65-27118

Manufactured in the United States of America

TABLE OF CONTENTS

ILLUSTRATIONS

PREFACE

ACHAPTER OF ERIE, by Charles Francis Adams, Jr., was first published in the *North American Review* of July, 1869. In the same year it was reprinted as a pamphlet of 152 pages, in Boston, by Fields, Osgood and Company.

The book, *Chapters of Erie and Other Essays,* which grew out of this article, was made up of eight essays, three of which were by Charles Francis Adams, Jr., four by Henry Adams, and one by Francis A. Walker and Henry Adams. It was published in Boston in 1871 by James R. Osgood and Company, and was reprinted without change by Henry Holt and Company in 1886.

The present volume retains only the first three of the essays,* which relate to the Erie Railway. Those omitted have been replaced by four articles published in 1871 and 1872. While written primarily on the one hand to condemn and on the other hand to defend David Dudley Field for his connection with the Erie litigations, they constitute enlightening additional Chapters of Erie.

Although the articles were written separately, they fall into a natural sequence. In order, however, further to unify them, there have been supplied an introduction, a table of events, additional footnotes, and a selected bibliography.   F. C. H.

New Haven, Connecticut
    June 1, 1929.

---

* The omitted essays are the following:—
By Henry Adams, ''Captaine John Smith''; ''The Bank of England Restriction''; ''British Finance in 1816.''
    By Francis A. Walker and Henry Adams, ''The Legal-Tender Act.''
    By C. F. Adams, Jr., ''The Railroad System.''

High Finance in the Sixties

BEING THREE "CHAPTERS OF ERIE"
AND OTHER PAPERS

THE VANTAGE POINT

THE decade immediately following the Civil War, because of its extraordinary happenings in speculative finance and in legislative and judicial corruption, has been called the fantastic era. It was a time of organized lawlessness under the forms of law, of reckless gambling with corporate securities as tools, of panics, and of "corners" in stock and in gold. The manipulators, fearless of public opinion, unrestrained and even aided by judges, lawmakers, and executives, treated investors' money as their own to repair their fortunes or destroy those of rival operators. Stockholders were indeed adventurers as they were in English colonial companies. A mania for railroad building in a time of unstable currency, when the concept of public service was not yet developed, an unjustified reliance on competition as a means of regulation, and an easy public complacency in the presence of sharp practices, set the stage for the entrance of a group of powerful, unscrupulous men as chief actors. Some of them laid the basis for American family fortunes, great today, and all of them seeking to center financial power in themselves, contributed to the movement which led to corporate consolidations and large-scale organization.

The leading characters in the drama of real life enacted in this period were Daniel Drew, "Speculative Director"; Commodore Cornelius Vanderbilt, giving up steamboating at the age of seventy speedily to become railroad king; Jay Gould, Wizard of Wall Street; James Fisk, Napoleon of Finance; William Tweed, Tammany boss; George G. Barnard, Tweed and Erie ring judge; Joseph H. Ramsey, railroad promoter; and David Dudley Field, eminent lawyer. Minor characters were the President of the United States; his brother-in-law, Abel R. Corbin; Secretary of the Treasury George S. Boutwell; and Assistant

United States Treasurer Daniel Butterfield. The supernumeraries included railroad men, stockbrokers, gamblers, sheriffs, policemen, judges, lawyers, legislators, editors, chorus girls, and a mob of "rough, rude, and dangerous men."

So fitted by nature for narration and biography are the episodes and the characters that their temptation to modern writers has become irresistible. Yet the story will never be better told than it was nearly sixty years ago by the two brothers Adams. Their three essays have become classics which cannot be superseded. To reprint them is a better service than to rewrite them. Likewise, extensive comment would only weaken their force. They are, therefore, republished exactly as they appeared in *Chapters of Erie,* including the footnotes.

Since the three essays overlap, their relation to each other should be explained. The first, "A Chapter of Erie," covers the period from the year 1866 to the end of 1868. The story opens with Daniel Drew in complete control of the Erie Railway, of which he was treasurer. He is systematically enriching himself at the expense of the road and its stockholders. In the autumn of 1867, Commodore Vanderbilt begins operations to oust Drew and add Erie to his New York Central properties. After preliminary skirmishes in which Drew's elusive character is demonstrated, Vanderbilt sets out to buy control of Erie in the open market. Now aided by Gould and Fisk, who had joined the Erie directorate in October, 1867, Drew breaks Vanderbilt's "corner," by issuing new stock in contempt of an injunction. Fleeing from arrest, the three conspirators establish themselves at "Fort Taylor" in Jersey City; but tiring of their imprisonment, Gould, who now takes the lead, defies arrest, goes to Albany, and by dint of bribery and the withdrawal of Vanderbilt's opposition, secures the passage of an act legalizing the unauthorized issues of stock. A compromise is now arranged in which there is a distribution of the spoils of war among Vanderbilt, Drew, Gould, and Fisk; but Drew is forced out of the Erie board. Gould and Fisk, now in full control, form an alliance with the Tweed Ring, they worst Drew in a stockjobbing battle, and renew the contest with Vanderbilt, this time over the former division of spoils. The courts are the weapons of both parties. Rival receivers are appointed, injunctions and counter-injunctions are granted, and a whole network of suits is constructed. The chapter ends, in December, 1868, with Drew definitely out of Erie and no longer a financial power, with Vanderbilt forced to keep his hands from Erie, and with Gould and Fisk flushed with victory.

The two next essays, "The New York Gold Conspiracy" and "An Erie Raid," by following separate threads, carry on the story to February, 1870. Drew and Vanderbilt drop out of the narrative, but Gould and Fisk remain as chief actors.

The "Gold Conspiracy," by Henry Adams, is a particular and personal account of Gould's most daring adventure, in which he seeks to corner the gold of the country. He has control of Erie, is in alliance with the Tweed Ring, and owns a joint-stock bank to certify his checks. Having subtly influenced the national government so that the supply of gold may not be increased, and having brought Fisk's millions to his aid, his success is, nevertheless, at the last minute thwarted. The unforgetable Black Friday, September 24, 1869, is the result. Gould, however, having been warned of impending events, keeps his own counsel, sells his gold through an intermediary to the unsuspecting Fisk, and averts his own ruin at the expense of his accomplice. Yet there is no break between these two men. They are engaged in other operations which require coöperation. These are described in the third of the essays.

In "An Erie Raid," Charles Francis Adams, Jr., takes the reader back to a time just subsequent to the formation of plans for the gold conspiracy. The raid is made by the Erie Ring, under the leadership of Fisk, to get possession of the Albany and Susquehanna Railroad. This line was projected by its promoter, Joseph H. Ramsey, a strong character and doughty fighter, to connect Albany and Binghamton, and while operating as an independent local road to serve as a feeder to Erie. After seventeen years of financial struggle it is completed on January 15, 1869. It has an empty treasury, and a strong opposition to Ramsey has developed in the board of directors. The Erie Ring seeks to take advantage of this situation. The road is wanted to connect the Erie with Albany and give access to New England in competition with the New York Central. As an independent coal-carrying line, it is also an impediment to Erie's new plans for controlling vast coal regions through control of transportation facilities. The raid begins in June, 1869, when Fisk undertakes to buy up stock and voting rights from investors and municipalities along the line, in preparation for the annual election to be held on September 7, 1869. The Ramsey party secretly removes the transfer books from the Company's office. Erie judge Barnard issues injunctions and appoints receivers, while other judges duplicate his action. Fisk tries to take possession of the Albany offices and is vigorously ejected from them. A contest for the physical possession of the road ensues in which engines crash head-on, armed forces fight, and the militia is called out. The Governor of the state appoints his own agent, but, nevertheless, two annual elections are held in the same room, two sets of directors are elected, while Ramsey is arrested, and freight-car loads of rough, hired, proxy-holders vote in the sardonic presence of Erie lawyer David Dudley Field. The sequel to the raid transpires in the courts by which Ramsey finally is vindicated. But before that happens, the road is leased in perpetuity to the Hudson and Delaware Canal Company.

The two articles by Charles Francis Adams, and that by Henry, dealing with the events which have just been summarized, are remarkable for the force of their searching criticism. They are even more remarkable for their courage; for they were written and published, not years afterward, but while the action was in progress, and while all the persons whose honor was impugned were alive and powerful. The Adamses, on the side of the public, were in the thick of the fight, actors in the drama, and their articles were themselves the subject of controversy. They are historical documents of the fantastic era, fighting articles, and not muckraking products of a later time. It is important, therefore, to know just how they came to be written and published.

At the close of the Civil War, Charles Francis Adams, Jr., the elder of the two brothers, was discharged from the army with the rank of colonel. His marriage in November, 1865, was followed by an eleven months' sojourn in Europe, from which he returned in October, 1866. Although feeling himself unfitted for the practice of the law, he opened an office in Boston. "I never had, in my recollection," he said in his *Autobiography*, "a bona-fide client." He was, therefore, virtually without employment, and anxious for something interesting to do. "I fixed on the railroad system," he wrote, "as the most developing force and largest field of the day, and determined to attach myself to it." One purpose, we learn from his own statements, was to promote the establishment of a railroad commission for Massachusetts with himself as one of the commissioners. He wrote article after article beginning in April, 1867, and in that way identified himself with railroads. While Charles was thus employed, in July, 1868, Henry Adams, who had been secretary to his father, the Ambassador to England, returned to the United States. He also was a man without occupation. Charles having identified himself with railroads, Henry decided "to strike for the press; and they hoped to play into each other's hands. They had great need, for they found no one else to play with" (*Education of Henry Adams*, p. 240). So he set off for Washington in October, 1868, while Charles opened house in Quincy, Massachusetts. "There, during that winter," says the latter, "I with infinite pains, sparing no labor, wrote my *Chapter of Erie*. That showed progress; it was really a careful piece of literary work." It had a widespread and deep political and economic effect, according to Henry Cabot Lodge, who says that it was the crowning stroke in the work which Charles had been doing by his writings for nearly three years. It made him the leader of the revolt against railroad domination, and helped him, says Charles, to put his "foot firmly on the rungs of the ladder." The article was published in July, 1869, and in the same month he became a member of the newly formed Massachusetts Railroad Commission, on which he served for ten years, during seven of which he was chairman. His official position did not, however, prevent him from writing hard-hitting articles against the railroad kings, as evidenced by the "Erie Raid," published in April, 1871.

Meanwhile, Henry Adams had been attracting attention by articles on finance in the United States, and by reviews of the sessions of Congress. He had supported the candidacy of Grant, and been shocked by the latter's choice of a cabinet. He had joined his brother in Massachusetts in the summer of 1869, when the details of Gould's great financial plot began to come out. Thirty-seven years afterward, in the *Education of Henry Adams,* he told in the following words how he came to write the "New York Gold Conspiracy."

Before he got back to Quincy, the summer was already half over, and in another six weeks the effects of President Grant's character showed themselves. They were startling—astounding—terrifying. The mystery that shrouded the famous, classical attempt of Jay Gould to corner gold in September, 1869, has never been cleared up—at least so far as to make it intelligible to Adams. Gould was led, by the change at Washington, into the belief that he could safely corner gold without interference from the Government. He took a number of precautions, which he admitted; and he spent a large sum of money, as he also testified, to obtain assurances which were not sufficient to have satisfied so astute a gambler; yet he made the venture. Any criminal lawyer must have begun investigation by insisting, rigorously, that no such man, in such a position, could be permitted to plead that he had taken, and pursued, such a course, without assurances which did satisfy him. The plea was professionally inadmissible.

This meant that any criminal lawyer would have been bound to start investigation by insisting that Gould had assurances from the White House or the Treasury, since none other could have satisfied him. To young men wasting their summer at Quincy for want of someone to hire their services at three dollars a day, such a dramatic scandal was

Heaven-sent. Charles and Henry Adams jumped at it like salmon at a fly, with as much voracity as Jay Gould, or his *âme damnée* Jim Fisk, had ever shown for Erie; and with as little fear of consequences. They risked something; no one could say what; but the people about the Erie office were not regarded as lambs.

The unraveling a skein so tangled as that of the Erie Railway was a task that might have given months of labor to the most efficient District Attorney, with all his official tools to work with. Charles took the railway history; Henry took the so-called Gold Conspiracy; and they went to New York to work it up. The surface was in full view. They had no trouble in Wall Street, and they paid their respects in person to the famous Jim Fisk in his Opera House Palace; but the New York side of the story helped Henry little. He needed to penetrate the political mystery, and for this purpose he had to wait for Congress to meet. At first he feared that Congress would suppress the scandal, but the Congressional Investigation was ordered and took place. He soon knew all that was to be known; the material for his essay was furnished by the Government.

Material furnished by a government seldom satisfies critics or historians, for it lies always under suspicion. Here was a mystery, and as usual, the chief mystery was the means of making sure that any mystery existed. All Adams's great friends—Fish, Cox, Hoar, Evarts, Sumner, and their surroundings—were precisely the persons most mystified. They knew less than Adams did; they sought information, and frankly admitted that their relations with the White House and the Treasury were not confidential. No one volunteered advice. No one offered suggestion. One got no light, even from the press, although press agents expressed in private the most damning convictions with their usual cynical frankness. The Congressional Committee took a quantity of evidence which it dared not probe, and refused to analyze. Although the fault lay somewhere on the Administration, and could lie nowhere else, the trail always faded and died out at the point where any member of the Administration became visible. Everyone dreaded to press inquiry. Adams himself feared finding out too much. He found out too much already, when he saw in evidence that Jay Gould had actually succeeded in stretching his net over Grant's closest surroundings, and that Boutwell's incompetence was the bottom of Gould's calculation. With the conventional air of assumed confidence, everyone in public assured everyone else that the President himself was the savior of the situation, and in private assured each other that if the President had not been caught this time, he was sure to be trapped the next, for the ways of Wall Street were dark and double. All this was wildly exciting to Adams. That Grant should have fallen, within six months, into such a morass—or should have let Boutwell drop him into it—rendered the outlook for the next four years—probably eight—possibly twelve—mysterious, or frankly opaque, to a young man who had hitched his wagon, as Emerson told him, to the star of reform. The country might outlive it, but not he. The worst scandals of the eighteenth century were relatively harmless by the side of this, which smirched executive, judiciary, banks, corporate systems, professions, and people, all the great active forces of society, in one dirty cesspool of vulgar corruption. Only six months before, this innocent young man, fresh from the cynicism of European diplomacy, had expected to enter an honorable career in the press as the champion and confidant of a new Washington, and already he foresaw a life of wasted energy, sweeping the stables of American society clean of the endless corruption which his second Washington was quite certain to breed.

In the Spring of 1870, Henry Adams went to Europe.

He had finished his New York "Gold Conspiracy," which he meant for his friend Henry Reeve and the *Edinburgh Review*. It was the best piece of work he had done, but this was not his reason for publishing it in England. The Erie scandal had provoked a sort of revolt among respectable New Yorkers, as well as among some who were not so respectable; and the attack on Erie was beginning to promise success. London was a sensitive spot for the Erie management, and it was thought well to strike them there, where they were socially and financially exposed. The tactics suited him in another way, for any expression about America in an English review attracted ten times the attention in America that the same article would attract in the *North American*. Habitually the American dailies reprinted such articles in full. Adams wanted to escape the terrors of copyright; his highest ambition was to be pirated and advertised free of charge, since, in any case, his pay was nothing. Under the excitement of chase, he was becoming a pirate himself, and liked it.

But his plans did not work out so easily.

The first shock came lightly, as though Nature were playing tricks on her spoiled child, though she had thus far not exerted herself to spoil him. Reeve refused the "Gold Conspiracy." Adams had become used to the idea that he was free of the quarterlies, and that his writing would be printed of course; but he was stunned by the reason of refusal. Reeve said it would bring half-a-dozen libel suits on him. One knew that the power of Erie was almost as great in England as in America, but one was hardly prepared to find it controlling the quarterlies. The English press professed to be shocked in 1870 by the Erie scandal, as it had professed in 1860 to be shocked by the scandal of slavery, but when invited to support those who were trying to abate these scandals, the English press said it was afraid. To Adams, Reeve's refusal seemed portentous. He and his brother and the *North American Review* were running greater risks every day, and no one thought of fear. That a notorious story, taken bodily from an official document, should scare the *Edinburgh Review* into silence for fear of Jay Gould and Jim Fisk, passed even Adams's experience of English eccentricity, though it was large.

He gladly set down Reeve's refusal of the "Gold Conspiracy" to respectability and editorial law, but when he sent the manuscript on to the *Quarterly*, the editor of the *Quarterly* also refused it. The literary standard of the two quarterlies was not so high as to suggest that the article was illiterate beyond the power of an active and willing editor to redeem it. Adams had no choice but to realize that he had to deal in 1870 with the same old English character of 1860, and the same inability in himself to understand it. As usual, when an ally was needed, the American was driven into the arms of the radicals. Respectability, everywhere and always, turned its back the moment one asked to do it a favor. Called suddenly away from England, he despatched the article, at the last moment, to the *Westminster Review* and heard no more about it for nearly six months.

Henry Adams sailed for the United States on September 1, 1870, and it was not until the October issue of the *Westminster Review* reached him that he knew that his article had been accepted. It was "instantly pirated on a great scale," he wrote.

This is not the place for a further account of the doings either of Henry or of Charles Francis Adams, Jr., but one cannot refrain from recording the fact that the latter, after being president of the Union Pacific Railroad for six and one-half years, was in November, 1890, ejected from that office by Jay Gould.

In all three of the Adams articles are uncomplimentary references to David Dudley Field, legal adviser to the Erie Railroad. One of these references touched Field in a tender spot, when Henry Adams said that he had "a silken halter round the neck of Judge Barnard, and a hempen one round that of Cardozo." Field, therefore, came to his own defense in a letter dated February 13, 1871, published in April, 1871, in the *Westminster Review*. Henry Adams summarized this letter and answered it in the last footnote to his "New York Gold Conspiracy," as it was reprinted in *Chapters of Erie* (see *post*, p. 152). He there says that the subject has "ceased to be one of consequence even to Mr. Field since the subsequent violent controversy which arose in March, 1871, in regard to other points of Mr. Field's professional conduct." That subsequent controversy grew up over Field's activities in connection with the Erie raid upon the Albany and Susquehanna Railroad, and is the subject matter of four additional articles reprinted in the present book.

The fat was thrown into the fire by Samuel Bowles, editor of the *Springfield Republican*, who permitted a critical editorial to be printed in his paper. Bowles, outspoken reformer, had had a taste of Erie Ring porridge when, on December 22, 1868, he spent a night in jail on a warrant procured by Jim Fisk. Perhaps, for this reason, he was less unhappy when in December, 1870, he deemed it to be his duty to attack Fisk's attorney. The editorial was the occasion for a long and caustic correspondence between David Dudley Field and his son, on the one side, and Bowles, on the other. The full set of letters was published in pamphlet form by Bowles early in 1871. The date of the last letter is January 28. On the thirty-first, the *New York Tribune* published a long article on "Erie Litigation," to which Mr. Field replied on February 2. Then entered the lists a champion on the side of Bowles and the *Tribune*. This was Francis C. Barlow, a major general in the Union army during the war, subsequently New York Secretary of State and United States Marshal, a founder of the Association of the Bar of the City of New York, and then, in 1871, practicing law in New York City. In that year, he was elected attorney-general, so that in the following year it became his duty, in the name of the state, to prosecute Tweed, who was defended by Field. Now, however, he was acting, not as an official, but as a member of the bar, anxious that the ethical standards of the profession might be upheld. Field had called upon Bowles to produce facts in support of his charges of professional misconduct. Barlow's "Facts for Mr. Field," contained in three letters, filling eight columns of the *Tribune* (March 7, 8, and 9), responded to this challenge. Field answered in three columns (March 13), and Barlow gave "More Facts," in six columns (March 24). This was the situation when, in April, 1871, appeared Charles Francis Adams' "Erie Raid," and in the same number of the *North American Review*, Albert Stickney's "Lawyer and His Clients" (reprinted *post*, p. 213).

Stickney was then only thirty-three years of age, a native of Boston, who after graduating from Harvard Law School, and serving as lieutenant colonel during the war, had opened his own law office in New York City. He came into prominence as junior counsel with Charles O'Connor and James C. Carter in the Jumel Will case, and he was soon, in 1872, to take part in the prosecution of the Tweed judges in opposition to David Dudley Field. He also, like the Adams brothers and General Barlow, was not merely a reporter and critic of events, but a participant in them. His article, "The Lawyer and His Clients," following up the Bowles-Field-Barlow correspondence, analyzed the situation from a lawyer's viewpoint, presenting evidence of unethical conduct on the part of the still-powerful Erie–Tweed judge Barnard, and on the part of Field, which the latter, with all his success and prestige, could not afford to leave unanswered. Incidentally, it clarified, for both layman and lawyer, the confusing happenings of the Erie raid and the resulting litigation.

Field had felt himself easily able to handle the criticisms of editor Bowles; but those of brother lawyers presented a different problem. He professed to think that they were opponents unworthy of his steel; yet they were both urging that his conduct be investigated by the City Bar Association. In the last of his

Tribune letters (March 13, 1871), Field had promised, "in another form," to go into all the particulars of the charges made against him. What "form" was referred to, was soon to appear. On April 10 George Ticknor Curtis, a leading New York lawyer, widely known as a legal author, who had declined judgeships and the ambassadorship to England, "was requested by an intimate friend of Mr. David Dudley Field, to examine the proceedings in the Albany and Susquehanna Railroad litigations (in 1869) in connection with the complaints made against him in reference thereto, in certain newspapers and other periodicals," and to give his "opinion" upon the whole matter. He spent exactly one month preparing his inquiry which was then published by D. Appleton and Company (see *post,* p. 246). It demonstrated conclusively that two lawyers, in possession of the same facts, can reach diametrically opposite conclusions.

Soon after the "opinion" was published, the question was raised whether it was "to be regarded merely as an argument," or as a paper expressing Mr. Curtis' personal convictions. He answered the query in a letter dated June 4, 1871, printed in *The World* and in the *New York Evening Express,* and when a second edition of the *Inquiry* was needed this letter was added as a supplement (see *post,* p. 347).

The whole controversy might have died down and smoldered out, if new events and the fighting instinct of Stickney and Barlow could have been eliminated. Field's connection with the Erie Ring continued; Stickney published an article in January, 1872, in the *American Law Review* on the "Erie Railway and the English Stock"; Jim Fisk was shot by Edward S. Stokes and Field drew his will by his deathbed; and from February 19 to April 11, 1872, the Judiciary Committee of the New York Assembly heard testimony in New York City on charges made by the Association of the Bar against Justices Barnard, Cardozo, and McCunn. The charges were drawn up by a committee made up of Joshua M. VanCott, John E. Parsons, and Albert Stickney, who also served as counsel for the Bar Association at the hear-ings. George Ticknor Curtis was chief counsel for Judge Barnard. The pages of the three volumes of testimony bristle with the spurs of contest between Stickney and Curtis as they examined and cross-examined such witnesses as David Dudley Field, his son Dudley, his partner Thomas G. Shearman, his client, Jay Gould, and Joseph H. Ramsey.

Although the charges were against Barnard, Cardozo, and McCunn and not against Field, the whole proceeding did not tend to reëstablish his professional standing. Indeed, as we learn from Theron G. Strong's *Landmarks of a Lawyer's Life,* pages 191–192, the Committee on Grievances of the Association of the Bar of the City of New York, at a meeting in 1872, presented a report so drawn "that the consequences to Mr. Field, if the recommendations had been adopted, would have been of the most serious character. The sentiment of the members and the general trend of the discussion seemed to make it a foregone conclusion that action unfavorable to Mr. Field would be taken." This result was averted only by a powerful address by William M. Evarts, President of the Association, whose counsel prevailed that no direct vote should be taken and that the report should be laid upon the table.

In March, 1872, Jay Gould was forced out of the Erie directorate, and Field's professional connection with the road ended. In the same month, evidence that Field still had powerful friends was presented in an article by Jeremiah S. Black, published in *The Galaxy* (see *post,* p. 351). This article took as its starting point *Chapters of Erie* and Curtis' *Inquiry,* and was entitled "A Great Lawsuit and a Field Fight." Black had been Chief Justice of the Pennsylvania Supreme Court, United States Attorney-General, and Secretary of State. He and Field had been associated as counsel in two famous cases in 1867 and 1868, the McArdle case and the Milligan case. While judicial in tone and showing the lawyer's careful attention to facts, it was undoubtedly a defense of Field, and somewhat prone to sweep aside with well-turned phrases and lawyer's reasoning the layman's doubts and questions. It must have come as a welcome change in Field's recent experiences.

Two months later, from May 13 to August 19, 1872, came the impeachment trial at Albany and Saratoga Springs of Judge Barnard. Curtis no longer was counsel for Barnard, and it was rumored and denied that he had advised his former client to resign on the conclusion of the Assembly investigation. He was replaced by eminent counsel headed by William O. Beach. Stickney was not engaged as counsel for the impeachment managers, but he served "without charge to the state" along with the employed counselors. At the close of the trial, Barnard was found guilty on twenty-five articles, was removed from office, and disqualified from ever again holding office under the state. Stickney, to whom a large share of credit for the success of the prosecution was given, must have felt that this result was a justification of his attack on Field, for there was an intimate connection between Field's professional activities and the disapproved judicial behavior of Barnard. Nevertheless, he did not let the matter rest there and found time to prepare an answer to Judge Black's defense of Field. It appeared in *The Galaxy* of October, 1872, with the title "The Truth of a 'Great Lawsuit'" (see *post*, p. 387). It sounds a note of triumph, perhaps of too-excited exultation, as though the young champion, having already helped to dispose of Judge Barnard, would annihilate Curtis, Black, and Field, all with one final sweeping gesture. In his closing paragraph he expresses the hope that the literature of the Albany and Susquehanna Railroad "will be hereafter confined to stock ledgers and cash books, and not stray into reviews and magazines." And so it was. He had had the last word.

As time has gone on, the general discussions of railroad problems by Charles Francis Adams, Jr., have been superseded by more detailed studies. His two controversial articles and that by Henry Adams have, however, in no sense lost their interest and importance. They would be worth preserving as literary productions even though they were not at the same time historical documents. The articles by Stickney, Curtis, and Black are also not without literary merit, although, at times, they fall short of that high quality possessed by the other articles. They constitute an evenly balanced debate on the subject of legal ethics as illustrated by an eminent lawyer's participation in the very events set down by the Adamses. Thus they serve two purposes, the most important of which is, in the present connection to analyze the events recounted in the Adams articles, and in combination with them to tell a more complete story than has heretofore, in one place, been available. An introduction was needed, not to add anything to their substance, but to raise the reader to a vantage point from which to view them before and after they have been read.

FREDERICK C. HICKS.

THE MARCH OF EVENTS

1832–33. Erie Railway chartered and organized.

1851. Erie Railway opened from Lake Erie to tidewater (Dunkirk to Piermont).

1852. Albany and Susquehanna Railroad organized.

1853. New York Central Railroad chartered.

1861–65. American Civil War.

1866. Treasurer Drew lends the Erie Railway $3,500,000.

1866–67. Vanderbilt gets control of New York Central.

1867, Autumn. Vanderbilt begins operations to gain control of the Erie.

1867, October 8. Gould and Fisk enter Erie board of directors.

1868, January 17. Injunction "war" begins between Vanderbilt and Drew.

1868, March 11. Drew, Gould, and Fisk flee to Jersey City.

1868, March 30. Gould goes to Albany to promote Erie legislation.

1868, April 1. Mattoon report, New York Senate, unfavorable to Drew faction of Erie directors.

1868, April 21. Act legalizing unauthorized Erie stock issues signed by New York Governor Fenton.

1868, July 1. Drew driven from Erie board. Gould elected president and treasurer, Fisk, vice-president and comptroller, and Frederick A. Lane, counsel.

1868, October. C. F. Adams' "The Erie Railroad Row" published in *American Law Review*.

1868, October 13. William M. Tweed and Peter B. Sweeny elected to Erie board.

1868, December 22. Samuel Bowles arrested on complaint of Fisk.

1869. New York Central and Hudson River Railroad organized.

1869, January 15. Albany and Susquehanna Railroad completed.

1869, March 4. President Grant inaugurated. George S. Boutwell appointed Secretary of the Treasury.

1869, May 20. Erie Classification Act passed by New York legislature.

1869, June. Erie Ring begins manipulations to get control of the Albany and Susquehanna Railroad.

1869, July. C. F. Adams' "Chapter of Erie" published in *North American Review*.

1869, July. Massachusetts Railroad Commission established.

1869, August 5. Albany and Susquehanna Railroad's transfer books secretly removed from the company's office.

1869, August 7. Fisk thrown out of Albany and Susquehanna Railroad's Albany office.

1869, August 9. David Dudley Field arrives in Albany.

1869, August 10. Erie and Ramsey parties, on two rival trains, crash head-on near Binghamton.

1869, September 2. President Grant instructs Boutwell not to force the price of gold down.

1869, September 2–27. New York gold conspiracy.

1869, September 7. Annual election of Albany and Susquehanna Railroad. Two rival sets of directors elected, the "Ramsey" directors headed by J. P. Morgan, and the "Fisk" directors by Charles Courter.

1869, September 24. Black Friday.

1869, November 29. Justice E. Darwin Smith, at Rochester, New York, hears *People* v. *Albany and Susquehanna Railroad Company*, a suit brought by the Attorney-General to determine the rights of the parties in the contested election of September 7.

1869, December. Justice Smith's decision (7 *Abb. Pr. N.S.* 265).

1870, January 15–February 15. Sessions of United States Committee on Banking, investigating the New York gold panic. Report ordered printed, March 1, 1870.

1870, February. Albany and Susquehanna Railroad leased in perpetuity to the Hudson and Delaware Canal Company.

1870, October 1. Henry Adams' "New York Gold Conspiracy" published in *Westminster Review.*

1870, December 27–January 28, 1871. Correspondence between David Dudley Field and Dudley Field, and Samuel Bowles.

1871, January–1873. Tweed Ring agitation and prosecutions.

1871, January 31. "The Erie Litigation" published in *New York Tribune.*

1871, February 2. Mr. Field's answer in *New York Tribune.*

1871, March 7, 8, 9, 11, 20, 25. Letters of General Francis C. Barlow, and Mr. Field's answers, published in *New York Tribune.*

1871, April. Albert Stickney's "Lawyer and His Clients," and C. F. Adams' "Erie Raid" published in *North American Review.* D. D. Field's letter answering Henry Adams' "Gold Conspiracy" published in *Westminster Review.*

1871, May 10. G. T. Curtis' *Inquiry into the Albany and Susquehanna Railroad Litigations* . . ., published (2d ed., June 15, 1871).

1872, January. Stickney's "Erie Railway and the English Stock" published in the *American Law Review.*

1872, January 6. James Fisk killed by Edward S. Stokes.

1872, February 19–April 11. Judiciary Committee of the New York Assembly hears testimony in New York City on charges made by the Association of the Bar against Justices Barnard, Cardozo, and McCunn.

1872, March. J. S. Black's "Great Lawsuit" published in *The Galaxy.*

1872, March 11. Field and Shearman replaced by S. L. M. Barlow as Erie counsel.

1872, March 12. Gould forced out of Erie.

1872, May 13–August 19. Impeachment trial of Justice Barnard.

1872, October. Stickney's "The Truth of a Great Lawsuit" published in *The Galaxy*.

1873. Panic of 1873.

1877. Cornelius Vanderbilt dies.

1878. William M. Tweed dies.
Samuel Bowles dies.

1879. Daniel Drew dies.
Justice George G. Barnard dies.

1879. United States returns to a gold basis.

1890, November. C. F. Adams is "ejected by Jay Gould from the presidency of the Union Pacific Railroad."

1892. Jay Gould dies.

1894. David Dudley Field dies.

I

A CHAPTER OF ERIE*

BY

CHARLES FRANCIS ADAMS, JR.

NOT a generation has passed away during the last six hundred years without cherishing a more or less earnest conviction that, through its efforts, something of the animal had been eliminated from the higher type of man. Probably, also, no generation has been wholly mistaken in nourishing this faith;—even the worst has in some way left the race of men on earth better in something than it found them. And yet it would not be difficult for another Rousseau to frame a very ingenious and plausible argument in support of the opposite view. Scratch a Russian, said the first Napoleon, and you will find a Cossack; call things by their right names, and it would be no difficult task to make the cunning civilization of the nineteenth century appear but as a hypocritical mask spread over the more honest brutality of the twelfth. Take, for instance, some of the cardinal vices and abuses of the imperfect past. Pirates are commonly supposed to have been battered and hung out of existence when the Barbary Powers and the Buccaneers of the Spanish Main had been finally dealt with. Yet freebooters are not extinct; they have only transferred their operations to the land, and conducted them in more or less accordance with the forms of law; until, at last, so great a proficiency have they attained, that the commerce of the world is more equally but far more heavily taxed in their behalf, than would ever have entered into their wildest hopes while, outside the law, they simply made all comers stand and deliver. Now, too,

---

* *North American Review*, CIX (July, 1869), 30–106.

DANIEL DREW

they no longer live in terror of the rope, skulking in the hiding-place of thieves, but flaunt themselves in the resorts of trade and fashion, and, disdaining such titles as once satisfied Ancient Pistol or Captain Macheath, they are even recognized as President This or Colonel That. A certain description of gambling, also, has ceased to be fashionable; it is years since Crawford's doors were closed, so that in this respect a victory is claimed for advancing civilization. Yet this claim would seem to be unfounded. Gambling is a business now where formerly it was a disreputable excitement. Cheating at cards was always disgraceful; transactions of a similar character under the euphemistic names of "operating," "cornering," and the like are not so regarded. Again, legislative bribery and corruption were, within recent memory, looked upon as antiquated misdemeanors, almost peculiar to the unenlightened period of Walpole and Fox, and their revival in the face of modern public opinion was thought to be impossible. In this regard at least a sad delusion was certainly entertained. Governments and ministries no longer buy the raw material of legislation;—at least not openly or with cash in hand. The same cannot be said of individuals and corporations; for they have of late not infrequently found the supply of legislators in the market even in excess of the demand. Judicial venality and ruffianism on the bench were not long since traditions of a remote past. Bacon was impeached, and Jeffries achieved an immortal infamy for offenses against good morals and common decency which a self-satisfied civilization believed incompatible with modern development. Recent revelations have cast more than doubt upon the correctness even of this assumption.*

No better illustration of the fantastic disguises which the worst

* See a very striking article entitled "The New York City Judiciary" in the *North American Review* for July, 1867. This paper, which, from its fearless denunciation of a class of judicial delinquencies which have since greatly increased both in frequency and in magnitude, attracted great attention when it was published, has been attributed to the pen of Mr. Thomas G. Shearman, of the New York bar.

and most familiar evils of history assume as they meet us in the actual movements of our own day could be afforded than was seen in the events attending what are known as the Erie wars of the year 1868. Beginning in February and lasting until December, raging fiercely in the late winter and spring, and dying away into a hollow truce at midsummer, only to revive into new and more vigorous life in the autumn, this strange conflict convulsed the money market, occupied the courts, agitated legislatures, and perplexed the country, throughout the entire year. These, too, were but its more direct and immediate manifestations. The remote political complications and financial disturbances occasioned by it would afford a curious illustration of the close intertwining of interests which now extends throughout the civilized world. The complete history of these proceedings cannot be written, for the end is not yet; indeed, such a history probably never will be written, and yet it is still more probable that the events it would record can never be quite forgotten. It was something new to see a knot of adventurers, men of broken fortune, without character and without credit, possess themselves of an artery of commerce more important than was ever the Appian Way, and make levies, not only upon it for their own emolument, but, through it, upon the whole business of a nation. Nor could it fail to be seen that this was by no means in itself an end, but rather only a beginning. No people can afford to glance at these things in the columns of the daily press, and then dismiss them from memory. For Americans they involve many questions;— they touch very nearly the foundations of common truth and honesty without which that healthy public opinion cannot exist which is the life's breath of our whole political system.

I

THE history of the Erie Railway has been a checkered one. Chartered in 1832, and organized in 1833, the cost of its construction was then estimated at three millions of dollars, of which but one million were subscribed. By the time the first report was made the estimated cost had increased to six millions, and the work of construction was actually begun on the strength of stock subscriptions of a million and a half, and a loan of three millions from the state. In 1842 the estimated cost had increased to twelve millions and a half, and both means in hand and credit were wholly exhausted. Subscription books were opened, but no names were entered in them; the city of New York was applied to, and refused a loan of its credit; again the legislature was besieged, but the aid from this quarter was now hampered with inadmissible conditions; accordingly work was suspended, and the property of the insolvent corporation passed into the hands of assignees. In 1845 the state came again to the rescue; it surrendered all claim to the three millions it had already lent to the company; and one-half of their old subscriptions having been given up by the stockholders, and a new subscription of three millions raised, the whole property of the road was mortgaged for three millions more. At last, in 1851, eighteen years after its commencement, the road was opened from Lake Erie to tidewater. Its financial troubles had, however, as yet only begun, for in 1859 it could not meet the interest on its mortgages, and passed into the hands of a receiver. In 1861 an arrangement of interests was effected, and a new company was organized. The next year the old New York & Erie Railroad Company disappeared under a foreclosure of the fifth mortgage, and the present Erie Railway Company rose from its ashes. Meanwhile the original estimate of three millions had developed into an actual outlay of fifty millions; the 470 miles of track opened in 1842 had expanded into 773 miles in 1868; and the revenue, which the projectors had "confidently" estimated at something less than two millions in 1833, amounted to over five millions when the road passed into the hands of a receiver in 1859, and in 1865 reached the enormous sum of sixteen millions and a half. The road was, in truth, a magnificent enterprise, worthy to connect the Great Lakes with the great seaport of America. Scaling lofty mountain ranges, running through fertile valleys and by the banks of broad rivers, connecting the Hudson, the Susquehanna, the St. Lawrence, and the Ohio, it stood forth a monument at once of engineering skill and of commercial enterprise.

The series of events in the Erie history which culminated in the struggle about to be narrated may be said to have had its origin some seventeen or eighteen years before, when Mr. Daniel Drew first made his appearance in the Board of Directors, where he remained down to the year 1868, generally holding also the office of treasurer of the corporation. Mr. Drew is what is known as a self-made man. Born in the year 1797, as a boy he drove cattle down from his native town of Carmel, in Putnam County, to the market of New York City, and, subsequently, was for years proprietor of the Bull's Head Tavern. Like his contemporary, and ally or opponent,—as the case might be,—Cornelius Vanderbilt, he built up his fortunes in the steamboat interest, and subsequently extended his operations over the rapidly developing railroad system. Shrewd, unscrupulous, and very illiterate,—a strange combination of superstition and faithlessness, of daring and timidity,—often good-natured and sometimes generous,—he ever regarded his fiduciary position of director in a railroad as a means of manipulating its stock for his own advantage. For years he had been the leading bear of Wall Street, and his favorite haunts were the secret recesses of Erie. As treasurer of that corporation, he had, in its frequently recurring hours of need, advanced it sums which it could not have obtained elsewhere, and the obtaining of which was a necessity. He had been at once a good friend of the road and the worst enemy it had as yet known. His management of his favorite stock had been cunning and recondite, and his ways inscrutable. Those who sought to follow him, and those who sought to oppose him, alike found food for sad reflection; until at last he won for himself the expressive *sobriquet* of the Speculative Director. Sometimes, though rarely, he suffered greatly in the complications of Wall Street; more frequently he inflicted severe damage upon others. On the whole, however, his fortunes had greatly prospered, and the outbreak of the Erie war found him the actual possessor of some millions, and the reputed possessor of many more.

In the spring of 1866 Mr. Drew's manipulations of Erie culminated in an operation which was at the time regarded as a masterpiece; subsequent experience has, however, so improved upon it that it is now looked upon as an ordinary and inartistic piece of what is called "railroad financiering," a class of operations formerly known by a more opprobrious name. The stock of the road was then selling at about 95, and the corporation was, as usual, in debt, and in pressing need of money. As usual, also, it resorted to its treasurer. Mr. Drew stood ready to make the desired advances—upon security. Some twenty-eight thousand shares of its own authorized stock, which had never been issued, were at the time in the hands of the company, which also claimed, under the statutes of New York, the right of raising money by the issue of bonds, convertible, at the option of the holder, into stock. The twenty-eight thousand unissued shares, and bonds for three millions of dollars, convertible into stock, were placed by the company in the hands of its treasurer, as security for a cash loan of $3,500,000. The negotiation had been quietly effected, and Mr. Drew's campaign now opened. Once more he was short of Erie. While Erie was buoyant,—while it steadily approximated to par,—while speculation was rampant, and that outside public, the delight and prey of Wall Street, was gradually drawn in by the fascination of amassing wealth without labor,—quietly and stealthily, through his agents and brokers, the grave, desponding operator was daily concluding his contracts for the future delivery of stock at current prices. At last the hour had come. Erie was rising, Erie was scarce, the great bear had many contracts to fulfil, and where was he to find the stock? His victims were not kept long in suspense. Mr. Treasurer Drew laid his hands upon his collateral. In an instant the bonds for three millions were converted into an equivalent amount of capital stock, and fifty-eight thousand shares, dumped, as it were, by the cartload in Broad Street, made Erie as plenty as even Drew could desire. Before the astonished bulls could rally their faculties, the quotations had fallen from 95 to 50, and they realized that they were hopelessly entrapped.*

The whole transaction, of course, was in no respect more creditable than any result, supposed to be one of chance or skill, which, in fact, is made to depend upon the sorting of a pack of cards, the dosing of a race-horse, or the selling out of his powers by a "walkist." But the gambler, the patron of the turf, or the pedestrian represents, as a rule, himself alone, and his character is generally so well understood as to be a warning to all the world. The case of the treasurer of a great corporation is different. He occupies a fiduciary position. He is a trustee,—a guardian. Vast interests are confided to his care; every shareholder of the corporation is his ward; if it is a railroad, the community itself is

* A bull, in the slang of the stock exchange, is one who endeavors to increase the market price of stocks, as a bear endeavors to depress it. The bull is supposed to toss the thing up with his horns, and the bear to drag it down with his claws. The vast majority of stock operations are pure gambling transactions. One man agrees to deliver, at some future time, property which he has not got, to another man who does not care to own it. It is only one way of betting on the price at the time when the delivery should be made; if the price rises in the meanwhile, the bear pays to the bull the difference between the price agreed upon and the price to which the property has risen; if it falls, he receives the difference from the bull. All operations, as they are termed, of the stock exchange are directed to this depression or elevation of stocks, with a view to the settlement of differences. A "pool" is a mere combination of men contributing money to be used to this end, and a "corner" is a result arrived at when one combination of gamblers, secretly holding the whole or greater part of any stock or species of property, induces another combination to agree to deliver a large further quantity at some future time. When the time arrives, the second combination, if the corner succeeds, suddenly finds itself unable to buy the amount of the stock or property necessary to enable it to fulfil its contracts, and the first combination fixes at its own will the price at which differences must be settled. The corner fails or is broken, when those who agree to deliver succeed in procuring the stock or property, and fulfilling their contracts. The *argot* of the exchange is, however, a language by itself, and very difficult of explanation to the wholly uninitiated. It can only be said that all combinations of interests and manipulations of values are mere weapons in the hands of bulls and bears for elevating or depressing values, with a view to the payment of differences.

his *cestui que trust*. But passing events, accumulating more thickly with every year, have thoroughly corrupted the public morals on this subject. A directorship in certain great corporations has come to be regarded as a situation in which to make a fortune, the possession of which is no longer dishonorable. The method of accumulation is both simple and safe. It consists in giving contracts as a trustee to one's self as an individual, or in speculating in the property of one's *cestui que trust*, or in using the funds confided to one's charge, as treasurer or otherwise, to gamble with the real owners of those funds for their own property, and that with cards packed in advance. The wards themselves expect their guardians to throw the dice against them for their own property, and are surprised, as well as gratified, if the dice are not loaded. These proceedings, too, are looked upon as hardly reprehensible, yet they strike at the very foundation of existing society. The theory of representation, whether in politics or in business, is of the essence of modern development. Our whole system rests upon the sanctity of the fiduciary relations. Whoever betrays them, a director of a railroad no less than a member of Congress or the trustee of an orphans' asylum, is the common enemy of every man, woman, and child who lives under representative government. The unscrupulous director is far less entitled to mercy than the ordinary gambler, combining as he does the character of the traitor with the acts of the thief.

No acute moral sensibility on this point, however, has for some years troubled Wall Street, nor, indeed, the country at large. As a result of the transaction of 1866, Mr. Drew was looked upon as having effected a surprisingly clever operation, and he retired from the field hated, feared, wealthy, and admired. This episode of Wall Street history took its place as a brilliant success beside the famous Prairie du Chien and Harlem "corners," and, but for subsequent events, would soon have been forgotten. Its close connection, however, with more important though later incidents of Erie history seems likely to preserve its memory fresh. Great events were impending; a new man was looming up in the railroad world, introducing novel ideas and principles, and it could hardly be that the new and old would not come in conflict. Cornelius Vanderbilt, commonly known as Commodore Vanderbilt, was now developing his theory of the management of railroads. Born in the year 1794, Vanderbilt was a somewhat older man than Drew. There are several points of resemblance in the early lives of the two men, and many points of curious contrast in their characters. Vanderbilt, like Drew, was born in very humble circumstances in the state of New York, and like him also received little education. He began life by ferrying passengers and produce from Staten Island to New York City. Subsequently, he too laid the foundation of his great fortune in the growing steamboat navigation, and likewise, in due course of time, transferred himself to the railroad interest. When at last, in 1868, the two came into collision as representatives of the old system of railroad management and of the new, they were each threescore and ten years of age, and had both been successful in the accumulation of millions,—Vanderbilt even more so than Drew. They were probably equally unscrupulous and equally selfish; but, while the cast of Drew's mind was somber and bearish, Vanderbilt was gay and buoyant of temperament, little given to thoughts other than of this world, a lover of horses and of the good things of life. The first affects prayer meetings, and the last is a devotee of whist. Drew, in Wall Street, is by temperament a bear, while Vanderbilt could hardly be other than a bull. Vanderbilt must be allowed to be by far the superior man of the two. Drew is astute and full of resources, and at all times a dangerous opponent; but Vanderbilt takes larger, more comprehensive views, and his mind has a vigorous grasp which that of Drew seems to want. While, in short, in a wider field, the one might have made himself a great and successful despot, the other would hardly have aspired beyond the control of the jobbing department of some corrupt government. Accordingly, while in Drew's connection with the railroad system his operations and manipulations evince no qualities calculated to excite even a vulgar admiration or respect, it is impossible to regard Vanderbilt's methods or aims without recognizing the magnitude of the man's ideas and conceding his abilities. He involuntarily excites feelings of admiration for himself and alarm for the public. His ambition is a great one. It seems to be nothing less than to make himself master in his own right of the great channels of communication which connect the city of New York with the interior of the continent, and to control them as his private property. Drew sought to carry to a mean perfection the old system of operating successfully from the confidential position of director, neither knowing anything nor caring anything for the railroad system, except in its connection with the movements of the stock exchange, and he succeeded in his object. Vanderbilt, on the other hand, as selfish, harder, and more dangerous, though less subtle, has by instinct, rather than by intellectual effort, seen the full magnitude of the system, and through it has sought to make himself a dictator in modern civilization, moving forward to this end step by step with a sort of pitiless energy which has seemed to have in it an element of fate. As trade now dominates the world, and railways dominate trade, his object has been to make himself the virtual master of all by making himself absolute lord of the railways. Had he begun his railroad operations with this end in view, complete failure would have been almost certainly his reward. Commencing as he did, however, with a comparatively insignificant objective,— the cheap purchase of a bankrupt stock,—and developing his ideas as he advanced, his power and his reputation grew, until an end which at first it would have seemed madness to entertain became at last both natural and feasible.

Two great lines of railway traverse the state of New York and connect it with the West,—the Erie and the New York Central. The latter communicates with the city by a great river and by two railroads. To get these two roads—the Harlem and the Hudson River—under his own absolute control, and then, so far as the connection with the Central was concerned, to abolish the river, was Vanderbilt's immediate object. First making himself master of the Harlem road, he there learned his early lessons in railroad management, and picked up a fortune by the way. A few years ago Harlem had no value. As late as 1860 it sold for eight or nine dollars per share; and in January, 1863, when Vanderbilt had got the control, it had risen only to 30. By July of that year it stood at 92, and in August was suddenly raised by a "corner" to 179. The next year witnessed a similar operation. The stock which sold in January at less than 90 was settled for in June in the neighborhood of 285. On one of these occasions Mr. Drew is reported to have contributed a sum approaching half a million to his rival's wealth. More recently the stock had been floated at about 130. It was in the successful conduct of this first experiment that Vanderbilt showed his very manifest superiority over previous railroad managers. The Harlem was, after all, only a competing line, and competition was proverbially the rock ahead in all railroad enterprise. The success of Vanderbilt with the Harlem depended upon his getting rid of the competition of the Hudson River railroad. An ordinary manager would have resorted to contracts, which are never carried out, or to opposition, which is apt to be ruinous. Vanderbilt, on the contrary, put an end to competition by buying up the competing line. This he did at about par, and, in due course of time, the stock was sent up to 180. Thus his plans had developed by another step, while through a judicious course of financiering and watering and dividing, a new fortune had been secured by him. By this time Vanderbilt's reputation as a railroad manager—as one who earned dividends, created stock, and invented wealth— had become very great, and the managers of the Central brought that road to him, and asked him to do with it as he had done with the Harlem and Hudson River. He accepted the proffered charge, and now, probably, the possibilities of his position and the magnitude of the prize within his grasp at last dawned on his mind. Unconsciously to himself, working more wisely than he knew, he had developed to its logical conclusion one potent element of modern civilization.

Gravitation is the rule, and centralization the natural consequence, in society no less than in physics. Physically, morally, intellectually, in population, wealth, and intelligence, all things tend to concentration. One singular illustration of this law is almost entirely the growth of this century. Formerly, either governments, or individuals, or, at most, small combinations of individuals, were the originators of all great works of public utility. Within the present century only has democracy found its way through the representative system into the combinations of capital, small shareholders combining to carry out the most extensive enterprises. And yet already our great corporations are fast emancipating themselves from the state, or rather subjecting the state to their own control, while individual capitalists, who long ago abandoned the attempt to compete with them, will next seek to control them. In this dangerous path of centralization Vanderbilt has taken the latest step in advance. He has combined the natural power of the individual with the factitious power of the corporation. The famous "L'état, c'est moi" of Louis XIV represents Vanderbilt's position in regard to his railroads. Unconsciously he has introduced Caesarism into corporate life. He has, however, but pointed out the way which others will tread. The individual will hereafter be engrafted on the corporation,—democracy running its course, and resulting in imperialism; and Vanderbilt is but the precursor of a class of men who will wield within the state a power created by the state, but too great for its control. He is the founder of a dynasty.

From the moment Vanderbilt stepped into the management of the Central, but a single effort seemed necessary to give the new railroad king absolute control over the railroad system, and consequently over the commerce, of New York. By advancing only one step he could securely levy his tolls on the traffic of a continent. Nor could this step have seemed difficult to take. It was but to repeat with the Erie his successful operation with the Hudson River road. Not only was it a step easy to take, but here again, as so many times before, a new fortune seemed ready to drop into his hand. The Erie might well yield a not less golden harvest than the Central, Hudson River, or Harlem. There was indeed but one obstacle in the way,—the plan might not meet the views of the one man who at that time possessed the wealth, cunning, and combination of qualities which could defeat it, that man being the Speculative Director of the Erie,—Mr. Daniel Drew.

The New York Central passed into Vanderbilt's hands in the winter of 1866–67, and he marked the Erie for his own in the succeeding autumn. As the annual meeting of the corporation approached, three parties were found in the field contending for control of the road. One party was represented by Drew, and might be called the party in possession, that which had long ruled the Erie, and made it what it was,—the Scarlet Woman of Wall Street. Next came Vanderbilt, flushed with success, and bent upon fully gratifying his great instinct for developing imperialism in corporate life. Lastly, a faction made its appearance composed of some shrewd and ambitious Wall Street operators and of certain persons from Boston, who sustained for the occasion the novel character of railroad reformers. This party, it is needless to say, was as unscrupulous, and, as the result proved, as able as either of the others; it represented nothing but a raid made upon the Erie treasury in the interest of a thoroughly bankrupt New England corporation, of which its members had the control. The history of this corporation, known as the Boston, Hartford, & Erie Railroad,—a projected feeder and connection of the Erie,—would be one curious to read, though very difficult to write. Its name was synonymous with bankruptcy, litigation, fraud, and failure. If the Erie was of doubtful repute in Wall Street, the Boston, Hartford, & Erie had long been of worse than doubtful repute in State Street. Of late years, under able and persevering, if not scrupulous management, the bankrupt, moribund company had been slowly struggling into new life, and in the spring of 1867 it had obtained, under certain conditions, from the Commonwealth of Massachusetts, a subsidy in aid of the construction of its road. One of the conditions imposed obliged the corporation to raise a sum from other sources still larger than that granted by the state. Accordingly, those having the line in charge looked abroad for a victim, and fixed their eyes upon the Erie.

As the election day drew near, Erie was of course for sale. A controlling interest of stockholders stood ready to sell their proxies, with entire impartiality, to any of the three contending parties, or to any man who would pay the market price for them. Nay, more, the attorney of one of the contending parties, as it afterward appeared, after an ineffectual effort to extort blackmail, actually sold the proxies of his principal to another of the contestants, and his doing so seemed to excite mirth rather than surprise. Meanwhile the representatives of the Eastern interest played their part to admiration. Taking advantage of some Wall Street complications just then existing between Vanderbilt and Drew, they induced the former to ally himself with them, and the latter saw that his defeat was inevitable. Even at this time the Vanderbilt party contemplated having recourse, if necessary, to the courts, and a petition for an injunction had been prepared, setting forth the details of the "corner" of 1866. On the Sunday preceding the election Drew, in view of his impending defeat, called upon Vanderbilt. That gentleman, thereupon, very amicably read to him the legal documents prepared for his benefit; whereupon the ready treasurer at once turned about, and, having hitherto been hampering the Commodore by his bear operations, he now agreed to join hands with him in giving to the market a strong upward tendency. Meanwhile the other parties to the contest were not idle. At the same house, at a later hour in the day, Vanderbilt explained to the Eastern adventurers his new plan of operations, which included the continuance of Drew in his directorship. These gentlemen were puzzled, not to say confounded, by this sudden change of front. An explanation was demanded, some plain language followed, and the parties separated, leaving everything unsettled; but only to meet again at a later hour at the house of Drew. There Vanderbilt brought the new men to terms by proposing to Drew a bold *coup de main*, calculated to throw them entirely out of the direction. Before the parties separated that night a written agreement had been entered into, providing that, to save appearances, the new board should be elected without Drew, but that immediately thereafter a vacancy should be created, and Drew chosen to fill it. He was therefore to go in as one of two directors in the Vanderbilt interest, that gentleman's nephew, Mr. Work, being the other.

This program was faithfully carried out, and on the 2d of October Wall Street was at once astonished by the news of the defeat of the notorious leader of the bears, and bewildered by the immediate resignation of a member of the new board and the election of Drew in his place. Apparently he had given in his submission, the one obstacle to success was removed, and the ever victorious Commodore had now but to close his fingers on his new prize. Virtual consolidation in the Vanderbilt interest seemed a foregone conclusion.

The reinstalment of Drew was followed by a period of hollow truce. A combination of capitalists, in pursuance of an arrangement already referred to, took advantage of this to transfer as much as possible of the spare cash of the "outside public" from its pockets to their own. A "pool" was formed, in view of the depressed condition of Erie, and Drew was left to manipulate the market for the advantage of those whom it might concern. The result of the Speculative Director's operations supplied a curious commentary on the ethics of the stock exchange, and made it questionable whether the ancient adage as to honor among a certain class in society is of universal application, or confined to its more persecuted members. One contributor to the "pool," in this instance, was Mr. ——, a friend of Vanderbilt. The ways of Mr. Drew were, as usual, past finding out; Mr. ——, however, grew impatient of waiting for the anticipated rise in Erie, and it occurred to him that, besides participating in the profits of the "pool," he might as well turn an honest penny by collateral operations on his own account, looking to the expected rise. Before embarking on his independent venture, however, he consulted Mr. Drew, it is said, who entirely declined to express any judgment as to the enterprise, but at the same time agreed to loan Mr. —— out of the "pool" any moneys he might require upon the security usual in such cases. Mr. —— availed himself of the means thus put at his disposal, and laid in a private stock of Erie. Still, however, the expected rise did not take place. Again he applied to Mr. Drew for information, but with no better success than before; and again, tempted by the cheapness of Erie, he borrowed further funds of the "pool," and made new purchases of stock. At last the long-continued depression of Erie aroused a dreadful suspicion in the bull operator, and inquiries were set on foot. He then discovered, to his astonishment and horror, that his stock had come to him through certain of the brokers of Mr. Drew. The members of the "pool" were at once called together, and Mr. Drew was appealed to on behalf of Mr. ——. It was suggested to him that it would be well to run Erie up to aid a confederate. Thereupon, with all the coolness imaginable, Mr. Drew announced that the "pool" had no Erie and wanted no Erie; that it had sold out its Erie and had realized large profits, which he now proposed to divide. Thereafter who could pretend to understand Daniel Drew? Who could fail to appreciate the humors of Wall Street? The controller of the "pool" had actually lent the money of the "pool" to one of the members of the "pool," to enable him to buy up the stock of the "pool"; and having thus quietly saddled him with it, the controller proceeded to divide the profits, and calmly returned to the victim a portion of his own money as his share of the proceeds. Yet, strange to say, Mr. —— wholly failed to see the humorous side of the transaction, and actually feigned great indignation.

This, however, was a mere sportive interlude between the graver scenes of the drama. The real conflict was now impending. Commodore Vanderbilt stretched out his hand to grasp Erie.

Erie was to be isolated and shut up within the limits of New York; it was to be given over, bound hand and foot, to the lord of the Central. To perfect this program, the representatives of all the competing lines met, and a proposition was submitted to the Erie party looking to a practical consolidation on certain terms of the Pennsylvania Central, the Erie, and the New York Central, and a division among the contracting parties of all the earnings from the New York City travel. A new illustration was thus to be afforded, at the expense of the trade and travel to and from the heart of a continent, of George Stephenson's famous aphorism, that where combination is possible competition is impossible. The Erie party, however, represented that their road earned more than half of the fund of which they were to receive only one third. They remonstrated and proposed modifications, but their opponents were inexorable. The terms were too hard; the conference led to no result; a ruinous competition seemed impending as the alternative to a fierce war of doubtful issue. Both parties now retired to their camps, and mustered their forces in preparation for the first overt act of hostility. They had not long to wait.

Vanderbilt was not accustomed to failure, and in this case the sense of treachery, the bitter consciousness of having been outwitted in the presence of all Wall Street, gave a peculiar sting to the rebuff. A long succession of victories had intensified his natural arrogance, and he was by no means disposed, even apart from the failure of his cherished plans, to sit down and nurse an impotent wrath in presence of an injured prestige. Foiled in intrigue, he must now have recourse to his favorite weapon,—the brute force of his millions. He therefore prepared to go out into Wall Street in his might, and to make himself master of the Erie, as before he had made himself master of the Hudson River road. The task in itself was one of magnitude. The volume of stock was immense; all of it was upon the street, and the necessary expenditure involved many millions of dollars. The peculiar difficulty of the task, however, lay in the fact that it had to be un-

dertaken in the face of antagonists so bold, so subtle, so unscrupulous, so thoroughly acquainted with Erie, as well as so
familiar with all the devices and tricks of fence of Wall Street,
as were those who now stood ready to take up the gage which
the Commodore so arrogantly threw down.

The first open hostilities took place on the seventeenth of February. For some time Wall Street had been agitated with forbod-
ings of the coming hostilities, but not until that day was recourse
had to the courts. Vanderbilt had two ends in view when he
sought to avail himself of the processes of law. In the first place,
Drew's long connection with Erie, and especially the unsettled
transactions arising out of the famous corner of 1866, afforded
admirable ground for annoying offensive operations; and, in the
second place, these very proceedings, by throwing his opponent
on the defensive, afforded an excellent cover for Vanderbilt's
own transactions in Wall Street. It was essential to his success
to corner Drew, but to corner Drew at all was not easy, and to
corner him in Erie was difficult indeed. Very recent experiences,
of which Vanderbilt was fully informed, no less than the memories of 1866, had fully warned the public how manifold and ingenious were the expedients through which the cunning treasurer
furnished himself with Erie, when the exigencies of his position
demanded fresh supplies. It was, therefore, very necessary for
Vanderbilt that he should, while buying Erie with one hand in
Wall Street, with the other close, so far as he could, that apparently inexhaustible spring from which such generous supplies of
new stock were wont to flow. Accordingly, on the seventeenth of
February, Mr. Frank Work, the only remaining representative of
the Vanderbilt faction in the Erie direction, accompanied by Mr.
Vanderbilt's attorneys, Messrs. Rapallo and Spenser, made his
appearance before Judge Barnard, of the Supreme Court of New
York, then sitting in chambers, and applied for an injunction
against Treasurer Drew and his brother directors, of the Erie
Railway, restraining them from the payment of interest or principal of the three and a half millions borrowed of the treasurer in

1866, as well as from releasing Drew from any liability or cause
of action the company might have against him, pending an investigation of his accounts as treasurer; on the other hand, Drew
was to be enjoined from taking any legal steps toward compelling
a settlement. A temporary injunction was granted in accordance
with the petition, and a further hearing was assigned for the
twenty-first. Two days later, however,—on the nineteenth of the
month,—without waiting for the result of the first attack, the
same attorneys appeared again before Judge Barnard, and now
in the name of the people, acting through the Attorney-General,
petitioned for the removal from office of Treasurer Drew. The
papers in the case set forth some of the difficulties which beset
the Commodore, and exposed the existence of a new fountain of
Erie stock. It appeared that there was a recently enacted statute
of New York which authorized any railroad company to create
and issue its own stock in exchange for the stock of any other
road under lease to it. The petition then alleged that Mr. Drew
and certain of his brother directors, had quietly possessed themselves of a worthless road connecting with the Erie, and called
the Buffalo, Bradford, & Pittsburgh Railroad, and had then, as
occasion and their own exigencies required, proceeded to supply
themselves with whatever Erie stock they wanted, by leasing
their own road to the road of which they were directors, and
then creating stock and issuing it to themselves, in exchange,
under the authority vested in them by law. The uncontradicted
history of this transaction, as subsequently set forth on the very
doubtful authority of a leading Erie director, affords, indeed,
a most happy illustration of brilliant railroad financiering,
whether true in this case or not. The road, it was stated, cost
the purchasers, as financiers, some $250,000; as proprietors, they
then issued in its name bonds for two million dollars, payable to
one of themselves, who now figured as trustee. This person, then,
shifting his character, drew up, as counsel for both parties, a
contract leasing this road to the Erie Railway for four hundred
and ninety-nine years, the Erie agreeing to assume the bonds; re-

appearing in their original character of Erie directors, these
gentlemen then ratified the lease, and thereafter it only remained for them to relapse into the rôle of financiers, and to
divide the proceeds. All this was happily accomplished, and the
Erie Railway lost and someone gained $140,000 a year by the
bargain. The skilful actors in this much-shifting drama probably
proceeded on the familiar theory that exchange is no robbery;
and the expedient was certainly ingenious.

Such is the story of this proceeding as told under oath by one
who must have known the whole truth. That the facts are correctly set forth by no means follows. Indeed, many parts of this
narrative are open to this criticism. The evidence on which it is
founded may be sufficiently clear, but unfortunately the witnesses are not seldom wholly unworthy of credence. The formality of an oath may accompany plausible statements without
giving to them the slightest additional weight. In this case the
sworn allegations were made, and they implicated certain respectable men; it can only be said of them that their falsehood is
not patent, and that they are thoroughly in character with other
transactions known to be true. If the facts of the case were correctly stated, or had in them an element of truth, it is difficult to
see what fiduciary relation these directors, as trustees, did not
violate. However this may be, it is indisputable that the supply
of Erie on the market had been largely increased from the source
indicated, and Commodore Vanderbilt naturally desired to put
some limit to the amount of the stock in existence, a majority of
which he sought to control. Accordingly it was now further ordered by Mr. Justice Barnard that Mr. Drew should show cause
on the twenty-first why the prayer of the petitioner should not
be granted, and meanwhile he was temporarily suspended from
his position as treasurer and director.

It was not until the third of March, however, that any decisive
action was taken by Judge Barnard on either of the petitions before him. Even then, that in the name of the Attorney-General
was postponed for final hearing until the tenth of the month;

but, on the application of Work, an injunction was issued restraining the Erie board from any new issue of capital stock, by conversion of bonds or otherwise, in addition to the 251,058 shares appearing in the previous reports of the road, and forbidding the guaranty by the Erie of the bonds of any connecting line of road. While this last provision of the order was calculated to furnish food for thought to the Boston party, matter for meditation was supplied to Mr. Drew by other clauses, which specially forbade him, his agents, attorneys, or brokers, to have any transactions in Erie, or fulfil any of his contracts already entered into, until he had returned to the company sixty-eight thousand shares of capital stock, alleged to be the number involved in the unsettled transaction of 1866, and the more recent Buffalo, Bradford, & Pittsburgh exchange. A final hearing was fixed for the tenth of March on both injunctions.

Things certainly did not now promise well for Treasurer Drew and the bear party. Vanderbilt and the bulls seemed to arrange everything to meet their own views; apparently they had but to ask and it was granted. If any virtue existed in the processes of law, if any authority was wielded by a New York court, it now seemed as if the very head of the bear faction must needs be converted into a bull in his own despite, and to his manifest ruin. He, in this hour of his trial, was to be forced by his triumphant opponent to make Erie scarce by returning into its treasury sixty-eight thousand shares,—one-fourth of its whole capital stock of every description. So far from manufacturing fresh Erie and pouring it into the street, he was to be cornered by a writ, and forced to work his own ruin in obedience to an injunction. Appearances are, however, proverbially deceptive, and all depended on the assumption that some virtue did exist in the processes of law, and that some authority was wielded by a New York court. In spite of the threatening aspect of his affairs, it was very evident that the nerves of Mr. Drew and his associates were not seriously affected. Wall Street watched him with curiosity not unmingled with alarm, for this was a conflict of Titans. Hedged all around with orders of the court, suspended, enjoined, and threatened with all manner of unheard-of processes, with Vanderbilt's wealth standing like a lion in his path, and all Wall Street ready to turn upon him and rend him,—in presence of all these accumulated terrors of the courtroom and of the exchange, the Speculative Director was not less speculative than was his wont. He seemed rushing on destruction. Day after day he pursued the same "short"* tactics; contract after contract was put out for the future delivery of stock at current prices, and this, too, in the face of a continually rising market. Evidently he did not yet consider himself at the end of his resources.

It was equally evident, however, that he had not much time to lose. It was now the third of March, and the anticipated "corner" might be looked for about the tenth. As usual, some light skirmishing took place as a prelude to the heavy shock of decisive battle. The Erie party very freely and openly expressed a decided lack of respect, and something approaching contempt, for the purity of that particular fragment of the judicial ermine which was supposed to adorn the person of Mr. Justice Barnard. They did not pretend to conceal their conviction that this magistrate was a piece of the Vanderbilt property, and they very plainly announced their intention of seeking for justice elsewhere. With this end in view they betook themselves to their own town of Binghamton, in the county of Broome, where they duly presented themselves before Mr. Justice Balcom, of the Supreme Court. The existing judicial system of New York divides the state into eight distinct districts, each of which has an independent Supreme Court of four judges, elected by the citizens of that district. The first district alone enjoys five judges, the fifth being the Judge Barnard already referred to. These local judges, however, are clothed with certain equity powers in actions commenced before them, which run throughout the state. As one subject of litigation, therefore, might affect many indi-

---

* An operator is said to be "short" when he has agreed to deliver that which he has not got. He wagers, in fact, on a fall.

viduals, each of whom might initiate legal proceedings before any of the thirty-three judges; which judge, again, might forbid proceedings before any or all of the other judges, or issue a state of proceedings in suits already commenced, and then proceed to make orders, to consolidate actions, and to issue process for contempt,—it was not improbable that, sooner or later, strange and disgraceful conflicts of authority would arise, and that the law would fall into contempt. Such a system can, in fact, be sustained only so long as coördinate judges use the delicate powers of equity with a careful regard to private rights and the dignity of the law, and therefore, more than any which has ever been devised, it calls for a high average of learning, dignity, and personal character in the occupants of the bench. When, therefore, the ermine of the judge is flung into the kennel of party politics and becomes a part of the spoils of political victory; when by any chance partisanship, brutality, and corruption become the qualities which especially recommend the successful aspirant to judicial honors, then the system described will be found to furnish peculiar facilities for the display of these characteristics.

Taking advantage of the occasion this system, so simple in theory, so complicated in practice, afforded for creating complications by obtaining conflicting orders from coördinate judges, the Erie party broke ground in a new suit. The injunction was no sooner asked of Judge Balcom than it was granted, and Mr. Frank Work, the Attorney-General, and all other parties litigant, were directed to show cause at Cortlandville on the seventh of March; and, meanwhile, Mr. Director Work, accused of being a spy in the councils of Erie, was temporarily suspended from his position, and all proceedings in the suits commenced before Judge Barnard were stayed. The moment, however, this order became known in New York, a new suit was commenced by the Vanderbilt interest in the name of Richard Schell; an urban judge cried check to the move of the rural judge, by forbidding any meeting of the Erie board, or the transaction of any business by it, unless Director Work was at full liberty to participate therein. The first move of the Drew faction did not seem likely to result in any signal advantage to its cause.

All this, however, was mere skirmishing, and now the decisive engagement was near at hand. The plans of the Erie Ring were matured, and, if Commodore Vanderbilt wanted the stock of their road, they were prepared to let him have all he desired. As usual the Erie treasury was at this time deficient in funds. As usual, also, Daniel Drew stood ready to advance all the funds required—on proper security. One kind of security, and only one, the company was disposed at this time to offer,—its convertible bonds under a pledge of conversion. The company could not issue stock outright, in any case, at less than par; its bonds bore interest, and were useless on the street; an issue of convertible bonds was another name for an issue of stock to be sold at market rates. The treasurer readily agreed to find a purchaser, and, in fact, he himself stood just then in pressing need of some scores of thousands of shares. Already at the meeting of the Board of Directors, on the nineteenth of February, a very deceptive account of the condition of the road, jockied out of the general superintendent, had been read and made public; the increased depot facilities, the projected double track, and the everlasting steel rails, had been made to do vigorous duty; and the board had, in the vaguest and most general language conceivable, clothed the Executive Committee with full power in the premises.* Immedi-

* This vote of the Board of Directors of the Erie Railway Company was the sole authority under which, without further consultation with the board, the stock of the road was increased four hundred and fifty thousand shares. It was worded as follows:—

"It being necessary for the finishing, completing, and operating the road of the company, to borrow money,

"*Resolved*, That under the provisions of the statute authorizing the loan of money for such purposes, the Executive Committee be authorized to borrow such sum as may be necessary, and to issue therefor such security as is provided for in such cases by the laws of this State; and that the president and secretary be authorized, under the seal of the company, to execute all needful and proper agreements and undertakings for such purpose."

The law referred to was Subdivision 10 of Section 28 of the General Railroad Act of 1850, which authorized the railroad companies to which it ap-

ately after the Board of Directors adjourned a meeting of the Executive Committee was held, and a vote to issue at once convertible bonds for ten millions gave a meaning to very ambiguous language of the directors' resolve; and thus, when apparently on the very threshold of his final triumph, this mighty mass of one hundred thousand shares of new stock was hanging like an avalanche over the head of Vanderbilt.

The Executive Committee had voted to sell the entire amount of these bonds at not less than 72½. Five millions were placed upon the market at once, and Mr. Drew's broker became the purchaser, Mr. Drew giving him a written guaranty against loss, and being entitled to any profit. It was all done in ten minutes after the committee adjourned,—the bonds issued, their conversion into stock demanded and complied with, and certificates for fifty thousand shares deposited in the broker's safe, subject to the orders of Daniel Drew. There they remained until the twenty-ninth, when they were issued, on his requisition, to certain others of that gentleman's army of brokers, much as ammunition might be issued before a general engagement. Three days later came the Barnard injunction, and Erie suddenly rose in the market. Then it was determined to bring up the reserves and let the eager bulls have the other five millions. The history of

plied "to borrow such sums of money as may be necessary for completing, finishing, and operating the road"; to mortgage their roads as security for such loans; and to "confer on any holder of any bond issued for money borrowed as aforesaid, the right to convert the principal due or owing thereon into stock of said company, at any time, not exceeding ten years from the date of the bond, under such regulations as the directors may see fit to adopt."

It was an open question whether this law applied at all to the Erie Railway Company, the amount of the capital stock of which was otherwise regulated by law; the bonds were issued and sold, not as bonds, but with a distinct pledge of immediate conversion into stock, and as an indirect way of doing that, the direct doing of which was clearly illegal; finally, as a matter of fact, the proceeds of these bonds were not used for "completing, finishing, or operating the road." As a matter of law the question is of no interest outside of New York, and is as yet undecided there. Of the good faith and morality of the transaction but one opinion exists anywhere.

this second issue was, in all respects, an episode worthy of Erie, and deserves minute relation. It was decided upon on the third, but before the bonds were converted Barnard's injunction had been served on everyone connected with the Erie road or with Daniel Drew. The tenth was the return day of the writ, but the Erie operators needed even less time for their deliberations. Monday, the ninth, was settled upon as the day upon which to defeat the impending "corner." The night of Saturday, the seventh, was a busy one in the Erie camp. While one set of counsel and clerks were preparing affidavits and prayers for strange writs and injunctions, the enjoined vice-president of the road was busy at home signing certificates of stock, to be ready for instant use in case a modification of the injunction could be obtained, and another set of counsel was in immediate attendance on the leaders themselves. Mr. Groesbeck, the chief of the Drew brokers, being himself enjoined, secured elsewhere, after one or two failures, a purchaser of the bonds, and took him to the house of the Erie counsel, where Drew and other directors and brokers then were. There the terms of the nominal sale were agreed upon, and a contract was drawn up transferring the bonds to this man of straw, who in return gave Mr. Drew a full power of attorney to convert or otherwise dispose of the bonds, in the form of a promissory note for their purchase money; Mr. Groesbeck, meanwhile, with the fear of injunctions before his eyes, prudently withdrew into the next room, and amused himself by looking at the curiosities and conversing with the lawyers' young gentlemen. After the contract was closed, the purchaser was asked to sign an affidavit setting forth his ownership of the bonds and the refusal of the corporation to convert them into stock in compliance with their contract, upon which affidavit it was in contemplation to seek from some justice a writ of mandamus to compel the Erie Railway to convert them, the necessary papers for such a proceeding being then in course of preparation elsewhere. This the purchaser declined to do. One of the lawyers present then said: "Well, you can make the demand now; here is Mr. Drew, the treasurer of the company, and Mr. Gould, one of the Executive Committee.'' In accordance with this suggestion a demand for the stock was then made, and, of course, at once refused; thereupon the scruples of the man of straw being all removed, the desired affidavit was signed. All business now being finished, the parties separated; the legal papers were ready, the convertible bonds had been disposed of, and the certificates of stock, for which they were to be exchanged, were signed in blank and ready for delivery.

Early Monday morning the Erie people were at work. Mr. Drew, the director and treasurer, had agreed to sell on that day fifty thousand shares of the stock, at 80, to the firms of which Mr. Fisk and Mr. Gould were members, these gentlemen also being Erie directors and members of the Executive Committee. The new certificates, made out in the names of these firms on Saturday night, were in the hands of the secretary of the company, who was strictly enjoined from allowing their issue. On Monday morning this official directed an employee of the road to carry these books of certificates from the West Street office of the company to the transfer clerk in Pine Street, and there to deliver them carefully. The messenger left the room, but immediately returned empty handed, and informed the astonished secretary that Mr. Fisk had met him outside the door, taken from him the books of unissued certificates, and ''run away with them.'' It was true;—one essential step toward conversion had been taken; the certificates of stock were beyond the control of an injunction. During the afternoon of the same day the convertible bonds were found upon the secretary's desk, where they had been placed by Mr. Belden, the partner in business of Director James Fisk, Jr.; the certificates were next seen in Broad Street.

Before launching the bolt thus provided, the conspirators had considered it not unadvisable to cover their proceedings, if they could, with some form of law. This probably was looked upon as an idle ceremony, but it could do no harm; and perhaps their next step was dictated by what has been called "a decent respect for the opinions of mankind," combined with a profound contempt for judges and courts of law.

Early on the morning of the ninth Judge Gilbert, a highly respected magistrate of the Second Judicial District, residing in Brooklyn, was waited upon by one of the Erie counsel, who desired to initiate before him a new suit in the Erie litigation,— this time, in the name of the Saturday evening purchaser of bonds and maker of affidavits. A writ of mandamus was asked for. This writ clearly did not lie in such a case; the magistrate very properly declined to grant it, and the only wonder is that counsel should have applied for it. New counsel were then hurriedly summoned, and a new petition, in a fresh name, was presented. This petition was for an injuction, in the name of Belden, the partner of Mr. Fisk, and the documents then and there presented were probably as eloquent an exposure as could possibly have been penned of the lamentable condition into which the once honored judiciary of New York had fallen. The petition alleged that some time in February certain persons, among whom was especially named George G. Barnard,—the justice of the Supreme Court of the First District,—had entered into a combination to speculate in the stock of the Erie Railway, and to use the process of the courts for the purpose of aiding their speculation; "and that, in furtherance of the plans of this combination," the actions in Work's name had been commenced before Barnard, who, the counsel asserted, was then issuing injunctions at the rate of half a dozen a day. It is impossible by any criticism to do justice to such audacity as this: the dumb silence of amazement is the only fitting commentary. Apparently, however, nothing that could be stated of his colleague across the river exceeded the belief of Judge Gilbert, for, after some trifling delays and a few objections on the part of the judge to the form of the desired order, the Erie counsel hurried away, and returned to New York with a new injunction, restraining all the parties to all the other suits from further proceedings, and from doing any acts in "furtherance of said conspiracy";—in one paragraph ordering the Erie directors, except Work, to continue in the discharge of their duties, in direct defiance of the injunction of one judge, and in the next, with an equal disregard of another judge, forbidding the directors to desist from converting bonds into stock. Judge Gilbert having, a few hours before signing this wonderful order, refused to issue a writ of mandamus, it may be proper to add that the process of equity here resorted to, compelling the performance of various acts, is of recent invention, and is known as a "mandatory injunction."

All was now ready. The Drew party were enjoined in every direction. One magistrate had forbidden them to move, and another magistrate had ordered them not to stand still. If the Erie board held meetings and transacted business, it violated one injunction; if it abstained from doing so, it violated another. By the further conversion of bonds into stock pains and penalties would be incurred at the hands of Judge Barnard; the refusal to convert would be an act of disobedience to Judge Gilbert. Strategically considered, the position could not be improved, and Mr. Drew and his friends were not the men to let the golden moment escape them. At once, before a new injunction could be obtained, even in New York, fifty thousand shares of new Erie stock were flung upon the market. That day Erie was buoyant,—Vanderbilt was purchasing. His agents caught at the new stock as eagerly as at the old, and the whole of it was absorbed before its origin was suspected, and almost without a falter in the price. Then the fresh certificates appeared, and the truth became known. Erie had that day opened at 80 and risen rapidly to 83, while its rise even to par was predicted; suddenly it faltered, fell off, and then dropped suddenly to 71. Wall Street had never been subjected to a greater shock, and the market reeled to and fro like a drunken man between these giants, as they hurled about shares by the tens of thousands, and money by the million. When night put an end to the conflict, Erie stood at 78, the shock of battle was over, and the astonished brokers drew breath as they waited for the events of the morrow. The attempted "corner" was a failure, and Drew was victorious,—no doubt existed in that point. The question now was, could Vanderbilt sustain himself? In spite of all his wealth, must he not go down before his cunning opponent?

The morning of the eleventh found the Erie leaders still transacting business at the office of the corporation in West Street. It would seem that these gentlemen, in spite of the glaring contempt for the process of the courts of which they had been guilty, had made no arrangements for an orderly retreat beyond the jurisdiction of the tribunals they had set at defiance. They were speedily roused from their real or affected tranquillity by trustworthy intelligence that processes for contempt were already issued against them, and that their only chance of escape from incarceration lay in precipitate flight. At ten o'clock the astonished police saw a throng of panic-stricken railway directors— looking more like a frightened gang of thieves, disturbed in the division of their plunder, than like the wealthy representatives of a great corporation—rush headlong from the doors of the Erie office, and dash off in the direction of the Jersey ferry. In their hands were packages and files of papers, and their pockets were crammed with assets and securities. One individual bore away with him in a hackney coach bales containing six millions of dollars in greenbacks. Other members of the board followed under cover of the night; some of them, not daring to expose themselves to the publicity of a ferry, attempted to cross in open boats concealed by the darkness and a March fog. Two directors, who lingered, were arrested; but a majority of the Executive Committee collected at the Erie station in Jersey City, and there, free from any apprehension of Judge Barnard's pursuing wrath, proceeded to the transaction of business.

Meanwhile, on the other side of the river, Vanderbilt was struggling in the toils. As usual in these Wall Street operations, there was a grim humor in the situation. Had Vanderbilt failed to sustain the market, a financial collapse and panic must have ensued which would have sent him to the wall. He had sustained it, and had absorbed a hundred thousand shares of Erie. Thus when Drew retired to Jersey City he carried with him seven millions of his opponent's money, and the Commodore had freely supplied the enemy with the sinews of war. He had grasped at Erie for his own sake, and now his opponents derisively promised to rehabilitate and vivify the old road with the money he had furnished them, so as more effectually to compete with the lines which he already possessed. Nor was this all. Had they done as they loudly claimed they meant to do, Vanderbilt might have hugged himself in the faith that, after all, it was but a question of time, and the prize would come to him in the end. He, however, knew well enough that the most pressing need of the Erie people was money with which to fight him. With this he had now furnished them abundantly, and he must have felt that no scruples would prevent their use of it.

Vanderbilt had, however, little leisure to devote to the enjoyment of the humorous side of his position. The situation was alarming. His opponents had carried with them in their flight seven millions in currency, which were withdrawn from circulation. An artificial stringency was thus created in Wall Street, and, while money rose, stocks fell, and unusual margins were called in. Vanderbilt was carrying a fearful load, and the least want of confidence, the faintest sign of faltering, might well bring on a crash. He already had a hundred thousand shares of Erie, not one of which he could sell. He was liable at any time to be called upon to carry as much more as his opponents, skilled by long practice in the manufacture of the article, might see fit to produce. Opposed to him were men who scrupled at nothing, and who knew every in and out of the money market. With every look and every gesture anxiously scrutinized, a position more trying than his can hardly be conceived. It is not known from what source he drew the vast sums which enabled him to surmount his difficulties with such apparent ease. His nerve, however, stood him in at least as good stead as his financial resources.

Like a great general, in the hour of trial he inspired confidence. While fighting for life he could "talk horse" and play whist. The manner in which he then emerged from his troubles, serene and confident, was as extraordinary as the financial resources he commanded.

Meanwhile, before turning to the tide of battle, which now swept away from the courts of law into the halls of legislation, there are two matters to be disposed of; the division of the spoils is to be recounted, and the old and useless lumber of conflict must be cleared away. The division of profits accruing to Mr. Treasurer Drew and his associate directors, acting as individuals, was a fit conclusion to the stock issue just described. The bonds for five millions, after their conversion, realized nearly four millions of dollars, of which $3,625,000 passed into the treasury of the company. The trustees of the stockholders had therefore in this case secured a profit for someone of $375,000. Confidence in the good faith of one's kind is very commendable, but possession is nine points of the law. Mr. James Fisk, Jr., through whom the sales were mainly effected, declined to make any payments in excess of the $3,625,000, until a division of profits was agreed upon. It seems that, by virtue of a paper signed by Mr. Drew as early as the nineteenth of February, Gould, Fisk, and others were entitled to one-half the profits he should make "in certain transactions." What these transactions were, or whether the official action of Directors Gould and Fisk was in any way influenced by the signing of this document, does not appear. Mr. Fisk now gave Mr. Drew, in lieu of cash, his uncertified check for the surplus $375,000 remaining from this transaction, with stock as collateral amounting to about the half of that sum. With this settlement, and the redemption of the collateral, Mr. Drew was fain to be content. Seven months afterward he still retained possession of the uncertified check, in the payment of which, if presented, he seemed to entertain no great confidence. Everything, however, showed conclusively the advantage of operating from interior lines. While the Erie treasury was once more re-

plete, three of the persons who had been mainly instrumental in
filling it had not suffered in the transaction. The treasurer was
richer by $180,000 directly, and he himself only knew by how
much more incidentally. In like manner his faithful adjutants
had profited to an amount as much exceeding $60,000 each as
their sagacity had led them to provide for.

The useless lumber of conflict, consisting chiefly of the numerous judges of the Supreme Court of New York and their conflicting processes of law, must next be disposed of. Judge Gilbert
was soon out of the field. His process had done its work, and
the Erie counselors hardly deigned upon the eighteenth, which
was the day fixed for showing cause, to go over to Brooklyn and
listen to indignant denunciations on the part of their Vanderbilt
brethren, as, with a very halting explanation of his hasty action,
Judge Gilbert peremptorily denied the request for further delay,
and refused to continue his injunction. It is due to this magistrate to say that he is one of the most respected in the state of
New York; and when that is said, much is implied in the facts
already stated as to his opinion of some of his brother judges.
Judicial demoralization can go no further. If Judge Gilbert was
out of the fray, however, Judge Barnard was not. The wrath and
indignation of this curious product of a system of elective judiciary cannot be described, nor were they capable of utterance.
They took strange forms of expression. At one time he sent all
the papers relating to the alleged conspiracy down to the grand
jury, and apparently sought thereby to indicate that he courted
an investigation. The prosecuting attorneys, however, better instructed in the law, seem to have doubted whether a matter which
was the proper subject for a legislative impeachment could satisfactorily be brought before a petty jury on an indictment, and
did not pursue the investigation. Then, at a later day, the judge
mysteriously intimated that the belief of both the counsel and the
affiants in the truth of the charges contained in the complaint
before Judge Gilbert was then a matter of investigation before a
criminal body, to see whether or not it constituted perjury. Fi-

nally, a heavy collection of counter-affidavits purified the judicial skirts from their taints, but not until fresh and more aggravated grounds for indignation had presented themselves. It is unnecessary to go into the details of the strange and revolting scenes which the next few months witnessed in the rooms of the Supreme Court. They read like some monstrous parody of the forms of law; some Saturnalia of bench and bar. The magistrate became more partisan than were the paid advocates before him, and all seemed to vie with one another in their efforts to bring their common profession into public contempt. Day and night detectives in the pay of suitors dogged the steps of the magistrate, and their sworn affidavits, filed in his own court, sought to implicate him in an attempt to kidnap Drew by means of armed ruffians, and to bring the fugitive by violence within reach of his process. Then, in retaliation, the judge openly avowed from the bench that his spies had penetrated into the consultations of the litigants, and he astonished a witness by angrily interrogating him as to an affidavit reflecting upon himself, to which that witness had declined to make oath.* At one moment he wept, as

---

* *Question by the Court to Mr. Belden.* Did not Mr. Field send you, two or three days ago, an affidavit filled with gross abuse of me, and you declined to sign it?

Witness (producing a paper). This is the affidavit. I said I would rather not sign it. . . .

Question by Mr. Field. Did you show that affidavit to Judge Barnard?

A. I did not.

Q. How, then, did he learn of its being sent to you?

Judge Barnard. He does not know, and never will in this world. I am now doing as other people have been doing; I have been followed by detectives for four or five weeks all over the city, and now I am following others. . . .

Q. Was it not stated openly to you, in a law office below Chambers Street, that you must prevent, at all hazards, Judge Barnard from hearing this case?

A. In hearing which case, Judge? I do not know which case you refer to.

Q. The case before me. . . .

Q. When you were present at the Metropolitan Hotel, did not one of the counsel, who was there, when he heard the complaint read, say that it was a shame to put Judge Barnard in as a defendant, and did not Dudley Field

counsel detailed before him the story of his own grievances and the insults to which he had been subjected, and then again he vindicated his purity by select specimens of pothouse rhetoric.* When the Vanderbilt counsel moved to fix a day on which their opponents should show cause why a receiver of the proceeds of the last overissue of stock should not be appointed, the judge astonished the petitioners by outstripping their eagerness, and appointing Vanderbilt's own son-in-law receiver on the spot. Then followed a fierce altercation in court, in which bench and bar took equal part, and which closed with the not unusual threat of impeaching the presiding judge.† When Mr. John B. Haskin was placed upon the stand, there ensued a scene which Barnard

say, that by doing so he could frighten him off the bench and overawe the balance?

A. I do not remember anything of it.

Q. See if one of the counsel did not tell you that it was a shame to put him in as one of the defendants, and whether another of the counsel did not tell you that that was the only way to scare him off the bench, and that you could overawe the balance of the judges?

A. I don't remember anything being said about overawing anyone.

* "In this wide city of a million or a million and a half of inhabitants, where a man can be hired for five dollars to swear any man's life away, there is not one so base as to come upon this stand and swear that I had anything to do with any conspiracy."

† The matter before the court, regarding the bail of the contumacious directors, being disposed of, Mr. Clark, of the Vanderbilt counsel, rose and referred to another matter, which proved to be no less than an application for an order appointing a receiver of all the property, amounting to millions of dollars, which had been issued in violation of the injunction.

Mr. Field. This is an *ex parte* application and we do not care anything about it. The worse you make the case the better it will be in the end.

Mr. Rapallo. I ask your honor to make this order returnable on Monday morning.

The Court. I do not think it necessary to wait till Monday morning. You had better have it returnable forthwith.

Mr. Clark. We ask that that paper (the order to show cause instantly) be served upon Mr. Diven, who is now in court.

The order was then served on an individual director then in court, and Mr. Clark moved the appointment of the receiver.

Judge Barnard. Is there any objection to this application?

Mr. Field sat smilingly in his chair, which was tipped back on its rear legs,

himself not inaptly characterized the next day as "outrageous and scandalous, and insulting to the court." Upon this occasion the late Mr. James T. Brady seemed to be on the verge of a personal collision with the witness in open court; the purity of the presiding magistrate was impugned, his venality openly implied through a long cross-examination, and the witness acknowledged that he had himself in the course of his career undertaken for money to influence the mind of the judge privately "on the side of right." All the scandals of the practice of the law, and the private immoralities of lawyers, were dragged into the broad light of day; the whole system of favored counsel, of private argument, of referees, and of unblushing extortion, was freely discussed.* On a subsequent day the judge himself made in-

and looked composed in the extreme, but made no response to the inquiry of the judge.

The Court. Draw up an order appointing George A. Osgood receiver of this fund, with security in the sum of $1,000,000, and requiring these defendants to appear before a referee in regard to the matter.

Mr. Field (rising). The court will understand that this was *ex parte.*

Mr. Clark. We have given notice, and therefore this is not *ex parte.*

Mr. Field. There has been no notice given; there has been no service. This is *ex parte,* and now if anyone will enter that order, I want to see him do it.

Mr. Fullerton (excitedly and earnestly). I dare enter that order, and will do it with your honor's permission.

Mr. Field. May it please the court, there have been no papers submitted in this case, and no affidavits presented on which this order is made. You have made it upon blank paper, and in complete absence of any regular proceeding whatever. I wish to say, however, that just so sure as this proceeding is being taken in this form, a day of reckoning will as surely come, when these parties will have to answer before someone for this action.

Mr. Fullerton (in a decidedly animated tone). Let that day come, and there will be a reckoning that you will have to bear, and so will every one of those men who have been engaged in this transaction.

* John B. Haskin was called as the next witness for the people, and examined by Mr. Clark, and testified that he was an attorney at law, and had practiced about twenty-six years.

Question by Mr. Clark. Were you ever employed by Mr. Dudley Field, professionally, prior to the 1st of March, or since?

A. I was applied to by Mr. Dudley Field, the attorney for Mr. Gould, on the 5th or 6th of March last, to accept a retainer in this Erie Railroad con-

quiries as to a visit of two of the directors to one gentleman supposed to have peculiar influence over the judicial mind, and

troversy, which I declined. I had never previous to that time been employed or requested to act as counsel by Mr. Field.

Mr. Brady, "on his own responsibility," objected to this line of examination; but after some discussion it was admitted, and the witness continued:—

Mr. Dudley Field, on the morning on the 5th or 6th of March, called at my office, and desired to retain me as counsel in this Erie controversy. I asked him on which side, and he said, "The Drew side." I asked him before whom, and he said, before Judge Barnard. I replied that my intimacy had been very great with Judge Barnard, and that I supposed he thought my influence as associate in this case would assist his side of the litigation.

Q. What further was said?

A. He said that he desired me to accept a retainer in the case, and said that if I would do so, it might be the means of avoiding serious trouble which would take place in the legislature, as I was Judge Barnard's friend, and if I would get that injunction modified I might, as his friend, prevent the terrible consequences which would result in this fight which was to take place, as Judge Barnard would be impeached; I then left him, and went into another office. In a short time Dudley Field came back, and handed me this book [producing a book], with his written modification of the injunction, as I believe, in his own handwriting, saying, "If you will get that signed by Judge Barnard, I will give you five thousand dollars; if that sum is not sufficient, I will make it more." I declined the offer; and having occasion to go to the City Hall to see Judge Barnard, I went, and met him at the Astor House, where he had gone with some friends,—John R. Hackett, Mr. Thomson, one of the directors of the Erie Railroad Company, and some others whom I do not recollect. I told him incidentally of this application to me, and he said: "Dudley Field must be a dirty fellow to apply to you for this modification in this way, for he applied to me in court this morning for this same modification, and I refused to grant it."

Q. Did you see Dudley Field again?

A. I did not see him again.

Q. Did you accept the retainer?

A. I did not accept the retainer or undertake the service.

.   .   .   .

Cross-examination by Mr. James T. Brady.

Q. Well, Mr. Haskin, have you ever in your life been applied to by anybody, to use your influence, personally or professionally, with Judge Barnard, to accomplish any result whatever?

A. Yes, sir; I think I have.

Q. Personally?

A. Yes.

evinced great familiarity with the negotiations then carried on,
and even showed some disposition to extend the inquiry indefi-

Q. Professionally?

A. Yes.

Q. To influence his action as a judge?

A. Well, no; not that.

Q. What, then?

A. Well, in cases where there were great interests at stake, to point out
to him certain objects that were entitled to consideration.

Q. Did you ever agree or undertake to influence his action as a judge?

A. I might have done so on the side of right. What do you mean, sir?

Mr. Brady. O well, you will understand what I mean, sir. Have you never
in all your life used your influence with Judge Barnard to induce him to
make a decision in favor of some person in litigation whose cause you espoused?

A. I don't recollect any case of that kind.

Q. Will you swear that you have never done so?

A. I won't swear I didn't, because I might have done it in some case in
the number of years I have been acquainted with him.

Q. Did you ever receive any kind of reward, directly or indirectly, for
using any species of influence, or promising to use any species of influence,
with Judge Barnard, or control or direct his action in any respect whatever?

A. I have never received anything; no, sir, except my legitimate fees,
which I have received in references and so forth.

.   .   .   .

He then asked him about his connection with the Christy will case.

Witness said he was general counsel in that.

Q. How did you earn your fee?

Witness. I will not answer; it is none of your business; it is impertinent.

Mr. Clark interposed, and said it was irrelevant.

Mr. Brady. I want to show that Mr. Haskin received a fee for his influence with the judge to gain a decision at the General Term.

Mr. Haskin said there was a suit pending about the matter.

Mr. Brady repeated that when he went into the case he knew the hostility
with which he would be met. He was prepared for it. He had known some
of the men a great many years, and he had hitherto kept still. He would
repeat the question about the Christy will case.

Witness. I refuse to answer; it is none of your business.

Witness further on gave some testimony as to what he said to Judge Barnard about the Merchants' Express Company case before that judge last
summer; he (witness) was not a counsel in it, but when on a fishing excur-
sion last summer he was talking with the court about the law of the case.
He told the judge there were some cases in which a judge could not afford

nitely into periodical literature.* Nor were the lawyers in any way behind the judge. At one moment they would indulge in personal wrangling, and accuse each other of the grossest malpractice, and the next, favor each other with remarks upon manners, more pointed than delicate. All this time injunctions were

to do a favor for a friend; I knew you were in the case, Mr. Brady; I told Judge Barnard that the newspapers were all down on the express monopoly.

Mr. Brady. Did you tell Judge Barnard in what cases a judge could afford to do a favor for a friend! You say you told him there were some in which a judge could not do a favor.

A. I did not say there were any.

.   .   .   .

The next day it was supposed that Mr. Field would be examined and the courtroom was crowded. Judge Barnard, however, declined to proceed any further, and ordered the evidence of the previous day to be stricken from the record. He further stated that he had already been busily engaged during the day in the other courtroom, and did not intend to sit here to gratify impertinent curiosity. . . . In regard to the examination of Mr. Field, he (Mr. Field) could make his affidavit *ex parte*, and would have the same publicity given to his testimony as had been given to that taken yesterday.

Mr. Brady said he appeared this afternoon exclusively to attend to the examination of Mr. Field. Of course he had had no notice on his side of the case that there had been any conference between his honor and other eminent gentlemen as to what course should be taken. He had come to take charge of Mr. Field's case, and as regards whatever had happened, he took the whole responsibility of it. It belonged to him exclusively,—every question, every suggestion,—as it would also belong to him hereafter. He simply asked now that Mr. Field have the opportunity to be heard in the matter publicly, as the other witnesses had been.

Mr. Clark, in reply, said that he would give Mr. Brady a promise that, if he lived, he (Mr. Brady) should have the opportunity of examining Mr. Field before a referee, if they could agree upon a gentleman who should be acceptable.

.   .   .   .

Judge Barnard, in reply to Mr. Field, who asked for the appointment of a referee, said that he had made the only order in the case he would make to-day, and that the matter would now stand adjourned until Thursday next, at three o'clock, P.M.

No affidavit of Mr. Field was ever taken, and the subject was allowed to drop.

* *Question by the Judge to Mr. Belden.* Do you know whether James Fisk, Jr., and William H. Marston, went in a carriage to John J. Crane's house and offered him $50,000 to vacate this injunction; and did you hear from a

flying about like hailstones; but the crowning injunction of all was issued, in reference to the appointment of a receiver, by Judge Clerke, a colleague of Judge Barnard, at the time sitting as a member of the Court of Appeals at Albany. The Gilbert injunction had gone, it might have seemed, sufficiently far, in enjoining Barnard the individual, while distinctly disavowing all reference to him in his judicial functions. Judge Clerke made no such exception. He enjoined the individual and he enjoined the judge; he forbade his making any order appointing a receiver, and he forbade the clerks of his court from entering it if it were made, and the receiver from accepting it if it were entered. The signing of this extraordinary order by any judge in his senses admits of no explanation. The Erie counsel served it upon Judge Barnard as he sat upon the bench, and, having done so, withdrew from the courtroom; whereupon the judge immediately proceeded to vacate the order, and to appoint a receiver. This appointment was then entered by a clerk, who had also been enjoined, and the receiver was himself enjoined as soon as he could be caught. Finally the maze had become so intricate, and the whole litigation so evidently endless and aimless, that by a sort of agreement of parties, Judge Ingraham, another colleague of Judge Barnard, issued a final injunction of universal application, as it were, and to be held inviolable by common consent,

director of the Erie Railroad that the Executive Committee had allowed that sum to be paid?

Answer. No one of the directors told me this; but I think I heard something of the kind. I can't tell from whom I heard it; there were numerous reports flying about at the time.

.   .   .   .

Judge Barnard. I haven't [addressing counsel] ruled the question out simply because I want to know whether I am fit to sit on the bench or not; if I have been engaged in a conspiracy, I am unfit to sit here.

Mr. Field said the question would open new evidence that had already been ruled out.

Judge Barnard. It was ruled out because I intend to have this *North American Review* [holding up the book] put in evidence, which contains an article about me, written by a clerk in your office. I intend to have this whole matter ferreted out.

under which proceedings were stayed, pending an appeal. It was
high time. Judges were becoming very shy of anything connected with the name of Erie, and Judge McCunn had, in a lofty
tone, informed counsel that he preferred to subject himself to
the liability of a fine of a thousand dollars rather than, by issuing
a writ of habeas corpus, allow his court "to have anything to do
with the scandal."

The result of this extraordinary litigation may be summed up
in a few words. It had two branches: one, the appointment of a
receiver of the proceeds of the hundred thousand shares of stock
issued in violation of an injunction; the other, the processes
against the persons of the directors for a contempt of court. As
for the receiver, every dollar of the money this officer was intended to receive was well known to be in New Jersey, beyond his
reach. Why one party cared to insist on the appointment, or why
the other party objected to it, is not very apparent. Mr. Osgood,
the son-in-law of Vanderbilt, was appointed, and immediately
enjoined from acting; subsequently he resigned, when Mr. Peter
B. Sweeney, the head of the Tammany Ring, was appointed in his
place, without notice to the other side. Of course he had nothing
to do, as there was nothing to be done, and so he was subsequently allowed by Judge Barnard $150,000 for his services. The
contempt cases had even less result than that of the receivership.
The settlement subsequently effected between the litigants seemed
also to include the courts. The outraged majesty of the law, as
represented in the person of Mr. Justice Barnard, was pacified,
and everything was explained as having been said and done in a
"Pickwickian sense"; so that, when the terms of peace had been
arranged between the high contending parties, Barnard's roaring
by degrees subsided, until he roared as gently as any sucking
dove, and finally he ceased to roar at all. The penalty for violating an injunction in the manner described was fixed at the not
unreasonable sum of ten dollars, except in the cases of Mr. Drew
and certain of his more prominent associates; their contumacy
his Honor held too gross to be estimated in money, and so they

escaped without any punishment at all. Probably being as well read a lawyer as he was a dignified magistrate, Judge Barnard bore in mind, in imposing these penalties, that clause of the fundamental law which provides that "no excessive fines shall be imposed, or cruel or unusual punishments inflicted." The legal profession alone had cause to regret the cessation of this litigation; and, as the Erie counsel had $150,000 divided among them in fees, it may be presumed that even they were finally comforted. And all this took place in the court of the state over which the immortal Chancellor Kent had once presided. His great authority was still cited there, the halo which surrounds his name still shed a glory over the bench on which he had sat, and yet these, his immediate successors, could

> On that high mountain cease to feed,
> And batten on this moor.

II.

It is now necessary to return to the real field of operations, which had ceased on the morning of the eleventh of March to be in the courts of law. As the arena widened the proceedings became more complicated and more difficult to trace, embracing as they did the legislatures of two states, neither of them famed for purity. In the first shock of the catastrophe it was actually believed that Commodore Vanderbilt contemplated a resort to open violence and acts of private war. There were intimations that a scheme had been matured for kidnapping certain of the Erie directors, including Mr. Drew, and bringing them by force within reach of Judge Barnard's process. It appeared that on the sixteenth of March some fifty individuals, subsequently described, in an affidavit filed for the special benefit of Mr. Justice Barnard, as "disorderly characters, commonly known as roughs," crossed by the Pavonia ferry and took possession of the Erie depot. From their conversation and inquiries it was divined that they came intending to "copp" Mr. Drew, or, in plainer phraseology, to take him by force to New York; and that they expected to receive the sum of $50,000 as a reward for so doing. The exiles at once loudly charged Vanderbilt himself with originating this blundering scheme. They simulated intense alarm. From day to day new panics were started, until, on the nineteenth, Drew was secreted, a standing army was organized from the employees of the road, and a small navy equipped. The alarm spread through Jersey City; the militia was held in readiness; in the evening the stores were closed and the citizens began to arm; while a garrison of about one hundred and twenty-five men intrenched themselves around the directors, in their hotel. On the twenty-first there was another alarm, and the fears of an attack continued, with lengthening intervals of quiet, until the thirty-first, when the guard was at last withdrawn. It is impossible to suppose that Vanderbilt ever had any knowledge of this ridiculous episode or of its cause, except through the press. A band of ruffians may have crossed the ferry, intending to kidnap Drew on speculation; but to suppose that the shrewd and energetic Commodore ever sent them to go gaping about a station, ignorant both of the person and the whereabouts of him they sought would be to impute to Vanderbilt at once a crime and a blunder. Such botching bears no trace of his clean handiwork.

The first serious effort of the Erie party was to intrench itself in New Jersey; and here it met with no opposition. A bill making the Erie Railway Company a corporation of New Jersey, with the same powers they enjoyed in New York, was hurried through the legislature in the space of two hours, and, after a little delay, signed by the Governor. The astonished citizens of the latter state saw their famous broad-gauge road thus metamorphosed before their eyes into a denizen of the kingdom of Camden and Amboy. Here was another dreadful hint to Wall Street. What further issues of stock might become legal under this charter, how the tenure of the present Board of Directors might be altered, what curious legal complications might arise, were questions more easily put than satisfactorily answered. The region of possibilities was considerably extended. The new act of incorporation, however, was but a precaution to secure for the directors of the Erie a retreat in case of need; the real field of conflict lay in the legislature of New York, and here Vanderbilt was first on the ground.

The corruption ingrained in the political system of New York City is supposed to have been steadily creeping into the legislature at Albany during several years past. The press has rung with charges of venality against members of this body; individuals have been pointed out as the recipients of large sums; men have certainly become rich during short terms in office; and, of all the rings which influence New York legislation, the railroad ring is currently supposed to be the most corrupt and corrupting. The mind of the unprejudiced inquirer, who honestly desires to ascertain the truth on this subject, will probably pass through several phases of belief before settling into conviction. In the first place, he will be overwhelmed by the broad, sweeping charges advanced in the columns of the press by responsible editors and well-informed correspondents. He will read with astonishment that legislation is controlled by cliques and is openly bought and sold; that the lobby is but the legislative broker's board, where votes are daily quoted; that sheep and bullocks are not more regularly in the market at Smithfield than Assemblymen and Senators at Albany. Amazed by such statements, the inquirer becomes incredulous, and demands evidence in support of them. This is never forthcoming. Committees of investigation —one or two in a session—are regularly appointed, and their reports are invariably calculated to confound the existing confusion. These committees generally express a belief in the existence of corruption and an utter inability to find it out; against some notoriously venal brother legislator they enter a Scotch verdict of "not proven"; and, having thus far been very guarded in their language, they then launch forth into tremendous denunciations of an unbridled and irresponsible press. Here they have it all their own way, and, indeed, too often make out an excellent case. Meanwhile the seeker after truth leaves both correspondents and committees, and tries to reach a conclusion by

other means. Public rumor he finds to be merely a reflection of
the press, or itself the impalpable form which the press reflects.
No conviction can be had on such evidence. He finds loose statements, unproved assertions, and unsustained charges, tending to
produce general incredulity. Where so much more is alleged than
is proved, nothing is finally believed; until individual corruption
may be almost measured by an ostentatious disregard of public
opinion. Passing through the phase of incredulity, the inquirer
may at last resort to the private judgment of the best informed.
Appealing to individuals in whose purity, judicial temper, and
means of information he has entire confidence, he will probably
find his conclusions as discouraging as they are inevitable. The
weight of opinion and of evidence gradually becomes irresistible,
until his mind settles down into a sad belief that probably no representative bodies were ever more thoroughly venal, more shame-
lessly corrupt, or more hopelessly beyond the reach of public
opinion, than are certain of those bodies which legislate for republican America in this latter half of the nineteenth century.
Certainly, none of the developments which marked the Erie conflict in the New York legislature of 1868 would tend to throw
doubts on this conclusion when once arrived at.

One favorite method of procedure at Albany is through the
appointment of committees to investigate the affairs of wealthy
corporations. The stock of some great company is manipulated
till it fluctuates violently, as was the case with Pacific Mail in
1867. Forthwith some member of the Assembly rises and calls
for a committee of investigation. The instant the game is afoot,
a rush is made for positions on the committee. The proposer, of
course, is a member, probably chairman. The advantages of the
position are obvious. The committee constitutes a little temporary
outside ring. If a member is corrupt, he has substantial advantages offered him to influence his action in regard to the report. If he is not open to bribery, he is nevertheless in possession
of very valuable information, and an innocent little remark,
casually let fall, may lead a son, a brother, or a loving cousin to

make very judicious purchases of stock. Altogether, the position is one not to be avoided.

The investigation phase was the first which the Erie struggle assumed at Albany. During the early stages of the conflict the legislature had scented the carnage from afar. There was "money in it," and the struggle was watched with breathless interest. As early as the fifth of March the subject had been introduced into the State Senate, and an investigation into the circumstances of the company was called for. A committee of three was ordered, but the next day a senator, by name Mattoon, moved to increase the number to five, which was done, he himself being naturally one of the additional members. This committee had its first sitting on the tenth, at the very crisis of the great explosion. But before the investigation was entered upon, Mr. Mattoon thought it expedient to convince the contending parties of his own perfect impartiality and firm determination to hold in check the corrupt impulses of his associates. With this end in view, upon the ninth or the tenth he hurried down to New York, and visited West Street, where he had an interview with the leading Erie directors. He explained to them the corrupt motives which had led to the appointment of the committee, and how his sole object in obtaining an increase of the number had been to put himself in a position in which he might be able to prevent these evil practices and see fair play. Curiously enough, at the same interview he mentioned that his son was to be appointed an assistant sergeant-at-arms to aid in the investigation, and proved his disinterestedness by mentioning the fact that this son was to serve without pay. The labors of the committee continued until the thirty-first of March, and during that time Mr. Mattoon, and at least one other senator, pursued a course of private inquiry which involved further visits to Jersey City. Naturally enough, Mr. Drew and his associates took it into their heads that the man wanted to be bought, and even affirmed subsequently that, at one interview, he had in pretty broad terms offered himself for sale. It has not been distinctly stated in evidence by anyone that an attempt was made on his purity or on that of his public-spirited son; and it is difficult to believe that one who came to New York so full of high purpose could have been sufficiently corrupted by metropolitan influences to receive bribes from both sides. Whether he did so or not his proceedings were terribly suggestive as regards legislative morality at Albany. Here was a senator, a member of a committee of investigation, rousing gamblers from their beds at early hours of the morning to hold interviews in the faro-bank parlor of the establishment, and to give "points" on which to operate upon the joint account. Even then the wretched creature could not even keep faith with his very "pals"; he wrote to them to "go it heavy" for Drew, and then himself went over to Vanderbilt,—he made agreements to share profits and then submitted to exposure sooner than meet his part of the loss. A man more thoroughly, shamefacedly contemptible and corrupt,—a more perfect specimen of a legislator on sale haggling for his own price, could not well exist. In this case he cheated everyone, including himself. Accident threw great opportunities in his way. On the thirty-first the draft of a proposed report, exonerating in great measure the Drew faction, was read to him by an associate, to which he not only made no objection, but was even understood to assent. On the same day another report was read in his presence, strongly denouncing the Drew faction, sustaining to the fullest extent the charges made against it, and characterizing its conduct as corrupt and disgraceful. Each report was signed by two of his associates, and Mr. Mattoon found himself in the position of holding the balance of power; whichever report he signed would be the report of the committee. He expressed a desire to think the matter over. It is natural to suppose that, in his eagerness to gain information privately, Mr. Mattoon had not confined his unofficial visits to the Drew camp. In any case his mind was in a state of painful suspense. Finally, after arranging in consultation on Tuesday for a report favoring the Drew party, on Wednesday he signed a report strongly denouncing it, and by doing so settled the action of

the committee. Mr. Jay Gould must have been acquainted with
the circumstances of the case, and evidently supposed that Mr.
Mattoon was "fixed," since he subsequently declared he was "astounded" when he heard that Mr. Mattoon had signed this report. The committee, however, with their patriotic sergeant-at-
arms, whose services, by the way, cost the state but a hundred
dollars, desisted at length from their labors, the result of which
was one more point gained by Commodore Vanderbilt.

Indeed, Vanderbilt had thus far as much outgeneraled Drew
in the manufacture of public opinion as Drew had outgeneraled
Vanderbilt in the manufacture of Erie stock. His whole scheme
was one of monopoly, which was opposed to every interest of the
city and state of New York, yet into the support of this scheme
he had brought all the leading papers of New York City, with a
single exception. Now again he seemed to have it all his own way
in the legislature, and the tide ran strongly against the exiles of
Erie. The report of the investigation committee was signed on
April 1, and may be considered as marking the high-water point
of Vanderbilt's success. Hitherto the Albany interest of the exiles
had been confided to mere agents, and had not prospered; but,
when fairly roused by a sense of danger, the Drew party showed
at least as close a familiarity with the tactics of Albany as with
those of Wall Street. The moment they felt themselves settled at
Jersey City they had gone to work to excite a popular sympathy
in their own behalf. The cry of monopoly was a sure card in their
hands. They cared no more for the actual welfare of commerce,
involved in railroad competition, than they did for the real
interests of the Erie Railway; but they judged truly that there
was no limit to the extent to which the public might be imposed
upon. An active competition with the Vanderbilt roads, by land
and water, was inaugurated; fares and freights on the Erie were
reduced on an average by one-third; sounding proclamations
were issued; "interviewers" from the press returned rejoicing
from Taylor's Hotel to New York City, and the Jersey shore
quaked under the clatter of this Chinese battle. The influence of

these tactics made itself felt at once. By the middle of March memorials against monopoly began to flow in at Albany.

While popular sympathy was thus roused by the bribe of active competition, a bill was introduced into the Assembly, in the Erie interest, legalizing the recent issue of new stock, declaring and regulating the power of issuing convertible bonds, providing for a broad-gauge connection with Chicago and the guaranty of the bonds of the Boston, Hartford, & Erie, and finally forbidding, in so far as any legislation could forbid, the consolidation of the Central and the Erie in the hands of Vanderbilt. This bill was referred to the Committee on Railroads on the thirteenth of March. On the twentieth a public hearing was begun, and the committee proceeded to take evidence, aided by a long array of opposing counsel, most of whom had figured in the proceedings in the courts of law. In a few days the bill was adversely reported upon, and the report adopted in the Assembly by the decisive vote of eighty-three to thirty-two. This was upon the twenty-seventh of March. The hint was a broad one; the exiles must give closer attention to their interests. As soon as the news of this adverse action reached Jersey City, it was decided that Mr. Jay Gould should brave the terrors of the law, and personally superintend matters at Albany. Neither Mr. Drew nor his associates desired to become permanent residents of Jersey City; nor did they wish to return to New York as criminals on their way to jail. Mr. Gould was to pave the way to a different return by causing the recent issue of convertible bonds to be legalized. That once done, Commodore Vanderbilt was not the man to wage an unavailing war, and a compromise, in which Barnard and his processes of contempt would be thrown in as a make-weight, could easily be effected. A rumor was therefore started that Mr. Gould was to leave for Ohio, supplied with the necessary authority and funds to press vigorously to completion the eighty miles of broad-gauge track between Akron and Toledo, which would open to the Erie the much-coveted connection with Chicago. Having hung out this false light, Mr. Jay Gould went on his mission, the president of the company having some time previously drawn half a million of dollars out of the overflowing Erie treasury.

This mission was by no means unattended by difficulties. In the first place, Judge Barnard's processes for contempt seemed to threaten the liberty of Mr. Gould's person. He left Jersey City and arrived at Albany on the thirtieth day of March, three days after the defeat of the Erie bill, and two days before Mr. Mattoon had made up his mind as to which report he would sign. Naturally his opponents were well satisfied with the present aspect of affairs, and saw no benefit likely to arise from Mr. Gould's presence in Albany. The day after his arrival, therefore, he was arrested, on the writ issued against him for contempt of court, and held to bail in half a million of dollars for his appearance in New York on the following Saturday. He was immediately bailed of course, and for the next few days devoted himself assiduously to the business he had in hand. On Saturday he appeared before Judge Barnard, and was duly put in charge of the sheriff to answer certain interrogatories. It would seem to have been perfectly easy for him to give the necessary bail, and to return from Barnard's presence at once to Albany; but the simple method seems never to have been resorted to throughout these complications: nothing was ever done without the interposition of a writ and the assistance of a crowd of counsel. In this case Judge Barrett of the Common Pleas was appealed to, who issued a writ of habeas corpus, by virtue of which Mr. Gould was taken out of the hands of the sheriff and again brought into court. Of course the hearing of the case was deferred, and it was equally a matter of course that Mr. Gould was bent on returning at once to his field of labor. The officer to whose care Mr. Gould was intrusted was especially warned by the court, in Mr. Gould's presence, that he was not to allow his charge to go out of his sight. This difficulty was easily surmounted. Mr. Gould went by an early train to Albany, taking the officer with him in the capacity of a traveling companion. Once in Albany he was naturally taken ill,—not too ill to go to the Capitol in the midst of a snow-storm, but much too ill to think of returning to New York. On the tenth the trusty official and traveling companion signified to Mr. Gould that his presence was much desired before Judge Barrett, and intimated an intention of carrying him back to New York. Mr. Gould then pleaded the delicate condition of his health, and wholly declined to undergo the hardships of the pro-posed journey. Whereupon the officer, stimulated, as was alleged, by Gould's opponents, returned alone to New York, and reported his charge to the court as a runaway. A new spectacle of judicial indignation ensued, and a new process for contempt seemed im-minent. Of course nothing came of it. A few affidavits from Al-bany pacified the indignant Barrett. The application for a habeas corpus was discharged, and Mr. Gould was theoretically returned into the custody of the sheriff. Thereupon the required security for his appearance when needed was given; and meanwhile, pending the recovery of his health, he assiduously devoted the tedious hours of convalescence to the task of cultivating a thor-ough understanding between himself and the members of the legislature.

A strange legislative episode occurred at this time, which for a day or two threatened to thwart Mr. Gould's operations, but in the end materially facilitated them. All through March the usual sensational charges had been flying through the press in relation to the buying of votes on the pending Erie measures. These were as vague and as difficult to sustain as usual, and it was very im-portant that no indiscreet friend of legislative purity should blunder out charges which could be triumphantly refuted. On the first of April, however, the second day after Mr. Gould ap-peared on the ground, a quiet country member named Glenn, remarkable for nothing but his advanced years and white hair, suddenly created an intense sensation by rising in his place in the Assembly and excitedly declaring that he had just been of-fered money for his vote on the Erie bill. He then sent up to the Speaker charges in writing, to the effect that the recent report on the bill in question was bought, that members of the House were engaged in purchasing votes, that reports of committees were habitually sold, and ended by charging "corruption, deep, dark, and damning on a portion of the House," of which he felt "degraded in being a member." A committee of investigation was, of course, appointed, and the press congratulated the public that at last specific charges had been advanced from a responsible quarter. On the ninth Mr. Glenn followed up the attack by charging, again in writing, that one member of the committee of investigation, whose name he gave, was the very member who had offered him money for his vote. Mr. Frear, the member in question, at once resigned his place upon the committee, and demanded an investigation. Then it turned out that the simple old gentleman, between his desire for notoriety and his eagerness to expose corruption, had been made the victim of a cruel joke. Some waggish colleagues had pointed out to him an itinerant Jew, who haunted the lobby and sold spectacles, as an agent of the fifth estate. From him the old gentleman, had, after some clumsy angling and many leading questions, procured what he supposed to be an offer of money for his vote, which, by a ludicrous misunderstanding, managed by his humorous colleagues, was made to appear in his eyes as having received Mr. Frear's indorsement. Mr. Glenn's charges ended, therefore, in a ridiculous fiasco, and in a tremendous outburst of offended legislative virtue. The committee reported on the tenth; everyone was exonerated; Mr. Glenn was brought to the bar and censured, and the next day he resigned. As for the astonished peddler, he was banished from the lobby, imprisoned, prosecuted, and forgotten. The display of indignation on the part of Mr. Glenn's brother legislators was, in view of the manifest absurdity of the whole affair, somewhat superfluous and somewhat suspicious; but one such false accusation protects a multitude of real sins. The trade of censor of morals fell into disrepute at Albany; and, under the shadow of this parody upon exposures of corruption, Mr. Gould was at liberty to devote himself to serious business without fear of interruption.

The full and true history of this legislative campaign will never be known. If the official reports of investigating committees are to be believed, Mr. Gould at about this time underwent a curious psychological metamorphosis, and suddenly became the veriest simpleton in money matters that ever fell into the hands of happy sharpers. Cunning lobby members had but to pretend to an influence over legislative minds, which everyone knew they did not possess, to draw unlimited amounts from this verdant habitué of Wall Street. It seemed strange that he could have lived so long and learned so little. He dealt in large sums. He gave to one man, in whom he said "he did not take much stock," the sum of $5,000, "just to smooth him over." This man had just before received $5,000 of Erie money from another agent of the company. It would, therefore, be interesting to know what sums Mr. Gould paid to those individuals in whom he did "take much stock." Another individual is reported to have received $100,000 from one side, "to influence legislation," and to have subsequently received $70,000 from the other side to disappear with the money; which he accordingly did, and thereafter became a gentleman of elegant leisure. One senator was openly charged in the columns of the press with receiving a bribe of $20,000 from one side, and a second bribe of $15,000 from the other; but Mr. Gould's foggy mental condition only enabled him to be "perfectly astounded" at the action of this senator, though he knew nothing of any such transactions. Other senators were blessed with a sudden accession of wealth, but in no case was there any jot or tittle of proof of bribery. Mr. Gould's rooms at the Delavan House overflowed with a joyous company, and his checks were numerous and heavy; but why he signed them, or what became of them, he seemed to know less than any man in Albany. This strange and expensive hallucination lasted until about the middle of April, when Mr. Gould was happily restored to his normal condition of a shrewd, acute, energetic man of business; nor is it known that he has since experienced any relapse into financial idiocy.

About the period of Mr. Gould's arrival in Albany the tide

turned, and soon began to flow strongly in favor of Erie and against Vanderbilt. How much of this was due to the skilful manipulations of Gould, and how much to the rising popular feeling against the practical consolidation of competing lines, cannot be decided. The popular protests did indeed pour in by scores, but then again the Erie secret-service money poured out like water. Yet Mr. Gould's task was sufficiently difficult. After the adverse report of the Senate committee, and the decisive defeat of the bill introduced into the Assembly, any favorable legislation seemed almost hopeless. Both Houses were committed. Vanderbilt had but to prevent action,—to keep things where they were, and the return of his opponents to New York was impracticable, unless with his consent; he appeared, in fact, to be absolute master of the situation. It seemed almost impossible to introduce a bill in the face of his great influence, and to navigate it through the many stages of legislative action and executive approval, without somewhere giving him an opportunity to defeat it. This was the task Gould had before him, and he accomplished it. On the thirteenth of April a bill, which met the approval of the Erie party, and which Judge Barnard subsequently compared not inaptly to a bill legalizing counterfeit money, was taken up in the Senate; for some days it was warmly debated, and on the eighteenth was passed by the decisive vote of seventeen to twelve. Senator Mattoon had not listened to the debate in vain. Perhaps his reason was convinced, or perhaps he had sold out new "points" and was again cheating himself or somebody else; at any rate, that thrifty senator was found voting with the majority. The bill practically legalized the recent issues of bonds, but made it a felony to use the proceeds of the sale of these bonds except for completing, furthering, and operating the road. The guaranty of the bonds of connecting roads was authorized, all contracts for consolidation or division of receipts between the Erie and the Vanderbilt roads were forbidden, and a clumsy provision was enacted that no stockholder, director, or officer in one of the Vanderbilt roads should be an officer or director in the Erie, and *vice versa*. The bill was, in fact, an amended copy of the one voted down so decisively in the Assembly a few days before, and it was in this body that the tug of war was expected to come.

The lobby was now full of animation; fabulous stories were told of the amounts which the contending parties were willing to expend; never before had the market quotations of votes and influence stood so high. The wealth of Vanderbilt seemed pitted against the Erie treasury, and the vultures flocked to Albany from every part of the state. Suddenly, at the very last moment, and even while special trains were bringing up fresh contestants to take part in the fray, a rumor ran through Albany as of some great public disaster, spreading panic and terror through hotel and corridor. The observer was reminded of the dark days of the war, when tidings came of some great defeat, as that on the Chickahominy or at Fredericksburg. In a moment the lobby was smitten with despair, and the cheeks of the legislators were blanched, for it was reported that Vanderbilt had withdrawn his opposition to the bill. The report was true. Either the Commodore had counted the cost and judged it excessive, or he despaired of the result. At any rate, he had yielded in advance. In a few moments the long struggle was over, and that bill which, in an unamended form, had but a few days before been thrown out of the Assembly by a vote of eighty-three to thirty-two, now passed it by a vote of one hundred and one to six, and was sent to the Governor for his signature. Then the wrath of the disappointed members turned on Vanderbilt. Decency was forgotten in a frenzied sense of disappointed avarice. That same night the *pro rata* freight bill, and a bill compelling the sale of through tickets by competing lines, were hurriedly passed, simply because they were thought hurtful to Vanderbilt; and the docket was ransacked in search of other measures, calculated to injure or annoy him. An adjournment, however, brought reflection, and subsequently, on this subject, the legislature stultified itself no more.

The bill had passed the legislature; would it receive the executive signature? Here was the last stage of danger. For some time doubts were entertained on this point, and the last real conflict between the opposing interests took place in the Executive Chamber at Albany. There, on the afternoon of the twenty-first of April, Commodore Vanderbilt's counsel appeared before Governor Fenton, and urged upon him their reasons why the bill should be returned by him to the Senate without his signature. The arguments were patiently listened to, but, when they had closed, the executive signature placed the seal of success upon Mr. Gould's labors at Albany. Even here the voice of calumny was not silent. As if this remarkable controversy was destined to leave a dark blot of suspicion upon every department of the civil service of New York, there were not wanting those who charged the Executive itself with the crowning act in this history of corruption. The very sum pretended to have been paid was named; the broker of executive action was pointed out, and the number of minutes was specified which should intervene between the payment of the bribe and the signing of the law.*

Practically, the conflict was now over, and the period of negotiation had already begun. The combat in the courts was indeed kept up until far into May, for the angry passions of the lawyers and of the judges required time in which to wear themselves out. Day after day the columns of the press revealed fresh scandals to the astonished public, which at last grew indifferent to such revelations. Beneath all the wrangling of the courts, however, while the popular attention was distracted by the clatter of lawyers' tongues, the leaders in the controversy were quietly approaching a settlement. In the early days of his exile Mr. Drew had been more depressed in spirit, more vacillating in counsel, than his younger and more robust associates. The publicity and

* It is but justice to Governor Fenton to say, that, though this charge was boldly advanced by respectable journals of his own party, it cannot be considered as sustained by the evidence. The testimony on the point will be found in the report of Senator Hale's investigating committee. Documents (Senate), 1869, No. 52, pp. 146–148, 151–155.

excitement which had sustained and even amused them had wearied and annoyed the old man. His mind had been oppressed with saucy doubts and tormented by officious advisers. Stronger wills than his were bearing him along with them; and though, perhaps, not more scrupulous than those about him, he was certainly less bold; their reckless daring shocked his more subtle and timid nature. He missed also his home comforts; he felt himself a prisoner in everything but in name; he knew that he was distrusted, and his every action watched by associates of whom he even stood in physical fear, who hardly allowed him to see his brokers alone, and did not respect the sanctity of his telegrams. After the first week or two, and as affairs began to assume a less untoward aspect, his spirits revived, and he soon began to make secret advances toward his angry opponent. The hostilities of the Stock Exchange are proverbially short-lived. A broker skilled in the ways of his kind gave it as his opinion, in one of these proceedings, that five minutes was the utmost period during which it was safe to count on the enmities or alliances of leading operators. Early in April Mr. Drew took advantage of that blessed immunity from arrest which the Sabbath confers on the hunted of the law, to revisit the familiar scenes across the river. His visit soon resulted in conferences between himself and Vanderbilt, and these conferences naturally led to overtures of peace. Though the tide was turning against the great railroad king, though an uncontrollable popular feeling was fast bearing down his schemes of monopoly, yet he was by no means beaten or subdued. His plans, however, had evidently failed for the present; as he expressed himself, he could easily enough buy up the Erie Railway, but he could not buy up the printing press. It was now clearly his interest to abandon his late line of attack, and to bide his time patiently, or to possess himself of his prey by some other method. The wishes of all parties, therefore, were fixed on a settlement, and no one was disposed to stand out except in order to obtain better terms. The interests, however, were multifarious. There were four parties to be taken care of,

CORNELIUS VANDERBILT

and the depleted treasury of the Erie Railway was doomed to suffer.

The details of this masterpiece of Wall Street diplomacy have never come to light, but Mr. Drew's visits to New York became more frequent and less guarded; by the middle of April he had appeared in Broad Street on a week day, undisturbed by fears of arrest, and soon rumors began to spread of misunderstandings between himself and his brother exiles. It was said that his continual absences alarmed them, that they distrusted him, that his terms of settlement were not theirs. It was even asserted that his orders on the treasury were no longer honored, and that he had in fact, ceased to be a power in Erie. Whatever truth there may have been in these rumors, it was very evident his associates had no inclination to trust themselves within the reach of the New York courts until a definitive treaty, satisfactory to themselves, was signed and sealed. This probably took place about the twenty-fifth of April; for on that day the Erie camp at "Fort Taylor," as their uninviting hotel had been dubbed, was broken up, the President and one of the Executive Committee took steamer for Boston, and the other directors appeared before Judge Barnard, prepared to purge themselves of their contempt.

Though the details of negotiation have never been divulged, yet it was clear enough what three of the four parties desired. Commodore Vanderbilt wished to be relieved of the vast amount of stock with which he was loaded, and his friends Work and Schell, in whose names the battle had been fought, must be protected. Mr. Drew desired to settle his entangled accounts as treasurer, and to obtain a release in full, which might be pleaded in future complications. Mr. Eldridge and his Boston friends were sufficiently anxious to be relieved of the elephant they found on their hands, in the Erie Railway of New York, and to be at leisure to devote the spoils of their victim to the development of the New England enterprise. Messrs. Gould and Fisk alone were unprovided for, and they alone presented themselves as obstacles to be overcome by railroad diplomacy.

At last, upon the second of July, Mr. Eldridge formally announced to the Board of Directors that the terms of peace had been agreed upon. Commodore Vanderbilt was, in the first place, provided for. He was to be relieved of fifty thousand shares of Erie stock at 70, receiving therefor $2,500,000 in cash, and $1,250,000 in bonds of the Boston, Hartford, & Erie at 80. He was also to receive a further sum of $1,000,000 outright, as a consideration for the privilege the Erie road thus purchased of calling upon him for his remaining fifty thousand shares at 70 at any time within four months. He was also to have two seats in the Board of Directors, and all suits were to be dismissed and offenses condoned. The sum of $429,250 was fixed upon as a proper amount to assuage the sense of wrong from which his two friends Work and Schell had suffered, and to efface from their memories all recollection of the unfortunate "pool" of the previous December. Why the owners of the Erie Railway should have paid this indemnity of $4,000,000 is not very clear. The operations were apparently outside of the business of a railway company, and no more connected with the stockholders of the Erie than were the butchers' bills of the individual directors.

While Vanderbilt and his friends were thus provided for, Mr. Drew was to be left in undisturbed enjoyment of the fruits of his recent operations, but was to pay into the treasury $540,000 and interest, in full discharge of all claims and causes of action which the Erie Company might have against him. The Boston party, as represented by Mr. Eldridge, was to be relieved of $5,000,000 of their Boston, Hartford, & Erie bonds, for which they were to receive $4,000,000 of Erie acceptances. None of these parties, therefore, had anything to complain of, whatever might be the sensations of the real owners of the railway. A total amount of some $9,000,000 in cash was drawn from the treasury in fulfilment of this *settlement,* as the persons concerned were pleased to term this remarkable disposition of property intrusted to their care.

Messrs. Gould and Fisk still remained to be taken care of,

and to them their associates left—the Erie Railway. These gentlemen subsequently maintained that they had vehemently opposed
this settlement, and had denounced it in the secret councils as a
fraud and a robbery. Mr. Fisk was peculiarly outspoken in relation to it, and declared himself "thunderstruck and dumb-
founded" that his brother directors whom he had supposed respectable men should have had anything to do with any such
proceeding. A small portion of this statement is not wholly improbable. The astonishment at the turpitude of his fellow-offi-
cials was a little unnecessary in one who had already seen "more
robbery" during the year of his connection with the Erie Railway than he had "ever seen before in the same space of time,"—
so much of it indeed that he dated his "gray hairs" from the
seventh of October which saw his election to the board. That Mr.
Fisk and Mr. Gould were extremely indignant at a partition of
plunder from which they were excluded is, however, very certain.
The rind of the orange is not generally considered the richest
part of the fruit; a corporation on the verge of bankruptcy is
less coveted, even by operators in Wall Street, than one rich in
valuable assets. Probably at this time these gentlemen seriously
debated the expediency of resorting again to a war of injunctions,
and carefully kept open a way for doing so; however this may
have been, they seem finally to have concluded that there was yet
plunder left in the poor old hulk, and so, after four stormy interviews, all opposition was at last withdrawn and the definitive
treaty was finally signed.* Mr. Eldridge thereupon counted out

* The account given of this affair by Mr. Fisk from the witness stand on
a subsequent occasion was characteristic: "Finally about twelve o'clock a
paper was passed round and we signed it; I don't know what it contained; I
didn't read it; I don't think I noticed a word of it; I remember the space
for the names was greater than that covered by the writing; my impression
is that I took my hat and left at once in disgust; I told Gould we had sold
ourselves to the Devil; I presume that was not the only document signed; I
remember seeing Mr. White, the cashier, come in with the check-book, and I
said to him, 'You are bearing in the remains of this corporation to be put
in Vanderbilt's tomb.' No; I didn't know the contents of the paper which
I signed, and I have always been glad that I didn't; I have thought of it a

his bonds and received his acceptances, which latter were cashed at once to close up the transaction, and at once he resigned his positions as director and president. The Boston raiders then retired, heavy with spoil, into their own North country, and there proceeded to build up an Erie influence for New England, in which task they labored with assiduity and success. Gradually they here introduced the more highly developed civilization of the land of their temporary adoption and boldly attempted to make good their private losses from the public treasury. A more barefaced scheme of plunder never was devised, and yet the executive veto alone stood between it and success. These, however, were the events of another year and unconnected with this narrative, from which these characters in the Erie management henceforth disappear. For the rest it is only necessary to say that Mr. Vanderbilt, relieved of his heavy load of its stock, apparently ceased to concern himself with Erie; while Daniel Drew, released from the anxieties of office, assumed for a space the novel character of a looker-on in Wall Street.

III.

THUS, in the early days of July, Messrs. Fisk and Gould found themselves beginning life, as it were, in absolute control of the Erie Railway, but with an empty treasury and a doubtful reputation. Outwardly things did not look unpromising. The legal complications were settled, and the fearful load imposed by the settlement upon the already overburdened resources of the road was not, of course, imparted to the public. It is unnecessary to add that the "outside" holders of the stock were, in the counsels of the managers, included in that public the inquiries of which

thousand times; I don't know what other documents I signed; I signed everything that was put before me; after once the Devil had hold of me I kept on signing; didn't read any of them and have no idea what they were; I don't know how many I signed; I kept no count after the first one; I went with the robbers then and I have been with them ever since; my impression is that after the signing I left at once; I don't know whether we sat down or not; we didn't have anything to eat, I know."

in regard to the affairs of the company were looked upon by the ring in control as downright impertinence. A calm—deceitful indeed, but yet a calm—succeeded the severe agitations of the money market. All through the month of July money was easy and ruled at 3 or 4 per cent; Erie was consequently high, and was quoted at about 70, which enabled the company to dispose without loss of the Vanderbilt stock. It may well be believed that Messrs. Fisk and Gould could not have regarded their empty treasury, just depleted to the extent of nine millions,—trust funds misapplied by directors in the processes of stock-gambling, —without serious question as to their ability to save the road from bankruptcy. The October election was approaching, Vanderbilt was still a threatening element in the future, and new combinations might arise. Millions were necessary, and must at once be forthcoming. The new officials were, however, men of resource, and were not men of many scruples. The money must be raised, and recent experience indicated a method of raising it. Their policy, freed from the influence of Drew's vacillating, treacherous, and withal timid nature, could now be bold and direct. The pretense of resistance to monopoly would always serve them, as it had served them before, as a plausible and popular cry. Above all, their councils were now free from interlopers and spies; for the first act of Messrs. Gould and Fisk had been to do away with the old board of auditors, and to concentrate all power in their own hands as president, treasurer, and controller. Fortunately for them it was midsummer, and the receipts of the road were very heavy, supplying them with large sums of ready money;* most fortunately for them, also, a strange infatuation at this time took possession of the English mind.

Shrewd as the British capitalist proverbially is, his judgment

---

* It will be remembered that the act of twenty-first April, legalizing the issue of bonds, made it a felony to devote the proceeds to any purpose except equipping, constructing, and operating the road. Mr. Gould's explanation of the effect he gave to this clause is not only amusing as a piece of impudence, but extremely suggestive as regards the efficacy of legislation. Mr. Gould, be it remembered, procured the passage of the law, and Mr. Gould thus explains

in regard to American investments has been singularly fallible. When our national bonds went begging at a discount of 60 per cent, he transmitted them to Germany and refused to touch them himself. At the very same time a class of railroad securities —such as those of this very Erie Railway, or, to cite a yet stronger case, those of the Atlantic & Great Western road—was gradually absorbed in London as an honest investment long after these securities had "gone into the street" in America. It was this strange fatuity which did much to bring on the crash of May, 1866. Even that did not seem to teach wisdom to the British bankers, who had apparently passed from the extreme of caution to the extreme of confidence. They now, after all the exposures of the preceding months, rushed into Erie, apparently because it seemed cheap, and the prices in New York were sustained by the steady demand for stock on foreign account. Not only did this curious infatuation, involving purchases to the extent of a hundred thousand shares, cover up the operations of the new ring, but, at a later period, the date of the possible return of this

to the railroad committee of the legislature the force he gave to its provisions.

Mr. Gould. . . . The law is, that you can only use the money realized on these bonds for the purpose of equipping, constructing, and operating the road, and therefore I had to use the earnings of the road to meet these large liabilities, which had been authorized by the board (the Eldridge-Vanderbilt settlement), and use the money realized from the bonds to equip, construct, and operate the road. . . .

Question by Mr. Waterman. In fact these twenty million of bonds were issued to meet these obligations, and not for the purpose of maintaining, operating, and constructing the road?

Answer. No, sir; I used the earnings of the road to meet these obligations. . . . We had to live up to the letter of the law, and use the money realized from the bonds for the purpose of operating, constructing, and equipping the road.

Q. But your pressing need of money was not for the purpose of operating the road, but for the purpose of meeting these obligations?

A. Yes, sir.

Q. The amount of money you sought to raise was the amount of these obligations?

A. Yes, sir.

stock to Wall Street was the hinge on which the success of its culminating plot was made to turn.

The appearance of calm lasted but about thirty days. Early in August it was evident that something was going on. Erie suddenly fell 10 per cent; in a few days more it experienced a further fall of 7 per cent, touching 44 by the nineteenth of the month, upon which day, to the astonishment of Wall Street, the transfer books of the company were closed preparatory to the annual election. As this election was not to take place until the thirteenth of October, and as the books had thus been closed thirty days in advance of the usual time, it looked very much as though the managers were satisfied with the present disposition of the stock, and meant, by keeping it where it was, to preclude any such unpleasantness as an opposition ticket. The courts and a renewed war of injunctions were of course open to any contestants, including Commodore Vanderbilt, who might desire to avail themselves of them; probably, however, the memory of recent struggles was too fresh to permit anyone to embark on these treacherous waters. At any rate, nothing of the sort was attempted. The election took place at the usual time, and the ring in control voted itself, without opposition, into a new lease of power. Two new names had meanwhile appeared in the list of Erie directors,—those of Peter B. Sweeny and William M. Tweed, the two most prominent leaders of that notorious ring which controls the proletariat of New York City and governs the politics of the state. The alliance was an ominous one, for the construction of the new board can be stated in few words, and calls for no comment. It consisted of the Erie Ring and the Tammany Ring, brought together in close political and financial union; and, for the rest, a working majority of supple tools and a hopeless minority of respectable figureheads. This formidable combination shot out its feelers far and wide: it wielded the influence of a great corporation with a capital of a hundred millions; it controlled the politics of the first city of the New World; it sent its representatives to the Senate of the state, and numbered among its agents the judges of the courts. Compact, disciplined, and reckless, it knew its own power and would not scruple to use it.

It was now the month of October, and the harvest had been gathered. The ring and its allies determined to reap their harvest also, and that harvest was to be nothing less than a contribution levied, not only upon Wall Street and New York, but upon all the immense interests, commercial and financial, which radiate from New York all over the country. Like the Caesar of old, they issued their edict that all the world should be taxed. The process was not novel, but it was effective. A monetary stringency may be looked for in New York at certain seasons of every year. It is generally most severe in the autumn months, when the crops have to be moved, and the currency is drained steadily away from the financial center toward the extremities of the system. The method by which an artificial stringency is produced is thus explained in a recent report of the Comptroller of the Currency: "It is scarcely possible to avoid the inference that nearly one-half of the available resources of the national banks in the city of New York are used in the operations of the stock and gold exchange; that they are loaned upon the security of stocks which are bought and sold largely on speculation, and which are manipulated by cliques and combinations, according as the bulls or bears are for the moment in the ascendency. . . . Taking advantage of an active demand for money to move the crops West and South, shrewd operators form their combination to depress the market by 'locking up' money,—withdrawing all they can control or borrow from the common fund; money becomes scarce, the rate of interest advances, and stocks decline. The legitimate demand for money continues; and, fearful of trenching on their reserve, the banks are strained for means. They dare not call in their demand loans, for that would compel their customers to sell securities on a falling market, which would make matters worse. Habitually lending their means to the utmost limit of prudence, and their credit much beyond that limit, to brokers and

speculators, they are powerless to afford relief;—their customers
by the force of circumstances become their masters. The banks
cannot hold back or withdraw from the dilemma in which their
mode of doing business has placed them. They must carry the
load to save their margins. A panic which should greatly reduce
the price of securities would occasion serious, if not fatal, results
to the banks most extensively engaged in such operations, and
would produce a feeling of insecurity which would be very dangerous to the entire banking interest of the country."[*]

All this machinery was now put in motion; the banks and their
customers were forced into the false position described, and
toward the end of October it had become perfectly notorious in
Wall Street that large new issues of Erie had been made, and
that these new issues were intimately connected with the sharp
stringency then existing in the money market. It was at last determined to investigate the matter, and upon the twenty-seventh
of the month a committee of three was appointed by the Stock
Exchange to wait upon the officers of the corporation with the view
of procuring such information as they might be willing to im-
part. The committee called on Mr. Gould and stated the object of
their visit. In reply to their inquiries Mr. Gould informed them
that Erie convertible bonds for ten millions of dollars had been
issued, half of which had already been, and the rest of which
would be, converted into stock; that the money had been devoted
to the purchase of Boston, Hartford, & Erie bonds for five millions, and also—of course—to payments for steel rails. The committee desired to know if any further issue of stock was in contemplation, but were obliged to rest satisfied with a calm assurance that no new issue was just then contemplated except "in
certain contingencies"; from which enigmatical utterances Wall
Street was left to infer that the exigencies of Messrs. Gould and
Fisk were elements not to be omitted from any calculations as to
the future of Erie and the money market. The amount of these
issues of new stock was, of course, soon whispered in a general

[*] Finance Report, 1868, pp. 20, 21.

way; but it was not till months afterward that a sworn statement of the secretary of the Erie Railway revealed the fact that the stock of the corporation had been increased from $34,265,300 on the first of July, 1868, the date when Drew and his associates had left it, to $57,766,300 on the twenty-fourth of October of the same year, or by two hundred and thirty-five thousand shares in four months.* This, too, had been done without consultation with the Board of Directors, and with no other authority than that conferred by the ambiguous resolution of February 19. Under that resolution the stock of the company had now been increased 138 per cent in eight months. Such a process of inflation may, perhaps, be justly considered the most extraordinary feat of financial legerdemain which history has yet recorded.

Now, however, when the committee of the Stock Exchange had returned to those who sent them, the mask was thrown off, and operations were conducted with vigor and determination. New issues of Erie were continually forced upon the market until the stock fell to 35; greenbacks were locked up in the vaults of the banks, until the unexampled sum of twelve millions was withdrawn from circulation; the prices of securities and merchandise declined; trade and the autumnal movement of the crops were brought almost to a standstill; and loans became more and more difficult to negotiate, until at length even 1½ per cent a day was paid for carrying stocks. Behind all this it was notorious that someone was pulling the wires, the slightest touch upon which sent a quiver through every nerve of the great financial organism, and wrung private gain from public agony. The strange proceeding reminds one of those scenes in the chambers of the Inquisition where the judges calmly put their victim to

* In April, 1871, although the stock was then nominally registered, a further secret issue was made by which some $600,000 in cash was realized on $3,000,000 of stock. Periodical issues had then carried the gross amount up to the neighborhood of $86,500,000; or from a total of 250,000 shares, when the management changed at the election of October 17, 1867, to 865,000 shares within four years. Apparently Mr. Fisk was more correct than usual in his statement, when he remarked, that, having once joined the robbers, "he had been with them ever since."

the question, until his spasms warned them not to exceed the limits of human endurance. At last the public distress reached the ears of the Government at Washington. While it was simply the gamblers of Wall Street who were tearing each other, their clamor for relief excited little sympathy. When, however, the suffering had extended through all the legitimate business circles of the country,—when the scarcity of money threatened to cut off the winter food of the poor, to rob the farmer of the fruits of his toil, and to bring ruin upon half the debtor class of the community,—then even Mr. McCulloch, pledged as he was to contraction, was moved to interfere. The very revenues of the government were affected by the operations of gamblers. They were therefore informed that, if necessary, fifty millions of additional currency would be forthcoming to the relief of the community, and then, and not till then, the screws were loosened.

The harvest of the speculators, however, was still but half gathered. Hitherto the combination had operated for a fall. Now was the moment to change the tactics and take advantage of the rise. The time was calculated to a nicety. The London infatuation had wonderfully continued, and as fast as certificates of stock were issued they seemed to take wings across the Atlantic. Yet there was a limit even to English credulity, and in November it became evident that the agents of foreign houses were selling their stock to arrive. The price was about 40; the certificates might be expected by the steamer of the twenty-third. Instantly the combination changed front. As before they had depressed the market, they now ran it up, and, almost as if by magic, the stock, which had been heavy at 40, astonished everyone by shooting up to 50. New developments were evidently at hand.

At this point Mr. Daniel Drew once more made his appearance on the stage. As was very natural, he had soon wearied of the sameness of his part as a mere looker-on in Wall Street, and had relapsed into his old habits. He was no longer treasurer of the Erie, and could not therefore invite the public to the game, while he himself with somber piety shook the loaded dice. But it had become with him a second nature to operate in Erie, and once more he was deep in its movements. At first he had combined with his old friends, the present directors, in their "locking-up" conspiracy. He had agreed to assist them to the extent of four millions. The vacillating, timid nature of the man, however, could not keep pace with his more daring and determined associates, and, after embarking a million, becoming alarmed at the success of the joint operations and the remonstrances of those who were threatened with ruin, he withdrew his funds from the operators' control and himself from their councils. But though he did not care to run the risk or to incur the odium, he had no sort of objection to sharing the spoils. Knowing, therefore, or supposing that he knew, the plan of campaign, and that plan jumping with his own bearish inclinations, he continued, on his own account, operations looking to a fall. One may easily conceive the wrath of the Erie operators at such a treacherous policy; and it is not difficult to imagine their vows of vengeance. Meanwhile all went well with Daniel Drew. Erie looked worse and worse, and the golden harvest seemed drawing near. By the middle of November he had contracted for the delivery of some seventy thousand shares at current prices, averaging, perhaps, 38, and probably was counting his gains. He did not appreciate the full power and resources of his old associates. On the fourteenth of November their tactics changed, and he found himself involved in terrible entanglements,—hopelessly cornered. His position disclosed itself on Saturday. Naturally the first impulse was to have recourse to the courts. An injunction—a dozen injunctions—could be had for the asking, but, unfortunately, could be had by both parties. Drew's own recent experience, and his intimate acquaintance with the characters of Fisk and Gould, were not calculated to inspire him with much confidence in the efficacy of the law. But nothing else remained, and, after hurried consultations among the victims, the lawyers were applied to, the affidavits were prepared, and it was decided to repair on the following Monday to the so-called courts of justice.

Nature, however, had not bestowed on Daniel Drew the steady nerve and sturdy gambler's pride of either Vanderbilt or of his old companions at Jersey City. His mind wavered and hesitated between different courses of action. His only care was for himself, his only thought was of his own position. He was willing to betray one party or the other, as the case might be. He had given his affidavit to those who were to bring the suit on the Monday, but he stood perfectly ready to employ Sunday in betraying their counsels to the defendants in the suit. A position more contemptible, a state of mind more pitiable, can hardly be conceived. After passing the night in this abject condition, on the morning of Sunday he sought out Mr. Fisk for purposes of self-humiliation and treachery.* He then partially revealed the difficulties of his situation, only to have his confidant prove to him how entirely he was caught, by completing to him the revelation. He betrayed the secrets of his new allies, and bemoaned his own hard fate; he was thereupon comforted by Mr. Fisk with the cheery remark that "he (Drew) was the last man who ought to whine over any position in which he placed himself in regard to Erie." The poor man begged to see Mr. Gould, and would take no denial. Finally Mr. Gould was brought in, and the scene was repeated for his edification. The two must have been satiated with revenge. At last they sent him away, promising to see him again that evening. At the hour named he again appeared, and, after waiting their convenience,—for they spared him no humiliation,—he again appealed to them, offering them great sums if they would issue new stock or lend him of their stock. He implored, he argued, he threatened. At the end of two hours of humiliation, persuaded that it was all in vain, that he was wholly in the power of antagonists without mercy, he took his hat, said, "I will bid you good night," and went his way.

There is a touch of nature about this scene which reads like

* It ought perhaps to be stated that this portion of the narrative has no stronger foundation than an affidavit of Mr. Fisk, which has not, however, been publicly contradicted.

fiction. Indeed, it irresistibly recalls the feebler effort of Dickens to portray Fagin's last night alive, and there is more pathos in the parting address than in the Jew's,—''An old man, my lord! a very, very old man.'' But the truth is stranger than fiction. Dickens did not dare picture the old ''fence'' in Oliver Twist turned out of his own house and stripped of his plunder by the very hands through which he had procured it. In the case of Daniel Drew, however, the ideal poetic justice was brought about in fact; the evil instructions returned to plague the inventor, and it is hard to believe that, as he left the Erie offices that night, his apt pupils, even as those of Fagin might have done, did not watch his retiring steps with suppressed merriment; and, when the door had closed upon him, that the one did not explode in loud bursts of laughter, while the other, with a quiet chuckle, plunged his hands into those capacious pockets which yawned for all the wealth of Erie. Bad as all these things are, terrible as is the condition of affairs only partially revealed, there is a grim humor running through them which ever makes itself felt.

But to return to the course of events. With the lords of Erie forewarned was forearmed. They knew something of the method of procedure in New York courts of law. At this particular juncture Mr. Justice Sutherland, a magistrate of such pure character and unsullied reputation that it is inexplicable how he ever came to be elevated to the bench on which he sits, was holding chambers, according to assignment, for the four weeks between the first Monday in November and the first Monday in December. By a rule of the court, all applications for orders during that time were to be made before him, and he only, according to the courtesy of the bench, took cognizance of such proceedings. Some general arrangement of this nature is manifestly necessary to avoid continual conflicts of jurisdiction. The details of the assault on the Erie directors having been settled, counsel appeared before Judge Sutherland on Monday morning, and petitioned for an injunction restraining the Erie directors from any new issue of stock or the removal of the funds of the company beyond the jurisdiction of the court, and also asking that the road be placed in the hands of a receiver. The suit was brought in the name of Mr. August Belmont, who was supposed to represent large foreign holders. The petition set forth at length the alleged facts in the case, and was supported by the affidavits of Mr. Drew and others. Mr. Drew apparently did not inform the counsel of the manner in which he had passed his leisure hours on the previous day; had he done so, Mr. Belmont's counsel probably would have expedited their movements. The injunction was, however, duly signed, and, doubtless, immediately served.

Meanwhile Messrs. Gould and Fisk had not been idle. Applications for injunctions and receiverships were a game which two could play at, and long experience had taught these close observers the very great value of the initiative in law. Accordingly, some two hours before the Belmont application was made, they had sought no less a person that Mr. Justice Barnard, caught him, as it were, either in his bed or at his breakfast, whereupon he had held a *lit de justice,* and made divers astonishing orders. A petition was presented in the name of one McIntosh, a salaried officer of the Erie road, who claimed also to be a shareholder. It set forth the danger of injunctions and of the appointment of a receiver, the great injury likely to result therefrom, etc. After due consideration on the part of Judge Barnard, an injunction was issued, staying and restraining all suits, and actually appointing Jay Gould receiver, to hold and disburse the funds of the company in accordance with the resolutions of the Board of Directors and the Executive Committee. This certainly was a very brilliant flank movement, and testified not less emphatically to Gould's genius than to Barnard's law; but most of all did it testify to the efficacy of the new combination between Tammany Hall and the Erie Railway. Since the passage of the bill "to legalize counterfeit money," in April, and the present November, new light had burst upon the judicial mind, and as the news of one injunction and a vague rumor of the other crept through Wall Street that day, it was no wonder that operators stood aghast and that Erie fluctuated wildly from 50 to 61 and back to 48.

The Erie directors, however, did not rest satisfied with the position which they had won through Judge Barnard's order. That simply placed them, as it were, in a strong defensive attitude. They were not the men to stop there: they aspired to nothing less than a vigorous offensive. With a superb audacity, which excites admiration, the new trustee immediately filed a supplementary petition. Therein it was duly set forth that doubts had been raised as to the legality of the recent issue of some two hundred thousand shares of stock, and that only about this amount was to be had in America; the trustee therefore petitioned for authority to use the funds of the corporation to purchase and cancel the whole of this amount at any price less than the par value, without regard to the rate at which it had been issued. The desired authority was conferred by Mr. Justice Barnard as soon as asked. Human assurance could go no further. The petitioners had issued these shares in the bear interest at 40, and had run down the value of Erie to 35; they had then turned round, and were now empowered to buy back that very stock in the bull interest, and in the name and with the funds of the corporation, at par. A law of the state distinctly forbade corporations from operating in their own stock; but this law was disregarded as if it had been only an injunction. An injunction forbade the treasurer from making any disposition of the funds of the company, and this injunction was respected no more than the law. These trustees had sold the property of their wards at 40; they were now prepared to use the money of their wards to buy the same property back at 80, and a judge had been found ready to confer on them the power to do so. Drew could not withstand such tactics, and indeed the annals of Wall Street furnished no precedent or parallel. They might have furnished one, but the opportunity had been lost. Had Robert Schuyler not lived fifteen years too soon,—had he, instead of flying his country and dying broken-hearted in exile, boldly attempted a change of front when his fraudulent issues had filled Wall Street with panic, and had he sought to use the funds of his company for a masterly upward movement in his own manufactured stock,—then, though in those uncultivated and illiberal days his scheme might have come to naught, and he himself might even have passed from the presence of an indignant jury into the keeping of a surly jailer, at least he would have evinced a mind in advance of his day, and could have comforted himself with the assurance that he was the first of a line of great men, and that the time was not far distant when his name and his fame would be cherished among the most brilliant recollections of Wall Street. But Schuyler lived before his time!

When this last, undreamed-of act was made public on Wednesday at noon, it was apparent that the crisis was not far off. Daniel Drew was cornered. Erie was scarce and selling at 47, and would not become plenty until the arrival of the English steamer on Monday; and so, at 47, Mr. Drew flung himself into the breach to save his endangered credit, and, under his purchases, the stock rapidly rose, until at five o'clock Wednesday afternoon it reached 57. Contrary to expectations, the "corner" had not yet culminated. It became evident the next morning that before two o'clock that day the issue would be decided. Drew fought desperately. The Brokers' Board was wild with excitement. High words passed; collisions took place; the bears were savage, and the bulls pitiless. Erie touched 62, and there was a difference of 16 per cent between cash stock and stock sold to be delivered in three days,—when the steamer would be in,—and a difference of 10 per cent between stock to be delivered on the spot and that to be delivered at the usual time, which was a quarter after two o'clock. Millions were handled like thousands; fabulous rates of interest were paid; rumors of legal proceedings were flying about, and forays of the Erie chiefs on the Vanderbilt roads were confidently predicted. New York Central suddenly shot up 7 per cent under these influences, and Vanderbilt seemed about to enter the field. The interest of the stock market centered in the combatants and on these two great corporations. All other stocks were quiet and neglected while the giants were fighting it out. The battle was too fierce to last long. At a quarter before three o'clock the struggle would be over. Yet now, at the very last moment, the prize which trembled before them eluded the grasp of the Erie Ring. Their opponent was not saved, but they shared his disaster. Their combination had turned on the fact, disclosed to them by the Erie books, that some three hundred thousand shares of its stock had been issued in the ten-share certificates which alone are transmitted to London. This amount they supposed to be out of the country; the balance they could account for as beyond the reach of Drew. Suddenly, as two o'clock approached, and Erie was trembling in the 60's, all Broadway—every tailor and bootmaker and cigar vender of New York—seemed pouring into Broad Street, and each newcomer held eagerly before him one or more of those ten-share certificates which should have been in London. Not only this, but the pockets of the agents of foreign bankers seemed bursting with them. Bedlam had suddenly broken loose in Wall Street. It was absolutely necessary for the conspirators to absorb this stock, to keep it from the hands of Drew. This they attempted to do, and manfully stood their ground, fighting against time. Suddenly, when the hour had almost come,—when five minutes more would have landed them in safety,—through one of those strange incidents which occur in Wall Street and which cannot be explained, they seemed smitten with panic. It is said their bank refused to certify their checks for the suddenly increased amount; the sellers insisted on having certified checks, and, in the delay caused by this unforeseen difficulty, the precious five minutes elapsed, and the crisis had passed. The fruits of their plot had escaped them. Drew made good his contracts at 57, the stock at once fell heavily to 42, and a dull quiet succeeded to the excitement of the morning. The hand of the Government had made itself felt in Wall Street.

The Broad Street conflict was over, and someone had reaped a harvest. Who was it? It was not Drew, for his losses, apart from a ruined prestige, were estimated at nearly a million and a half of dollars. The Erie directors were not the fortunate men, for their only trophies were great piles of certificates of Erie stock, which had cost them "corner" prices, and for which no demand existed. If Drew's loss was a million and a half, their loss was likely to be nearer three millions. Who, then, were the recipients of these missing millions? There is an ancient saying, which seems to have been tolerably verified in this case, that when certain persons fall out certain other persons come by their dues. The "corner" was very beautiful in all its details, and most admirably planned; but, unfortunately, those who engineered it had just previously made the volume of stock too large for accurate calculation. For once the outside public had been at hand and Wall Street had been found wanting. A large portion of the vast sum taken from the combatants found its way into the pockets of the agents of English bankers, and a part of it was accounted for by them to their principals; another portion went to relieve anxious holders among the American outside public; the remainder fell to professional operators, probably far more lucky than sagacious. Still, there had been a fall before there was a rise. The subsequent disaster, perhaps, no more than counterbalanced the earlier victory; at any rate, Messrs. Gould and Fisk did not succumb, but preserved a steady front, and Erie was more upon the street than ever. In fact, it was wholly there now. The recent operations had proved too outrageous even for the Brokers' Board. A new rule was passed, that no stock should be called, the issues of which were not registered at some respectable banking house. The Erie directors declined to conform to this rule, and their road was stricken from the list of calls. Nothing daunted at this, these Protean creatures at once organized a new board of their own, and so far succeeded in their efforts as to have Erie quoted and bought and sold as regularly as ever.

Though the catastrophe had taken place on the nineteenth, the struggle was not yet over. The interests involved were so enormous, the developments so astounding, such passions had been aroused, that some saftey-valve through which suppressed wrath could work itself off was absolutely necessary, and this the courts of law afforded. The attack was stimulated by various motives. The *bona fide* holders of the stock, especially the foreign holders, were alarmed for the existence of their property. The Erie Ring had now boldly taken the position that their duty was, not to manage the road in the interests of its owners, not to make it a dividend-paying corporation, but to preserve it from consolidation with the Vanderbilt monopoly. This policy was openly proclaimed by Mr. Gould, at a later day, before an investigating committee at Albany. With unspeakable effrontery,—an effrontery so great as actually to impose on his audience and a portion of the press, and make them believe that the public ought to wish him success,—he described how stock issues at the proper time, to any required amount, could alone keep him in control of the road, and keep Mr. Vanderbilt out of it; it would be his duty, therefore, he argued, to issue as much new stock, at about the time of the annual election, as would suffice to keep a majority of all the stock in existence under his control; and he declared that he meant to do this.* The strangest thing of all was,

---

* *Question to Mr. Gould.* For the information, of the committee, would you give us your opinion as to the utility of that section of the general railroad law, under which so many issues of convertible bonds have been made?

Answer. I could only speak as to the Erie Road; that law saved the Erie Road from bankruptcy; and as long as that law is unrepealed, I should do what I did again. I should save the road. I think it is a good law.

Q. Is it not liable to abuse?

A. I have never known it to be abused; if that was repealed, I think that Mr. Vanderbilt would have the road; but as long as it is not repealed it is held *in terrorem* over him.

Q. Suppose the section was amended so as to require the consent of the stockholders?

A. Suppose he owned all the stock, what would be the difference? . . .

Q. What other effect would it (the repeal of Section 10) have?

A. I think it would lay the State open to a great monopoly,—the greatest the world has ever seen.

Much more followed in the same style. One remark of Mr. Gould's, how-that it never seemed to occur to his audience that the propounder of this comical sophistry was a trustee and guardian for the stockholders, and not a public benefactor; and that the owners of the Erie road might possibly prefer not to be deprived of their property, in order to secure the blessing of competition. So unique a method of securing a reëlection was probably never before suggested with a grave face, and yet, if we may believe the reporters, Mr. Gould, in developing it, produced a very favorable impression on the committee. It was hardly to be expected that such advanced views as to the duties and powers of railway directors would favorably impress commonplace individuals who might not care to have their property scaled down to meet Mr. Gould's views of public welfare. These persons accordingly, popularly supposed to be represented by Mr. Belmont, wished to get their property out of the hands of such fanatics in the cause of cheap transportation and plentiful stock, with the least possible delay. Combined with these were the operators who had suffered in the late ''corner,'' and who desired to fight for better terms and a more equal division of plunder. Behind them all, Vanderbilt was supposed to be keeping an eager eye on the long-coveted Erie. Thus the materials for litigation existed in abundance.

On Monday, the twenty-third, Judge Sutherland vacated Judge Barnard's order appointing Jay Gould receiver, and, after seven hours' argument and some exhibitions of vulgarity and indecency on the part of counsel, which vied with those of the previous April, he appointed Mr. Davies, a former chief justice of the Court of Appeals, receiver of the road and its franchise, leaving the special terms of the order to be settled at a future day. The seven hours' struggle had not been without an object; that day Judge Barnard had been peculiarly active. The morning hours he had beguiled by the delivery to the grand jury of one of the most astounding charges ever recorded; and now, as the shades

ever, in this examination, bore the stamp of truth and perspicuity. It is recorded as follows: ''The Erie road won't be a dividend-paying road for a long time on its common stock.''

of evening were falling, he closed the labors of the day by issuing
a stay of the proceedings then pending before his associate.*
Tuesday had been named by Judge Sutherland, at the time he
appointed his receiver, as the day upon which he would settle
the details of the order. His first proceeding upon that day, on
finding his action stayed by Judge Barnard, was to grant a motion to show cause, on the next day, why Barnard's order should
not be vacated. This style of warfare, however, savored altogether too much of the tame defensive to meet successfully the
bold strategy of Messrs. Gould and Fisk. They carried the war
into Africa. In the twenty-four hours during which Judge
Sutherland's order to show cause was pending three new actions
were commenced by them. In the first place, they sued the suers.

* The charge referred to is altogether too curious to be forgotten; it was
couched in the following terms:—
   "GENTLEMEN OF THE GRAND JURY,—I deem it not inappropriate at the
present time to call your attention to three or four subjects that, in my
judgment, the grand jury should look into: First, in regard to alleged frauds
at elections; second, in regard to the alleged corruptions of the judiciary
here; third, as to the action of certain newspapers in New York in perpetrat-
ing daily and hourly libels. I had intended, gentlemen, at the commencement
of this term, to have gone over many of these subjects more fully than I can
now; but I am led to-day not to delay it any longer in consequence of the
annoyance I am subjected to by newspapers and letter-writers, not borne out,
of all sorts of vilifications and abuses for offences of which I certainly know
nothing, and see if the writers of some of these articles cannot be made to
come before you and substantiate some among the many of the different allegations that they have made against the judge that now addresses you. In
to-day's *Tribune* and to-day's *Times*, along with articles in the Jersey papers
and elsewhere, are charges of the most atrocious character made against corruptions, in interfering with the duties of electors, and charging the judge
with being in a combination in Wall Street. Now, it is unnecessary for me to
say to you that he never bought or sold or owned a share of stock in his life,
and as for the large fortune of $5,000,000 which one of the papers charges
him with being possessed of, he has not now, nor did he ever have, belonging
to him, separate from his wife, a single dollar's worth of property, and is
to-day dependent upon his salary as a judge and the charity of his wife; and
why these particular and atrocious charges at this particular time should be
made with such boldness and audacity is a matter I hope you as grand jurors,
whose duty it is, will look into, so that if you find them to be substantial, or
even a suspicion that they are true, that you will give the judge a chance to

Alleging the immense injury likely to result to the Erie road from actions commenced, as they alleged, solely with a view of extorting money in settlement, Mr. Belmont was sued for a million of dollars in damages. Their second suit was against Messrs. Work, Schell, and others, concerned in the litigations of the previous spring, to recover the $429,250 then paid them, as was alleged, in a fraudulent settlement. These actions were, however, commonplace, and might have been brought by ordinary men. Messrs. Gould and Fisk were always displaying the invention of genius. The same day they carried their quarrels into the United States courts. The whole press, both of New York and of the country, disgusted with the parody of justice enacted in the state courts, had cried aloud to have the whole matter trans-

resign. For infamy means one thing, and it ought to be ferreted out; and if a man or a newspaper editor will sit down deliberately and make a charge without any proof, let us see whether the rigor and terror of the law will not stop this thing in future. For eleven years this judge has submitted to it without any notice, and now, having arrived at a period of life when his usefulness is impaired by such charges, he deems it his duty, and yours, gentlemen, to look into the matter whenever you have leisure, and say whether a combination of thieves, scoundrels, and rascals, who have infested Wall Street and Broad Street for years, and are now quarrelling among themselves, shall be permitted to turn around and endeavor to hide their own tracks by abuse and vilification of the judge.''

It may be interesting to record how this fulmination affected the papers referred to. The *Times* the next morning commented on it as follows: ''What we have said and done in the matter we have said and done deliberately; . . . we believe we have said nothing that is not true, and nothing that cannot be proved to be true. At all events, we shall very willingly accept the responsibility of establishing its truth and of vindicating ourselves from the judge's imputations for having said it.'' A few days later it was reported that a true bill had been found against the *Times*, and that paper on the twenty-sixth congratulated the public on the fact. Finally, when Judge Barnard determined to drop the matter, the *Times*, in its issue of December 1, discoursed as follows on the subject: ''We beg the judge to understand that we are quite ready to meet the issue that he tendered us, and to respond to such an indictment as he first urged the grand jury to find against us, or to a suit for damages, which would, perhaps, better suit the deplorable condition of pecuniary dependence to which he says he is reduced.'' Nothing further came of the matter.

88883

ferred to the United States tribunals, the decisions of which
might have some weight, and where, at least, no partisans upon
the bench would shower each other with stays, injunctions, vacat-
ings of orders, and other such pellets of the law. The Erie Ring, as
usual, took time by the forelock. While their slower antagonists
were deliberating, they acted. On this Monday, the twenty-third,
one Henry B. Whelpley, who had been a clerk of Gould's, and
who claimed to be a stockholder in the Erie and a citizen of New
Jersey, instituted a suit against the Erie Railway before Judge
Blatchford, of the United States District Court. Alleging the
doubts which hung over the validity of the recently issued stock,
he petitioned that a receiver might be appointed, and the company
directed to transfer into his hands enough property to secure
from loss the plaintiff as well as all other holders of the new
issues. The Erie counsel were on the ground, and, as soon as the
petition was read, waived all further notice as to the matters contained in it; whereupon the court at once appointed Jay Gould
receiver, and directed the Erie Company to place eight millions
of dollars in his hands to protect the rights represented by the
plaintiff. Of course the receiver was required to give bonds with
sufficient sureties. Among the sureties was James Fisk, Jr. The
brilliancy of this move was only surpassed by its success. It fell
like a bombshell in the enemy's camp, and scattered dismay
among those who still preserved a lingering faith in the virtue
of law as administered by any known courts. The interference of
the court was in this case asked for on the ground of fraud. If
any fraud had been committed, the officers of the company alone
could be the delinquents. To guard against the consequences of
that fraud, a receivership was prayed for, and the court appointed as receiver the very officer in whom the alleged frauds,
on which its action was based, must have originated. It is true,
as was afterward observed by Judge Nelson in setting it aside,
that a *prima facie* case, for the appointment of a receiver "was
supposed to have been made out," that no objection to the person suggested was made, and that the right was expressly re-

served to other parties to come into court, with any allegations they saw fit against Receiver Gould. The collusion in the case was, nevertheless, so evident, the facts were so notorious and so apparent from the very papers before the court, and the character of Judge Blatchford is so far above suspicion, that it is hard to believe that this order was not procured from him by surprise, or through the agency of some counsel in whom he reposed a misplaced confidence. The Erie Ring, at least, had no occasion to be dissatisfied with this day's proceedings.

The next day Judge Sutherland made short work of his brother Barnard's stay of proceedings in regard to the Davies receivership. He vacated it at once, and incontinently proceeded, wholly ignoring the action of Judge Blatchford on the day before, to settle the terms of the order, which, covering as it did the whole of the Erie property and franchise, excepting only the operating of the road, bade fair to lead to a conflict of jurisdiction between the state and federal courts.

And now a new judicial combatant appears in the arena. It is difficult to say why Judge Barnard, at this time, disappears from the narrative. Perhaps the notorious judicial violence of the man, which must have made his eagerness as dangerous to the cause he espoused as the eagerness of a too swift witness, had alarmed the Erie counsel. Perhaps the fact that Judge Sutherland's term in chambers would expire in a few days had made them wish to intrust their cause to the magistrate who was to succeed him. At any rate, the new order staying proceedings under Judge Sutherland's order was obtained from Judge Cardozo,—it is said, somewhat before the terms of the receivership had been finally settled. The change spoke well for the discrimination of those who made it, for Judge Cardozo is a very different man from Judge Barnard. Courteous but inflexible, subtle, clear headed, and unscrupulous, this magistrate conceals the iron hand beneath the silken glove. Equally versed in the laws of New York and in the mysteries of Tammany, he had earned his place by a partisan decision on the excise law, and was nominated for the bench by

Mr. Fernando Wood, in a few remarks concluding as follows: "Judges were often called on to decide on political questions, and he was sorry to say the majority of them decided according to their political bias. It was therefore absolutely necessary to look to their candidate's political principles. He would nominate, as a fit man for the office of Judge of the Supreme Court, Albert Cardozo." Nominated as a partisan, a partisan Cardozo has always been, when the occasion demanded. Such was the new and far more formidable champion who now confronted Sutherland, in place of the vulgar Barnard. His first order in the matter—to show cause why the order of his brother judge should not be set aside—was not returnable until the thirtieth, and in the intervening five days many events were to happen.

Immediately after the settlement by Judge Sutherland of the order appointing Judge Davies' receiver, that gentleman had proceeded to take possession of his trust. Upon arriving at the Erie building, he found it converted into a fortress, with a sentry patrolling behind the bolts and bars, to whom was confided the duty of scrutinizing all comers, and of admitting none but the faithful allies of the garrison. It so happened that Mr. Davies, himself unknown to the custodian, was accompanied by Mr. Eaton, the former attorney of the Erie corporation. This gentleman was recognized by the sentry, and forthwith the gates flew open for himself and his companion. In a few moments more the new receiver astonished Messrs. Gould and Fisk, and certain legal gentlemen with whom they happened to be in conference, by suddenly appearing in the midst of them. The apparition was not agreeable. Mr. Fisk, however, with a fair appearance of cordiality, welcomed the strangers, and shortly after left the room. Speedily returning, his manner underwent a change, and he requested the newcomers to go the way they came. As they did not comply at once, he opened the door, and directed their attention to some dozen men of forbidding aspect who stood outside, and who, he intimated, were prepared to eject them forcibly if they sought to prolong their unwelcome stay. As an indication of the lengths to

which Mr. Fisk was prepared to go, this was sufficiently signifi-
cant. The movement, however, was a little too rapid for his companions; the lawyers protested, Mr. Gould apologized, Mr. Fisk
cooled down, and his familiars retired. The receiver then proceeded to give written notice of his appointment, and the fact
that he had taken possession; disregarding, in so doing, an order
of Judge Cardozo, staying proceedings under Judge Sutherland's order, which one of the opposing counsel drew from his
pocket, but which Mr. Davies not inaptly characterized as a
"very singular order," seeing that it was signed before the
terms of the order it sought to affect were finally settled. At
length, however, at the earnest request of some of the subordinate
officials, and satisfied with the formal possession he had taken,
the new receiver delayed further action until Friday. He little
knew the resources of his opponents, if he vainly supposed that
a formal possession signified anything. The succeeding Friday
found the directors again fortified within, and himself a much
enjoined wanderer without. The vigilant guards were now no
longer to be beguiled. Within the building, constant discussions
and consultations were taking place; without, relays of detectives
incessantly watched the premises. No rumor was too wild for
public credence. It was confidently stated that the directors were
about to fly the state and the country,—that the treasury had
already been conveyed to Canada. At last, late on Sunday night,
Mr. Fisk with certain of his associates left the building, and
made for the Jersey ferry; but on the way he was stopped
by a vigilant lawyer, and many papers were served upon him.
His plans were then changed. He returned to the office of the
company, and presently the detectives saw a carriage leave the
Erie portals, and heard a loud voice order it to be driven to the
Fifth Avenue Hotel. Instead of going there, however, it drove to
the ferry, and presently an engine, with an empty directors' car
attached, dashed out of the Erie station in Jersey City, and disappeared in the darkness. The detectives met and consulted; the
carriage and the empty car were put together, and the inference,

announced in every New York paper the succeeding day, was that
Messrs. Fisk and Gould had absconded with millions of money
to Canada.

That such a ridiculous story should have been published, much
less believed, simply shows how utterly demoralized the public
mind had become, and how prepared for any act of high-handed
fraud or outrage. The libel did not long remain uncontradicted.
The next day a card from Mr. Fisk was telegraphed to the newspapers, denying the calumny in indignant terms. The eternal
steel rails were again made to do duty, and the midnight flitting
became a harmless visit to Binghamton on business connected
with a rolling mill. Judge Balcom, however, of injunction
memory in the earlier records of the Erie suits, resides at Binghamton, and a leading New York paper not inaptly made the
timid inquiry of Mr. Fisk, "If he really thought that Judge Balcom was running a rolling-mill of the Erie Company, what did he
think of Judge Barnard?" Mr. Fisk, however, as became him in
his character of the Maecenas of the bar, instituted suits claiming
damages in fabulous sums, for defamation of character, against
some half-dozen of the leading papers, and nothing further was
heard of the matter, nor, indeed, of the suits either. Not so of
the trip to Binghamton. On Tuesday, the first of December, while
one set of lawyers were arguing an appeal in the Whelpley case
before Judge Nelson in the federal courts, and another set were
procuring orders from Judge Cardozo staying proceedings authorized by Judge Sutherland, a third set were aiding Judge Balcom
in certain new proceedings instituted in the name of the Attorney-General against the Erie road. The result arrived at was, of
course, that Judge Balcom declared his to be the only shop where
a regular, reliable article in the way of law was retailed, and
then proceeded forthwith to restrain and shut up the opposition
establishments. The action was brought to terminate the existence
of the defendant as a corporation, and, by way of preliminary,
application was made for an injunction and the appointment of
a receiver. His Honor held that, as only three receivers had as

yet been appointed, he was certainly entitled to appoint another. It was perfectly clear to him that it was his duty to enjoin the defendant corporation from delivering the possession of its road, or of any of its assets, to either of the receivers already appointed; it was equally clear that the corporation would be obliged to deliver them to any receiver he might appoint. He was not prepared to name a receiver just then, however, though he intimated that he should not hesitate to do so if necessary. So he contented himself with the appointment of a referee to look into matters, and, generally, enjoined the directors from omitting to operate the road themselves, or from delivering the possession of it to ''any person claiming to be a receiver.''

This raiding upon the agricultural judges was not peculiar to the Erie party. On the contrary, in this proceeding it rather followed than set an example; for a day or two previous to Mr. Fisk's hurried journey, Judge Peckham of Albany had, upon papers identical with those in the Belmont suit, issued divers orders, similar to those of Judge Balcom, but on the other side, tying up the Erie directors in a most astonishing manner, and clearly hinting at the expediency of an additional receiver to be appointed at Albany. The amazing part of these Peckham and Balcom proceedings is, that they seem to have been initiated with perfect gravity, and neither to have been looked upon as jests, nor intended by their originators to bring the courts and the laws of New York into ridicule and contempt. Of course the several orders in these cases were of no more importance than so much waste paper, unless, indeed, some very cautious counsel may have considered an extra injunction or two very convenient things to have in his house; and yet, curiously enough, from a legal point of view, those in Judge Balcom's court seem to have been almost the only properly and regularly initiated proceedings in the whole case.

These little rural episodes in no way interfered with a renewal of vigorous hostilities in New York. While Judge Balcom was appointing his referee, Judge Cardozo granted an order for a reargument in the Belmont suit,—which brought up again the appointment of Judge Davies as receiver,—and assigned the hearing for the sixth of December. This step on his part bore a curious resemblance to certain of his performances in the notorious case of the Wood leases, and made the plan of operations perfectly clear. The period during which Judge Sutherland was to sit in chambers was to expire on the fourth of December, and Cardozo himself was to succeed him; he now, therefore, proposed to signalize his associate's departure from chambers by reviewing his orders. No sooner had he granted the motion, than the opposing counsel applied to Judge Sutherland, who forthwith issued an order to show cause why the reargument ordered by Judge Cardozo, should not take place at once. Upon which the counsel of the Erie road instantly ran over to Judge Cardozo, who vacated Judge Sutherland's order out of hand. The lawyers then left him and ran back to Judge Sutherland with a motion to vacate this last order. The contest was now becoming altogether too ludicrous. Somebody must yield, and when it was reduced to that, the honest Sutherland was pretty sure to give way to the subtle Cardozo. Accordingly the hearing on this last motion was postponed until the next morning, when Judge Sutherland made a not undignified statement as to his position, and closed by remitting the whole subject to the succeeding Monday, at which time Judge Cardozo was to succeed him in chambers. Cardozo, therefore, was now in undisputed possession of the field. In his closing explanation Judge Sutherland did not quote, as he might have done, the following excellent passage from the opinion of the court, of which both he and Cardozo were justices, delivered in the Schell case as recently as the last day of the previous June: "The idea that a cause, by such manoeuvres as have been resorted to here, can be withdrawn from one judge of this court and taken possession of by another; that thus one judge of the same and no other powers can practically prevent his associate from exercising his judicial functions; that thus a case may be taken from judge to judge whenever one of

the parties fears that an unfavorable decision is about to be rendered by the judge who, up to that time, had sat in the cause, and
that thus a decision of a suit may be constantly indefinitely postponed at the will of one of the litigants, only deserves to be noticed as being a curiosity in legal tactics,—a remarkable exhibition of inventive genius and fertility of expedient to embarrass
a suit which this extraordinarily conducted litigation has developed. . . . Such a practice as that disclosed by this litigation,
sanctioning the attempt to counteract the orders of each other in
the progress of the suit, I confess is new and shocking to me,
. . . and I trust that we have seen the last in this high tribunal
of such practices as this case has exhibited. No apprehension, real
or fancied, that any judge is about, either wilfully or innocently,
to do a wrong, can palliate, much less justify it.''* Neither
did Judge Sutherland state, as he might have stated, that this
admirable expression of the sentiments of the full bench was
written and delivered by Judge Albert Cardozo. Probably also
Judge Cardozo and all his brother judges, rural and urban, as
they used these bowstrings of the law, right and left,—as their
reckless orders and injunctions struck deep into business circles
far beyond the limits of their state,—as they degraded themselves in degrading their order, and made the ermine of supreme
justice scarcely more imposing than the motley of the clown,—
these magistrates may have thought that they had developed at
least a novel, if not a respectable, mode of conducting litigation.
They had not done even this. They had simply, so far as in them
lay, turned back the wheels of progress and reduced the America
of the nineteenth century to the level of the France of the sixteenth. ''The advocates and judges of our times find bias enough
in all causes to accommodate them to what they themselves think
fit. . . . What one court has determined one way another determines quite contrary, and itself contrary to that at another time;
of which we see very frequent examples, owing to that practice
admitted among us, and which is a marvellous blemish to the

* *Schell* v. *Erie Railway Co.*, 51 Barbour's S. C., 373, 374.

ceremonious authority and lustre of our justice, of not abiding by one sentence, but running from judge to judge, and court to court, to decide one and the same cause.''*

It was now very clear that Receiver Davies might abandon all hope of operating the Erie Railway, and that Messrs. Gould and Fisk were borne upon the swelling tide of victory. The prosperous aspect of their affairs encouraged these last-named gentlemen to yet more vigorous offensive operations. The next attack was upon Vanderbilt in person. On Saturday, the fifth of December, only two days after Judge Sutherland and Receiver Davies were disposed of, the indefatigable Fisk waited on Commodore Vanderbilt, and, in the name of the Erie Company, tendered him fifty thousand shares of Erie common stock at 70.† As the stock was then selling in Wall Street at 40, the Commodore naturally declined to avail himself of this liberal offer. He even went further, and, disregarding his usual wise policy of silence, wrote to

* *Montaigne's Works*, Vol. II, p. 316.

† Throughout these proceedings glimpses are from time to time obtained of the more prominent characters in their undress, as it were, which have in them a good many elements both of nature and humor. The following description of the visit in which this tender was made was subsequently given by Fisk on the witness stand: ''I went to his (Vanderbilt's) house; it was a bad, stormy day, and I had the shares in a carpet-bag; I told the Commodore I had come to tender 50,000 shares of Erie and wanted back the money which we had paid for them and the bonds, and I made a separate demand for the $1,000,000 which had been paid to cover his losses; he said he had nothing to do with the Erie now, and must consult his counsel; . . . Mr. Shearman was with me; the date I don't know; it was about eleven o'clock in the morning; don't know the day, don't know the month, don't know the year; I rode up with Shearman, holding the carpet-bag tight between my legs; I told him he was a small man and not much protection; this was dangerous property, you see, and might blow up; . . . besides Mr. Shearman the driver went in with the witnesses, and besides the Commodore I spoke with the servant-girl; the Commodore was sitting on the bed with one shoe off and one shoe on; . . . don't remember what more was said; I remember the Commodore put on his other shoe; I remember those shoes on account of the buckles; you see there were four buckles on that shoe, and I know it passed through my mind that if such men wore that kind of shoe I must get me a pair; this passed through my mind, but I did not speak of it to the Commodore; I was very civil to him.''

the *New York Times* a short communication, in which he referred
to the alleged terms of settlement of the previous July, so far as
they concerned himself, and denied them in the following explicit
language: "I have had no dealings with the Erie Railway Company, nor have I ever sold that company any stock or received
from them any *bonus*. As to the suits instituted by Mr. Schell
and others, I had nothing to do with them, nor was I in any way
concerned in their settlement." This was certainly an announce-
ment calculated to confuse the public; but the confusion became
confounded, when, upon the tenth, Mr. Fisk followed him in a
card in which he reiterated the alleged terms of settlement, and
reproduced two checks of the Erie Company, of July 11, 1868,
made payable to the treasurer and by him indorsed to C. Vanderbilt, upon whose order they had been paid. These two checks
were for the sum of a million of dollars. He further said that
the company had a paper in Mr. Vanderbilt's own handwriting,
stating that he had placed fifty thousand shares of Erie stock in
the hands of certain persons, to be delivered on payment of
$3,500,000, which sum he declared had been paid. Undoubtedly
these apparent discrepancies of statement admitted of an explanation; and some thin veil of equivocation, such as the transaction of the business through third parties, justified Vanderbilt's statements to his own conscience. Comment, however, is
wholly superfluous, except to call attention to the amount of
weight which is to be given to the statements and denials, apparently the most general and explicit, which from time to time
were made by the parties to these proceedings. This short controversy merely added a little more discredit to what was already
not deficient in that respect. On the tenth of December the Erie
Company sued Commodore Vanderbilt for $3,500,000, specially
alleging in their complaint the particulars of that settlement, all
knowledge of or connection with which the defendant had so
emphatically denied.

None of the multifarious suits which had been brought as yet
were aimed at Mr. Drew. The quondam treasurer had apparently

wholly disappeared from the scene on the nineteenth of November. Mr. Fisk took advantage, however, of a leisure day, to remedy this oversight, and a suit was commenced against Drew, on the ground of certain transactions between him, as treasurer, and the railway company, in relation to some steamboats concerned in the trade of Lake Erie. The usual allegations of fraud, breach of trust, and other trifling and, technically, not state-prison offenses, were made, and damages were set at a million of dollars.

Upon the eighth the argument in Belmont's case had been reopened before Judge Cardozo in New York, and upon the same day, in Oneida County, Judge Boardman, another justice of the Supreme Court, had proceeded to contribute his share to the existing complications. Counsel in behalf of Receiver Davies had appeared before him, and, upon their application, the Cardozo injunction, which restrained the receiver from taking possession of the Erie Railway, had been dissolved. Why this application was made, or why it was granted, surpasses comprehension. However, the next day, Judge Boardman's order having been read in court before Judge Cardozo, that magistrate suddenly revived to a full appreciation of the views expressed by him in June in regard to judicial interference with judicial action, and at once stigmatized Judge Boardman's action as "extremely indecorous." Neglecting, however, the happy opportunity to express an opinion as to his own conduct during the previous week, he simply stayed all proceedings under this new order, and applied himself to the task of hearing the case before him reargued.

This hearing lasted many days, was insufferably long and inexpressibly dull. While it was going on, upon the fifteenth Judge Nelson, in the United States court, delivered his opinion in the Whelpley suit, reversing, on certain technical grounds the action of Judge Blatchford, and declaring that no case for the appointment of a receiver had been made out; accordingly he set aside that of Gould, and, in conclusion, sent the matter back to the state court, or, in other words, to Judge Cardozo, fo decision. Thus the gentlemen of the ring, having been most fortunate in getting their case into the federal court before Judge Blatchford, were now even more fortunate in getting it out of that court when it had come before Judge Nelson. After this, room for doubt no longer existed. Brilliant success at every point had crowned the strategy of the Erie directors. For once Vanderbilt was effectually routed and driven from the field. That he shrank from continuing the contest against such opponents is much to his credit. It showed that he, at least, was not prepared to see how near he could come to the doors of a state prison and yet not enter them; that he did not care to take in advance the opinion of leading counsel as to whether what he meant to do might place him in the felons' dock. Thus Erie was wholly given over to the control of the ring. No one seemed any longer to dispute their right and power to issue as much new stock as might seem to them expedient. Injunctions had failed to check them; receivers had no terrors for them. Secure in their power, they now extended their operations over sea and land, leasing railroads, buying steamboats, ferries, theaters, and rolling mills, building connecting links of road, laying down additional rails, and, generally, proving themselves a power wherever corporations were to be influenced or legislatures were to be bought.

Christmas, the period of peace and good will, was now approaching. The dreary arguments before Judge Cardozo had terminated on December 18, long after the press and the public had ceased to pay any attention to them, and already rumors of a settlement were rife. Yet it was not meet that the settlement should be effected without some final striking catastrophe, some characteristic concluding tableau. Among the many actions which had incidentally sprung from these proceedings was one against Mr. Samuel Bowles, the editor of the *Springfield Republican,* brought by Mr. Fisk in consequence of an article which had appeared in that paper, reflecting most severely on Fisk's proceedings and private character,—his past, his present, and his probable future. On the twenty-second of December, Mr. Bowles happened to be in New York, and, as he was standing in the office of his hotel, talking with a friend, was suddenly arrested on the warrant of Judge McCunn, hurried into a carriage, and driven to Ludlow Street Jail, where he was locked up for the night. This excellent jest afforded intense amusement, and was the cause of much wit that evening at an entertainment given by the Tammany Ring to the newly elected mayor of New York, at which entertainment Mr. James Fisk, Jr., was an honored guest. The next morning the whole press was in a state of high indignation, and Mr. Bowles had suddenly become the best-advertised editor in the country. At an early hour he was, of course, released on bail, and with this outrage the second Erie contest was brought to a close. It seemed right and proper that proceedings which, throughout, had set public opinion at defiance, and in which the Stock Exchange, the courts, and the legislature had come in for equal measures of opprobrium for their disregard of private rights, should be terminated by an exhibition of petty spite, in which bench and bar, judge, sheriff, and jailer, lent themselves with base subserviency to a violation of the liberty of the citizen.

It was not until the tenth of February that Judge Cardozo published his decision setting aside the Sutherland receivership, and establishing on a basis of authority the right to overissue stock at pleasure. The subject was then as obsolete and forgotten as though it had never absorbed the public attention. And another "settlement" had already been effected. The details of this arrangement have not been dragged to light through the exposures of subsequent litigation. But it is not difficult to see where and how a combination of overpowering influence may have been effected, and a guess might even be hazarded as to its objects and its victims. The fact that a settlement had been arrived at was intimated in the papers of the twenty-sixth of December. On the nineteenth of the same month a stock dividend of 80 per cent in the New York Central had been suddenly declared by Vanderbilt. Presently the legislature met. While the Erie Ring seemed to have good reasons for apprehending hostile legislation, Vanderbilt, on his part, might have feared for the success of a bill which was to legalize his new stock. But hardly a voice was raised against the Erie men, and the bill of the Central was safely carried through. This curious absence of opposition did not stop here, and soon the two parties were seen united in an active alliance. Vanderbilt wanted to consolidate his roads; the Erie directors wanted to avoid the formality of annual elections. Thereupon two other bills went hastily through this honest and patriotic legislature, the one authorizing the Erie Board, which had been elected for one year, to classify itself so that one fifth only of its members should vacate office during each succeeding year, the other consolidating the Vanderbilt roads into one colossal monopoly. Public interests and private rights seem equally to have been the victims. It is impossible to say that the beautiful unity of interests which led to such results was the fulfilment of the December settlement; but it is a curious fact that the same paper which announced in one column that Vanderbilt's two measures, known as the consolidation and Central scrip bills had gone to the Governor for signature, should, in another, have reported the discontinuance of the Belmont and Whelpley suits by the consent of all interested.* It may be that public and private interests were not thus balanced and traded away in a servile legislature, but the strong probabilities are that the settlement of December made white even that of July. Meanwhile the conquerors—the men whose names had been made notorious through the whole land in all these infamous proceedings—were at last undisputed masters of the situation, and no man questioned the firmness of their grasp on the Erie Railway. They walked erect and proud of their infamy through the streets of our great cities; they voluntarily subjected themselves to that to which other depredators are compelled to submit, and, by exposing their portraits in public conveyances, converted noble steamers into branch galleries of a police office; nay, more, they bedizened their persons with gold lace, and assumed honored

* See the *New York Tribune* of May 10, 1869.

titles, until those who witnessed in silent contempt their strange antics were disposed to exclaim in the language of poor Doll Tearsheet: "An Admiral! God's light, these villains will make the word as odious as the word 'occupy,' which was an excellent good word before it was ill sorted; therefore, Admirals had need look to 't."

The subsequent history of the Erie Railway, under the management of the men who had thus succeeded in gaining absolute control over it, forms no part of this narrative. The attempt has been made simply to trace the course of events which resulted in placing a national thoroughfare in the hands of unscrupulous gamblers, and to describe the complications which marked their progress to power. The end was finally attained, when, after every opponent had, by fair means or by foul, been driven from the conflict, that strange law was enacted which assured these men, elected for one year, a five years' term of power, beyond the control of their stockholders. From that moment all the great resources of the Erie Railway became mere engines with which to work their lawless will.

Comment would only weaken the force of this narrative. It sufficiently suggests its own moral. The facts which have been set forth cannot but have revealed to every observant eye the deep decay which has eaten into our social edifice. No portion of our system was left untested, and no portion showed itself to be sound. The stock exchange revealed itself as a haunt of gamblers and a den of thieves; the offices of our great corporations appeared as the secret chambers in which trustees plotted the spoliation of their wards; the law became a ready engine for the furtherance of wrong, and the ermine of the judge did not conceal the eagerness of the partisan; the halls of legislation were transformed into a mart in which the price of votes was higgled over, and laws, made to order, were bought and sold; while under all, and through all, the voice of public opinion was silent or was disregarded.

It is not, however, in connection with the present that all this
has its chief significance. It speaks ominously for the future. It
may be that our society is only passing through a period of ugly
transition, but the present evil has its root deep down in the
social organization, and springs from a diseased public opinion.
Failure seems to be regarded as the one unpardonable crime, success as the all-redeeming virtue, the acquisition of wealth as the
single worthy aim of life. Ten years ago such revelations as these
of the Erie Railway would have sent a shudder through the community, and would have placed a stigma on every man who had
had to do with them. Now they merely incite others to surpass
them by yet bolder outrages and more corrupt combinations.
Were this not so, these things would be as impossible among us
now as they are elsewhere, or as they were here not many years
ago. While this continues it is mere weakness to attribute the
consequences of a lax morality to a defective currency, or seek to
prevent its outward indications by statute remedies. The root of
the disease is deep; external applications will only hide its dangerous symptoms. It is well to reform the currency, it is well to
enact laws against malefactors; but neither the one nor the other
will restore health to a business community which tolerates successful fraud, or which honors wealth more than honesty.

One leading feature of these developments, however, is, from
its political aspect, especially worthy of the attention of the
American people. Modern society has created a class of artificial
beings who bid fair soon to be the masters of their creator. It is
but a very few years since the existence of a corporation controlling a few millions of dollars was regarded as a subject of
grave apprehension, and now this country already contains single organizations which wield a power represented by hundreds
of millions. These bodies are the creatures of single states; but in
New York, in Pennsylvania, in Maryland, in New Jersey, and
not in those states alone, they are already establishing despotisms
which no spasmodic popular effort will be able to shake off.
Everywhere, and at all times, however, they illustrate the truth

of the old maxim of the common law, that corporations have no souls. Only in New York has any intimation yet been given of what the future may have in store for us should these great powers become mere tools in the hands of ambitious, reckless men. The system of corporate life and corporate power, as applied to industrial development, is yet in its infancy. It tends always to development,—always to consolidation,—it is ever grasping new powers, or insidiously exercising covert influence. Even now the system threatens the central government. The Erie Railway represents a weak combination compared to those which day by day are consolidating under the unsuspecting eyes of the community. A very few years more, and we shall see corporations as much exceeding the Erie and the New York Central in both ability and will for corruption as they will exceed those roads in wealth and in length of iron track. We shall see these great corporations spanning the continent from ocean to ocean,—single, consolidated lines, not connecting Albany with Buffalo, or Lake Erie with the Hudson, but uniting the Atlantic and the Pacific, and bringing New York nearer to San Francisco than Albany once was to Buffalo. Already the disconnected members of these future leviathans have built up states in the wilderness, and chosen their attorneys senators of the United States. Now their power is in its infancy; in a very few years they will reënact, on a larger theater and on a grander scale, with every feature magnified, the scenes which were lately witnessed on the narrow stage of a single state. The public corruption is the foundation on which corporations always depend for their political power. There is a natural tendency to coalition between them and the lowest strata of political intelligence and morality; for their agents must obey, not question. They exact success, and do not cultivate political morality. The lobby is their home, and the lobby thrives as political virtue decays. The ring is their symbol of power, and the ring is the natural enemy of political purity and independence. All this was abundantly illustrated in the events which have just been narrated. The existing coalition between the Erie Railway and the Tammany Ring is a natural one, for the former needs votes, the latter money. This combination now controls the legislature and courts of New York; that it controls also the Executive of the state, as well as that of the city, was proved when Governor Hoffman recorded his reasons for signing the infamous Erie Directors' Bill. It is a new power, for which our language contains no name. We know what aristocracy, autocracy, democracy are; but we have no word to express government by moneyed corporations. Yet the people already instinctively seek protection against it, and look for such protection, significantly enough, not to their own legislatures, but to the single autocratic feature retained in our system of government,— the veto by the Executive. In this there is something more imperial than republican. The people have lost faith in themselves when they cease to have any faith in those whom they uniformly elect to represent them. The change that has taken place in this respect of late years in America has been startling in its rapidity. Legislation is more and more falling into contempt, and this not so much on account of the extreme ignorance manifested in it as because of the corrupt motives which are believed habitually to actuate it. Thus the influence of corporations and of class interests is steadily destroying that belief in singleness of purpose which alone enables a representative government to exist, and the community is slowly accustoming itself to look for protection, not to public opinion, but to some man in high place and armed with great executive powers. Him they now think they can hold to some accountability. It remains to be seen what the next phase in this process of gradual development will be. History never quite repeats itself, and, as was suggested in the first pages of this narrative, the old familiar enemies may even now confront us, though arrayed in such a modern garb that no suspicion is excited. Americans are apt pupils, and among them there are probably some who have not observed Fisk and Vanderbilt and Hoffman without a thought of bettering their instructions. No successful military leader will repeat in America the threadbare experiences of Europe;—the executive power is not likely to be seized while the legislative is suppressed. The indications would now seem rather to point toward the corruption of the legislative and a quiet assumption of the executive through some combination in one vigorous hand of those influences which throughout this narrative have been seen only in conflict. As the Erie Ring represents the combination of the corporation and the hired proletariat of a great city; as Vanderbilt embodies the autocratic power of Caesarism introduced into corporate life, and as neither alone can obtain complete control of the government of the state, it, perhaps, only remains for the coming man to carry the combination of elements one step in advance, and put Caesarism at once in control of the corporation and of the proletariat, to bring our vaunted institutions within the rule of all historic precedent.

It is not pleasant to take such views of the future; yet they are irresistibly suggested by the events which have been narrated. They seem to be in the nature of direct inferences. The only remedy lies in a renovated public opinion; but no indication of this has as yet been elicited. People did indeed, at one time, watch these Erie developments with interest, but the feeling excited was rather one of amazement than of indignation. Even where a real indignation was excited, it led to no sign of any persistent effort at reform; it betrayed itself only in aimless denunciation or in sad forebodings. The danger, however, is day by day increasing, and the period during which the work of regeneration should begin grows always shorter. It is true that evils ever work their own cure, but the cure for the evils of Roman civilization was worked out through ten centuries of barbarism. It remains to be seen whether this people retains that moral vigor which can alone awaken a sleeping public opinion to healthy and persistent activity, or whether to us also will apply these words of the latest and best historian of the Roman republic: "What Demosthenes said of his Athenians was justly applied to the Romans of this period; that people were very zealous for action so long as they stood round the platform and listened to proposals of reform; but, when they went home, no one thought further of what he had heard in the market-place. However those reformers might stir the fire, it was to no purpose, for the inflammable material was wanting."*

* Mommsen, IV, 91, referring to the early Ciceronian period, B.C. 75.

II

THE NEW YORK GOLD CONSPIRACY*

BY

HENRY ADAMS

THE Civil War in America, with its enormous issues of depreciating currency, and its reckless waste of money and credit by the Government, created a speculative mania such as the United States, with all its experience in this respect, had never before known. Not only in Broad Street, the center of New York speculation, but far and wide throughout the northern states, almost every man who had money at all employed a part of his capital in the purchase of stocks or of gold, of copper, of petroleum, or of domestic produce, in the hope of a rise in prices, or staked money on the expectation of a fall. To use the jargon of the street, every farmer and every shopkeeper in the country seemed to be engaged in "carrying" some favorite security "on a margin." Whoever could obtain five pounds sent it to a broker with orders to buy fifty pounds' worth of stocks, or whatever amount the broker would consent to purchase. If the stock rose, the speculator prospered; if it fell until the five pounds of deposit or margin were lost, the broker demanded a new deposit, or sold the stock to protect himself. By means of this simple and smooth machinery, which differs in no essential respect from the processes of *roulette* or *rouge-et-noir*, the whole nation flung itself into the Stock Exchange, until the "outsiders," as they were called, in opposition to the regular brokers of Broad Street, represented nothing less than the entire population of the American Republic. Everyone speculated, and for a time everyone speculated successfully.

* *Westminster Review*, XCIV (October, 1870), 411–436.

The inevitable reaction began when the Government, about a year after the close of the war, stopped its issues and ceased borrowing. The greenback currency had for a moment sunk to a value of only 37 cents to the dollar. It is even asserted that on the worst day of all, the eleventh of July, 1864, one sale of £20,000 in gold was actually made at 310, which is equivalent to about 33 cents in the dollar.* At this point, however, the depreciation stopped; and the paper which had come so near falling into entire discredit steadily rose in value, first to 50 cents, then to 60, to 70, and within the present year to more than 90 cents. As soon as the industrious part of the public felt the touch of this return to solid values, the whole fabric of fictitious wealth began to melt away under their eyes.

Thus it was not long before the so-called "outsiders," the men who speculated on their own account, and could not act in agreement or combination, began to suffer. One by one, or in great masses, they were made the prey of the larger operators; their last margins were consumed, and they dropped down to the solid level of slow, productive industry. Some lost everything; many lost still more than they had, and there are few families of ordinary connection and standing in the United States which cannot tell, if they choose, some dark story of embezzlement, or breach of trust, committed in these days. Some men, who had courage and a sense of honor, found life too heavy for them; others went mad. But the greater part turned in silence to their regular pursuits, and accepted their losses as they could. Almost every rich American could produce from some pigeonhole a bundle of worthless securities, and could show check books representing the only remaining trace of margin after margin consumed in vain attempts to satisfy the insatiable broker. A year or two of incessant losses swept the weaker gamblers from the street.

But even those who continued to speculate found it necessary

* See *Men and Mysteries of Wall Street*, by James K. Medbery, pp. 250, 251.

to change their mode of operations. Chance no longer ruled over the Stock Exchange and the gold market. The fate of a battle, the capture of a city, or the murder of a President, had hitherto been the influences which broke through the plans of the strongest combinations, and put all speculators, whether great or small, on fairly even ground; but as the period of sudden and uncontrollable disturbing elements passed away, the market fell more and more completely into the hands of cliques which found a point of adhesion in some great mass of incorporated capital. Three distinct railways, with all their enormous resources, became the property of Cornelius Vanderbilt, who, by means of their credit and capital, again and again swept millions of dollars into his pocket by a process curiously similar to gambling with loaded dice. But Vanderbilt was one of the most respectable of these great operators. The Erie Railway was controlled by Daniel Drew, and while Vanderbilt at least acted in the interests of his corporations, Drew cheated equally his corporation and the public. Between these two men and the immense incorporated power they swayed, smaller operators, one after another, were crushed to pieces, until the survivors learned to seek shelter within some clique sufficiently strong to afford protection. Speculation in this manner began to consume itself, and the largest combination of capital was destined to swallow every weaker combination which ventured to show itself in the market.

Thus, between the inevitable effect of a currency which steadily shrank the apparent wealth of the country, and the omnipotence of capital in the stock market, a sounder and healthier state of society began to make itself felt. Nor could the unfortunate public, which had been robbed with such cynical indifference by Drew and Vanderbilt, feel any sincere regret when they saw these two cormorants reduced to tearing each other. In the year 1867 Mr. Vanderbilt undertook to gain possession of the Erie road, as he had already obtained possession of the New York Central, the second trunk line between New York and the West. Mr. Vanderbilt was supposed to own property to the value of some £10,000,000, all of which might be made directly available for stock operations. He bought the greater part of the Erie stock; Drew sold him all he could take, and then issued as much more as was required in order to defeat Vanderbilt's purpose. After a violent struggle, which overthrew all the guaranties of social order, Drew triumphed, and Mr. Vanderbilt abandoned the contest. The Erie corporation paid him a large sum to reimburse his alleged losses. At the same time it was agreed that Mr. Drew's accounts should be passed, and he obtained a release in full, and retired from the direction. And the Erie road, almost exhausted by such systematic plundering, was left in the undisturbed, if not peaceful, control of Mr. Jay Gould and Mr. James Fisk, Jr., whose reign began in the month of July, 1868.

Mr. Jay Gould was a partner in the firm of Smith, Gould, & Martin, brokers, in Wall Street. He had been engaged before now in railway enterprises, and his operations had not been of a nature likely to encourage public confidence in his ideas of fiduciary relations. He was a broker, and a broker is almost by nature a gambler, perhaps the very last profession suitable for a railway manager. In character he was strongly marked by his disposition for silent intrigue. He preferred as a rule to operate on his own account, without admitting other persons into his confidence, and he seemed never to be satisfied except when deceiving everyone as to his intentions. There was a reminiscence of the spider in his nature. He spun huge webs, in corners and in the dark, which were seldom strong enough to resist a serious strain at the critical moment. His disposition to this subtlety and elaboration of intrigue was irresistible. It is scarcely necessary to say that he had not a conception of a moral principle. In speaking of this class of men it must be fairly assumed at the outset that they do not and cannot understand how there can be a distinction between right and wrong in matters of speculation, so long as the daily settlements are punctually effected. In this respect Mr. Gould was probably as honest as the mass of his fellows, according to the moral standard of the street; but without entering upon technical questions of roguery, it is enough to say that he was an uncommonly fine and unscrupulous intriguer, skilled in all the processes of stock gambling, and passably indifferent to the praise or censure of society.

James Fisk, Jr., was still more original in character. He was not yet forty years of age, and had the instincts of fourteen. He came originally from Vermont, probably the most respectable and correct state in the Union, and his father had been a peddler who sold goods from town to town in his native valley of the Connecticut. The son followed his father's calling with boldness and success. He drove his huge wagon, made resplendent with paint and varnish, with four or six horses, through the towns of Vermont and western Massachusetts; and when his father remonstrated in alarm at his reckless management, the young man, with his usual bravado, took his father into his service at a fixed salary, with the warning that he was not to put on airs on the strength of his new dignity. A large Boston firm which had supplied his goods on credit, attracted by his energy, took him into the house; the war broke out; his influence drew the firm into some bold speculations which were successful; in a few years he retired with some £20,000, which he subsequently lost. He formed a connection with Daniel Drew in New York, and a new sign, ominous of future trouble, was raised in Wall Street, bearing the names of Fisk & Belden, brokers.

Personally Mr. Fisk was coarse, noisy, boastful, ignorant; the type of a young butcher in appearance and mind. Nothing could be more striking than the contrast between him and his future associate Gould. One was small and slight in person, dark, sallow, reticent, and stealthy, with a trace of Jewish origin. The other was large, florid, gross, talkative, and obstreperous. Mr. Fisk's redeeming point was his humor, which had a strong flavor of American nationality. His mind was extraordinarily fertile in ideas and expedients, while his conversation was filled with unusual images and strange forms of speech, which were caught up and made popular by the New York press. In respect to honesty as between Gould and Fisk, the latter was, perhaps, if possible, less deserving of trust than the former. A story not without a keen stroke of satirical wit is told by him, which illustrates his estimate of abstract truth. An old woman who had bought of the elder Fisk a handkerchief which cost ninepence in the New England currency, where six shillings are reckoned to the dollar, complained to Mr. Fisk, Jr., that his father had cheated her. Mr. Fisk considered the case maturely, and gave a decision based on *a priori* principles. "No!" said he, "The old man wouldn't have told a lie for ninepence"; and then, as if this assertion needed some reasonable qualification, he added, "though he would have told eight of them for a dollar!" The distinction as regards the father may have been just, since the father seems to have held old-fashioned ideas as to wholesale and retail trade; but in regard to the son even this relative degree of truth cannot be predicated with any confidence, since, if the Investigating Committee of Congress and its evidence are to be believed, Mr. Fisk seldom or never speaks truth at all.

An intrigue equally successful and disreputable brought these two men into the Erie Board of Directors, whence they speedily drove their more timid predecessor Drew. In July, 1868, Gould made himself president and treasurer of the corporation. Fisk became comptroller. A young lawyer, named Lane, became counsel. These three directors made a majority of the Executive Committee, and were masters of Erie. The Board of Directors held no meetings. The Executive Committee was never called together, and the three men—Fisk, Gould, and Lane—became from this time the absolute, irresponsible owners of the Erie Railway, not less than if it had been their personal property and plaything.

This property was in effect, like all the great railway corporations, an empire within a republic. It consisted of a trunk line of road 459 miles in length, with branches 314 miles in extent, or 773 miles of road in all. Its capital stock amounted to about £7,000,000. Its gross receipts exceeded £3,000,000 per annum. It employed not less than fifteen thousand men, and supported their families. Over all this wealth and influence, greater than that directly swayed by any private citizen, greater than is absolutely and personally controlled by most kings, and far too great for the public safety either in a democracy or in any other form of society, the vicissitudes of a troubled time placed two men in irresponsible authority; and both these men belonged to a low and degraded moral and social type. Such an elevation has been rarely seen in modern history. Even the most dramatic of modern authors, even Balzac himself, who so loved to deal with similar violent alternations of fortune, or Alexandre Dumas, with all his extravagance of imagination, never have reached a conception bolder or more melodramatic than this, nor have they ever ventured to conceive a plot so enormous, or a catastrophe so original, as was now to be developed.

One of the earliest acts of the new rulers was precisely such as Balzac or Dumas might have predicted and delighted in. They established themselves in a palace. The old offices of the Erie Railway were in the lower part of the city, among the wharves and warehouses; a situation, no doubt, convenient for business, but by no means agreeable as a residence; and the new proprietors naturally wished to reside on their property. Mr. Fisk and Mr. Gould accordingly bought a huge building of white marble, not unlike a European palace, situated about two miles from the business quarter, and containing a large theater or opera house. They also purchased several smaller houses adjoining it. The opera house cost about £140,000, and a large part of the building was at once leased, by the two purchasers, to themselves as the Erie corporation, to serve as offices. This suite of apartments was then furnished by themselves, as representing the corporation, at an expense of some £60,000, and in a style which, though called vulgar, is certainly not more vulgar than that of the President's official residence, and which would be magnificent in almost any palace in Europe. The adjoining houses were connected with the main building; and in one of these Mr. Fisk had his private apartments, with a private passage to his opera box. He also assumed direction of the theater, of which he became manager in chief. To these royal arrangements he brought tastes which have been commonly charged as the worst results of royal license. The atmosphere of the Erie offices was not supposed to be disturbed with moral prejudices; and as the opera itself supplied Mr. Fisk's mind with amusement, so the opera troupe supplied him with a permanent harem. Whatever Mr. Fisk did was done on an extraordinary scale.

These arrangements, however, regarded only the pleasures of the American Aladdin. In the conduct of their interests the new directors showed a capacity for large conceptions, and a vigor in the execution of their schemes, such as alarmed the entire community. At the annual election in 1868, when Gould, Fisk, and Lane, having borrowed or bought proxies for the greater part of the stock, caused themselves to be elected for the ensuing year, the respectable portion of the public throughout the country was astonished and shocked to learn that the new Board of Directors contained two names peculiarly notorious and obnoxious to honest men,—the names of William M. Tweed and Peter B. Sweeny. To English ears these commonplace, not to say vulgar, titles do not seem singularly alarming; but to every honest American they conveyed a peculiar sense of terror and disgust. The state of New York in its politics is much influenced, if not controlled, by the city of New York. The city politics are so entirely in the hands of the Democratic party as to preclude even the existence of a strong minority. The party organization centers in a political club, held together by its patronage and the money it controls through a system of jobbery unequaled elsewhere in the world. And the Tammany Club, thus swaying the power of a small nation of several million souls, is itself ruled by William M. Tweed and Peter B. Sweeny, absolute masters of this terrible system of theft and fraud, and to American eyes the incarnation of political immorality.

The effect of this alliance was felt in the ensuing winter in the passage of a bill through the state legislature, and its signature by the Governor, abolishing the former system of annual elections of the entire board of Erie directors, and authorizing the board to classify itself in such a manner that only a portion should be changed each year. The principle of the bill was correct. Its practical effect, however, was to enable Gould and Fisk to make themselves directors for five years, in spite of any attempt on the part of the stockholders to remove them. The formality of annual reëlection was spared them; and so far as the stockholders were concerned, there was no great injustice in the act. The Erie road was in the peculiar position of being without an owner. There was no *cestui que trust,* unless the English stockholders could be called such. In America the stock was almost exclusively held for speculation, not for investment; and in the morals of Wall Street speculation means, or had almost come to mean, disregard of intrinsic value. In this case society at large was the injured party, and society knew its risk.

This step, however, was only a beginning. The Tammany Ring, as it is called, exercised a power far beyond politics. Under the existing constitution of the state, the judges of the state courts are elected by the people. There are thirty-three such judges in New York, and each of the thirty-three is clothed with equity powers running through the whole state. Of these judges Tammany Hall elected several, and the Erie Railway controlled others in country districts. Each of these judges might forbid proceedings before any and all the other judges, or stay proceedings in suits already commenced. Thus the lives and the property of the public were in the power of the new combination; and two of the city judges, Barnard and Cardozo, had already acquired a peculiarly infamous reputation as so-called "slaves to the ring," which left no question as to the depths to which their prostitution of justice would descend.

The alliance between Tammany and Erie was thus equivalent to investing Mr. Gould and Mr. Fisk with the highest attributes of sovereignty; but in order to avail themselves to the utmost of their judicial powers, they also required the ablest legal assistance. The degradation of the bench had been rapidly followed by the degradation of the bar. Prominent and learned lawyers were already accustomed to avail themselves of social or business relations with judges to forward private purposes. One whose partner might be elevated to the bench was certain to be generally retained in cases brought before this special judge; and litigants were taught by experience that a retainer in such cases was profitably bestowed. Others found a similar advantage resulting from known social relations with the court. The debasement of tone was not confined to the lower ranks of advocates; and it was probably this steady demoralization of the bar which made it possible for the Erie Ring to obtain the services of Mr. David Dudley Field as its legal adviser. Mr. Field, a gentleman of European reputation, in regard to which he is understood to be peculiarly solicitous, was an eminent law reformer, author of the New York Code, delegate of the American Social Science Association to the European International Congress, and asserted by his partner, Mr. Shearman, in evidence before a committee of the New York legislature, to be a man of quixotic sense of honor. Mr. Shearman himself, a gentleman of English parentage, had earned public gratitude by arraigning and deploring, with unsurpassed courage and point, the condition of the New York judiciary, in an admirable essay which will be found in the *North American Review* for July, 1867. The value of Mr. Field's services to Messrs. Fisk and Gould was not to be measured even by the enormous fees their generosity paid him. His power over certain judges became so absolute as to impress the popular imagination; and the gossip of Wall Street insists that he has a silken halter round the neck of Judge Barnard, and a hempen one round that of Cardozo. It is certain that he who had a year before threatened Barnard on his own bench with impeachment now appeared in the character of Barnard's master, and issued as a matter of course the edicts of his court.

One other combination was made by the Erie managers to extend their power, and this time it was credit that was threatened.

They bought a joint-stock bank in New York City, with a capital of £200,000. The assistance thus gained was purchased at a very moderate price, since it was by no means represented by the capital. The great cliques and so-called "operators" of Wall Street and Broad Street carry on their transactions by a system of credits and clearing houses with a very limited use of money. The banks certify their checks, and the certified checks settle all balances. Nominally and by law the banks only certify to the extent of *bona fide* deposits, but in reality the custom of disregarding the strict letter of the law is not unknown, and in regard to the bank in question, the Comptroller of the Currency, an officer of the National Treasury, testifies that on an examination of its affairs in April, 1869, out of fifteen checks deposited in its hands as security for certifications made by it, selected at hazard for inquiry, and representing a nominal value of £300,000, three only were good. The rest represented accommodation extended to brokers and speculators without security. As an actual fact it is in evidence that this same bank on Thursday, September 24, 1869, certified checks to the amount of nearly £1,500,000 for Mr. Gould alone. What sound security Mr. Gould deposited against this mass of credit may be left to the imagination. His operations, however, were not confined to this bank alone, although this was the only one owned by the ring.

Thus Mr. Gould and Mr. Fisk created a combination more powerful than any that has been controlled by mere private citizens in America or in Europe since society for self-protection established the supreme authority of the judicial name. They exercised the legislative and the judicial powers of the state; they possessed almost unlimited credit, and society was at their mercy. One authority alone stood above them, beyond their control; and this was the distant but threatening figure of the National Government.

Nevertheless, powerful as they were, the Erie managers were seldom in funds. The huge marble palace in which they lived, the theater which they supported, the reckless bribery and profu-

sion of management by which they could alone maintain their defiance of public opinion, the enormous schemes for extending
their operations into which they rushed with utter recklessness,
all required greater resources than could be furnished even by
the wholesale plunder of the Erie road. They were obliged from
time to time to issue from their castle and harry the industrious
public or their brother freebooters. The process was different
from that known to the dark ages, but the objects and the results
were equally robbery. At one time Mr. Fisk is said to have ordered heavy speculative sales of stock in an express company
which held a contract with the Erie Railway. The sales being effected, the contract was declared annulled. The stock naturally
fell, and Mr. Fisk realized the difference. He then ordered heavy
purchases, and having renewed the contract the stock rose again,
and Mr. Fisk a second time swept the street.* In the summer and
autumn of 1869 the two managers issued and sold 235,000 new
shares of Erie stock, or nearly as much as its entire capital when
they assumed power in July, 1868. With the aid of the money
thus obtained, they succeeded in withdrawing about £2,500,000
in currency from circulation at the very moment of the year
when currency was most in demand in order to harvest the crops.
For weeks the whole nation writhed and quivered under the tor-
ture of this modern rack, until the National Government itself
was obliged to interfere and threaten a sudden opening of the
treasury. But whether the Erie speculators operated for a rise or
operated for a fall, whether they bought or sold, and whether
they were engaged in manipulating stocks, or locking up currency,
or cornering gold, they were always a public nuisance and
scandal.

In order to explain the operation of a so-called corner in gold
to ordinary readers with the least possible use of slang or technical phrases, two preliminary statements are necessary. In the
first place it must be understood that the supply of gold immediately available for transfers is limited within distinct bounds in

* *Men and Mysteries of Wall Street,* p. 168.

America. New York and the country behind it contain an amount usually estimated at about £4,000,000. The National Government commonly holds from £15,000,000 to £20,000,000, which may be thrown bodily on the market if the President orders it. To obtain gold from Europe or other sources requires time.

In the second place, gold in America is a commodity bought and sold like stocks, in a special market or gold room which is situated next the Stock Exchange in Broad Street and is practically a part of it. In gold as in stocks, the transactions are both real and speculative. The real transactions are mostly purchases or loans made by importers who require coin to pay customs on their imports. This legitimate business is supposed to require from £1,000,000 to £1,500,000 per day. The speculative transactions are mere wagers on the rise or fall of price, and neither require any actual transfer of gold, nor even imply its existence, although in times of excitement hundreds of millions nominally are bought, sold, and loaned.

Under the late administration Mr. McCulloch, then Secretary of the Treasury, had thought it his duty at least to guarantee a stable currency, although Congress forbade him to restore the gold standard. During four years gold had fluctuated little, and principally from natural causes, and the danger of attempting to create an artificial scarcity in it had prevented the operators from trying an experiment which would have been sure to irritate the Government. The financial policy of the new administration was not so definitely fixed, and the success of a speculation would depend on the action of Mr. Boutwell, the new secretary, whose direction was understoood to have begun by a marked censure on the course pursued by his predecessor.

Of all financial operations, cornering gold is the most brilliant and the most dangerous, and possibly the very hazard and splendor of the attempt were the reasons of its fascination to Mr. Jay Gould's fancy. He dwelt upon it for months, and played with it like a pet toy. His fertile mind even went so far as to discover that it would prove a blessing to the community, and on this in-

genious theory, half honest and half fraudulent, he stretched
the widely extended fabric of the web in which all mankind was
to be caught. This theory was in itself partially sound. Starting
from the principle that the price of grain in New York is regulated by the price in London and is not affected by currency
fluctuations, Mr. Gould argued that if it were possible to raise
the premium on gold from thirty to forty cents at harvest time,
the farmers' grain would be worth $1.40 instead of $1.30, and as
a consequence the farmer would hasten to send all his crop to
New York for export, over the Erie Railway, which was sorely in
need of freight. With the assistance of another gentleman, Mr.
Gould calculated the exact premium at which the western farmer
would consent to dispose of his grain, and thus distance the three
hundred sail which were hastening from the Danube to supply
the English market. Gold, which was then heavy at 34, must be
raised to 45.

This clever idea, like all the other ideas of these gentlemen of
Erie, seems to have had the single fault of requiring that someone,
somewhere, should be swindled. The scheme was probably feasible; but sooner or later the reaction from such an artificial
stimulant must have come, and whenever it came someone must
suffer. Nevertheless, Mr. Gould probably argued that as long as
the farmer got his money, the Erie Railway its freights, and he
himself his small profits on the gold he bought, it was of little
consequence who else might be injured; and, indeed, by the time
the reaction came, and gold was ready to fall as he expected, Mr.
Gould would probably have been ready to assist the process by
speculative sales in order to enable the western farmer to buy
his spring goods cheap as he had sold his autumn crops dear.
He himself was equally ready to buy gold cheap and sell it dear
on his private account; and as he proposed to bleed New York
merchants for the benefit of the western farmer, so he was willing to bleed Broad Street for his own. The patriotic object was,
however, the one which for obvious reasons Mr. Gould preferred
to put forward most prominently, and on the strength of which
he hoped to rest his ambitious structure of intrigue.

In the operation of raising the price of gold from 133 to 145, there was no great difficulty to men who controlled the resources of the Erie Railway. Credit alone was needed, and of credit Mr. Gould had an unlimited supply. The only serious danger lay in the possible action of the National Government, which had not taken the same philanthropic view of the public good as was peculiar to the managers of Erie. Secretary Boutwell, who should have assisted Mr. Gould in "bulling" gold, was gravely suspected of being a bear, and of wishing to depress the premiums to nothing. If he were determined to stand in Mr. Gould's path, it was useless even for the combined forces of Erie and Tammany to jostle against him; and it was therefore essential that Mr. Gould should control the Government itself, whether by fair means or foul, by persuasion or by purchase. He undertook the task; and now that his proceedings in both directions have been thoroughly drawn into light, it is well worth while for the public to see how dramatic and how artistically admirable a conspiracy in real life may be, when slowly elaborated from the subtle mind of a clever intriguer, and carried into execution by a band of unshrinking scoundrels.

The first requisite for Mr. Gould's purpose was some channel of direct communication with the President; and here he was peculiarly favored by chance. Mr. Abel Rathbone Corbin, formerly lawyer, editor, speculator, lobby agent, familiar, as he claims, with everything, had succeeded, during his varied career, in accumulating from one or another of his hazardous pursuits a comfortable fortune, and he had crowned his success, at the age of sixty-seven or thereabouts, by contracting a marriage with General Grant's sister, precisely at the moment when General Grant was on the point of reaching the highest eminence possible to an American citizen. To say that Mr. Corbin's moral dignity had passed absolutely pure through the somewhat tainted atmosphere in which his life had been spent, would be flattering him too highly; but at least he was now no longer engaged in any active occupation, and he lived quietly in New York, watching the course of public affairs, and remarkable for an eminent respectability which became the President's brother-in-law. Mr. Gould enjoyed a slight acquaintance with Mr. Corbin, and he proceeded to improve it. He assumed, and he asserts that he really felt, a respect for Mr. Corbin's shrewdness and sagacity. It is amusing to observe that Mr. Corbin claims to have first impressed the famous crop theory on Mr. Gould's mind; while Mr. Gould testifies that he himself indoctrinated Mr. Corbin with this idea, which became a sort of monomania with the President's brother-in-law, who soon began to preach it to the President himself. On the fifteenth of June, 1869, the President came to New York, and was there the guest of Mr. Corbin, who urged Mr. Gould to call and pay his respects to the Chief Magistrate. Mr. Gould had probably aimed at precisely this result. He called; and the President of the United States not only listened to the president of Erie, but accepted an invitation to Mr. Fisk's theater, sat in Mr. Fisk's private box, and the next evening became the guest of these two gentlemen on their magnificent Newport steamer, while Mr. Fisk, arrayed, as the newspapers reported, "in a blue uniform, with a broad gilt cap band, three silver stars on his coat-sleeve, lavender gloves, and a diamond breast pin as large as a cherry, stood at the gangway, surrounded by his aids, bestarred and bestriped like himself," and welcomed his distinguished friend.

It had been already arranged that the President should on this occasion be sounded in regard to his financial policy; and when the selected guests—among whom were Mr. Gould, Mr. Fisk, and others—sat down at nine o'clock to supper, the conversation was directed to the subject of finance. "Someone," says Mr. Gould, "asked the President what his view was." The "someone" in question was, of course, Mr. Fisk, who alone had the impudence to put such an inquiry. The President bluntly replied, that there was a certain amount of fictitiousness about the prosperity of the country, and that the bubble might as well be tapped in one way as another. The remark was fatal to Mr. Gould's plans, and he felt it, in his own words, as a wet blanket.

Meanwhile the post of assistant treasurer at New York had become vacant, and it was a matter of interest to Mr. Gould that some person friendly to himself should occupy this position, which, in its relations to the public, is second in importance only to the secretaryship of the treasury itself. Mr. Gould consulted Mr. Corbin, and Mr. Corbin suggested the name of General Butterfield,—a former officer in the volunteer army. The appointment was not a wise one; nor does it appear in evidence by what means Mr. Corbin succeeded in bringing it about. There is a suggestion that he used Mr. A. T. Stewart, the wealthy importer, as his instrument for the purpose; but whatever the influence may have been, Mr. Corbin appears to have set it in action, and General Butterfield entered upon his duties toward the first of July.

The elaborate preparations thus made show that some large scheme was never absent from Mr. Gould's mind, although between the months of May and August he made no attempt to act upon the markets. But between the twentieth of August and the first of September, in company with Messrs. Woodward and Kimber, two large speculators, he made what is known as a pool, or combination, to raise the premium on gold, and some ten or fifteen millions were bought, but with very little effect on the price. The tendency of the market was downward, and it was not easily counteracted. Perhaps under ordinary circumstances he might have now abandoned his project; but an incident suddenly occurred which seems to have drawn him headlong into the boldest operations.

Whether the appointment of General Butterfield had any share in strengthening Mr. Gould's faith in Mr. Corbin's secret powers does not appear in evidence, though it may readily be assumed as probable. At all events, an event now took place which would have seemed to authorize an unlimited faith in Mr. Corbin, as well as to justify the implicit belief of an Erie treasurer in the corruptibility of all mankind. The unsuspicious President again passed through New York, and came to breakfast at Mr. Corbin's house on the second of September. He saw no one but Mr. Corbin while there, and the same evening at ten o'clock departed for Saratoga. Mr. Gould declares, however, that he was told by Mr. Corbin that the President, in discussing the financial situation, had shown himself a convert to the Erie theory about marketing the crops, and had "stopped in the middle of a conversation in which he had expressed his views, and written a letter" to Secretary Boutwell. This letter is not produced; but Secretary Boutwell testifies as follows in regard to it:—

I think on the evening of the fourth of September I received a letter from the President dated at New York, as I recollect it; I am not sure where it is dated. I have not seen the letter since the night I received it. I think it is now in my residence in Groton. In that letter he expressed an opinion that it was undesirable to force down the price of gold. He spoke of the importance to the West of being able to move their crops. His idea was that if gold should fall, the West would suffer, and the movement of the crops would be retarded. The impression made on my mind by the letter was that he had rather a strong opinion to that effect. . . . Upon the receipt of the President's letter on the evening of the fourth of September, I telegraphed to Judge Richardson [Assistant Secretary at Washington] this despatch: "Send no order to Butterfield as to sales of gold until you hear from me."

Mr. Gould had therefore succeeded in reversing the policy of the National Government; but this was not all. He knew what the Government would do before any officer of the Government knew it. Mr. Gould was at Corbin's house on the second of September; and although the evidence of both these gentlemen is very confused on this point, the inference is inevitable that Gould saw Corbin privately, unknown to the President, within an hour or two after this letter to Mr. Boutwell was written, and that it was at this interview, while the President was still in the house, that Mr. Corbin gave him the information about the letter; perhaps showed him the letter itself. Then followed a transaction worthy of the French stage. Mr. Corbin's evidence gives his own account of it:—

On the second of September (referring to memoranda) Mr. Gould

offered to let me have some of the gold he then possessed. . . . He
spoke to me as he had repeatedly done before, about taking a certain
amount of gold owned by him. I finally told Mr. Gould that for the sake
of a lady, my wife, I would accept of $500,000 of gold for her benefit,
as I shared his confidence that gold would rise. . . . He afterwards insisted that I should take a million more, and I did so on the same conditions for my wife. He then sent me this paper.

The paper in question is as follows:—

Smith, Gould, Martin, & Co., Bankers,
11 Broad Street, New York, September 2, 1869.

Mr. ——
    Dear Sir: we have bought for your account and risk—

500,000, gold, 132, R.
1,000,000, gold, 135⅝, R.

which we will carry on demand with the right to use.

SMITH, GOULD, MARTIN, & CO.

This memorandum meant that for every rise of 1 per cent
in the price of gold Mr. Corbin was to receive £3,000, and his
name nowhere to appear. If the inference is correct that Gould
had seen Corbin in the morning and had learned from him what
the President had written, it is clear that he must have made his
bargain on the spot, and then going directly to the city, he must
in one breath have ordered this memorandum to be made out and
large quantities of gold to be purchased, before the President
had allowed the letter to leave Mr. Corbin's house.

No time was lost. On this same afternoon, Mr. Gould's brokers
bought large amounts in gold. One testifies to buying $1,315,000
at 134⅛. On the third the premium was forced up to 36; on the
fourth, when Mr. Boutwell received his letter, it had risen to 37.
Here, however, Mr. Gould seems to have met a check, and he describes his own position in nervous Americanisms, as follows:—

I did not want to buy so much gold. In the spring I put gold up
from 32 to 38 and 40, with only about seven millions. But all these
fellows went in and sold short, so that in order to keep it up I had to
buy, or else to back down and show the white feather. They would sell

it to you all the time. I never intended to buy more than four or five millions of gold, but these fellows kept purchasing it on, and I made up my mind that I would put it up to 40 at one time. . . . We went into it as a commercial transaction, and did not intend to buy such an amount of gold. I was forced into it by the bears selling out. They were bound to put it down. I got into the contest. All these other fellows deserted me like rats from a ship. Kimber sold out and got short. . . . He sold out at 37. He got short of it, and went up (or, in English, he failed).

It was unfortunate that the bears would not consent to lie still and be flayed, but this was unquestionably the fact. They had the great operators for once at a disadvantage, and they were bent on revenge. Mr. Gould's position was very hazardous. When Mr. Kimber sold out at 37, which was probably on the seventh of September, the market broke; and on the eighth the price fell back to 35. Nor was this all. At the same moment, when the "pool" was ended by Mr. Kimber's desertion, Mr. Corbin, with his eminent shrewdness and respectability, told Mr. Gould "that gold had gone up to 37," and that he "should like to have this matter realized," which was equivalent to saying that he wished to be paid something on account. This was on the sixth; and Gould was obliged this same day to bring him a check for £5,000, drawn to the order of Jay Gould, and indorsed in blank by him with a touching regard for Mr. Corbin's modest desire not to have his name appear. There are few financiers in the world who will not agree that this transaction does great credit to Mr. Corbin's sagacity. It indicates at least that he was acquainted with the men he dealt with. Undoubtedly it placed Mr. Gould in a difficult position; but as Mr. Gould already held some fifteen millions of gold and needed Mr. Corbin's support, he preferred to pay £5,000 outright rather than allow Corbin to throw his gold on the market. Yet the fabric of Gould's web had now been so seriously injured that, for a whole week, from the eighth to the fifteenth of September, he was at a loss what to do, unable to advance and equally unable to retreat without very severe losses. He sat at his desk in the opera house, silent as usual, and tearing little slips of paper which he threw on the floor in his abstraction, while he revolved new combinations in his mind.

Down to this moment Mr. James Fisk, Jr., has not appeared in the affair. Gould had not taken him into his confidence; and it was not until after the tenth of September that Gould appears to have decided that there was nothing else to be done. Fisk was not a safe ally in so delicate an affair, but apparently there was no choice. Gould approached him; and, as usual, his touch was like magic. Mr. Fisk's evidence begins here, and may be believed when very strongly corroborated:

Gold having settled down to 35, and I not having cared to touch it, he was a little sensitive on the subject, feeling as if he would rather take his losses without saying anything about it. . . . One day he said to me, "Don't you think gold has got to the bottom?" I replied that I did not see the profit in buying gold unless you have got into a position where you can command the market. He then said he had bought quite a large amount of gold, and I judged from his conversation that he wanted me to go into the movement and help strengthen the market. Upon that I went into the market and bought. I should say that was about the fifteenth or sixteenth of September. I bought at that time about seven or eight millions, I think.

The market responded slowly to these enormous purchases; and on the sixteenth the clique was still struggling to recover its lost ground.

Meanwhile Mr. Gould had placed another million and a half of gold to the account of General Butterfield, and notified him of the purchase. So Mr. Gould swears in spite of General Butterfield's denial. The date of this purchase is not fixed. Through Mr. Corbin a notice was also sent by Gould about the middle of September to the President's private secretary, General Porter, informing him that half a million was placed to his credit. General Porter instantly wrote to repudiate the purchase, but it does not appear that Butterfield took any notice of Gould's transaction on his account. On the tenth of September the President had again come to New York, where he remained his brother-in-law's

guest till the thirteenth; and during this visit Mr. Gould appears
again to have seen him, although Mr. Corbin avers that on this
occasion the President intimated his wish to the servant that this
should be the last time Mr. Gould obtained admission. "Gould
was always trying to get something out of him," he said; and if
he had known how much Mr. Gould had succeeded in getting out
of him, he would have admired the man's genius, even while
shutting the door in his face. On the morning of the thirteenth
the President set out on a journey to the little town of Washington, situated among the mountains of western Pennsylvania,
where he was to remain a few days. Mr. Gould, who now consulted Mr. Corbin regularly every morning and evening, was
still extremely nervous in regard to the President's policy; and
as the crisis approached, this nervousness led him into the fatal
blunder of doing too much. The bribe offered to Porter was a
grave mistake, but a greater mistake yet was made by pressing
Mr. Corbin's influence too far. He induced Mr. Corbin to write
an official article for the New York press on the financial policy
of the Government, an article afterward inserted in the *New York
Times* through the kind offices of Mr. James McHenry, and he
also persuaded or encouraged Mr. Corbin to write a letter directly
to the President himself. This letter, written on the seventeenth
under the influence of Gould's anxiety, was instantly sent away
by a special messenger of Fisk's to reach the President before
he returned to the capital. The messenger carried also a letter of
introduction to General Porter, the private secretary, in order
to secure the personal delivery of this important dispatch.

We have now come to the week which was to witness the explosion of all this elaborately constructed mine. On Monday, the
twentieth, gold again rose. Throughout Tuesday and Wednesday
Fisk continued to purchase without limit, and forced the price
up to 40. At this time Gould's firm of Smith, Gould, & Martin,
through which the operation was conducted, had purchased some
$50,000,000; and yet the bears went on selling, although they
could only continue the contest by borrowing Gould's own gold.

Gould, on the other hand, could no longer sell and clear himself, for the very reason that the sale of $50,000,000 would have broken the market to nothing. The struggle had become intense. The whole country was looking on with astonishment at the battle between the bulls and the bears. All business was deranged, and all values unsettled. There were indications of a panic in the stock market; and the bears in their emergency were vehemently pressing the Government to intervene. Gould now wrote to Mr. Boutwell a letter so inconceivably impudent that it indicates desperation and entire loss of his ordinary coolness. He began:—

SIR,—There is a panic in Wall Street, engineered by a bear combination. They have withdrawn currency to such an extent that it is impossible to do ordinary business. The Erie Company requires eight hundred thousand dollars to disburse. . . . Much of it in Ohio, where an exciting political contest is going on, and where we have about ten thousand employed, and the trouble is charged on the administration. . . . Cannot you, consistently, increase your line of currency?

From a friend such a letter would have been an outrage; but from a member of the Tammany Ring, the principal object of detestation to the Government, such a threat or bribe—whichever it may be called—was incredible. Mr. Gould was, in fact, at his wits' end. He dreaded a panic, and he felt that it could no longer be avoided.

The scene now shifts for a moment to the distant town of Washington, among the hills of western Pennsylvania. On the morning of the nineteenth of September, President Grant and his private secretary, General Porter, were playing croquet on the grass, when Fisk's messenger, after twenty-four hours of travel by rail and carriage, arrived at the house, and sent in to ask for General Porter. When the President's game was ended, General Porter came, received his own letter from Corbin, and called the President, who entered the room and took his brother-in-law's dispatch. He then left the room, and after some ten or fifteen minutes' absence returned. The messenger, tired of waiting, then asked, "Is it all right?" "All right," replied the President; and the messenger hastened to the nearest telegraph station, and sent word to Fisk, "Delivered; all right."

The messenger was, however, altogether mistaken. Not only was all not right, but all was going hopelessly wrong. The President, it appears, had at the outset supposed the man to be an ordinary post-office agent, and the letter an ordinary letter which had arrived through the post office. Nor was it until Porter asked some curious question as to the man, that the President learned of his having been sent by Corbin merely to carry this apparently unimportant letter of advice. The President's suspicions were at once excited; and the same evening, at his request, Mrs. Grant wrote a hurried note to Mrs. Corbin, telling her how greatly the President was distressed at the rumor that Mr. Corbin was speculating in Wall Street, and how much he hoped that Mr. Corbin would "instantly disconnect himself with anything of that sort."

This letter, subsequently destroyed or said to have been destroyed by Mrs. Corbin, arrived in New York on the morning of Wednesday the twenty-second, the same day on which Gould and his enemies the bears were making their simultaneous appeals to Secretary Boutwell. Mrs. Corbin was greatly excited and distressed by her sister-in-law's language. She at once carried the letter to her husband, and insisted that he should instantly abandon his interest in the gold speculation. Mr. Corbin, although he considered the scruples of his wife and her family to be highly absurd, assented to her wish; and when Mr. Gould came that evening as usual, with $50,000,000 of gold on his hands, and extreme anxiety on his mind, Corbin read to him two letters: the first, written by Mrs. Grant to Mrs. Corbin; the second, written by Mr. Corbin to President Grant, assuring him that he had not a dollar of interest in gold. The assurance of this second letter was, at any sacrifice, to be made good.

Mr. Corbin proposed that Mr. Gould should give him a check for £20,000, and take his $1,500,000 off his hands. A proposition more calmly impudent than this can scarcely be imagined. Gould had already paid Corbin £5,000, and Corbin asked for £20,000 more, at the very moment when it was clear that the £5,000 he had received had been given him under a misunderstanding of his services. He even had the impudence to represent himself as doing Gould a favor by letting him have a million and a half more gold at the highest market price, at a time when Gould had fifty millions which it was clear he must sell or be ruined. What Gould might, under ordinary circumstances, have replied, may be imagined; but at this moment he could say nothing. Corbin had but to show this note to a single broker in Wall Street, and the whole fabric of Gould's speculation would have fallen to pieces. Gould asked for time and went away. He consulted no one. He gave Fisk no hint of what had happened. The next morning he returned to Corbin, and made him the following offer:—

"Mr. Corbin, I cannot give you anything if you will go out. If you will remain in, and take the chances of the market, I will give you my check [for £20,000]." "And then," says Mr. Corbin, "I did what I think it would have troubled almost any other business man to consent to do,—refuse one hundred thousand dollars on a rising market. If I had not been an old man married to a middle-aged woman, I should have done it (of course with her consent) just as sure as the offer was made. I said, 'Mr. Gould, my wife says "No!" Ulysses thinks it wrong, and that it ought to end.' So I gave it up. . . . He looked at me with an air of severe distrust, as if he was afraid of treachery in the camp. He remarked, 'Mr. Corbin, I am undone if that letter gets out.' . . . He stood there for a little while looking very thoughtful, exceedingly thoughtful. He then left and went into Wall Street, . . . and my impression is that he it was, and not the Government, that broke that market."

Mr. Corbin was right; throughout all these transactions his insight into Mr. Gould's character was marvelous.

It was the morning of Thursday, the third; Gould and Fisk went to Broad Street together, but as usual Gould was silent and secret, while Fisk was noisy and communicative. There was now a complete separation in their movements. Gould acted entirely through his own firm of Smith, Gould, & Martin, while Fisk operated principally through his old partner, Belden. One of Smith's principal brokers testifies:—

"Fisk never could do business with Smith, Gould, & Martin very comfortably. They would not do business for him. It was a very uncertain thing of course where Fisk might be. He is an erratic sort of genius. I don't think anybody would want to follow him very long. I am satisfied that Smith, Gould, & Martin controlled their own gold, and were ready to do as they pleased with it without consulting Fisk. I do not think there was any general agreement. . . . None of us who knew him cared to do business with him. I would not have taken an order from him nor had anything to do with him." Belden was considered a very low fellow. "I never had anything to do with him or his party," said one broker employed by Gould. "They were men I had a perfect detestation of; they were no company for me. I should not have spoken to them at all under any ordinary circumstances." Another says, "Belden is a man in whom I never had any confidence in any way. For months before that, I would not have taken him for a gold transaction."

And yet Belden bought millions upon millions of gold. He himself says he had bought twenty millions by this Thursday evening, and this without capital or credit except that of his brokers. Meanwhile Gould, on reaching the city, had at once given secret orders to sell. From the moment he left Corbin, he had but one idea, which was to get rid of his gold as quietly as possible. "I purchased merely enough to make believe I was a bull," says Gould. This double process continued all that afternoon. Fisk's wild purchases carried the price up to 144, and the panic in the street became more and more serious as the bears realized the extremity of their danger. No one can tell how much gold which did not exist they had contracted to deliver or pay the difference in price. One of the clique brokers swears that on this Thursday evening the street had sold the clique one hundred and eighteen millions of gold, and every rise of one per cent on this sum implied a loss of more than £200,000 to the bears. Naturally the terror was extreme, for half Broad Street and thousands of speculators would have been ruined if compelled to settle gold at 150 which they had sold at 140. It need scarcely be said that by this time nothing more was heard in regard to philanthropic theories of benefit to the western farmer.

Mr. Gould's feelings can easily be imagined. He knew that Fisk's reckless management would bring the Government upon his shoulders, and he knew that unless he could sell his gold before the order came from Washington he would be a ruined man. He knew, too, that Fisk's contracts must inevitably be repudiated. This Thursday evening he sat at his desk in the Erie offices at the opera house, while Fisk and Fisk's brokers chattered about him.

I was transacting my railway business. I had my own views about the market, and my own fish to fry. I was all alone, so to speak, in what I did, and I did not let any of those people know exactly how I stood. I got no ideas from anything that was said there. I had been selling gold from 35 up all the time, and I did not know till the next morning that there would probably come an order about twelve o'clock to sell gold.

He had not told Fisk a word in regard to Corbin's retreat, nor his own orders to sell.

When the next day came, Gould and Fisk went together to Broad Street, and took possession of the private back office of a principal broker, "without asking the privilege of doing so," as the broker observes in his evidence. The first news brought to Gould was a disaster. The Government had sent three men from Washington to examine the bank which Gould owned, and the bank sent word to Mr. Gould that it feared to certify for him as usual, and was itself in danger of a panic, caused by the presence of officers, which created distrust of the bank. It barely managed to save itself. Gould took the information silently, and his firm redoubled sales of gold. His partner, Smith, gave the orders to one broker after another,—"Sell ten millions!" "The order was given as quick as a flash, and away he went," says one of these men. "I sold only eight millions." "Sell, sell, sell! do nothing but sell!—only don't sell to Fisk's brokers," were the orders which Smith himself acknowledges. In the gold room Fisk's brokers were shouting their rising bids, and the packed crowd grew frantic with terror and rage as each successive rise showed their increasing losses. The wide streets outside were thronged with excited people; the telegraph offices were overwhelmed with messages ordering sales or purchases of gold or stocks; and the whole nation was watching eagerly to see what the result of this convulsion was to be. All trade was stopped, and even the President felt that it was time to raise his hand. No one who has not seen the New York gold room can understand the spectacle it presented; now a perfect pandemonium, now silent as the grave. Fisk, in his dark back office across the street, with his coat off, swaggered up and down, "a big cane in his hand," and called himself the Napoleon of Wall Street. He really believed that he directed the movement, and while the street outside imagined that he and Gould were one family, and that his purchases were made for the clique, Gould was silently flinging away his gold at any price he could get for it.

Whether Fisk really expected to carry out his contract, and force the bears to settle, or not, is doubtful; but the evidence seems to show that he was in earnest, and felt sure of success. His orders were unlimited. "Put it up to 150," was one which he sent to the gold room. Gold rose to 150. At length the bid was made—"160 for any part of five millions," and no one any longer dared take it. "161 for five millions,"—"162 for five millions." No answer was made, and the offer was repeated,— "162 for any part of five millions." A voice replied, "Sold one million at 62." The bubble suddenly burst, and within fifteen minutes, amid an excitement without parallel even in the wildest excitements of the war, the clique brokers were literally swept away, and left struggling by themselves, bidding still 160 for gold in millions which no one would any longer take their word for; while the premium sank rapidly to 135. A moment later the telegraph brought from Washington the Government order to sell, and the result was no longer possible to dispute. Mr. Fisk had gone too far, while Mr. Gould had secretly weakened the ground under his feet.

Gould, however, was saved. His fifty millions were sold; and although no one yet knows what his gains or losses may have been, his firm was now able to meet its contracts and protect its brokers. Fisk was in a very different situation. So soon as it became evident that his brokers would be unable to carry out their contracts, everyone who had sold gold to them turned in wrath to Fisk's office. Fortunately for him it was protected by armed men whom he had brought with him from his castle of Erie; but nevertheless the excitement was so great that both Mr. Fisk and Mr. Gould thought it best to retire as rapidly as possible by a back entrance leading into another street, and to seek the protection of the opera house. There nothing but an army could disturb them; no civil mandate was likely to be served without their permission within these walls, and few men would care to face Fisk's ruffians in order to force an entrance.

The subsequent winding up of this famous conspiracy may be stated in few words. But no account could possibly be complete which failed to reproduce in full the story of Mr. Fisk's last interview with Mr. Corbin, as told by Fisk himself.

I went down to the neighborhood of Wall Street, Friday morning, and the history of that morning you know. When I got back to our office, you can imagine I was in no enviable state of mind, and the moment I got up street that afternoon I started right round to old Corbin's to rake him out. I went into the room, and sent word that Mr. Fisk wanted to see him in the dining-room. I was too mad to say anything civil, and when he came into the room, said I, "You damned old scoundrel, do you know what you have done here, you and your people?" He began to wring his hands, and, "Oh!" he says, "this is a horrible position. Are you ruined?" I said I didn't know whether I was or not; and I asked him again if he knew what had happened? He had been crying, and said he had just heard; that he had been sure everything was all right; but that something had occurred entirely different from what he had anticipated. Said I, "That don't amount to anything; we know that gold ought not to be at 31, and that it would not be but for such performances as you have had this last week; you know damned well it would not if you had not failed." I knew that somebody had run a saw right into us, and said I, "This

whole damned thing has turned out just as I told you it would." I
considered the whole party a pack of cowards, and I expected that
when we came to clear our hands they would sock it right into us. I
said to him, "I don't know whether you have lied or not, and I don't
know what ought to be done with you." He was on the other side of
the table, weeping and wailing, and I was gnashing my teeth. "Now,"
he says, "you must quiet yourself." I told him I didn't want to be quiet.
I had no desire to ever be quiet again, and probably never should be
quiet again. He says, "But, my dear sir, you will lose your reason."
Says I, "Speyers [a broker employed by him that day] has already lost
his reason; reason has gone out of everybody but me." I continued,
"Now what are you going to do? You have got us into this thing, and
what are you going to do to get out of it?" He says, "I don't know.
I will go and get my wife." I said, "Get her down here!" The soft talk
was all over. He went up stairs and they returned, tottling into the
room, looking older than Stephen Hopkins. His wife and he both looked
like death. He was tottling just like that. [Illustrated by a trembling
movement of his body.] I have never seen him from that day to this.

This is sworn evidence before a committee of Congress; and its
humor is perhaps the more conspicuous, because there is every
reason to believe that there is not a word of truth in the story
from beginning to end. No such interview ever occurred, except
in the unconfined apartments of Mr. Fisk's imagination. His
own previous statements make it certain that he was not at Corbin's house at all that day, and that Corbin did come to the Erie
offices that evening, and again the next morning. Corbin himself
denies the truth of the account without limitation; and adds, that
when he entered the Erie offices the next morning Fisk was
there. "I asked him how Mr. Gould felt after the great calamity
of the day before. He remarked, 'Oh, he has no courage at all.
He has sunk right down. There is nothing left of him but a heap
of clothes and a pair of eyes.'" The internal evidence of truth in
this anecdote would support Mr. Corbin against the world.*

* Mr. Fisk to the Editor of the *Sun:*—

Erie Railway Company, Comptroller's Office,
NEW YORK, October 4, 1869.

TO THE EDITOR OF THE *Sun.*

   Dear Sir,— . . . Mr. Corbin has constantly associated with me; . . . *he*

In regard to Mr. Gould, Fisk's graphic description was probably again inaccurate. Undoubtedly the noise and scandal of the moment were extremely unpleasant to this silent and impenetrable intriguer. The city was in a ferment, and the whole country pointing at him with wrath. The machinery of the gold exchange had broken down, and he alone could extricate the business community from the pressing danger of a general panic. He had saved himself, it is true; but in a manner which could not have been to his taste. Yet his course from this point must have been almost self-evident to his mind, and there is no reason to suppose that he hesitated.

His own contracts were all fulfilled. Fisk's contracts, all except one, in respect to which the broker was able to compel a settlement, were repudiated. Gould probably suggested to Fisk that it was better to let Belden fail, and to settle a handsome fortune on him, than to sacrifice something more than £1,000,000 in sustaining him. Fisk therefore threw Belden over, and swore

spent more than an hour with me in the Erie Railway office on the afternoon of Saturday, September 25th, the day after the gold panic. . . . . I enclose you a few affidavits which will give you further information concerning this matter.

I remain your obedient servant,

JAMES FISK, JR.

Affidavit of Charles W. Pollard.

"State of New York, City and County of New York, ss.

"C. W. Pollard, being duly sworn, says: 'I have frequently been the bearer of messages between Mr. James Fisk, Jr., and Mr. Abel R. Corbin, brother-in-law of President Grant. . . . Mr. Corbin called on me at the Erie building on Thursday, 23d September, 1869, telling me he came to see how Messrs. Fisk and Gould were getting along. . . . He called again on Friday, the following day, at about noon; appeared to be greatly excited and said he feared *we* should lose a great deal of money. The following morning, Saturday, September 25, Mr. Fisk told me to take his carriage and call upon Mr. Corbin and say to him that he and Mr. Gould would like to see him (Corbin) at their office. I called and saw Mr. Corbin. He remarked upon greeting me: "How does Mr. Fisk bear his losses?" and added, "*It is terrible for us.*" He then asked me to bring Mr. Fisk up to his house immediately, as he was indisposed, and did not feel able to go down to his

that he had acted only under Belden's order; in support of which statement he produced a paper to the following effect:—

September 24.

DEAR SIR,—I hereby authorize you to order the purchase and sale of gold on my account during this day to the extent you may deem advisable, and to report the same to me as early as possible. It is to be understood that the profits of such order are to belong entirely to me, and I will, of course, bear any losses resulting.

Yours,

WILLIAM BELDEN.

JAMES FISK, JR.

This document was not produced in the original, and certainly never existed. Belden himself could not be induced to acknowledge the order; and no one would have believed him if he had done so. Meanwhile the matter is before the national courts, and Fisk may probably be held to his contracts: but it will be far more difficult to execute judgment upon him, or to discover his assets.

One of the first acts of the Erie gentlemen after the crisis was to summon their lawyers, and set in action their judicial powers. The object was to prevent the panic-stricken brokers from using legal process to force settlements, and so render the entanglement inextricable. Messrs. Field and Shearman came, and instantly prepared a considerable number of injunctions, which were sent to their judges, signed at once, and immediately served. Gould then was able to dictate the terms of settlement; and after a week of complete paralysis, Broad Street began at last to show signs of returning life. As a legal curiosity, one of these docu-

(Fisk's) office. I went after Mr. Fisk, who returned immediately with me to Mr. Corbin's residence, but shortly after came out with Mr. Corbin, who accompanied him to Mr. Fisk's office, where he was closeted with him and Mr. Gould for about two hours. . . .' ''

There are obvious inconsistencies among these different accounts, which it is useless to attempt to explain. The fact of Saturday's interview appears, however, to be beyond dispute.

ments, issued three months after the crisis, may be reproduced, in order to show the powers wielded by the Erie managers :—

SUPREME COURT.

H. N. SMITH, JAY GOULD, H. H. MARTIN,
and J. B. BACH, Plaintiffs,
against
JOHN BONNER and ARTHUR L. SEWELL,
Defendants,

| Injunction by order.

It appearing satisfactorily to me by the complaint duly verified by the plaintiffs that sufficient grounds for an order of injunction exist, I do hereby order and enjoin . . . That the defendants, John Bonner and Arthur L. Sewell, their agents, attorneys, and servants, refrain from pressing their pretended claims against the plaintiffs, or either of them, before the Arbitration Committee of the New York Stock Exchange, or from taking any proceedings thereon, or in relation thereto, except in this action.

GEORGE G. BARNARD, J. S. C.

NEW YORK, December 29, 1869

Mr. Bonner had practically been robbed with violence by Mr. Gould, and instead of his being able to bring the robber into court as the criminal, the robber brought him into court as criminal, and the judge forbade him to appear in any other character. Of all Mr. Field's distinguished legal reforms and philanthropic projects, this injunction is beyond a doubt the most brilliant and the most successful.*

* These remarks on Mr. Field's professional conduct as counsel of the Erie Railway have excited a somewhat intemperate controversy, and Mr. Field's partisans in the press have made against the authors of the *Chapters of Erie* a charge which certainly has the merit of even exaggerated modesty on the part of the New York bench and bar, namely, that these writers "have indelicately interfered in a matter alien to them in every way"; the administration of justice in New York being, in this point of view, a matter in which Mr. Field and the Erie Railway are alone concerned. Mr. Field himself has published a letter in the *Westminster Review* for April, 1871, in which, after the general assertion that the passages in the "New York Gold Conspiracy" which relate to him "cover about as much untruth as could be crowded into so many lines," he proceeds to make the following corrections:
First, he denies, what was never suggested, that he was in any way a party

The fate of the conspirators was not severe. Mr. Corbin went to Washington, where he was snubbed by the President and at once disappeared from public view, only coming to light again before the Congressional Committee. General Butterfield, whose share in the transaction is least understood, was permitted to resign his office without an investigation. Speculation for the next six months was at an end. Every person involved in the affair seemed to have lost money, and dozens of brokers were swept from the street. But Mr. Jay Gould and Mr. James Fisk, Jr., continued to reign over Erie, and no one can say that their power or their credit was sensibly diminished by a shock which for the time prostrated all the interests of the country.

Nevertheless it is safe to predict that sooner or later the last

to the origin or progress of the Gold Conspiracy; until (secondly) he was consulted on the twenty-eighth of September; when (thirdly) he gave an opinion as to the powers of the members of the Gold and Stock Exchanges. Fourthly, he denies that he has relations of any sort with any judge in New York, or any power over these judges, other than such as English counsel have in respect to English judges. Fifthly, he asserts that out of twenty-eight injunctions growing out of the gold transaction, his partners obtained only ten, and only one of these ten, the one quoted above, from Justice Barnard. Sixthly, that this injunction was proper to be sought and granted. Seventhly, that Mr. Bonner was not himself the person who had been "robbed with violence," but the assignee of the parties.

On the other hand it does not appear that Mr. Field denies that the injunction as quoted is genuine, or that he is responsible for it, or that it did, as asserted, shut the defendants out of the courts as well as out of the Gold Exchange Arbitration Committee, or that it compelled them to appear only as defendants in a case where they were the injured parties.

In regard to the power which Mr. Field, whether as a private individual or as Erie counsel, has exercised over the New York bench, his modest denial is hardly calculated to serve as a final answer. And in regard to Mr. Bonner, the fact of his being principal or representative scarcely affects the character of Mr. Field's injunction. Finally, so far as the text is concerned, after allowing full weight to all Mr. Field's corrections, the public can decide for itself how many untruths it contains. The subject has, however, ceased to be one of consequence even to Mr. Field since the subsequent violent controversy which arose in March, 1871, in regard to other points of Mr. Field's professional conduct, and in another month after his letter was written he would perhaps have thought the comments of the *Westminster Review* so comparatively trifling in importance as not to deserve his attention.

traces of the disturbing influence of war and paper money will disappear in America, as they have sooner or later disappeared in every other country which has passed through the same evils. The result of this convulsion itself has been in the main good. It indicates the approaching end of a troubled time. Messrs. Gould and Fisk will at last be obliged to yield to the force of moral and economical laws. The Erie Railway will be rescued, and its history will perhaps rival that of the great speculative manias of the last century. The United States will restore a sound basis to its currency, and will learn to deal with the political reforms it requires. Yet though the regular process of development may be depended upon, in its ordinary and established course, to purge American society of the worst agents of an exceptionally corrupt time, there is in the history of this Erie corporation one matter in regard to which modern society everywhere is directly interested. For the first time since the creation of these enormous corporate bodies, one of them has shown its power for mischief, and has proved itself able to override and trample on law, custom, decency, and every restraint known to society, without scruple, and as yet without check. The belief is common in America that the day is at hand when corporations far greater than the Erie—swaying power such as has never in the world's history been trusted in the hands of mere private citizens, controlled by single men like Vanderbilt, or by combinations of men like Fisk, Gould, and Lane, after having created a system of quiet but irresistible corruption—will ultimately succeed in directing government itself. Under the American form of society, there is now no authority capable of effective resistance. The National Government, in order to deal with the corporations, must assume powers refused to it by its fundamental law, and even then is always exposed to the chance of forming an absolute central government which sooner or later is likely to fall into the very hands it is struggling to escape, and thus destroy the limits of its power only in order to make corruption omnipotent. Nor is this danger confined to America alone. The corporation is in its nature a threat against the popular institutions which are spreading so rapidly over the whole world. Wherever there is a popular and limited government this difficulty will be found in its path, and unless some satisfactory solution of the problem can be reached, popular institutions may yet find their very existence endangered.

III

AN ERIE RAID*

BY

CHARLES FRANCIS ADAMS, JR.

HISTORY scarcely affords a parallel to the rapid development of character which took place in America during the five years of the late Civil War. At its close the ordinary results of long internal strife were conspicuous only by their absence. No chronic guerrilla warfare was sustained in the South, and in the North no unusual license or increase of crime revealed the presence of a million of men unaccustomed to habits of industry and inured to a life of arms. Yet while these superficial indications of change would be sought in vain, other and far more suggestive phases of development cannot but force themselves on the attention of any thoughtful observer. The most noticeable of these is perhaps to be found in a greatly enlarged grasp of enterprise and increased facility of combination. The great operations of war, the handling of large masses of men, the influence of discipline, the lavish expenditure of unprecedented sums of money, the immense financial operations, the possibilities of effective cooperation, were lessons not likely to be lost on men quick to receive and to apply all new ideas. Those keen observers who looked for strange and unexpected phenomena when the struggle in the field was over have indeed witnessed that which must have surpassed all anticipation.

If the five years that succeeded the war have been marked by no exceptional criminal activity, they have witnessed some of the most remarkable examples of organized lawlessness, under the

* *North American Review*, CXII (April, 1871), 241–291.

JAY GOULD

forms of law, which mankind has yet had an opportunity to study. If individuals have, as a rule, quietly pursued their peaceful vocations, the same cannot be said of certain single men at the head of vast combinations of private wealth. This has been peculiarly the case as regards those controlling the rapidly developed railroad interests. These modern potentates have declared war, negotiated peace, reduced courts, legislatures, and sovereign states to an unqualified obedience to their will, disturbed trade, agitated the currency, imposed taxes, and, boldly setting both law and public opinion at defiance, have freely exercised many other attributes of sovereignty. Neither have the means at disposal proved at all inadequate to the ends in view. Single men have controlled hundreds of miles of railway, thousands of men, tens of millions of revenue, and hundred of millions of capital. The strength implied in all this they wielded in practical independence of the control both of governments and of individuals; much as petty German despots might have governed their little principalities a century or two ago. Thus by degrees almost the whole of the system of internal communication through the northern half of the United States has practically been partitioned out among a few individuals, and, as proximity, or competition on certain debatable grounds,—the Belgiums of the system, —brought the interests represented by these men into conflict, a series of struggles have ensued replete with dramatic episodes. No history of the present time will be complete in which these do not occupy much space, and any condensed record of them has, therefore, much more than a passing value. Not history in itself, it contains the material of history; yet the thread of these episodes is so difficult to trace, lying concealed in such dull volumes of evidence and records of the law, or preserved only in the knowledge of individuals, that unless it be found at once it is in danger of being lost forever. The speedy oblivion which covers up events that, for a time, fasten public attention and seem big with great results, is indeed one of the noticeable indications of the times. The practical experience of this fact has tended greatly to encourage all sorts of violations both of law and of morals. There seems no longer to be any Nemesis to dog the evildoer. Men are today in all mouths infamous from active participation in some great scandal or fraud,—some stock operation or gambler's conspiracy, some gold combination or Erie Railway war, some Credit Mobilier's contractor's job or Hartford & Erie scandal,—and tomorrow a new outrage, in another quarter, works a sudden condonation of each offense.

Nothing could more fully illustrate the rapidity with which such episodes as those referred to are forgotten than the complete oblivion into which the struggle in 1869 for the possession of the Albany & Susquehanna Railroad has fallen. This contest, marked by legal scandals almost unparalleled, and actually resulting in an attempt at armed warfare between corporations, though not yet finally passed upon by the courts,* is fairly forgotten by the world. It was, however, not without elements of a permanent interest, though no consecutive account of it has yet been attempted. The following narrative, drawn almost exclusively from the sworn evidence and official records in the case, probably presents the story with as near an approach to accuracy as is now likely ever to be arrived at.

The business of transportation by rail naturally divides itself into the two great elements of through and local traffic. The Erie Railway was especially constructed with a view to through traffic, and the New York Central, though originally consisting in a chain of disconnected local roads, through the force of circumstances and by a natural process of development, early became one of the great trunk lines of the continent. The Albany & Susquehanna, on the contrary, was designed by its projectors as a purely local road. As such its history could never have been a very interesting one, except to its projectors and owners. It happened, however, to occupy a bit of debatable territory between the two great trunk lines just mentioned, and hence de-

* See note, *post*, p. 212.

rived its importance. New England has always been in railroad
history a sort of an appanage of the Central Railroad of New
York. Both freight and passengers passing to and fro between
Boston and the West naturally took Albany on their way, and
the Central Road, monopolizing as it did the one natural gap
in the mountain ranges which divided the interior basin from
the sea, looked upon this traffic as its inalienable property. The
Albany & Susquehanna Railroad started from this eastern terminus of the Central, and was intended to open it to the Erie at
the city of Binghamton, some one hundred and forty miles from
the point of departure. In the early days of the enterprise
through traffic was less regarded by railroad managers than it
now is, and the future significance of this link in their system
was hardly realized by either of the great trunk lines. The carriage of freight was then but little understood, and grades were
of far greater importance than they now are. Valley roads, it
was supposed, might safely ignore the mountain track. This
the Albany & Susquehanna certainly was. The region through
which it passes is very broken, though it ranks among the finest
of the agricultural districts of New York. Starting from that
point where the great Alleghany Range gradually sinks away
into the valley of the Mohawk, the road skirts the base of the
heights of Helderberg, an outlying spur of the Catskills, famous
once as the seat of the anti-rent troubles, and then, passing among
the large rolling hills of southeastern New York, it gradually
climbs the watershed. The route was a difficult one, and the road
was costly of construction; laid out on the broad-gauge principle,
as a contemplated feeder of the Erie, it was forced to scale ridge
after ridge in working its way from one picturesque valley to
another, through which to find a natural roadway to its destination. The country along the line is of a hilly rather than a mountainous character, partaking more of the appearance of Vermont
than of New Hampshire; timbered lands and cultivated fields
alternate over the loftiest summits, and there is something peculiarly attractive in the primitive nestling appearance of the

towns and villages. The road thus was projected through a difficult and sequestered region, neither wealthy nor of varied industries, opening to a new trade neither great markets nor a peculiarly active people. It encountered, therefore, even more than the average amount of those financial tribulations which mark the early history of all railroads.

The company was organized in 1852, and the work of construction was begun in 1853, with $1,000,000 raised by individual subscription along the line of the road; further sums in aid of construction were subsequently received from the towns likely to be benefited by the line, which, by an act of special legislation, were authorized to subscribe to its stock; a loan of $1,000,000 was likewise obtained from the city of Albany, upon a pledge of the first-mortgage bonds of the company. The process of construction was, however, very slow. The work begun in 1853 was suspended in 1854 on account of the failure of the contractors; it was recommenced in 1857, and then slowly dragged along to completion, a very contractors' Golgotha. Eight times did acts extending to it the financial aid of the state pass the legislature; but they were encountered by six executive vetoes, and from this source the company realized but $750,000. That the scheme was successfully carried out at all was mainly due to the good pluck and untiring industry of one man, Joseph H. Ramsey,—at once the originator, president, financial agent, legal adviser, and guiding spirit of the enterprise.

The close of the seventeenth year of corporate life found all the available means of the company exhausted, and everyone connected with it, except Mr. Ramsey, thoroughly discouraged and despondent, with the twenty-two last and most difficult miles of the work yet unfinished. In this emergency the company once more looked to the state for assistance. Through the management of Mr. Ramsey, who had himself in former times more than once assumed the duties of a state legislator in behalf of the enterprise, the necessary act was passed. Most unexpectedly it encountered a veto, the sixth of the series. With an empty treasury

with heavy payments to contractors and on account of interest
already due, and with other similar payments rapidly maturing,
—with bankruptcy staring him in the face, and with all sources
of supply apparently exhausted,—under all these disheartening
aspects of the case Mr. Ramsey did not despair. The company
had in its safe two classes of securities and two only on which the
further necessary loans could possibly be effected. It had a portion of its own second-mortgage bonds and some nine thousand
shares of its capital stock, on which various instalments ranging
from 10 to 40 per cent had been paid by the original subscribers. This stock and the subscriptions upon it had subsequently been declared forfeited by a vote of the Board of Directors, with the consent of the holders, for the non-payment of
the balance of subscriptions. A law of New York prescribed that
no railroad should issue its stock for less than its par value. This
law, however, the courts had held did not apply to forfeited
stock in the treasury of the company. The difficulty in the case
was not in putting the stock on the market, but in finding a
purchaser for it when it got there; it had no market price; as an
investment it ranked far from high, and, unlike the Erie, it had
at this time no value for "speculative purposes." Under these
circumstances it seemed possible to the directors to make this
one of their two securities available only as a make-weight,—a
douceur, it might be said, to the other. Two loans were effected
accordingly, under a resolution which received the unanimous
approval of the Board of Directors on the third of June, 1868.
The first was with Azro Chase, who became the purchaser of
$50,000 of the second-mortgage bonds at 70 per cent of their
par value, with the additional right or option of taking at any
time three hundred shares of the forfeited stock at $20 per
share. This loan was negotiated through one of the directors of
the company named Leonard, acting as its financial agent, and
amounted to the sale of $80,000, in the nominal securities of the
company, for the sum of $41,000 in cash. Two hundred shares of
the stock, as it afterward appeared, passed into the pockets of

the director and financial agent as a species of brokerage commission. The second loan was negotiated by Mr. Ramsey himself
with Mr. David Groesbeck, the head of a well-known brokers'
firm in the city of New York, and formerly the business associate
of Mr. Daniel Drew. This loan was upon terms somewhat more
favorable to the company than the other, and there were no indications of brokerage in the case. The company received $560,-
000, and pledged as collateral its second-mortgage bonds at 70
per cent, with the privilege of purchasing them at any time
within eighteen months at 80, and a similar privilege as regarded
twenty-four hundred shares of the forfeited stock at $25 per
share. In other words, if the lenders availed themselves of the
option, as they subsequently did, securities to the nominal value
of $1,040,000 were sold to them for $700,000 in cash. This must
certainly be considered as a very advantageous bargain for the
company; 30 per cent is a large profit, but it here represented a
very unusual risk. Both of these loans received the unanimous
sanction of the Board of Directors, and that to Groesbeck played
a most important part in the subsequent struggle for the possession of the road.

With the money thus raised the enterprise was at last carried
through, and, on the fifteenth of January, 1869, seventeen years
after the organization of the company, the cities of Binghamton
and Albany were brought into direct communication. Meanwhile
those seventeen years of construction had greatly altered all the
conditions of that railroad system of which the Albany & Susquehanna Railroad was now for the first time to become an in-
tegral part. In 1853 both the Erie and the Central were but feebly
entering on their great careers. The Erie was just completed to
Dunkirk: the Central was not yet consolidated; the whole receipts of the first were but one third part of what the completion
of Mr. Ramsey's road found them, while, during the same interval, the receipts of the last had swollen from less than six millions per annum to considerably over fifteen. As for the men who
managed the great trunk lines when Mr. Ramsey had completed

his work, their names had never been mentioned in connection
with railroads when he began it. In fact, the whole aspect of the
problem had changed. In 1853 all the roads in the country were
local roads; in 1869 no local road was suffered to exist, unless
the great through roads were satisfied that it could serve no purpose in their hands; nay, more, unless they were also satisfied
that it could serve no purpose in the hands of their competitors.
When, therefore, the projectors of the Albany & Susquehanna
line had completed it to Binghamton, they suddenly found themselves involved in all the complications and controversies of an
intricate system. The intended local road was an element of
strength or a source of danger not to be ignored by the managers
of the great trunk lines.

Messrs. Jay Gould and James Fisk, Jr., had at this time already succeeded in firmly establishing themselves in the practical
ownership of the Erie Railway. Mr. Daniel Drew, some six
months before, had been driven out of its treasurership, and even
Commodore Vanderbilt had been compelled by fair means and
by foul to abandon all idea of controlling its management. When
the Susquehanna road was completed it became at once a most
important element in the successful prosecution of the plans of
Messrs. Gould and Fisk. It was so from two points of view,—
either as regarded their competition with the Central Road for
the carriage of the produce of the West to New England; or,
still more important, as regarded their competition with other
agencies for the carriage of coal to the same region. The anthracite coal deposits of America lie but a short distance to the south
of the Erie Railway. Disappointed in the hope of successfully
competing with the Central Road for the carriage of the produce
of the West, convinced at last by hard experience that the more
of this business the road undertook to do the more hopelessly
bankrupt it became, the Erie managers had more and more
turned their attention to the business of transporting coal. In
this also they were subject to a very sharp competition, particularly from the wealthy companies which themselves owned the

coal beds, and which now proposed to supplement their business
as colliers with that of carriers also. This by no means met the
views of the Erie people. They were now entering into vast contracts with various coal companies to haul many hundreds of
thousands of tons per annum; they naturally wished to extend
their connection, as by doing so they accomplished two ends,—
they shut the coal companies up in their mines, making them dependent on the Erie Railway for access to their markets, and at
the same time they secured to themselves a monopoly in so far as
the consumers were concerned; they, in fact, placed themselves
as an indispensable medium between producer and consumer.
The Albany & Susquehanna Road might well develop into an
independent and competing line; hence they greatly coveted the
possession of it. By it they would not only secure an access to
Albany, but would forge the link which was to unite the Erie
with a whole network of roads running north and east from Albany throughout coal-consuming New England.

It is wholly unnecessary to dwell upon the public considera-
tions which rendered it unadvisable that the adventurers then
representing the Erie Railway should be intrusted with a practical control over the winter supply of such an article as anthracite
coal. However amiable or otherwise they might be in their domestic characters, their course had not been such as to make unprejudiced observers anxious to repose in them so delicate a duty
as that of sole purveyors at any season of an article of prime
necessity. The coal companies naturally did not look with any
favor at a policy which threatened their lines of communication.
Finally Mr. Ramsey, as the controlling influence in the Albany &
Susquehanna management, neither desired to surrender the independence of his road, nor, in view of the recent experience of
others, did he impose implicit faith in either the verbal or written assurances or obligations of the Erie representatives. Possession was with them considerably more than nine points of the
law, and Mr. Ramsey evinced a marked repugnance to surrender
the property intrusted to his charge into their possession, regard-

less of any liberal promises held out as to subsequent beneficial results, public and private, likely to ensue from his doing so.

The position of Mr. Ramsey in his own board of direction was not, however, perfectly secure. Certain enmities and jealousies had, little by little, not unnaturally grown up along the line of the road, and, at the election of directors in 1868, a ticket had been chosen partly in the opposition interest. What these parties represented when they came into the board it is difficult to say; it may have been a restless feeling of discontent at the slow progress of the enterprise, or a vague desire for change; or, perhaps, a personal dislike and mistrust of Mr. Ramsey. Whatever the cause, the direction at the time of the completion of the road was divided not unevenly. This condition of affairs was very unsatisfactory to Mr. Ramsey. He maintained that at the previous election he and his friends had been taken by surprise; that no wish for a change in management really existed in the minds of the bulk of the stockholders; but, finally, whether it existed or not, he let it be distinctly understood that he did not intend to belong to a divided direction, and that at the coming election either he or his opponents were to go out. The materials for a lively contest for the control of the company in September, 1869, thus existed in great abundance and on all sides.

The road was completed in January, and early in June the Erie manipulators began their preparations to obtain possession of it, or, as they more graphically would have said, to "gobble" it. The stock of the road was nominally quoted at about 25 per cent of its par value; it was rarely bought or sold, and was supposed to possess little real value, except as representing the control of the enterprise. It was almost exclusively in the hands of three classes of owners,—the directors and those dwelling along the line of the road, subscribing municipalities, and certain capitalists who held it as security for money advanced and expended in construction. The subscription books of the company had never been closed, as but $2,800,000 of the $4,000,000 of authorized capital had ever been subscribed, and of the amount of stock which had been subscribed for, $800,000 had been forfeited in the manner already mentioned. Whoever desired to get possession of the property had, therefore, to obtain the control for a longer or shorter period, to include the election day, of a majority of this stock. The Erie party wishing to come in, and the opposition minority determined not to go out, thus had natural affinities to each other. But though when united they controlled a formidable minority of the whole stock, yet it was by no means the majority, and the Ramsey party was now thoroughly alive to the danger of the situation. The plan for the approaching campaign was soon matured. Under a sudden demand for election purposes the stock, which for years had been nominally quoted at 20, rose rapidly in July to 40 and 50 and even to 60 and 65 per cent. All parties were buying. The issue was, however, to be decided by stock held by municipalities, and it was to the control of this that the greatest efforts were devoted. Here lay the stronghold of the Ramsey party; and here they felt secure, for the law authorized the town commissioners, who held this stock as trustees, to sell it only for cash and at its par value, and forbade them to sell it for less unless specially authorized to do so by a town vote. This was a point which it seemed hardly likely to touch. Suddenly, and to their great dismay, Mr. Ramsey and his friends heard of agents out among the towns offering the commissioners par for the stock, provided the offer was accepted at once. Naturally this was a great temptation to commissioners who represented towns which grievously felt the weight of railroad loans. These men were suddenly called upon to accept or reject, on their own responsibility, an offer which, a few days before, would have seemed incredible, but the acceptance of which, while it would relieve the town of debt, would also deprive it of all voice in the management of the road waited for so long. In a number of cases the commissioners considered it their duty to accept the offer, and the control of several hundred shares was in this way secured. The Ramsey party was thus forced into the field, and the stock of towns rose to a premium. This process, however, involved a very considerable outlay of money and no inconsiderable risk of loss. Buying up a majority of the stock was altogether too much like paying for a road. Why should that be obtained at great cost which could equally well be got for nothing? Stimulated by the passion which Mr. Fisk has happily described as an inherited disposition "to rescue things out of somebody else," one Sunday afternoon, early in August, a party of gentlemen met at the Fifth Avenue Hotel in New York and arranged a new plan, involving the certain transfer of the road into their hands, but avoiding the necessity of further pecuniary outlay. A negotiation was successfully concluded for the purchase of $450,000 of the stock of various towns on the following terms: no money was to pass, but the bonds of Messrs. Gould and Fisk were given, binding them to purchase and pay for the stock after the election, provided the commissioners should at the election vote as the givers of the bond should direct. The legal effect of such an arrangement may well have escaped the town commissioners, but Messrs. Fisk and Gould had not as a rule up to this time been found deficient in matters of technical nicety. These bonds had no binding force whatever. It was not a sale for cash, it was contrary to law and to public policy; it was an arrangement wholly beyond the powers of the commissioners to make, and one which the courts would not sustain. The commissioners who accepted these bonds and who subsequently did vote as those who gave them dictated, were public officials, as such their duties were prescribed and were sufficiently simple; they could sell, and they could vote, but if they sold it was to be for cash down, and if they voted it was to be on their own judgments, and not on those of other people. In this case, indeed, what security had they that, after they had voted the road into the hands of the Erie managers, the conditions of the bond in regard to the purchase of the stock would be fulfilled? As a matter of fact they did vote as they agreed, but nothing further was ever done to complete the transfer of the stock.

Events now moved rapidly on both sides. On the third of August the certificates of town stock were presented for transfer. It was a new question; Mr. Ramsey was away, and the treasurer hesitated. Finally, all stock sold for cash and paid for by either side was transferred; but the transfer was denied where, in the opinion of the treasurer, the transaction was not completed. It was evident they were pressing the Ramsey party heavily. It now occurred to Ramsey that the subscription books had never been closed, and that twelve thousand shares of the capital stock of the company were as yet unissued. On the fifth he took the subscription book home with him, held a meeting of a few of his friends, and, among them, they wrote down their names for nine thousand five hundred shares of stock. It was fully understood that this subscription bound those who made it to no immediate payments; 10 per cent was to be paid in at once, and for this Ramsey was to provide; the remainder would only be called in as should be ordered by the board of directors whom this very stock would elect. Meanwhile, if any of the subscribers desired to get rid of their stock, Ramsey undertook to relieve them of it. That this subscription, made by directors in secret on the eve of an election, and with a view of affecting that election, should have subsequently been held legal is open to criticism; its good faith even might well have been suspected; but that, on grave consideration, it should be justifiable is perhaps as severe a censure as could be passed on the condition of affairs existing in the community in which it was made. Yet, under the circumstances, unnecessary and unfortunate as the step afterward proved to have been, Mr. Ramsey and his friends were justified in taking it. It is simply necessary to refer to those who now sought to obtain control of the Albany & Susquehanna Railroad. Their position in the community, their standing in the courts, their financial and fiduciary relations, were notorious. They had reduced society to a condition in which any man brought into conflict with them could not but realize that he had only himself to rely on, that a species of lynch law prevailed, and that might and possession alone counted for anything. The first duty of Mr. Ramsey then, unquestionably, was to keep the property intrusted to his charge out of the hands of those men; this every consideration of honor and responsibility bound him to do at any cost and by all legal means, certain that, whatever he might scruple at, his opponents, once in control, would scruple at nothing. This step was legal, and, however questionable in many aspects, Mr. Ramsey and his friends were justified in taking it, provided they made their subscriptions in good faith to their company, and held themselves responsible for them. At best, however, it was an error in judgment. By it Mr. Ramsey sacrificed much of the strength of his position, which lay in the fact that he was fighting men who had set the most infamous precedents ever known for transactions of a not dissimilar character. As usual in dealing in measures of questionable right and expediency, one doubtful step soon led to another which admitted of no doubt.

Ten per cent of the amount of the subscriptions had at once to be provided, and that, too, by Ramsey, whose resources were already strained to the utmost. Again he had recourse to Groesbeck, and drew on him for $100,000; he had also subscribed for more stock in Groesbeck's name. The subscription, involving as it did further possible calls to the full value of the stock, Groesbeck politely declined; the draft he honored, receiving as collateral for it a deposit of $150,000 of the equipment bonds of the Albany & Susquehanna Railroad Co., which belonged to the road, and which Mr. Ramsey procured from the treasurer for the purpose of so pledging them. The 10 per cent of the subscription was thus paid in, and the nine thousand five hundred shares were placed on the books of the company to the credit of the nominal subscribers, each of whom gave Ramsey a voting proxy for the coming election. Months afterward Mr. Groesbeck defended this transaction, and declared that, under the same circumstances and fighting the same men, he himself would have gone as far, and farther too, if necessary. The proceeding was, however, none the less indefensible. The securities which had thus been misap-

plied were shortly after, at Groesbeck's own suggestion, returned
to the officials of the company, and their place supplied by collateral of inferior value; and as for the stock, it was never voted
on, and the issue of it only served to endanger the case of the
Ramsey party.*

This took place on the fifth of August, but already the usual
storm of judicial orders and injunctions had begun. The stock
of the towns being, so far as possible, secured, the next blow was
directed at the stock reissued and held as collateral. Two blocks
of this were outstanding,—one in the hands of Chase, the other
in those of Groesbeck. On the application of Messrs. Gould and
Fisk's counsel, an injunction was issued by Mr. Justice Barnard,
of the Supreme Court, forbidding any votes being cast upon this
stock, and ordering its transfer to a receiver pending judicial
investigation; all this upon the ground that the stock was unlawfully issued. The books were to close upon the seventh, the order
was procured on the fourth. While this was going on in the city,
the Ramsey party was not idle in the country. On the same day
they appeared before Judge Parker of Owego and commenced a

* This and the previous paragraph are republished in the form in which
they originally appeared. Yet it may well be questioned whether even the
modified censure implied upon Mr. Ramsey's proceedings would bear examination. Ordinary rules cannot always govern exceptional cases. If a man
finds himself involved in an everyday controversy, however angry, he is
very properly expected to confine himself to recognized remedies; if, however, he is suddenly roused from his sleep by the assault of midnight robbers,
he cannot, if he is a man of courage, be called upon to exercise any nice
judgment as to the use he may make of the weapons nearest at hand;—it is
a case of self-preservation. Especially would this be true if his assailants
were notoriously in collusion with the watch. If Ramsey had hesitated, even
for an instant, his friends would have lost courage, and he could never have
recovered himself; under the circumstances it is very difficult to see why he
was not as fully justified in the use of any and every weapon as a man
would be in a struggle for his life. Of course in the one case or the other he
would be amenable to the law for any illegal act. The question is one purely
of moral accountability; legally, a man so circumstanced must act at his own
peril. He may infringe laws, and, if he does, he must be prepared to undergo
the penalty of so doing, but it may yet be his duty to incur that penalty in
defense of his trust.

suit, resulting, of course, in the inevitable injunction, by which all parties were restrained and enjoined from transferring on the books of the company seven hundred shares of stock belonging to the town of Oneonta, and which the Erie party claimed to have purchased. No sooner did the news of this move arrive in New York, than Mr. Thomas G. Shearman, a member of the firm of Field, Shearman, & Co., and one of the most trusted legal advisers of those now controlling the Erie Railway, was dispatched to Owego, where he succeeded in getting the injunction dissolved. Hitherto the engagement had been at long range, as it were, but it now lacked a few days only of the date when transfers previous to the election were to cease; it was time for close quarters. Not content with the success of his defensive operations, the Erie counselor at once assumed a vigorous offensive. Two new suits were initiated,—one to compel the immediate transfer of that very Oneonta stock which the company had just previously sought to prevent; and the other, a more vital thrust still, sought to restrain Ramsey himself from the further performance of his duties as president of the company. It is almost unnecessary to say that both the desired orders were almost immediately obtained. The board of direction was divided into two hostile camps exactly equal in strength,—they stood seven to seven. The suspension of Mr. Ramsey thus turned the scale and placed the Erie opposition in the majority. It remained only to call a meeting of the directors, over which the vice-president, whose sympathy with the Erie movement was pronounced, would preside, and this meeting would vote out of office the present treasurer, who hesitated about the desired transfers, and would replace him by a suitable successor. Absolute control of the books thus secured, the election might be regarded as a mere matter of detail. All the day of that meeting the offices of the company swarmed with indignant directors and opposing counsel; angry words passed, loud threats were uttered; the suspended president was informed that his presence was undesired, and the unsuspended vice-president showed a strong disposition to assume

also the duties of treasurer in so far as these involved the entering of transfers and the issuing of certificates of stock. At last
a sort of tussle took place over the books, and then the police
were called in, who established an angry truce. All this took
place on the fifth; on the seventh the books were to be closed.

The control of those books, it was well understood, implied the
control of the road. The presence of James Fisk, Jr., and of Jay
Gould in the struggle was no mystery, and the officers of the
road could not fail to recall how, only a few months before, the
vault of the Union Pacific Railroad had been forced, in a vain
search for the books of the company, under cover of a judicial
process and at the dictation of these very men. That the records
were not in safety while in the offices of the corporation was notorious. That night, in the presence of counsel, and with the
knowledge of the treasurer, they were removed from the building. The law guaranteed to stockholders access to the books of
the corporation; the judicial abuse of the processes of law had
converted this right into a facility for fraud. Whether those who
would now insist upon the right were likely to avail themselves
of that opportunity was a question in regard to which recent experience in other quarters might warrant the formation of an
opinion. In any case the books were now surreptitiously removed
under the advice of counsel, and the action of the officials who
assented to this removal was indorsed by public opinion, and
throughout the subsequent proceedings, was not censured by the
courts.

The next day the opposition wing of the direction met and
organized with the vice-president in the chair. Just as they were
proceeding to business, however, an attorney of the other wing
quietly entered the room and served upon four of those present
a new judicial order, restraining them from acting as directors
of the company, or from interfering with its affairs. This unexpected move, leaving them without a quorum, fell like a thunderbolt on the Albany members of the Erie party, and they precip-

tately retired from the field and took the first train to New York
in search of counsel and assistance.

Reaching the Grand Opera House and the offices of the Erie
counsel, the fugitives laid their case before Mr. Shearman. The
quick eye of that gentleman at once took in the whole situation,
and he was not unequal to the emergency. The president, vice-
president, and a majority of the board of direction were now
suspended, and the Albany & Susquehanna Railroad was suspended with them; everyone was enjoined; there was no one
authorized to give an order or to pay out a dollar; chaos was
come again. Recognizing the fact that a court of equity had done
this mischief through the exercise of one of its powers, Mr.
Shearman was inspired with a conviction that the same court
must repair it by the exercise of another power,—injunctions had
occasioned the deadlock, a receivership must dissolve it. A new
suit was at once commenced, the complaint in which set forth
he existing condition of affairs, and prayed for the appointment of receivers who should operate the road, and so avert the
disastrous consequences otherwise sure to ensue. This paper was
drawn up by Mr. Shearman at his office in the Twenty-third
Street Opera House, on the afternoon of Friday the sixth of
August. It was not ready for signature until the hour of
10.00 P.M. The Grand Opera House is not in the immediate
vicinity of any court of law, nor do judges generally frequent
their courtrooms at late hours on August evenings. The private
residence of Mr. Justice Barnard was on Twenty-first Street, at
least half a mile away, and on the morning of this day the justice
himself was at the bedside of his dying mother at Poughkeepsie,
seventy-five miles from New York. Telegraphs from Mr. Fisk
had, however, found him there and summoned him to the city.
The order was ready for signature at 10.20 P.M., when it was delivered to a junior partner of the firm of Field, Shearman, & Co.,
who thereupon left the Grand Opera House and, in fifteen minutes, returned with what purported to be Judge Barnard's signature appended to it. A strange obscurity hangs over this part of

the transaction. It was never stated throughout the subsequent proceedings where this order was signed; it was never proved that it had then been signed by Judge Barnard at all. Diligent inquiry at a date long subsequent failed to discover any trace of it in the records of the court; no evidence was ever elicited that Judge Barnard was in New York at any time during that day. It was subsequently said to have been signed at the house of Fisk's mistress; but this strange statement only called forth a bare denial unaccompanied by any explanation.* That this order, whether there signed by him or not, was subsequently adopted as his own by Judge Barnard admits of no doubt. Under the most favorable supposition it would appear that the surprisingly brief period of fifteen minutes had sufficed to go through all the forms and make all the inquiries necessary to satisfy the judicial mind in regard to so trifling a matter as the receivership of some one hundred and fifty miles of railroad, involving millions of capital. This order appointed Charles Courter, of whom the judge probably knew absolutely nothing, and James Fisk, Jr., of whom he undoubtedly knew a great deal, receivers of the Albany & Susquehanna Railroad Co. Criticism is wholly unnecessary. The whole proceeding reflects the highest credit on the energy of all concerned: it speaks volumes. The law's delay is an ill of which the citizens of New York, certainly, have no cause to complain, at all times and under all circumstances.

By half after ten o'clock all was settled, and at eleven the two receivers, accompanied by a select bodyguard of directors, friends, and lawyers, were on their way by the night train to take possession of their charge. Their opponents had, however, already

---

* It has since been stated, on the authority of Judge Barnard, that he accidentally met the counsel on his way from the cars to his house, and was asked by him to sign the order; that he did so, stepping into a neighboring real estate office for the purpose. The meeting was certainly a singular coincidence, and the method indicated of transacting judicial business of the first importance is calculated to excite surprise, if not consternation. The "explanation" seems, however, to have been considered perfectly satisfactory by those to whom it was made.

got an inkling of the summary process impending over them from New York, and, while Mr. Shearman was busy with the preparation of his order in the Grand Opera House, other counsel were no less busy in the opposing camp at Albany preparing a counter-order, appointing another receiver in their own interest. This, when completed, was duly submitted to Mr. Justice Peckham, of the Supreme Court of the Albany district, between nine and ten o'clock of the same (Friday) evening. The signature of this magistrate was affixed to it, and a Mr. Pruyn, of Albany, was by him appointed receiver of the Albany & Susquehanna Railroad Co. It was close work. Each order took effect when signed, and there certainly was no delay in their preparation, and even less in procuring signatures to them. The evidence seemed subsequently to indicate that the Albany receivership had about one hour's priority in time; it had, however, one hundred and fifty miles of distance in its favor, and the great weight which attaches to possession as an element of success in litigation has long since passed into a proverb.

Thus, on Saturday, the seventh of August, everything indicated a collision of forces. No sooner had Receiver Fisk reached Albany, and received the reports of his scouts, than he hastened with his friends to the offices of the company. He arrived there toward eight o'clock. In spite of this praiseworthy activity on their part, Messrs. Fisk and Courter, on proceeding to take possession of the premises, encountered a somewhat unexpected obstacle in the person of a Mr. Van Valkenburg, the superintendent of the road, who, upon being informed of their errand, announced that he was already in possession under the orders of Receiver Pruyn, and further intimated that he did not propose to abandon it. A very amusing and somewhat exciting scene then ensued. The junior appointee of Mr. Justice Barnard presented his papers to the superintendent, seated himself on the table, announced himself as Mr. James Fisk, Jr., of New York, come to take possession and prepared to do so if it required "millions of money and an unlimited number of men." He further added that this was his twenty-sixth raid of the same character, and that he proposed ''to take you fellows''; to all of which Mr. Van Valkenburg pleasantly replied that he ''hoped he would have a good time doing it.'' His companions Mr. Fisk introduced as his ''boys,'' and invited them in to possess themselves. Quite a lively colloquy ensued, which was not satisfactory to Mr. Fisk, who from words gradually proceeded to overt acts, and finally ordered his ''boys'' to put the other ''boys'' out. Unfortunately the preponderance of force was not on his side. Instead of ejecting his opponents, he was summarily ejected himself, and, after being ignominiously and very roughly hustled downstairs, he found himself in the street in a very disheveled condition. Nor did his discomfiture stop here; no sooner did he reach the pavement than he was arrested by a fiery little individual, claiming to be a policeman, and ignominiously marched off to the station-house. As no complaint was preferred he was speedily released, but probably not until he had discovered that his arrest, like his ejectment, was the work, not of a policeman, but of an employee of the company. No sooner was he again a free man than he returned to the charge. Mr. Pruyn was now at the offices in person, claiming to be in possession as receiver, and a crowd of lawyers, officers, and parties in interest had also assembled there. The heads of the opposing factions met face to face. No further riotous demonstrations were attempted, but, pending advices from New York, Mr. Fisk kept up the semblance of a possession. He evidently bore no ill will to Mr. Van Valkenburg, on account of the rough treatment of the morning, as he even went so far as to compliment that gentleman on his display of energy, and to signify a desire to extend to him his personal favor. As to Mr. Ramsey, Mr. Fisk, as a happy solution of existing complications, suggested that the possession of the road should be decided, not as of old by a personal contest between the two heads of the opposing factions, but by the goddess of chance, or whatever other divinity may preside over the issue of a game of ''seven up''; and, with such interchange of amenities and pleasant sallies of wit, with now and again the service of some notice or order of court, and perhaps an injunction or two, the *protégé* of Barnard beguiled the weary monotony of the day.

The cessation of active hostilities did not last long. The discomfiture of the morning had been at once telegraphed to Mr. Shearman, in the recesses of the Grand Opera House, and that gentleman had forthwith proceeded to discover and apply the suitable remedies of the law. Recourse was at once had, or is alleged to have been had, to Judge Barnard, sitting at special term in the courthouse. Again, however, a curious obscurity hangs over the actual whereabouts of that magistrate. On this day his mother was still lingering at Poughkeepsie, and another judge was sitting at special term in the courthouse. In any case a most unusual and indeed well-nigh antiquated writ, never before granted to meet such an exigency as that which had now arisen, was at once exhumed and prepared. In the first place a new and sweeping injunction, purporting to have been granted by Judge Barnard, was obtained, by virtue of which Mr. Receiver Pruyn, the sheriff of the county, the Albany police, and all the railroad employees, were restrained from any interference with receivers Courter and Fisk. Not satisfied with this, a writ of assistance* was likewise ordered to issue, by which the sheriff, and, if need be, the *posse comitatus*, were placed at the disposal of Messrs. Fisk and Courter. This was a sufficiently unusual proceeding, but the service of the process was so extraordinary that the ordering it was at once reduced to the commonplace. Now, probably for the first time on record, both injunction and writ were forwarded to their destination for service by electric telegraph. That afternoon officers in Albany actually undertook to

---

* "Writs to the sheriff, to assist a receiver, sequestrator, or other party to a suit in chancery, to get possession, under a decree of the court, of lands withheld from him by another party to the suit. These writs, which issue from the equity side of the Court of Exchequer, or from any other court of chancery, are at least as old as the reign of James I, and are still in common use in England, Ireland, and some of the United States."—*Quincy's (Mass.) Reports*, p. 396.

serve upon parties to a suit processes which had been issued in
New York not an hour before, on the strength of affidavits as to
facts which had that day occurred in Albany. In place of making
service with the original, bearing the seal of the court and the
signature of the judge, the very ink of the copies which the
officers had in their hands was not yet dry. Of course such a
service was contemptuously disregarded, nor did the sheriff presume to insist upon it.

It was now afternoon, and it was very evident that nothing
further could be effected this day; both parties, however, claimed
to be in possession, and neither would yield the ground. Finally
a species of truce was arranged to hold good over the coming
Sunday. A representative of each party was to be left in the
offices, and, before nine o'clock of the coming Monday, no act of
hostility, open or covert, in so far as possession was concerned,
was to be attempted by either side.

The interval of Sunday was passed in active preparation.
While the representatives of the receivers tarried in the deserted
offices, the principals themselves were busy with their plans of
campaign. Mr. Fisk and his friends among the directors retired
to New York to get advice and the originals of the telegraphed
writs; Mr. Pruyn and the Ramsey party stoutly prepared themselves in Albany for such trials as the morrow might bring forth.
The issue now presented was, in plain language, one simply of
judicial nerve. It was a conflict between the judiciary of New
York City and that of the country. The system of electing judges
by the popular vote had at last brought forth bitter fruit, and
men had been elevated to the bench who should have ornamented
the dock. These selections did not perhaps extend beyond one or
two districts out of the eight into which the state was divided,
but each of the thirty-three judges who composed those eight
courts exercised throughout the state the extensive and delicate
powers of a chancellor. All were magistrates of coördinate powers, and technically of one court; an order made by one could be
dissolved by another, an officer appointed by this magistrate

could be suspended in the exercise of his duties by that, what one justice could do the next could undo. Everything under such a system depended on judicial respect for judicial action; courtesy and confidence were the essence of it. All these had, in certain quarters, now long passed away. The judges of the country had felt bitterly the discredit brought upon the common bench by the action of more than one judge in the city; there were among them those who had been deeply mortified by a contemptuous disregard of their process. Hence a conflict had become inevitable, and nowhere was it so likely to arise as out of. the litigations originating with the managers of the Erie Railway. A peculiar discredit had now long attached to these, and certain names, both on the bench and at the bar, were always associated with them. There are facts which are of public notoriety; the community recognizes them and no justice can ignore them. When, therefore, James Fisk, Jr., was appointed, as a matter of course, by Judge Barnard, receiver of a railway, no part of which lay within a hundred miles of that magistrate's judicial district, and when this appointment was made on the eve of a contested election for directors of that railway, and must have been decisive of the contest, then, at last, a case was presented which could not be ignored. The conflict was not likely to be a pleasant one. Recent proceedings in other causes had indicated with sufficient clearness the lengths to which certain justices of the first district were not indisposed to go. Neither the scandal certainly involved, nor the defeat not unlikely to ensue, were pleasant to contemplate; but the stand must be made. Circumstances had already designated Judge Peckham, of Albany, as the magistrate to whom the Ramsey people must almost necessarily have recourse. The public estimation in which this gentleman is held was shown by his election, shortly after the events here narrated took place, as one of the new Court of Appeals organized under the judiciary clause of the rejected Constitution of 1869. The scandal which arose out of the Albany & Susquehanna case most materially contributed to the adoption of this single clause. It is probable, therefore, that the action of Judge Peckham on this occasion had a direct influence on his own future elevation; it certainly received the public indorsement.

Receiver Fisk might confidently be expected back, well armed with injunctions and with the original of his writ of assistance on Monday morning. It was necessary that Receiver Pruyn should be prepared to meet him. The last New York suit had enjoined the Albany receiver from any interference with the New York receivers, and had been accompanied by a writ of assistance. This was now met in the usual way. A new Albany suit enjoined the New York receiver from any interference with Mr. Pruyn, and at the same time an order was issued by Judge Peckham restraining the sheriffs from taking any action under the writs of assistance. It was further sought to punish Mr. Fisk for a contempt of court in interfering with its receiver on the previous Saturday, but this the judge held it necessary to send to a referee to take evidence and report. A temporary injunction was granted, and Mr. Fisk was ordered to appear and show cause on the thirteenth why this should not be made permanent. Such were the legal complications encountered by Mr. Fisk on his return to the scene of his labors early on Monday morning. He had left New York on the boat the evening before, in company with fifteen friends and advisers, and was fully prepared for vigorous operations. The condition of affairs did not look propitious. He was distinctly checkmated at Albany, and the order checkmating him, and forbidding the sheriffs to interfere to put him in possession, was already on the express train which had left Albany at 8.00 A.M., and would be due in Binghamton, at the other end of the coveted road, at three o'clock that afternoon. A party to a conflict, however, who operates by steam, is at a manifest disadvantage when acting against one who dispatches writs by telegraph. In the present case Mr. Fisk, baffled at one end of the line, went vigorously to work a hundred and forty miles away at the other end of it. While the express train was toiling along to

Binghamton, enjoining as it went all sheriffs and others from paying any attention to his writs of assistance, the telegraph was flashing those writs direct to Binghamton, and commanding that immediate possession should be given to his representatives. Accordingly just before two o'clock, and as the afternoon train for Albany was on the point of leaving Binghamton, the sheriff of Broome County made his appearance, and, by virtue of a writ of Judge Barnard's, fresh from the telegraph wires, proceeded to take possession of all the property of the Albany & Susquehanna Railroad Co., including the train then standing at the station. Three locomotives belonging to the same company were also at Binghamton. These he undertook to seize next; of two of them he obtained possession, but the agent of the road was before him with the third; for, just as he was approaching his prey, writ in hand and borne upon one locomotive, the ingenious employee switched him off, and, while his own path suddenly led into space, he saw his prize gently slide down the grade out of his reach, and there get up the steam necessary to make good its escape.

The Barnard receivers were thus fairly installed in possession of the Binghamton end of the road, of the point where it connected with the Erie. An assistant superintendent of the Erie Railway was at once appointed superintendent of the Albany & Susquehanna, and a conductor of the same road was ordered to take out the regular train to Albany, which was still standing at the platform where it was seized. Matters were evidently approaching a crisis. Different sets of receivers were operating the two ends of the road, and two sheriffs, bearing conflicting processes, were rapidly approaching each other on trains drawn by the locomotives and directed by the officers of the hostile factions. This condition of affairs was telegraphed to the Ramsey train at Harpersville, twenty-five miles from Binghamton, and, after some consideration, it was determined to proceed no farther. Meanwhile the news of the Binghamton proceedings caused Superintendent Van Valkenburg to decide on vigorous measures. In the first place he proceeded to clear the offices of all hostile influences. Mr. Fisk had not that day been allowed within the premises. Repeatedly, in company with the sheriff and others, had he presented himself and energetically demanded admission. It was of no avail. It was different with Mr Courter, his fellow receiver; he had been treated with a degree of courtesy, and indeed had been permitted to sustain the character of a nominal receiver within the offices. This gentleman was, however, now notified by Mr. Van Valkenburg that the farce of a double possession was to terminate then and there. On Saturday, in the little unpleasantness with Mr. Fisk, Van Valkenburg had given some indications that he was a man of few words and decided action. The hint had not been thrown away. Mr. Courter, after a formal resistance just sufficient to establish the fact of forcible ejectment, withdrew from the premises, and the Barnard receivers abandoned every pretence of actual possession of the Albany end of the line. Van Valkenburg's next move was to telegraph an order over the road, stopping every train where it then was; all movement was thus brought to a stand. An extra train, carrying a hundred and fifty men from the workshops, under command of the master mechanic, was then sent up the road to be ready for any emergency. Having thus cleared everything away for action, the next move of the other side was in order.

The representatives of this other side were meanwhile advancing from the opposite direction; upon the train were the sheriff of Broome County, the Erie superintendent of the road, and some twenty men. As they moved along, the orders of Judge Barnard were served at each way station, the old officials of the road were displaced, and Erie men were substituted for them. So eager, indeed, was the sheriff in the discharge of his duties, under the electro-writ of assistance, that he not only served an order, the illegal character of which he must have more than suspected, throughout his own county, but he continued to do so throughout the adjacent county, and, indeed, seemed not indisposed to extend his bailiwick to Albany. At Afton, about thirty miles from

Binghamton, a dispatch was received from Mr. Van Valkenburg, notifying the party that any further advance would be at its own peril. The Albany people were then lying at Bainbridge, six miles farther down the track. After some hesitation, which involved a great deal of rapid telegraphing and no inconsiderable delay, positive orders for an advance came to the Erie party, followed shortly after by reinforcements. It was now deep in the night, but the train at last was started, and moved slowly and cautiously toward Bainbridge. The Albany party was prepared to receive it. They lay on a siding, with a patent frog—a little machine made to slide trains on to the rails, but equally calculated to slide them off—attached at a convenient point to the main track. In total ignorance of this bit of strategy, the Erie people felt their way along, when, just as Bainbridge, to their very great relief, seemed safely reached, their locomotive gently and suddenly glided off the track, and their train was brought to a standstill. The instant this took place the Albany train moved up the siding, passed triumphantly by its disabled opponents and on to the main track above them, where it took its position in their rear, effectually cutting off all retreat. As the Erie party tumbled out of their train, they were met by Mr. Smith, one of the counsel of their opponents, who glanced at the process under which they were acting, and at once pronounced it worthless. There was no alternative; they had fallen into a trap, unconditional surrender was all that remained. This was accordingly submitted to, and Sheriff Browne of Broome County, and all his *posse comitatus,* were helped off their train and duly served with the order of Judge Peckham, restraining them from doing or attempting anything in aid of the receivers appointed by Judge Barnard.

Having disposed of this little party by capture, and it being now broad day, the Ramsey commander decided vigorously to follow up his advantage, steaming up the road toward Binghamton. On the way he displaced the recently appointed Fisk men, and replaced the ejected Ramsey men in charge of the various stations. Everything proceeded well until the train approached the long tunnel, near Binghamton. This was the battle ground chosen by the Erie party. Here, close to their base of operations, and near their supplies, they had massed their reserves, after the total and ignominious capture of their advance guard.

The tunnel is some twenty-two hundred feet in length, and is about fifteen miles from Binghamton. It marks the last summit the road crosses in going west, and, on either side, is approached by a heavy ascending grade and round a sharp curve. The Albany party arrived at this point at about ten o'clock, and here halted. On the other side of the hill, trains were bringing up workmen from the Erie shops, under the officers of the Erie road, until Mr. Fisk's threat in regard to "any number of men" seemed tolerably certain to be verified. It was a motley collection, the control of which must have considerably puzzled the general superintendent of the Erie Railway, who found himself in command. A more unwieldy body could not well have been got together. The men were wholly unarmed, except, perhaps, with sticks, which one party was detailed to cut in the neighboring woods; they had been hastily summoned from the shops, and were ignorant as children of the crazy errand they were about, nor had they the slightest enmity toward those opposite to whom they stood in ludicrous array. This, however, was not the case with the Susquehanna people. They were now thoroughly stirred up and ready for anything. Most of them had for years been in the employ of the road, and many were personally attached to Mr. Ramsey; they regarded the effort to dispossess him as aimed also at themselves. They were, too, flushed with the success at Bainbridge, and possessed with a strong *esprit de corps*. Such being the opposing elements, they lay waiting for preëmptory orders, which in any case had to come from Albany, for there both Fisk and Van Valkenburg kept their headquarters. From time to time reinforcements came up, until by seven o'clock the Erie party was raised to an unwieldy mob of some eight hundred men, while their opponents numbered hardly less than four hundred and fifty. The Erie people now decided to try an advance, and accordingly a train well loaded with combatants was set in motion. It moved slowly through the tunnel and emerged safely from the eastern end, merely having to replace a single rail. This done, the advance was continued. Meanwhile the Albany people were fully notified of the impending danger. Accordingly, when the Erie people had replaced the rail and started, they started too, and thus the first intimation the raiders had of danger was the discovery, on rounding the sharp curve, of an approaching locomotive, angrily puffing up the grade, and apparently bent on mischief. This was more than they were prepared for. Their whistle at once signaled danger, which the Albany locomotive replied to by signaling to them to get out of the way. In vain the Erie conductor jumped off his train and gesticulated like a madman; in vain the Erie engineer tried to back out of the way; the curve was here so sharp and the incline up which it was necessary to back in order to return into the tunnel was so great, that it was instantly evident, not only that the Albany people wanted a collision, but that their wish was to be gratified. Though the Erie engine could not reverse, it had stopped, and the heavy grade kept down the speed of the Albany train, so that the collision rather indicated an *animus* than inflicted an injury; nevertheless, in a moment the two locomotives came together with a sharp shock. The damage done was not great; guards and cowcatchers were swept away, headlights were broken, and the attacking locomotive was roughly thrown from the track; but the collision of engines was the signal for a collision of men. Before the trains had met they were emptied of their loads. Such a system of opposition was something on which the Erie people had not counted, and when, simultaneously with the collision, the Albany men rushed upon them with loud shouts, they were at once completely demoralized, and broke into a precipitate flight. Their locomotive, with broken lights and a pistol bullet through its cab, vigorously reversed, until it had reversed itself out of the *mêlée* and back into the tunnel, while they themselves took to their heels and scampered back toward Binghamton. A few remained on board the train, a few stumbled back through the darkness of the tunnel, but the greater part, to whom their terror perhaps lent wings, scaled the mountain like a sand hill in their flight.

Victory had again rested on the Albany banners; the Ramsey star was in the decided ascendant. While one party of the Albany men followed up the disorganized enemy, others busied themselves in getting the locomotive on the track. This was soon done, and then they, in their turn, locomotive and all, advanced through the tunnel to complete the rout of Erie. The last-named party had, however, rallied a little in the breathing time afforded them, and were now at least equal to the task of making a very considerable noise. This, it is true, was not much, but in the growing darkness it was enough. In fact it might be said that one party was afraid to go forward, and the other did not dare to attack. The element of the ludicrous was becoming very pronounced, notwithstanding the earnestness of the combatants. Thus, as the shades of night deepened, they stood apart and defied each other with loud shouts and excessive profanity. A few conflicts of the more daring, a few scattering pistol shots, a few wounds, none of them serious, told the whole story. Yet it was a riot, and a shockingly lawless one; nay, more, it was an alarming one. It was not a sudden fight between ignorant and angry mobs; it was the attempt of two great corporations to levy war on each other with organized force. How far it might have gone cannot be said, for, in the midst of the tumult, the drums of the Forty-fourth Regiment of State Militia were heard approaching, and at this not unwelcome sound the combatants desisted. The Erie people held possession of the field. The Albany party sullenly withdrew, locomotive and all, through the tunnel, which they blocked up with a freight car, and then, after breaking down a trestlework or two, with a view of preventing another attack, they retired to Harpersville, where they established themselves for the night.

Meanwhile the whole state was in an uproar over the scandal of these lawless acts. All along the line of the road, and indeed almost everywhere, the feeling was strongly in sympathy with Mr. Ramsey. It could not well be otherwise; without knowing anything of the circumstances of the particular case, a strong presumption was now inevitable wherever the Erie management made its appearance in any complication. At Albany the public sentiment was peculiarly strong; meetings were held, a perfect ovation greeted the arrival of the runaway locomotive from Binghamton and the captured Erie train; crowds collected round the station, and were addressed from the cars by city demagogues on their way "to the front." At last, also, the point was reached at which, if the authorities did not interfere, the people would organize and take matters into their own hands. The militia had already been called upon by the civil authorities of Broome County and had responded to the call, and now Governor Hoffman was recalled from his summer sojourning place by telegraph, and reached Albany at almost the very time that the Forty-fourth Regiment arrived at the scene of riot. He at once took decisive measures. Orders were telegraphed to the sheriffs along the line of the road, directing them, in all cases of doubt, to treat any party in actual possession under a judicial order as being in rightful possession. The military were to be called upon only in case of extreme emergency, but, if the disorders continued, the whole district was to be placed under martial law.

In spite of these new developments, the Erie party was neither discouraged nor idle. The papers of Tuesday contained a long letter from Mr. James Fisk, Jr., setting forth at great length the magnitude of the public interests for which he claimed to be contending. The literary shortcomings of this production were excused on the ground of "quick, sharp work on a stamping ground new to me." Not content with this bid for moral support, on the evening of Tuesday, when the offices of the company would naturally have been deserted, Fisk and Courter made another effort to obtain possession of them. Armed with an order of

Judge Barnard's, staying all proceedings under Judge Peckham's writ of Monday, and further fortified with an additional writ of assistance, the brother receivers made their appearance in a carriage accompanied by the sheriff. Van Valkenburg was, however, on the ground, and, for a moment or two, things had an unpleasant look; so unpleasant, indeed, that Mr. Fisk now changed his tactics. Instead of bullying he attempted bribing; all the braggart confidence of Saturday was gone, and his demeanor was chiefly marked by an excessive care for his personal safety. As for the sheriff, the indications of violence were sufficiently pronounced to induce him to think it inexpedient to proceed further. Probably they would have gone away empty handed, had not a new judicial power just then stepped into the arena. This was Mr. Justice Clute, of the Albany County Court, who issued his order directing the arrest of the Barnard receivers for conspiring to take possession of the Albany & Susquehanna Railroad by force of arms. In obedience to this order the two indignant receivers were at once taken to Judge Clute's office, whence they were not released until they gave bail for their appearance next morning. The *coup de main* was a failure; but Mr. Fisk relieved his feelings by graphically describing the attempts which had been made to assassinate him.

The next morning Judge Peckham began the day, not exactly by setting aside his brother Barnard's recent orders, but, more courteously, by fixing a day on which cause should be shown why they should not be vacated, and, meanwhile, granting a temporary stay of all proceedings under them. The judicial equilibrium was thus restored. At last Governor Hoffman put a final stop to the judicial farce by notifying the sheriff of Albany that he was included in the directions of the previous day. The Ramsey party, being in actual possession at Albany under a judicial order, forthwith applied to the police for protection, which was immediately granted them. Meanwhile, Governor Hoffman received information of the tunnel conflict. He at once notified the counsel that such proceedings must stop, and that some agreement must be arrived at. In due time the counsel notified the Governor, in reply, that they were utterly unable to, agree on anything. His Excellency thereupon very emphatically and very properly replied that he neither knew nor cared anything for their complications, but he did propose to preserve the public peace. If those interested could not agree on some other course, it only remained for him to declare the whole district in a state of insurrection, and to operate the road as a military one. This declaration produced a document, signed by all the receivers, requesting his Excellency, as a species of nondescript superintendent, mutually agreed upon, to take possession of and operate the road. This very anomalous trust was accepted by Governor Hoffman, who issued a *quasi* military order, detailing Inspector-General McQuade as his deputy superintendent, and directing him to take possession. This was certainly a fitting climax to all that had gone before. A receiver is an officer of the court. His possession is the possession of the court. The courts in this case were fighting over the control of a railroad, and were forced to ask the Executive to hold the bone of contention while the judiciary "had it out" among themselves. Thus the Executive, in the utter breakdown of the law, had to accept a trust which did not belong to it, and proceed to perform duties which it had no right to perform, under an authority conferred by certain persons who had no such authority to confer. And all this because a man was selected in caucus and elected at the polls a judge in the first judicial district of New York, who fairly represented the moral and intellectual level of the majority of the voters who had elevated him into infamy. It was no accident; there was no element of chance in the case; it was the working of a system which produced a logical and natural result.

Though the possession of the road was thus disposed of, certain little outstanding accounts remained to be adjusted. The vacating of Judge Peckham's orders by Judge Barnard, and the staying of proceedings under Judge Barnard's orders by Judge Peckham, were matters of too common occurrence to call for notice. The interference of Judge Clute, however, a mere county judge, was something "most tolerable and not to be endured." And now for the first time in these proceedings Judge Barnard appeared upon the stage as something more than a name. The funeral of his mother had taken place at Poughkeepsie on the previous day; on that day, also, orders had been forthcoming from him in these Susquehanna suits, purporting to be granted on the behest of Mr. Shearman, between 11 A.M. and 1 P.M., at special term at the courthouse in New York City. The minutes of the courthouse show that the special term at the courthouse in New York City was held on this day by another magistrate. Upon the morning of the eleventh, however, he at length appeared in proper person, and, after obtaining from him the usual order, setting aside Judge Peckham's action of the day before, Mr. David Dudley Field, of counsel for the Erie Railway, read to the court the return of the sheriff, setting forth the resistance he had encountered on the previous afternoon in his attempt on the Susquehanna offices. Upon his motion the court ordered a peremptory writ, not bailable, to issue, commanding the sheriff to arrest Messrs. Pruyn, Ramsey, and Van Valkenburg, and to produce their bodies in court without delay. Under this process these gentlemen were arrested that afternoon, while in the executive chamber, and were held in duress awaiting conveyance to New York. Of course they none of them, at this time, seriously contemplated any such journey. Recourse was again had to Judge Clute, and the nonbailable prisoners were carried before that magistrate on a habeas corpus. The subject was taken under consideration by him until next morning. The opponents of Mr. Fisk had shown themselves not inapt scholars, and it naturally occurred to them that processes for contempt might be made to apply to him as well as to themselves. The same thought suggested itself to Mr. Fisk, as soon as he found time to relax from the efforts incident to "quick, sharp work on a stamping ground new to him." He had once before fled to Jersey City, pursued by Barnard; he now incontinently retired to New York, terrified by

Peckham. In fact, he abandoned his new "stamping ground" with great precipitation. Flying on board his own steamer, which was lying in the stream ready to serve either as an ark of refuge or a stronghold for prisoners, he was conveyed at once to New York, where he secured himself in the recesses of Castle Erie.

The next morning Judge Clute incontinently discharged the prisoners held under Judge Barnard's writ. It is almost unnecessary to say that his action was apparently in disregard of law; these proceedings throughout were open to this criticism. It was perfectly proper for Judge Clute to issue his writ of habeas corpus; when it came, however, to releasing prisoners held by a sheriff on a writ issued for contempt from a court superior to his own, the action of his Honor was, perhaps, more spirited than correct in practice. The prisoners, however, were released, and it only remained for the sheriff to make a return of the facts by mail to Judge Barnard. The matter was then brought once more before that magistrate, this time by Mr. Shearman. The colloquy that then took place was characteristic and well calculated to fill with terror the hearts of Peckham and Clute, no less than of Pruyn and Ramsey. The counsel began with a comparison. Judge Peckham, it appeared, had signed certain of his orders at his office; Judge Barnard, it will be remembered, was supposed to have signed his somewhere in the immediate neighborhood of a theater. Bearing these facts in mind, one cannot but appreciate the delicate sense of honor implied in the following opening remark of the counsel: "Unlike our opponents, who invite the judge to their private office, and from which he issues his orders as if from the court, we have never sought to consult your Honor in private, and whatever we have asked has been asked openly in court, and in accordance with our firm conviction of our legal rights." The peculiarly elevated tone of Judge Barnard's court being thus established, the colloquy proceeded as follows:—

Judge Barnard. I have been looking into this matter with some degree of care, and am of opinion that J. H. Clute, signing himself as county judge of Albany County, entertained jurisdiction of this matter as a criminal contempt, well knowing that it was a civil contempt. I am not quite sure but he should be brought before me to be punished for contempt.

Mr. Shearman. I intend to follow these men as I have followed others. Four months ago we were in pursuit of certain parties, and they were finally overtaken as their coat tails were disappearing behind a safe. I shall follow these men, if it is necessary and possible, to the end of time.

Judge Barnard. I have some years to sit on this bench, and would as soon devote them to this as to anything else.

Mr. Shearman. I am a young man also, having perhaps forty years at my disposal, and I am willing to devote them all to the pursuit of these men.

The first step in this forty years of persistent strife was thereupon at once taken by directing the sheriff to make a more detailed return. The individuals in question had, however, already fled the state, and Judge Barnard does not seem finally to have made up his mind to try conclusions with Judge Clute. Meanwhile the friends of the fugitives began to think that these proceedings had exceeded the limits of a jest. To fly the state was an ignominious thing; it seemed to imply a confession of wrongdoing; it could only be justified by the uncertainty which existed in regard to the limits of judicial power in cases of contempt, and especially of the exercise of that power by Barnard himself. He had indicated his *animus* by his remarks in court. Resort was had to negotiation. One of the Ramsey counsel went to New York and threw himself in Barnard's way. The Judge assured him that there was no vindictiveness in his mind, and this interview led finally to some distinct understanding, reassured by which the fugitives one by one came back and presented themselves in court. After this the matter took the usual course. A reference was ordered, a mass of evidence was taken, the case dragged its slow length along, bail was reduced, a multiplicity of orders were issued, the wrath of Barnard gradually subsided, and, at last, the battle of the judges died away in a faint rumble of evidence, affidavits, explanations, and orders, and then was heard of no more.

One further order, and one only, was made at about this time, to which subsequent events lent a deep consequence. The Erie party had been completely foiled in its efforts to get possession of the much-coveted books. Now and again they would obtain some clew which led them to suspect their presence somewhere, but when they were sought they were gone. Agents went out of the state hunting for them, parties were examined in the state concerning them; a strange ignorance apparently existed as to their whereabouts. They seemed ubiquitous; at one time in Albany, at another in Pittsfield, and then suddenly in Troy; but always in the undisturbed possession of some friend of Mr. Ramsey. The Erie party was, in their absence, wholly unable to estimate its own relative strength as compared with that of its opponents. It was known, however, that a portion of the forfeited stock had been reissued, and now stood in the names of Leonard, Groesbeck, and others. Leonard was a director, and in negotiating the sale for the company of certain of its second-mortgage bonds and stock had reserved to himself a portion of the stock as a species of brokerage commission. Mr. Leonard, however, was one of the directors in close sympathy and alliance with the Erie management, and, in regard to the stock reissued and standing in his name, for which in reality no consideration had been paid to the company, it seemed unnecessary to institute any proceedings. Not so as regarded that issued to Groesbeck and paid for by him. The reissue of this last stock was pronounced flagrantly illegal and void, and Judge Barnard was accordingly petitioned to appoint a receiver for it. The order was immediately granted, and Mr. William J. A. Fuller, an individual who had once been a clerk in Mr. Field's office, was named receiver, and directed to take immediate possession of the property. Armed with this order, and accompanied by a sheriff's officer, the new receiver proceeded at once to Mr. Groesbeck's office and demanded his scrip. Upon Mr. Groesbeck's demurring somewhat at being deprived of

his property in this summary way, Receiver Fuller proceeded to
explain to him the mysterious terrors of a writ of assistance,
which almost unknown process he darkly intimated he had somewhere at hand. Mr. Groesbeck was tolerably familiar from long
experience with all the usual judicial processes which are auxil-
iary to New York financial combinations, but writs of assistance
were implements strange to him. The element of the unknown
seems to have produced the desired effect, and Mr. Groesbeck
delivered to Mr. Fuller certificates for nine hundred shares of
stock. Under the same authority this gentleman further collected
other certificates representing sixteen hundred additional shares.
His duty was simply, at the most, to hold these shares pending
the result of litigation as to the legality of their issue; he subsequently, as will be seen, took what may be called very enlarged
views of these duties. Both parties had now gathered up their
strength for the election which was to take place on the seventh
of September.

It was provided in the by-laws of the company that the polls
should be opened at twelve o'clock on the day of election, and
should continue open for one hour; no transfers of shares were
to take place during the thirty days next preceding the election;
three inspectors were provided for, to be chosen each year by the
stockholders; it was their duty to conduct the election; they
were to be provided by the secretary with a list of stockholders
entitled to vote, and to them also upon that day the transfer book
was to be submitted. To this state of the law and the facts the
two parties prepared to conform their plans. It was in the first
place incumbent on the Ramsey party to restore the books to the
offices of the company. This was done very secretly on the night
preceding the election. A certain fictitious consequence was
sought to be attached to the way in which this was done, owing to
the fact that, when the messengers arrived with the books, instead of finding everything quiet and deserted as they had hoped,
they discovered a large crowd gathered in front of the offices
watching a conflagration across the river. The nature of their

business was thus sure to be discovered. This was just what they wished to avoid. After a moment's reflection it was decided to drive with the books to the rear of the building and put them in through a window. A basket and cord were found, the books were hauled up to the second story window by the secretary, and by him secured in the safe of the company. Had the books, under the circumstances, been carried in through the front door, an officer armed with a warrant, and accompanied, if need be, by picklocks and blacksmiths, would, in all probability, have been after them before morning. As it was, their return was a secret until it ceased to be of importance. Many unjustifiable features were assigned to the proceeding by the Fisk counsel; the one thoroughly unjustifiable one in their eyes was probably its success. It was never denied that the secretary of the company had, after the removal of the books and while they were secreted, made many entries in them. These, however, were all of transactions concluded prior to the day when the books were to be closed, and included all of those transactions, whether favoring Ramsey or Fisk. Though much was hinted in regard to these entries, during the searching investigation they were subjected to in the subsequent trial, no instance of abuse of trust was even specifically alleged, much less proved. Nor indeed is it probable in itself that any such improper entries were made, as those who made them must at the time have known that they were unnecessary as far as securing a majority of the stock was concerned.

The aspect of affairs was not, on the whole, propitious to the Erie party as the day of election drew near. Their opponents held the books, which forced them to act very much in the dark, and the inspectors of election were understood to incline to the Ramsey interest. That a majority of the stock also inclined to it was a matter of less moment. The situation was full of difficulty; but the men called upon to meet it were full of resource. Their preliminary step was naturally to lay in a sufficient supply of judicial orders. The regular inspectors must, in the first place, be got out of the way. It was ascertained that they were not

stockholders; the by-laws required that the inspectors should be
chosen from among the stockholders. The Fisk-Gould counsel at
once applied to Judge Clerke, a colleague of Judge Barnard's,
in the First District, and that magistrate granted, as a matter
of course, an *ex parte* order, restraining the inspectors from acting as such. Having obtained this process from Judge Clerke, and
filed it away for use at the proper moment, the counsel next applied to Judge Barnard. They quietly commenced a suit in the
name of the Albany & Susquehanna Railroad Co. against Messrs.
Ramsey, Pruyn, Phelps, and Smith, the president, receiver, secretary, and leading counsel of the company, to recover damages
for the abstraction of its books. On this complaint they obtained
from Judge Barnard, on the evening of the day preceding the
election, an order of arrest against the defendants, with bail
fixed at $25,000. This, be it remembered, was a judicial proceed-
ing in New York, and not in Constantinople. Thus panoplied in
orders, all parties repaired on the sixth to Albany. Mr. David
Dudley Field came from the pleasant shades of his summer retreat among the hills of Berkshire, and Mr. Shearman, his associate in the practice of the law, had, for the nonce, quitted his
offices in the Grand Opera House, in order himself to be at the
right hand of his chief in conducting those delicate proceedings
so skilfully and secretly planned in New York. The former gentleman was doubtless actuated only by a high sense of his professional duty to his clients, but Mr. Shearman may have been
braced for the approaching crisis by the fell purpose he had
recently avowed of pursuing even for forty years the miscreants
who had failed properly to respect the orders of the distinguished magistrate with whom his own relations were such
models of propriety. Having arrived in Albany, the last-named
gentleman repaired at once to the capitol, where he carefully
informed himself as to the details of the election. This done, a
general conference was held at the Delavan House, and the plan
of operations was matured. The first object was to secure the
organization of the meeting; that once done, arrangements of a

satisfactory nature had been made to hold it. The trap was to be
sprung just before the hour appointed for the election, when the
regular inspectors were to be enjoined by the service upon them
of Judge Clerke's *ex parte* order. The whole regular machinery
being thus dislocated, a preliminary organization was to be effected, three new and thoroughly sound inspectors were to be
chosen, which would insure the control of the election and the
subsequent possession of the Susquehanna Railway. Every detail
was arranged, every person who was to play a part was designated and carefully taught his rôle. Such was the extreme caution used that Mr. Shearman himself wrote out the appropriate
resolutions, and indorsed upon them the order in which, and the
very second at which, they were to be offered; while Mr. David
Dudley Field personally handed certain of them to the leading
performers, with further verbal instruction. Early the next
morning there took place one of the most remarkable comparisons of watches on record. A special messenger visited the Dudley Observatory, and obtained the exact time, which was by him
communicated to every active performer in the approaching
farce; or, rather, to all except the vulgar majority, to whom time
was of no consequence, they being hired by the day, and constituting the fierce democracy of the occasion. These gentlemen
arrived by the morning train from New York; they were a very
singular party, such as is more frequently seen in the neighborhood of the riotous election precincts of New York City than in
the offices of respectable corporations. A breakfast was negotiated
for them by an employee of the Fall River line of steamers,
which constituted ''Admiral'' Fisk's naval command, at the
saloon in the station; and there they stood and fed at the counter,
as rough a set of patriots as ever stuffed a ballot or hit from the
shoulder. Some of them had coats, and some had not; their
clothes were in various stages of dilapidation, as also were their
countenances; open shirts disclosed muscular breasts, and rolled-
up trousers stockingless feet; one man saved himself the trouble
of rolling up both legs of his trousers by having only one; they

emphatically belonged to that class technically known as "roughs," a class subsequently defined by a witness as "men with scarred faces and noses, and black eyes." Under the circumstances it was little to be wondered at, that, while they indulged in a "square meal," the keeper of the saloon gave directions to have his silver counted. Pending the feeding of the democracy, their proxies were in course of preparation; at last all was ready, and between eleven and twelve o'clock they were marched up fifty strong to the offices of the company.

Everywhere things proceeded exactly according to plan. On his way in a carriage to the corporation offices, Mr. Shearman happened to see the injunction of Judge Clerke served on two of the three inspectors as they were on their way to the meeting. This settled two points; the injunction was a surprise; and the regular inspectors were disposed of. Judge Barnard's more important order was meanwhile sent to the sheriff, and the messenger was specially instructed by Mr. Shearman himself to hand it to him with this Roman injunction, "Sheriff, do your duty!" This instruction was given at nine o'clock, but, curiously enough, the official had to consult his lawyer about the service of the process, and this lawyer happened to be one of Mr. Fisk's numerous legal advisers; with that gentleman he remained in counsel until half past eleven o'clock, when at last he was advised to make his arrests at once. By this time all the parties were collected at the offices of the company. It might fairly be called a mixed society. Mr. Van Valkenburg had tendered to the Governor's receivers a guard of men from the shops of the road, but these had been refused, and a large force of Albany police were on duty in the building. Some thirty of the employees of the company were on hand against an emergency, but under positive orders not to enter the offices until sent for. Upstairs was a large array of stockholders, directors, real and contingent, a few receivers, and a score or two of counsel. Then came the New York importation of ruffians, who were divided into squads under the command of divers officials of the Fall River boats, the

Erie Railway and the Grand Opera House; thus marshaled, and each man proxy in hand, they were marched into the room and formed in line at one end of it. Besides these there was present a choice collection of Albanians of somewhat similar character, either neutrals or inclined to Mr. Ramsey. How they got there did not appear, but if the instructions to the police to allow no one but holders of certificates of stock to pass upstairs were enforced that day, these certificates were certainly held by a great many strange characters. The Erie party, prominent among whom were Messrs. David Dudley Field, Thomas G. Shearman, and James Fisk, Jr., took possession of the directors' room, which their assortment of "New York stockholders" well-nigh filled; in the adjoining room were Messrs. Ramsey, Pruyn, and their friends and advisers.

Exactly at fifteen minutes before twelve o'clock, by observatory time, one Colonel North, to whom that rôle in the Erie parts had been assigned, moved the organization of the meeting. No opposition was encountered, and the gentleman cast for the part of chairman was duly installed. The resolve indorsed "No. 1, Immediate," was then recited by Colonel North, Mr. Shearman standing at his side watch in hand, and the old inspectors were voted out of office and the new ones in. The officers thus elected at once retired to the treasurer's room, where the poll was to be held, whither they were immediately followed by Mr. Shearman, still watch in hand; having satisfied himself that all was in readiness there, this master of ceremonies immediately returned to the side of Colonel North and resumed his comparison of time-pieces. At last he said: "It is now one minute of twelve; keep your watch open and be sure that you offer these resolutions at a little after twelve, and not before; and, in order to make sure, wait a few seconds after twelve, but not more than fifteen seconds." With this parting injunction he left the Colonel to his own devices, and "at thirty seconds of twelve" returned to the inspectors' room, just in time to find an injunction served on those officials. It was issued on the complaint of David Groesbeck, and enjoined an election unless the stock held by him was first voted on. Now, at last, was developed the entire significance of the *ex parte* order under which Mr. William J. A. Fuller was made receiver of this stock. There were twenty-five hundred shares of it; Mr Groesbeck had paid for several hundred of them; he was at that very moment in the next room; he was on every ground bitterly opposed to the Erie direction, and to the parody of an election then in process; Mr. William J. A. Fuller was the receiver of the stock, and it was to this receiver, now conveniently standing at his elbow, that Mr. Shearman turned and remarked: "An injunction has been served restraining this election from going on, unless the votes on the twenty-four hundred shares which you hold are first received, and you had better vote." Thus appealed to, Mr. Fuller modestly replied that he had not intended to vote at this election, but, having been appointed receiver, he deemed it his duty to do all in his power to preserve the property, and concluded his statement by giving as a reason for his vote that the ticket which he offered was composed of men of the highest character and ability, whose election would best secure the rights of all parties to the litigation. At the close of these remarks he actually voted, and the curious spectacle was exhibited of a court of equity taking a man's stock away from him on the ground that it was illegally issued and could not be voted on at all, and then proceeding to vote on it itself, before the man's face and against his wishes. Viewed calmly, and after the event, such a proceeding strikes one chiefly as an extremely droll joke. The climax of the humorous, however, was not attained until some months later, when Mr. Fuller gravely stated in court that, as a receiver, he considered it his duty to vote on stock without consulting the wishes of its ostensible owner, and that for his services as receiver in this case he had as yet received no remuneration, but expected the regular fees, amounting to $15,000. After Mr. Fuller had thus relieved Mr. Groesbeck of the trouble of voting, and after the meeting in the next room had gone through a nominal reorganization to meet the letter of the law, the polls were declared open. The inspectors were withal curiously careless, or too intent on the passage of time to think of aught else; they certainly neglected to be qualified by taking oath as to the performance of their duties, which was specially prescribed in the by-laws; neither did they use any ballot box, other than the straw hat of one of their number. In this, however, the ballots were deposited, and the election went briskly on for some fifteen minutes, when, under the names of John Doe, Richard Roe, and James Jackson, the inspectors were again enjoined, this time from any further proceedings. Most of their tickets had, however, already been voted, and this injunction was violated by the reception of others, subsequently offered, only in a moderate degree.

Meanwhile events did not stand still in the little library adjoining the directors' room, where Mr. Ramsey and his friends were collected. The sheriff of Albany, after leaving the office of his legal adviser, proceeded to "do his duty." As Mr. Ramsey was intently listening in the president's office to Colonel North, who was moving the organization in the next room, someone suddenly touched his arm, and he became conscious of the sheriff at his side. Here was a thunderbolt. At the very instant when his presence was most necessary, when all depended on the full possession of his liberty and his faculties, he found himself, the secretary of the company and its legal adviser, under arrest. The thing could not have been better timed. To understand the full possible effect of this move, it is necessary to bear in mind a remark made by Mr. Shearman in his subsequent testimony, though in another connection: "I didn't want to lose a second's time, because I knew the value of time in this case, and I knew that the whole question would have to depend upon the question of which meeting was organized first." The officials of the road were therefore arrested, by mere accident, as it was claimed, just when they should have been organizing their meeting. Nor did the possible benefit to be derived from this measure stop here. The election was limited to one hour, and the sheriff was instructed "to do his duty." He might have effected his arrest at ten o'clock; but had he done so, the parties would have been bailed at once, and the arrest might as well not have been made. Having been made at exactly the right moment, the sheriff might now further construe it to be his duty to remove the prisoners to his office, there to arrange their bail. The votes on which Mr. Ramsey relied were, of course, held by him in the usual form of proxies; they were, in fact, on this day so cast by him. Could he, therefore, be held in durance, away from the offices, by any fictitious delays and objections, for one short hour, the election would be over and irrevocably decided against him. The construction the sheriff should give to "his duty" in the premises was very vital, and fully warranted his lengthy interview with that gentleman who was the common adviser of himself and the Erie Railway Company. The whole proceeding certainly spoke volumes for the ingenuity and resource of those who engineered it. In its style it could not have been improved.

Mr. Ramsey was thus a prisoner. He proposed at first to leave the room to consult his friends, but was requested by the sheriff to remain in it, and here he was soon visited by Mr. David Dudley Field, of counsel for the Erie Railway Company, who satisfied himself that the sheriff was doing "his duty" by taking a comprehensive glance at the situation. Finding this greatly to his mind, he then proceeded, with a smile indicative of profound satisfaction and with his thumbs in the armholes of his waistcoat, to inquire of Mr. Ramsey as to the present condition of his health. Mr. Ramsey has the reputation of being a remarkably cool and imperturbable man, so that now, when his counsel, Mr. Smith, entered the room in a state of intense excitement and indignation, and also under arrest, he received simply a direction to go back and attend to the election, while Mr. Ramsey himself effected the bail arrangements. It is not clear whether the sheriff lacked nerve to construe his duty as he might have done, or whether the delay already occasioned was considered sufficient; at any rate, though he certainly arrested his prisoners at exactly

the proper moment, he did not remove them from the building.
He was, indeed, even provided with blank bail bonds, which
were produced and filled, though not until objection had been
made to the security of one or two gentlemen notoriously worth
millions; and this done the prisoners were released. All this had
occupied half an hour; on the theory of Mr. Shearman it was
now too late, the moment had passed; the *coup* had been completely successful. Mr. Smith had, indeed, gone back and organized a stockholders' meeting in the hall of the building; but not
until ten minutes after twelve, and when the polls of the other
organization had been long open. The Erie party were, in their
own belief, in possession of the Albany & Susquehanna Railroad
beyond a peradventure.

Before going on with the narrative, a few words may here be
not out of place concerning the much-discussed question of the
limits, if there be any, of the duty which counsel owe to their
clients. The celebrated dictum of Lord Brougham in this regard
is sufficiently general in its terms: "An advocate, by the sacred
duty which he owes his client, knows, in the discharge of that
office, but one person in the world, THAT CLIENT AND NONE OTHER.
To save that client by all expedient means, to protect that client
at all hazards and costs to all others, and among others to himself, is the highest and most unquestioned of his duties; and he
must not regard the alarm, the suffering, the torment, the destruction which he may bring on any other. Nay, separating
even the duties of a patriot from those of an advocate, and casting them, if need be, to the wind, he must go on reckless of the
consequences, if his fate it should unhappily be to involve his
country in confusion for his client's sake!"

Certainly no counsel could have acted more fully up to both
the letter and spirit of this famous rule than did Messrs. David
Dudley Field and Thomas G. Shearman, of counsel for the Erie
Railway Company, on this notable occasion. They even "cast to
the wind" the single faint limitation conveyed by Lord Brougham in the words "to *save*" and "to *protect*" by all "expedient

means"; and, in the intense fervor of their devotion to their clients, had recourse in aggressive proceedings to processes of law which were subsequently judicially characterized as procured "in aid of fraudulent purposes." Attending one's clients to corporation meetings, at the head of a band of "rude, rough, and dangerous persons" and there acting as the master of ceremonies, through the parody of an election, was a case which undoubtedly Brougham would have included in his definition, had it occurred to him; but it probably escaped his notice, from the fact that, since the fall of the Roman Republic, such proceedings have not been usual. The ingenious device, also, of arresting one's opposing counsel and holding him to $25,000 bail, at the moment when his professional services are likely to become peculiarly necessary, is a feature in legal amenities with which the English barrister could not have been expected to be familiar. A high authority has now, however, established these as part of the duties of the American advocate. Instances of similar devotion will, therefore, unless the now obsolete practice of disbarring should chance to be revived, probably hereafter become more common than they hitherto have been. The use of unusual processes of court, unpleasantly suggestive of *lettres de cachet*, quietly procured and suddenly brought in play, would seem also to have met of late with an undeserved odium. Whether these will again arrive at the great efficiency as an element in litigation which they once attained in France will, perhaps, depend upon the degree of fidelity with which sheriffs do their duty. For the shortcomings of such officials, advocates naturally cannot be held accountable, even by the most exacting of clients. The client, moreover, in whose defense Brougham was prepared, if need be, "to involve his country in confusion" was the Queen of England; which, indeed, cannot but cause the deeper sense of a professional devotion, no less reckless, exerted in furtherance of the schemes of Mr. James Fisk, Jr.*

---

* It ought, perhaps, to be stated in this connection, that the opinion commonly entertained of the transactions with which the names of Fisk and Gould are associated was not apparently shared by their counsel. These

To return from this abstract digression to the narrative, little remains to be said of the election after the release of Mr. Ramsey was effected. While bail was being procured, and the necessary bonds executed, a second meeting had been organized by Mr. Smith in the hall before the offices, and this meeting had proceeded to choose inspectors, who were duly sworn and received from the secretary the prescribed list of stockholders. They then opened their polls in the same room and at the same desk at which the opposition inspectors were still sitting. Mr. Shearman immediately stepped in front of them and began, on various grounds, to challenge every vote. Of course his challenge was dis-

gentlemen, whose close acquaintance with the facts in the case must certainly have qualified them to form an intelligent judgment, have made no concealment of what that extra professional judgment was. Upon this point Mr. Shearman expressed himself very explicitly before a legislative committee at Albany on the thirty-first of March, 1870, six months subsequent to the Susquehanna proceedings. He then paid the following high tribute to himself and to Messrs. Field, Fisk, and Gould:—

"If I were to speak from my own personal judgment of the management of the Erie road, I should say that I have never been able to find where these fraudulent acts charged were committed. I have never been able to find where the villainy comes in. I have been looking for it very anxiously. I have thought that the newspapers were edited by men so much wiser than myself that they must know all about it, and I confess that when I entered upon the service of the company, amid a perfect clamor on the part of the newspapers, I thought they were edited by such wise men that there must be something wrong, and I entered upon my duties with fear and trembling, but I found no occasion for fear and trembling."

Mr. Littlejohn. You are speaking as a lawyer now?

Mr. Shearman. No, sir,—as a man; and now as a lawyer I say that I think it is no slight tribute to the character of the gentlemen who are in the management of the Erie Company, that, knowing as they did how particular I was in regard to the management of its officers, how careful I was that no injustice should be done to the company, and how strongly determined I was that its interests should not suffer, they confided their affairs in my hands. And they have confided also in a gentleman of superior age and of very high character, a gentleman with a Quixotic sense of honor, a gentleman who has never done a dishonorable action, a gentleman whom the other side would have been glad to engage for themselves if they could have done so,—Mr. David Dudley Field. Mr. Field has been chosen by the Erie Railway Company as their adviser, and, trained with Mr. Field, I have learned something of his high sense of professional honor, etc.

regarded, but the process was kept up by himself or others, until, toward one o'clock, both polls were declared closed. Neither party attempted to vote at the polls of the other, nor was there any disorder or disturbance. The two boards then canvassed their votes; the Erie board declared that the ticket voted for at their polls had received 13,400 votes, and was elected. Shortly afterward the Ramsey board declared that the ticket voted for at their poll had received 10,742 votes, and was elected. The two boards of directors thus chosen then met and organized, the one by the choice of Colonel Church as president, and the other by the reëlection of Mr. Ramsey; and having then sufficiently regarded each other from the opposite sides of the directors' room, in due time they adjourned.

The election was over, and apparently nothing was decided by it. Each of the boards elected claimed to be the regular and only lawful one, and neither of them in any way recognized the other. Fortunately the agents of Governor Hoffman were still in actual possession. The Erie party had, indeed, endeavored to take advantage of this fact, by including in their list of directors both Messrs. McQuade and Banks, who were then operating the road under the authority of the Governor. This move wholly failed. Both of these gentlemen instantly and peremptorily withdrew from the board when notified of their election. Governor Hoffman was the one person now responsible, and he very wisely called upon the courts to decide who was legally entitled to the possession of the road. At his direction the Attorney-General, immediately after the election, began a new suit, in which all parties litigant were included, and a general decision on the merits was prayed for. This was the only way to cut the knot. The previous litigation was in a state of hopeless chaos. Twenty-two suits had been begun, a score of injunctions had been issued, numberless orders had been made, and both parties now stood ready to continue the same style of warfare, just as long as any judge could be found who disregarded the duties of his position on the one side, or who did not lack nerve on the other.

The action brought by the Attorney-General came on for trial before Justice E. Darwin Smith, at Rochester, on the twenty-ninth of November succeeding the election. The intervening time had been wasted by neither party. Messrs. Fisk and Gould had utilized it in those manipulations of the gold market, which had resulted in the celebrated explosion of September 24, long to be famous as the "black Friday" in Wall Street annals. Mr. Ramsey, meanwhile, had confined his attention to the quarrel already existing, and had carried the war vigorously into Africa, assailing the Erie management in its own stronghold through the suit of *Ramsey* vs. *Erie et als.* Writs, orders, injunctions, receiverships, and conflicts of jurisdiction had become matters of such daily occurrence as hardly to excite a passing notice, and the complications which had grown up around the Erie Ring were only exceeded by the scandal they caused. Hitherto, strong in the protection of the more reckless of the city judges, Messrs. Gould and Fisk had suffered no material defeat; they had, indeed, in so far as the law was concerned, carried all before them; for to them the law was simply a process for annoying others, and obstructing all that was calculated to annoy them. Foiled in their attempt to get control of the Susquehanna road by force, they did, indeed, now try to get it by negotiation; they proposed a compromise of all existing disputes on the basis of a lease of this road by the Erie for a term of ninety-nine years, at a rent equal to 7 per cent on its bonds and stock outstanding, with a 30 per cent stock dividend flung in as a bonus. The Susquehanna people listened to the proposal, but it finally appeared that no further guaranty than the word of the Erie managers was contemplated. The Altlantic & Great Western Railroad had already illustrated the value of that. Like Falstaff's tailor, the Susquehanna people "liked not the security"; and the other party, like the fat old knight himself, "had as lief they would put ratsbane in my mouth as offer to stop it with security." The negotiation fell wholly through, and nothing remained but the arbitrament of a country justice of the Supreme Court.

At the end of November the case was in order for trial. The Executive, the Attorney-General, the court, and the Ramsey counsel were ready and in earnest. The usual motions for delay from the other side were received with little favor. It was shown that another suit, in which Messrs. Fisk and Gould and their leading counsel were engaged, was then on trial before Judge Barnard. It was of no avail; the parties were ordered to proceed, and the case before Judge Barnard had to be postponed. The trial lasted ten days, and a vast amount of evidence was put in. Mr. Fisk and Mr. Gould were conspicuous by their absence from the witness stand, but their counsel were put upon it, and Messrs. Harris and Shearman each told his own story. Some features of the evidence and incidents of the trial were far from creditable. Among these may especially be mentioned an attempt to create an impression that Mr. Ramsey had once been under an indictment for forgery. So grave a charge seemed most unlikely to be made without some shadow of reason. In this case, however, it was wantonly advanced, and even the machinery through which it was manufactured was subsequently exposed. Naturally this proceeding and others reacted violently on those who had sought to derive advantage from them. Public feeling in the courtroom and in the city of Rochester grew very strong as the case proceeded, showing itself in ways not to be mistaken. As the case was on the equity side of the court, there was no intervention of a jury, no chance of an inability to agree on a verdict. After the evidence was all in, and the case had been elaborately argued by Mr. David Dudley Field for the Erie party, and by Mr. Henry Smith for the Susquehanna party, Judge Smith took the papers, but reserved his decision. It was January before this was made public.

There are cases where a judge upon the bench is called upon to vindicate in no doubtful way the purity as well as the majesty of the law; cases in which the parties before the court should be made to feel that they are not equal, that fraud is fraud even in a court of law,—that caviling and technicalities and special pleading cannot blind the clear eye of equity. It is possible that even a judicial tone may be overdone or be out of place. There are occasions when the scales of justice become almost an incumbrance, and both hands clutch at the sword alone. Whether the magistrate upon whom the decision of this cause devolved was right in holding this to be such an occasion is not now to be discussed; it is enough to say that his decision sustained at every point the Ramsey board, and crushed in succession all the schemes of the Erie Ring. The opinion was most noticeable in that it approached the inquiry in a large spirit. Its conclusion was not made to turn on the question of a second of time, or a rigid adherence to the letter of the law, or any other technicality of the pettifogger; it swept all these aside and spoke firmly and clearly to the question of fraud and fraudulent conspiracy. All the elaborate comparison of watches, and noting of fractional parts of a minute, which marked the organization of the Erie meeting were treated with contempt, but the meeting itself was pronounced to be organized in pursuance of a previous conspiracy, and the election held by it was "irregular, fraudulent, and void." The scandals of the law—the strange processes, injunctions, orders, and conflicts of jurisdiction—were disposed of with the same grasp, whenever they came in the path of the decision. The appointment of Fuller as receiver was declared to have been made in a "suit instituted for a fraudulent purpose," and it was pronounced in such "clear conflict with the law and settled practice of the court" as to be explicable only on a supposition that the order was "granted incautiously, and upon some mistaken oral representation or statement of the facts of the case." The order removing the regular inspectors of election was "improvidently granted" and was "entirely void"; and the keeping it back by counsel, and serving it only at the moment of election, was "an obvious and designed surprise on the great body of stockholders." The suit under which the Barnard order of arrest was issued against Ramsey and Phelps was instituted without right, the order of arrest was unauthorized, the order to hold to bail "most extraordinary and exorbitant," and was procured "in aid of fraudulent purposes." The injunction forbidding Ramsey to act as president of the company was "entirely void." The three thousand shares of forfeited stock reissued to Mr. Groesbeck were pronounced "valid stock," and numerous precedents were cited in which the principle had been sustained. Even the subscription for the nine thousand five hundred new shares of stock by Ramsey and his friends, on which they had not even attempted to vote at the election, was declared, in point of law, regular, valid, and binding. Upon the facts of the case the decision was equally outspoken; it was fraud and conspiracy everywhere. "The importation and crowding into a small room" of a large number of "rude, rough, and dangerous persons," and furnishing them with proxies that they might participate in the proceedings of the meeting, "was a gross perversion and abuse of the right to vote by proxy and a clear infringement of the rights of stockholders, tending, if such proceedings are countenanced by the courts, to convert corporation meetings into places of disorder, lawlessness, and riot." Finally, costs were decreed to the Ramsey Board of Directors, and a reference was made to Samuel L. Selden, late a judge of the Court of Appeals, to ascertain and report a proper extra allowance in the case, and to which of the defendants it was to be paid.

The legal scandals of the case were not yet quite exhausted. No sooner was this decision announced and telegraphed to New York, than the Erie counsel at once had recourse to the judges of that city. As a matter of course, an *ex parte* order was instantly granted, staying the entry of judgment. It reached Rochester a few hours too late; the judgment was entered. The next day a new order was obtained, staying all proceedings under the judgment; and this was served on Messrs. Banks and McQuade, who were still in possession of the road. Recourse was had to Judge Peckham, who quietly declared the stay of no effect, and granted an order putting the Ramsey board in possession. Then at last the keys were delivered to them. The Erie counsel were not yet satisfied. A motion was made to vacate the judgment. This was supported by affidavits of counsel of the most unusual nature. Imputations of unfairness, irregularity, bias, and conduct otherwise wholly unbecoming a magistrate, were advanced against Judge Smith. The four leading lawyers of the defeated party then united in a certificate, which concluded with these singular words: "We have examined the opinion of Mr. Justice Smith in this cause, and, in our judgment, it is in every material part erroneous, either in fact or in law." It may be necessary to mention here that this was a certificate of counsel on the losing side of a decided case, applying to one judge of the Supreme Court of New York, to vacate a judgment just entered by another judge of the same court. It ought to be unnecessary to add that the assumptions on which the motion was based were pronounced "simply monstrous"; and the affidavits were ordered to be stricken from the record as "irrelevant and impertinent." Nothing now remained to the Erie faction but the slow process of appeal, with their opponents in actual possession.

The struggle was over. Long before any action could be taken on the decision of Judge Smith, at the general term of the court, the Albany & Susquehanna Railroad was beyond the reach of Fisk or Gould or the Erie Railway. Early in February, 1870, the Ramsey direction leased the whole property in perpetuity, and on very favorable terms, to the Hudson & Delaware Canal Company. This arrangement transferred the struggle from the comparatively weak shoulders of the railroad itself to those of one of the most powerful and wealthy corporations in the country. With it the Erie managers could not afford to quarrel, so they were fain to profess themselves satisfied with the result, and to desist from the contest.

Meanwhile the Hon. Samuel L. Selden was busy over his reference; and the case was well-nigh forgotten before he made his report. When it was made, it was calculated to revive a very fresh recollection of the litigation in the minds of Mr. Fisk's Board of Directors. This was composed of thirteen individuals, of whom Messrs. Fisk and Gould were two. The report of Mr. Selden was long and very minutely drawn; it was a document likely to be accepted by the court, and not easily overthrown on appeal. "In view of the whole history of this extraordinary case," and in consideration of the assumption by the Albany & Susquehanna Railroad Company of the entire expenses of the litigation, the sum of $92,000 was fixed upon as a just and proper extra allowance to be paid by the persons constituting the Fisk Board of Directors to those persons constituting the Ramsey board.*

* An appeal was taken by the Fisk Board of Directors from the decision of Judge Smith, referred to in the text, and reported in 7 *Abbot's Pr. Rep. N. S.*, p. 265. The decision of the General Term was not announced until May, 1871. It turned wholly upon technical points, and in no respect entered into the merits of the controversy; upon these the findings of the court below were apparently accepted as conclusive. The decision of Judge Smith was affirmed in so far as it declared the election of the Fisk board fraudulent and void, and that of the Ramsey board valid, on the ground that this question was properly before the court, and it was competent to pass upon it. Judge Smith had also decreed that the proceedings in all the suits on either side between the parties defendant should be stayed and discontinued. This relief, it was held, upon technical grounds, the court below was not competent to grant, and upon this point the decision was reversed. It was also reversed upon the question of costs, upon the ground that in an action brought by the People against two sets of defendants the court had no power to grant costs to one set against the other.

The Ramsey party, was, therefore, sustained in the possession of the property; but the Fisk party escaped the payment of costs under the Selden reference. As far as the scandals in litigation were concerned, which gave so great a notoriety to this case between the preparation and publication of this paper, the court at General Term confined itself to a simple closing reference to them. Profound regret was expressed at the occurrences which had preceded the action then before the court, which in itself, however, it was declared had been marked by no unbecoming conduct on the part of counsel.

[The sequence of decisions in *People* v. *The Albany and Susquehanna Railroad Company* is shown by the following citations to the law reports:—

7 *Abb. Pr. N. S.*, 265 (Special Term, Supreme Court, December, 1869).

8 *Abb. Pr. N. S.*, 122 (Special Term, Supreme Court, January, 1870).

2 *Lans.*, 459 (General Term, Supreme Court, June, 1870).

5 *Lans.*, 25 (General Term, Supreme Court, May, 1871).

57 *N. Y.*, 161 (Commissioners of Appeal, January Term, 1874).

In the last of these decisions, Commissioner Johnson opened the door for retrial of the issues relating to the title of the several claimants to the office of director; but there is no record of such a retrial, and, therefore, Adams' statement in the above footnote remains substantially correct.]

IV

THE LAWYER AND HIS CLIENTS*

BY

ALBERT STICKNEY

BOSWELL gives this account of a conversation with Doctor Johnson :—

I asked him whether, as a moralist, he did not think that the practice of the law in some degree hurt the nice feeling of honesty.

Johnson. Why, no, sir, if you act properly. You are not to deceive your clients with false representations of your opinion; you are not to tell lies to a judge.

Boswell. But what do you think of supporting a cause which you know to be bad?

Johnson. Sir, you do not know it to be good or bad till the judge determines it. I have said that you are to state facts fairly; so that your thinking, or what you call knowing, a cause to be bad must be from reasoning, must be from your supposing your arguments to be weak and inconclusive. But, sir, that is not enough. An argument which does not convince yourself may convince the judge to whom you urge it; and if it does convince him, why then, sir, you are wrong and he is right. It is his business to judge; and you are not to be confident in your own opinion that a cause is bad, but to say all you can for your client, and then hear the judge's opinion.

Boswell. But, sir, does not affecting a warmth when you have no warmth, and appearing to be clearly of one opinion when you are in reality of another opinion,—does not such dissimulation impair one's honesty? Is there not some danger that a lawyer may put on the same mask in common life, in the intercourse with his friends?

Johnson. Why, no, sir. Everybody knows you are paid for affecting warmth for your client; and it is therefore properly no dissimulation; the moment you come from the bar you resume your usual behavior.

* *North American Review*, CXII (April, 1871), 392–421.

And it is continually said: "One side of a case is right and the other side is wrong. Counsel, then, on one side or the other in a cause, is always arguing against the right and in favor of the wrong."

The question of the duties of counsel has recently had a special interest given it by the correspondence between Mr. David Dudley Field and Mr. Samuel Bowles. No one, at this day, will claim for counsel the latitude allowed them by Doctor Johnson, in the extract just given. But what is all this talk of affecting warmth when you do not feel it, of supporting the wrong side of a cause, of arguing against your belief, of the insincerity or dishonesty of the advocate? Where is the blame to be placed of prosecuting bad causes? What do counsel commonly do? What can counsel rightly do? And what have counsel, in fact, of late years been doing?

It is yet to be learned how a lawyer can argue a cause without a client, how he can argue a point of fact without having witnesses, how he can argue a point of law without citing cases. Perhaps, even if counsel go into court with a bad cause, there is as much guilt on the client's shoulders, who brought the cause to the counsel, as on the counsel's shoulders, who took the cause from the client. Moreover, it is one of the commonest things in the world for judges to differ in their views of the law of the same case, for jurymen to differ in their views of the facts of the same case, for clients to differ in their views of the justice of the same case, and for witnesses to differ in their stories of the same case, all being equally honest. If, then, judges, jurymen, clients, and witnesses can honestly err, why are the counsel deprived of the same very reasonable privilege? For, be it remembered, a counsel goes to trial, hearing one side of his case from one client, and judges and jury are often in doubt and utterly unable to agree, after hearing from both clients both sides. It may, then, be possible for counsel to be on what is finally adjudged to be the wrong side of a cause, and still have been honest in his advocacy of it.

And what does the counsel, in conducting the trial of an

ordinary cause in a court really do? For, of course, the abnormal knaves of the profession, as in any general discussion, are here to be thrown out of consideration. In the case of *Ryves* v. *The Attorney-General,* which attracted so much notice a few years since, where Mrs. Ryves attempted to establish her claim to royal lineage, this occurrence is reported:—

Dr. Smith then proceeded to address the jury for the petitioner, and was beginning to say that "on his honor he believed his client's case to be well founded," when the Lord Chief Justice interfered, and peremptorily said he "could not allow the learned counsel to pledge his honor on his own belief. To do so were a violation of the rules of the profession, and a dishonor to counsel." Dr. Smith apologized.

And this same thing would be done in any rightly ordered court. It is understood, that counsel, in arguing cases, do not make statements of matters of fact on their own authority. They comment on what witnesses have sworn to. They are not allowed to do more than that. And as to arguments on points of law, generally, if counsel have no points of law in their cause that deserve a hearing, they do not get a hearing. And few intelligent counsel will take up the time of a heedless judge by talking nonsense. Moreover, there remains, behind all these points, the one fact, that counsel who often argue losing causes very soon argue no causes at all.

And as to the question what counsel can rightly do, it is plain in the beginning that, on many points, the duties of counsel and client present precisely the same questions.

It is wrong for a client to take away another man's property, or keep him out of his rights. It is wrong for counsel to help his client do either of these things by the use or abuse of the process of the court. And, as to the mere argument of causes in court, if a counsel never knowingly misstate facts or law, he can have a very clear conscience.

There remains one other point. If it be considered settled what a counsel has a right to do for his clients, there still remains the point in some minds to be decided, what clients counsel has a right to have. And, on this point, the choice of the lawyer must be absolutely unlimited, and for his choice he can be blamed by no one. A lawyer has the right to take any clients he chooses. Sinners do have rights and must have justice. They cannot have justice without counsel. In a criminal proceeding no lawyer has a right to see a prisoner condemned contrary to the law and the evidence, for lack of counsel to protect him. In a civil cause every lawyer does, as a matter of fact, and does rightly, consult his own wishes as to accepting or rejecting particular cases or particular clients. The want of a sufficiently large retainer is a ground which will appeal at once to the reason of any professional man, and very rightly. Men of reputation cannot be asked to give the power they have gained after long years of toil and study without being paid for it. Any lawyer is at perfect liberty to take any client that he chooses, with blame from no one. But what he may do for his client, after he takes him, is not matter to be unquestioned by others.

This brings us to the correspondence between Mr. David Dudley Field and Mr. Bowles. In December, 1870, in the New York correspondence of the *Springfield Republican* appeared some very severe remarks in relation to Mr. Field's professional conduct and reputation. Mr. Field wrote to Mr. Bowles, complaining of the publication, and asking a disavowal of the offensive matter. Thereupon ensued a long correspondence. It is here possible only to give a very brief statement of the points made or attempted to be made on either side.

Mr. Bowles makes two charges against Mr. Field: first, that Mr. Field has, in Mr. Fisk and Mr. Gould, clients notoriously bad men, who have robbed and are now robbing other men of their property; and second, that Mr. Field, as their counsel, has aided them in so doing. This is the substance.

To this Mr. Field replies that he is not responsible to anyone for his choice of clients, and that, assuming his clients to be bad men, it is not only his, Mr. Field's, right, but his bounden duty,

to defend them in their rights, and that he never has done anything but defend them in their rights. He says:—

To give this as a reason for not defending them, is equivalent to
saying that the saints must have a monopoly of lawsuits. If a saint
sues a sinner, the sinner shall not be defended. If it should happen that
a saint wrongs a sinner, the sinner shall not sue the saint. . . . In
this state of things I know no better general rule than this: that the
lawyer, being intrusted by government with the exclusive function of
representing litigants before the courts, *is bound* to represent any
person who has any rights to be asserted or defended. If a person
has no rights, the lawyer is not bound to assist. If he has any rights,
the lawyer is bound to see them respected, if he can. . . . I do not
assent to the theory of Brougham, that the lawyer should know nobody
but his client. I insist that he should defend his client *per fas* and not
per nefas. By this rule I am willing to be judged.

. . . I am quite willing to leave to time the formation of a just
public opinion. When that time comes, it will be known that, whatever
may be the faults of the clients, their counsel, or that one of them for
whom I speak with knowledge, has been governed by nothing but a
sense of duty. . . . You have ventured to arraign my professional
conduct. I repel your charge, and challenge you to specify an instance.
You fail to specify any, but say public opinion is against me. . . .
That will not do; you must go further or submit to be branded as a
libeller. . . . I have never been consulted beforehand about the management of the Erie Railway, or the issue of any of its stock or bonds,
or the payment of any dividend to any stockholder or class of stockholders, or about what is known as the Erie classification bill, or about
the gold operations of 1869, or any of the private transactions of
Messrs. Gould and Fisk, or either of them, or about any transaction
whatever of this company or these gentlemen, to which, so far as I
now recollect, any exception has been taken.

And, finally, Mr. Bowles goes so far as to admit:—

I am only impressed with the fact that you believe yourself right,
and that you are acting sincerely, if not intelligently. . . .

You have sinned against no statute; I will not undertake to say, even,
that you have violated any prescript of the code professional. Within
those lines you are wiser than I, and I shall not follow you. . . .

Thus I dismiss the most of your argument as purely technical, and
not pertinent to my view of the subject.

It has been here attempted to give with fairness, in the words of the disputants themselves, the main points of this correspondence. And it must, it would seem, be admitted that Mr. Bowles does not make a very strong case. Mr. Field is a very cunning master of fence. Mr. Bowles had not the knowledge necessary for him on these points to cope with his opponent; and, as far as this controversy with Mr. Bowles is concerned, Mr. Field is undoubtedly right. Neither Mr. Bowles nor anyone else has the slightest right to question Mr. Field's choice of clients. Nor has Mr. Bowles any right to publish, as he did, this statement about Mr. Field, that "his connection with Fisk and Gould secures him the favor of Barnard and the other ring judges, though it has destroyed his reputation as a high-toned lawyer with the public," unless he can, when called on, come forward with the facts to prove his statements.

This dispute has drawn to itself great attention, and rightly. Mr. Field has as nearly a cosmopolitan reputation as any member of the bar in this country. He is a man of great acuteness of mind, a very thoroughly read lawyer, has a muscular strong grasp of legal principles, and he well deserves the highest opinions that have ever been held of his ability. Moreover, he was educated in a day when the purity of the bench in New York was never for an instant questioned, when the most honorable traditions of the profession were taught and practiced. He continually shows in court his thorough acquaintance with these traditions, when an adversary violates the least of them. Mr. Field belongs to the time when, as Mr. Evarts said in his address at the meeting called for the organization of the Bar Association of New York, "for a lawyer to come out from the chambers of a judge with an *ex parte* writ that he could not defend before the public, would have occasioned the same sentiment towards him as if he came out with a stolen pocket-book." Beyond a doubt, Mr. Field knows very well what the honor of his profession demands of him. If there have been professional sins on his part, they surely have not been sins of ignorance. If such a man as Mr. Field has been guilty of the outrages with which Mr. Bowles and other men continually charge him, the public should know it, and should well ponder on it. For it shows something "rotten in the state of Denmark."

It is proposed, then, here to briefly examine some of the legal features of one of Mr. Fisk's "raids," as he calls them,—the contest for the control of the Albany & Susquehanna Railroad. This litigation, in its activity, lasted only about two months. But in this space of time there was a perfect meteoric shower of suits, injunctions, and receiverships, that has not been surpassed in any of the Erie wars. It is not intended here to give a history of them, or even any mention of more than three or four of these suits, but simply to examine, at no great length, the character of a very few of the legal proceedings taken by counsel on Mr. Fisk's side of this controversy, and then to examine Mr. David Dudley Field's part in some of these proceedings.

And it will be necessary, for the right understanding of the legal proceedings here mentioned, to give a very short statement of some of the cardinal unquestioned principles of the law in relation to the granting of injunctions and receiverships, which, under the New York Code, are both called provisional remedies. But these principles here to be stated are very rudimentary and simple, and easily understood by any layman.

Under the New York Code the pleading made by the plaintiff is called the complaint, and in its form it is somewhat like the old bill in chancery; and it has ordinarily a verification on the part of the plaintiff, to the effect that "it is true except as to the matters therein stated on information and belief, and as to those matters he believes it to be true." This complaint proves nothing. It is merely the plaintiff's statement, for the purposes of the trial, of what he conceives to be the facts constituting his cause of action. And they must be proved by him on the trial, before he can have his judgment or decree.

The writ of injunction, or injunction order, as it is termed in the practice under the New York Code, is an order enjoining or forbidding, pending the suit, some act on the part of the defendant which would be specially injurious to the plaintiff, and against which the plaintiff has no other protection or remedy. And, under the New York practice, this injunction order is continually granted, and rightly granted, *ex parte*, or on the application of one party without hearing the other.

Of course, however, in such cases, the court, under the decisions, and in accordance with every principle of law and justice, requires the clearest proof, on the part of the plaintiff, of his rights, and of the damage to his rights, which would ensue without the injunction. This proof, too, must be by affidavit. The affidavit, too, must show facts. It must be, too, the affidavit of a party testifying of his own knowledge, and not of hearsay. The necessity of an affidavit no one would ever question; but, under the circumstances, it may be well to cite one New York authority. Mr. Justice Ingraham says, in the case of *Hecker* v. *The Mayor, etc.*, 18 *Abbott Rep.* 371: "I have repeatedly held, that an injunction should not be granted on the mere verification of the complaint. This has always been the rule. And such rule has been adhered to since the adoption of the code." These points are law and common sense. And it is even questionable whether a judge has any jurisdiction to grant an injunction without an affidavit, and whether, if he does so, the injunction is not absolutely void.

And in granting receiverships of property, the plaintiff, both under the old equity practice and under the New York code, is required clearly to establish two points,—first, that he himself has some right in the property which is the subject of the action; and, second, that the property is in danger of being lost or materially injured, pending the suit, if left in the possession of the defendant. And this is very reasonable. For no plaintiff can, with reason, ask a court to take possession of property for him, unless he has himself some right in the property. Nor can he ask a court to take such property from the possession of the defendant, unless there is danger of injury if the property stays where it is. And in the case of a receivership as well as of an injunction, these points, required to be proved, must be proved by affidavit. The affidavit, too, must show facts. It must be, too, the affidavit of a person testifying of his own knowledge, and not of hearsay.

These points being stated, some parts of the Albany & Susquehanna litigation may be considered. The contest was between the Fisk party and the Ramsey party for the control of the road, and the main point, finally, was to carry the election for directors, on the seventh of September, 1869. It was decided, in the case of *The People* v. *The Albany & Susquehanna Railroad Company and Others*, that, out of about thirty thousand shares of stock of the company, Mr. Fisk and his friends controlled only about 6,500 shares. The court, too, further decides that Mr. Fisk and his associates, owning only about one-fifth of the stock, in order to get control of the road on the day of the election, "took possession of one of the rooms of the office of the company, and filled the same, and made an unlawful organization of themselves, as a pretended stockholders' meeting; that the holding thereof was in pursuance of a previous conspiracy and fraudulent design between said associates, made for the purpose of interfering with and hindering a lawful election, and procuring an unlawful and sham election; that in pursuance of said conspiracy they brought from the city of New York a large number of men, who were not stockholders of the company, and who were rough, rude, and dangerous persons, and placed them in said room, with the intent and design that they should participate in said meeting, and prevent lawful stockholders from attending said meeting; that in further execution of said conspiracy, and with intent to hinder the defendant, Ramsey, the president of said company, and William L. M. Phelps, the secretary and treasurer of said company, and Henry Smith, the counsel of said company, from performing their duties at said annual election, and with intent thereby to hinder a lawful stockholders' meeting, they did, on the sixth day of September, 1869, fraudulently procure an order for the arrest of said Ramsey, Phelps, and Smith at or about the time of the organization of the said pretended stockholders' meeting.'' The foregoing statement is condensed, by simply leaving out from the decision of the court words and phrases here useless, but there necessary, which do not in the least vary the meaning.

But general statements are not enough, nor do they, at all, by themselves, concern Mr. David Dudley Field. Three or four of these proceedings will themselves be examined.

The first proceeding, worthy of notice, was the suit of Mr. Joseph Bush. Mr. David Groesbeck and some other gentlemen held three thousand shares of this Susquehanna stock, which they had purchased of the company. In his complaint, Bush stated that, ''as he is informed and believes,'' this Groesbeck stock was illegally issued, and he asked to have a receiver of this stock appointed by the court.

Now in this suit of Mr. Bush, brought by Messrs. Field and Shearman, there were three peculiarities: first, there was no affidavit as to any point; second, the plaintiff did not pretend to any interest whatever in this stock; third, the plaintiff did not pretend that there was any danger whatever of injury to the stock. However, on the fourteenth of August, 1869, an order was granted, without a hearing, by Mr. Justice Barnard, appointing William J. A. Fuller receiver of these three thousand shares of stock. Mr. Fuller had been a clerk in Mr. Field's office. He took possession of the stock, under this order, for the purpose and with the intent, as Mr. Justice Smith says in his decision, of voting on it in the Fisk interest, in opposition to the wishes of the rightful owners; and he did so vote.

Now, even if it had been clearly proved, by affidavit, that this stock had been illegally issued, the most that anyone could by possibility have claimed, was that an injunction should issue restraining anyone from voting on it. But such an injunction would only have hindered Mr. Groesbeck from voting on the stock. The receivership allowed Mr. Bush, through his receiver, to vote on it himself. And the result of this maneuver was, that three thousand votes were taken from the Ramsey interest and given to the Fisk interest, and were used in the Fisk interest, by an order obtained, on no proof whatever, by any person whatever, of any fact whatever.

Mr. Ramsey was himself, however, the head and front of the opposition to Mr. Fisk's plans. He was the president and a director of the company.

A suit was commenced in the name of David Wilber, who lived in Otsego County. There are courts and counsel in Otsego County quite able to give Mr. Wilber justice, if he wished justice. Mr. Wilber, however, begins his suit in New York City. Messrs. Field and Shearman are his attorneys. Mr. Wilber, in his complaint, alleges that, "as he is informed and believes," Mr. Ramsey has done certain things and has not done certain other things. No affidavit of any person to any fact is offered. And on the fourth of August an injunction order is obtained *ex parte* from Mr. Justice Barnard, ordering "that the defendant, Joseph H. Ramsey, refrain from exercising the offices of president and director, or either of them, and from issuing any stock of said company, or in any way interfering in its affairs, until the further order of this court."

Now if it had been clearly proved, by affidavit, of some person, that some party defendant had done or was about to do something which would injure the plaintiff, a court of equity might have enjoined such defendant from doing some particular wrong. No proof whatever was given, by any party, of any wrong, and Mr. Ramsey was enjoined from doing any act.

The Ramsey party met this by a counter-injunction, restraining four members of the Board of Directors from acting as such, on the allegations that these four directors had fraudulently entered into a conspiracy to transfer the property and control of the railroad to the Erie Railway Company.

The four enjoined Fisk directors, as they were called, were Leonard, Herrick, North, and Wilber. The injunction is served on them, on the morning of the sixth of August, in Albany. Leonard and Herrick live in Albany. They wish justice speedily from the nearest source. They go at once to New York City. They go to Mr. Fisk's Grand Opera House. They find there Mr. Fisk, Mr. Gould, and Mr. Shearman. As to what follows, Mr. Thomas G. Shearman's version of the events will first be given, with the assumption that it is true.

A complaint is prepared, the plaintiff this time being Azro Chase. Mr. Chase also lives in Otsego County, where there are courts and counsel quite able to give him justice if he wishes it. The same attorneys, Messrs. Field and Shearman, appear for Mr. Chase, and his suit is brought in New York City. On his complaint an order is obtained from Mr. Justice Barnard, appointing Charles Courter and James Fisk, Jr., receivers "of all the property of the Albany & Susquehanna Railroad Company." Messrs. Field and Shearman obtained this order that took away 142 miles of railroad and the entire property of a large corporation, amounting to several millions of dollars, from a judge, at chambers, without notice and without a hearing.

The order suspending Mr. Ramsey was served on him on the morning of the fifth of August. The order suspending Leonard and his three codirectors was served on the morning of the sixth of August. The order for the Fisk receivership was granted about half past ten o'clock on the evening of the sixth. The receivers at once started from the Grand Opera House to take the night train for Albany.

But on the arrival of these receivers in Albany on the morning of the seventh, the road was already in the possession of Mr. Pruyn, a receiver appointed in an action commenced the day before in the Supreme Court at Albany, where the property was. And here came, on the part of the Fisk party, what is, so far as the writer is aware, the most extraordinary proceeding recorded in the history of English or American law. And to make clear the nature of the proceeding, it will be necessary to explain briefly what is a writ of assistance.

Where an order directing the delivery of certain property to a receiver has been properly served, and the receiver is still unable to get possession of the property, in certain cases a writ of assistance issues, directing the sheriff to put the receiver in possession of that property. To warrant the issuing of the writ, two points must be established: first, that the order appointing the receiver has been duly served; and, second, that the delivery of the property has been refused after such service. Moreover, as in the other cases before mentioned, the points must be clearly proved by the affidavit of a person swearing to them positively of his own knowledge.

In this Chase suit Mr. Fisk was unable to get possession of the property of the railroad. He and his counsel were in Albany. The property was in Albany. Mr. Chase, the plaintiff, was in Albany. If they had not their rights, and speed were necessary in getting them their rights, the nearest court was, of course, to be found. But application, in this case, for the writ of assistance, is made by Mr. Thomas G. Shearman in New York City, on this same seventh of August, to Mr. Justice Barnard. So Mr. Shearman testifies. Of course he has himself no knowledge of what has been doing in Albany an hour before. But this Prospero, in his lonely cell at the Grand Opera House, hath a weird potency. Mr. Shearman makes an affidavit. He does not swear that the order appointing the receivers has ever been served on anyone. He does not swear that he has "knowledge" of anything. Mr. Shearman makes his affidavit that he has received a telegram from Albany, and that he "is informed" that opposition is made to the receivers by certain persons; that attempts have been made to eject the receivers from the office of the company by force. And on no other affidavit than this, Mr. Shearman testifies that he obtained a writ of assistance from Mr. Justice Barnard, directed to the sheriff of Albany County, and all other counties where the company had property, directing them to put Mr. Fisk and Mr. Courter in possession of that property.

This is not quite enough, however. Mr. Shearman, by a supplemental complaint, brings in new parties. And then appears, with the writ of assistance, on no affidavit but the one before mentioned of Mr. Shearman that he is "informed" of something by a telegram, what purports to be an injunction, of which the terms are so singular that two clauses of it will be given verbatim. The order enjoins the railroad company, its president, all its directors, the receiver appointed in another action, the plaintiff in that other action, the sheriff, and the *Police Commissioners of Albany* "from disturbing or interfering with Charles Courter and James Fisk, Jr., receivers appointed in this action, in the performance of their duties as such receivers; from interfering with the possession of such receivers; from hindering or delaying them in taking possession of any property or effects of the above-named railroad company, or held in trust for it; from refusing or neglecting to deliver to the said receivers all and every the property and effects of the said company, or that may be held in trust for the same, of any name and nature, real or personal; and from inciting or encouraging any opposition, or *permitting any opposition to be made* to the said receivers in the discharge of their duties as such." "That all the defendants refrain from commencing or prosecuting any action for the purpose of obtaining an injunction against said company, or its officers, agents, or servants, or against said plaintiff herein, or said receivers appointed herein, and also from commencing or prosecuting any action for the appointment of a receiver or receivers of said company, or from making any application therefor, except to this court, in this action."

As has been stated, the police commissioners of the city of Albany were made parties defendant by this supplemental complaint. The only allegation in this complaint which even mentions or refers to these commissioners is as follows: "That, as the plaintiff is *informed and believes* . . . , the said . . . , have attempted to eject the said receivers by force and violence, and are still attempting so to do." Not one word of evidence was laid before Mr. Justice Barnard when he granted this injunction.

The papers which were laid before him showed clearly that there could be no evidence.

It must be admitted to have a kind of grim grotesque humor. Armed with two or three injunctions of this kind, one might with safety say, with Alexander Selkirk, "I am monarch of all I survey." But, after all, this injunction is partial, incomplete. It is applicable to only one particular case. It is better to find at once a formula for an injunction for all cases. And, none being found in the books, the writer takes the liberty of suggesting the following, which is doubtless capable of great improvement. Have in the beginning the ordinary complaint, that, "as the plaintiff is informed and believes," someone, no matter who, has done something, no matter what. Leave out altogether the names of parties defendant, to be inserted as need arises. Let the injunction read, "It is ordered that the defendants, and each of them, refrain from refusing or neglecting to do anything that the plaintiff may request." Or, in order to have definiteness of evidence in case of a proceeding for contempt, it might be well to amend the last clause thus: "That the plaintiff may request in writing." And, of course, there must be the invariable protective provision, "that the defendants bring no suit, and make no application for relief, *except to this court in this action.*" Add a receivership of the defendants' property. And if injunctions of this kind are adopted, it will at once do away with the necessity of any examination as to the limits of the powers of a court of equity. And the terms of such an injunction are no broader than those of the one already cited.

But the manner of serving this new Chase injunction, and of executing this writ of assistance, is another novelty. Most persons know that an injunction order cannot be served without producing the original order. Nor can a writ be executed by the sheriff until he has it in his possession. The injunction was to be served and the writ executed in Albany. Both writ and injunction, as a matter of fact, were in New York. Inconvenient it was, surely. The inconvenience might, perhaps, have been avoided, had application been made to a nearer court. However, the order and writ had been obtained by telegraph; why not serve and execute them by telegraph?

About nine o'clock in the morning Mr. Fisk has his misadventure in not getting possession of the property of the road. About three o'clock in the afternoon the sheriff in Albany has in his hands what purports to be the writ of assistance, issued in New York City; and the counsel of Mr. Gould is with him, urging him to execute it. The counsel of the railroad company calls the attention of the sheriff to the fact that the ink is not dry on the writ, signed in New York by a New York justice, reciting on its face matters that had taken place in Albany only five or six hours before. And the sheriff very wisely concluded that, on such process, it would be dangerous to try to take away the entire property of a large railroad corporation. The words of the writ had been sent by telegraph, by Mr. Shearman, from New York. The original writ was sent from New York by the train that left there at 4.00 P.M. and reached Albany about ten o'clock in the evening. So Mr. Shearman testifies.

This is, perhaps, the nearest approach yet made, on the part of the ordinary human being of the period, to omniscience and omnipotence. But how far is this to go? You can obtain your writ, with the evidence at one end of the telegraph and the writ at the other end. You can execute your writ with the original at one end and the sheriff with the copy at the other end. Why not do away altogether with the two useless elements, the evidence and the original writ, and get on with copies alone? Or may we make our own originals? Or may we have our writs and orders signed in blank? Among the glorious inventions of the nineteenth century will be recorded that of obtaining process of court without evidence, and executing process of court without having it. The name of the inventor is unknown; but the glory of the invention lies, as far as yet appears, between Mr. Thomas G. Shearman and Mr. David Dudley Field.

Non nostrum inter vos tantas componere lites.

Who will say, hereafter, that law is merely a science of precedents?

But were these orders and writs ever signed in New York? And were they signed anywhere on the days of their date? Testimony was, during this litigation, taken in regard to the circumstances under which these orders, which were served in so extraordinary a manner, were obtained. The testimony was very peculiar. It was substantially as follows.

Mr. Shearman, during these proceedings, gave his testimony in relation to the obtaining the first order, of the sixth of August, which appointed the receivers. According to this testimony, the first thing done, to his knowledge, as to the appointment of Fisk and Courter as receivers, was done in the treasurer's office at Mr. Fisk's Grand Opera House, on the evening of the sixth of August, about 8.00 P.M. The order was taken by his partner from the treasurer's room, in order to procure Mr. Justice Barnard's signature, and this partner was not absent from his (Mr. Shearman's) presence longer than from 10.20 to 10.35 P.M.; and this partner returned with what purported to be Mr. Justice Barnard's signature at the foot of the order. Mr. Shearman also stated that he was then informed by Mr. Fisk that Judge Barnard was at the house of a friend in the neighborhood. Neither this partner, who is stated to have obtained Judge Barnard's signature, nor Mr. James Fisk, who is stated to have given Mr. Shearman information as to Judge Barnard's whereabouts, were at any time produced as witnesses.

Mr. Courter, too, one of the receivers, testified that on the morning of the seventh, when they reached Albany, he had no paper relating to the receivership in his possession; nor could he swear that Fisk had the original order at the railroad office on that morning.

Nor can this order, the place of which in space and time it is so hard to determine, be anywhere found in the minutes or records of the court.

It did not appear in evidence that Judge Barnard was in New

York at all on the sixth of August. It did appear in evidence that he was in Poughkeepsie as late as 7.00 P.M., on the evening of that day. The distance from Poughkeepsie to New York is about seventy-five miles by rail.

The injunction order of the seventh of August, even Mr. Shearman swears, was not in Albany when it was pretended to serve it there. The writ of assistance of the same day, Mr. Shearman swears, was not in Albany when it was pretended to execute it there.

This writ of assistance, Mr. Shearman swears, "purports to have been granted by Judge Barnard, sitting at special term in the court-house, and such was my information and belief." The order for leave to file a supplemental complaint, Mr. Shearman swears, was made on the same day. And he says, "I drew the papers and sent them to the court-house."

The minutes of the "special term in the court-house" for the seventh of August show that this "special term" was held, not by Mr. Justice Barnard, but by Mr. Justice Ingraham.

When and where were this writ and this order granted?

Of another order, bearing date the tenth of August, Mr. Shearman swears: "It was granted by a special term of the Supreme Court, held by Judge Barnard. I cannot remember on what day, but it was between 11.00 A.M. and 1.00 P.M., at the court-house in New York City."

The minutes of the "special term of the Supreme Court," held on this tenth of August, "at the court-house in New York City," show that this "special term" on that day was held, not by Mr. Justice Barnard, but by Mr. Justice Ingraham. On Friday, the sixth of August, Judge Barnard was in Poughkeepsie, where his mother was dangerously ill. She died on Sunday, the eighth, and her funeral was on Tuesday, the tenth.

Was this order of the tenth of August granted by Mr. Justice Barnard? And if so, when and where was it granted?

It has not been here attempted to give an account of every step in these legal proceedings, so called. Merely those which are most pertinent to the matter in hand are here related. And the only remaining occurrences that call for notice here are the proceedings connected with the election on the seventh of September, 1869. These proceedings, on the part of the Fisk party, embraced several points.

The inspectors for the election had been chosen, as they always were, at the preceding annual meeting of stockholders, and the facts making their appointment regular or irregular had been long known to the Fisk party and their counsel. An injunction was obtained enjoining these inspectors from acting as inspectors at the election. This injunction, with printed copies ready for service, was in Albany on the sixth, the day before the election. Of this injunction Mr. Justice Smith says: "It seems to me quite clear that this injunction was improvidently granted. . . . The use that was made of this injunction is, I think, the more serious ground of objection to it."

This would dispose of the inspectors, who were supposed to be unfriendly to the Church-Fisk interest, and friendly to the Ramsey interest. But further "legal process" was necessary.

A suit was commenced in the name of the Albany & Susquehanna Railroad Company, as plaintiff, against Mr. Ramsey, the president, Mr. Phelps, the secretary and treasurer, Mr. Henry Smith, the counsel of the company, and Mr. Pruyn, the receiver, who was also a stockholder in the Ramsey interest. Messrs. Field and Shearman commenced this action, as attorneys for the plaintiff, although there was regular counsel of the railroad company, regularly appointed, and they must have known it. It was stated in the complaint, which no one, either attorney or client, ventured to swear to, that these defendants had, "with intent to cheat and defraud the plaintiff, clandestinely and without authority removed" from the office of the company certain of the company's books. As matter of fact, these books had, on the night of the fifth of August, been removed for the purpose of securing them from Mr. Fisk, whether unnecessarily or not needs no discussion here. This action was not brought to recover the books, nor was there any pretense that it was brought for that purpose. It was brought to recover damages, laid at the sum of fifty thousand dollars, for the removal of these books, which were, as matter of fact, returned uninjured before service of process on either of the defendants. And in this suit an order of arrest was granted by Mr. Justice Barnard, holding each of the defendants to bail in the sum of $25,000.

The authority of Messrs. Field and Shearman to bring this action, and the purpose in bringing it, will more fully appear hereafter. Mr. Justice Smith says of it:

> The order of arrest was unauthorized. But assuming it to be otherwise, the order to hold to bail in the sum of $25,000 was most extraordinary and exorbitant, and must have been procured to be used, as it was used, on the day of election, in aid of the fraudulent purposes of Mr. Fisk and his associates.

These election proceedings are the ones that specially concern Mr. David Dudley Field.

The election was announced for twelve o'clock, noon, of the seventh of September. On that day Mr. Fuller, the receiver of the Groesbeck stock, an impartial officer of the court, meets Mr. Fisk and Mr. Shearman at breakfast, receives his Fisk ballots from Mr. Shearman, and rides to the company's offices with him, about half-past eleven o'clock. So Mr. Fuller testifies. On their way they see the injunction served on one or two of the inspectors, and it was about the same time served on all three of them, within less than half an hour of the time of the election. At half-past eleven o'clock, Mr. James Fisk, Jr., and Mr. David Dudley Field enter the railroad company's office together, and immediately behind them Mr. Fisk's band of "rough, rude, and dangerous" men, to the number of forty or fifty; Mr. Fisk saying to them, as one witness testifies, "Come on, boys, follow me." According to the testimony, the appearance of these men was much like that of Sir John Falstaff's levies, of whom the Knight said: "No eye hath seen such scarecrows. . . . There's but a shirt and a half in all my company." And Sir John's final determination, as given in the play, "I'll not march through Coventry with them," might have been a safe precedent, for both client and counsel, in the case in question. These men nearly filled the directors' room, where the stockholders' meeting had been appointed. They had just come from New York, and each of them had received his proxy on one or two shares of stock. Mr. Field and Mr. Shearman were both there, advising as counsel through the whole proceeding.

At a quarter before twelve, Colonel Church, one of Mr. Fisk's proposed codirectors, was chosen chairman of this stockholders' meeting.

Immediately thereafter the first set of resolutions was passed. One of them was to the effect that,

WHEREAS, Samuel Hand, Ralph Lathrop, and William Haskell were declared inspectors at the last annual meeting, and whereas they have not been and are not now stockholders, and *have been enjoined* from acting as inspectors, *Resolved,* That . . . the offices of inspectors of election be and the same are hereby declared vacant.

And another resolution was then passed, appointing, as inspectors, three of Mr. Fisk's friends, one of them being Mr. Gould's counsel throughout this whole contest, and another being Mr. Bush, the plaintiff in the receiver suit. This was the first set of resolutions.

A second set was offered and passed, at twelve o'clock, or a few seconds after, to the effect "that this meeting proceed with the annual election of directors and inspectors." The newly appointed inspectors had proceeded to the treasurer's room immediately after their election, ready to begin receiving votes, precisely at twelve o'clock, and they did so begin to receive votes. Mr. Field and Mr. Shearman were at their side to advise them, and these "rough" men, according to the testimony, voted under the eyes of Messrs. Shearman and David Dudley Field, until Mr. Fisk said, "Let them boys go back. There is enough of them voted. Drive them back."

Just at this time the sheriff appeared, arrested the president, the secretary, and the counsel of the company, under (as the court say) an "unauthorized" order, holding them to bail in the "extraordinary and exorbitant" sum of $25,000, in pursuance of this "fraudulent conspiracy." Surely there was an artistic completeness to this plan, by whomsoever it may have been arranged.

Saith my Lord Bacon, in his essay "Of Cunning," "There be, that can pack the cards, and yet cannot play well."

Mr. Groesbeck and his friends seemed to think that they had some rights in relation to their three thousand shares of stock. They had consequently begun a suit, in which they set forth that they were the owners of these three thousand shares of stock (as the court say they undoubtedly were) ; that through a fraudulent conspiracy on the part of Mr. Fisk and his associates a receiver had been illegally appointed, who had taken possession of their shares (as the court decided was the case) ; and that this receiver intended to vote thereon (which was also the case, for he did so vote). They thereupon asked and obtained an injunction order, enjoining the holding of any election, unless they, the plaintiffs, were first allowed to vote on their three thousand shares of stock "free from injunction," and this injunction was duly served on the newly made inspectors, before they had received a single vote. Mr. Bush, one of these inspectors, testifies that he did not read the injunction, but handed it over to his counsel and proceeded with the election. A moment's delay seems to have been all the result. A copy of the injunction was handed to Mr. Shearman, who was standing next the inspectors. He examined it, simply said to Receiver Fuller that an election was enjoined unless the votes on the three thousand shares were first received, and Mr. Fuller, who had been waiting to deposit his votes, at once voted, as he himself testifies, on stock which was by him claimed to be void, in opposition to what he knew to be the wishes of its owners. And Mr. Bush, the plaintiff in the suit where the receiver was appointed, made inspector at a sham election, by the votes of rough men, who were not stockholders, brought from New York by Mr. James Fisk, in pursuance of a conspiracy to prevent the true stockholders from electing the directors of their own corporation, received votes, in disobedience of an injunction of the Supreme Court, on stock which he had sworn no one had a right to vote on, in which he himself claimed no interest, in direct opposition to the wishes, as he knew, of the owners of the stock, who were there with their hands tied by injunctions which they obeyed. This was done under the advice of Mr. Thomas G. Shearman, given at the time, as Mr. Shearman himself testifies, in the presence of Mr. David Dudley Field.

The voting then went on at the Fisk poll. But Mr. Ramsey had wealthy friends present. Bail was immediately given for himself, the secretary, and the counsel, a meeting of the legal stockholders was then organized, a new poll opened, the election there went on, in (as the court held) a perfectly regular manner, the Ramsey ticket, as the court decides, was elected, and Mr. Fisk defeated.

And Mr. Justice Smith says in his opinion:

Upon the whole evidence upon this branch of the case, I think I am bound to find, as matter of fact, that there was a preconceived scheme, combination, or conspiracy to carry the election of directors appointed to be held at the time and place aforesaid, by the use and abuse of legal process and proceedings.

"A conspiracy," the court say, "to carry the election by the use and abuse of legal process and proceedings."

The judgment of the court in this cause may possibly be reversed. Be that as it may. For the first time, so far as the writer is aware, in the history of English or American law, a court has decided that there was a "conspiracy and fraudulent design . . . for the purpose of interfering with and hindering a lawful election, and procuring an unlawful and sham election" of the directors of a corporation; that in the "execution of said conspiracy" parties did "fraudulently procure an order for the arrest" of the officers and counsel of the company; and that there was a "fraudulent conspiracy to carry the election of directors by the abuse of legal process." Grave charges are these against the parties. On their face they would seem to deeply concern counsel. Any court would naturally require very clear evidence before ever giving such a decision. The evidence in this case was very clear. And a slight examination of some points of this evidence will give the means of deciding whether or not the opinion of the court was well founded, and what share Mr. David Dudley Field had in these matters.

In all these suits and proceedings which were taken, in the names of different parties, in the interest of Mr. Fisk, the plaintiff's attorneys were Messrs. Field and Shearman. In this firm Mr. David Dudley Field is a partner, according to the sworn testimony of Mr. Shearman. It does not appear by the evidence that Mr. David Dudley Field personally advised or directed every one of these proceedings. He did personally advise and direct some of them, some of the earliest and some of the latest. But in order to hold him personally responsible for the character of these proceedings, whatever they were, it needs not to show that he personally procured, or directed the procuring of, all the obnoxious orders.

No sane man supposes for an instant that any counsel of ordinary shrewdness engages in a litigation like the Susquehanna contest without advising continually at each successive stage of the affair, without being carefully and minutely informed of the contents of every single paper, without thoroughly examining every single fact. Mr. Field is one of the most acute practitioners that has ever been known at the New York bar. Any person who has heard him try a cause in court is well aware how exactly he knows and remembers the slightest particulars of the most unimportant testimony connected with his case, how his unceasing watchfulness never loses a single point of fact or law. Mr. Field assuredly would consider it an insult to his shrewdness if anyone should suppose that he was engaged for one day in this Susquehanna litigation without thoroughly knowing every the least point in it from the beginning to the end.

Now, even if Mr. Field had not himself examined an order or process of court before it was obtained by his firm, as soon as he did examine it, if it had been wrongly obtained, he was bound neither to use it himself nor to allow anyone else to use it. And if it had been rightly obtained, he was bound neither to "abuse" it himself nor to allow anyone else to "abuse" it. In such cases it is not enough for him to say that he is not the whole of the firm of Field and Shearman, and that he did not in person procure the obnoxious order or process. Perhaps any ordinary layman can see that, if the order of arrest for Mr. Ramsey and his counsel, after it was signed, had been quietly laid away in a drawer, no one would have been greatly injured. Probably Mr. Ramsey and his counsel would have been quite content for Messrs. Field and Shearman to obtain orders without number, of all kinds, if they were never used. Mr. Field did himself use these orders. As to some, at least, of these orders and proceedings here related, Mr. Field was "consulted beforehand," and himself advised and directed them.

On the evening of the sixth of August, when the Fisk directors, who had been suspended, came to New York, it will be remembered they went at once to the Grand Opera House, and reached there about 6.00 P.M. They did not come to hear the witching strains of Offenbach. They were seeking the halls of justice.

This order of the sixth Mr. Field says he did not procure. But did anyone procure it? Mr. Field did, in his own person, go to Albany on the ninth, to help get possession, under this order, of this railroad. Mr. Field did, in his own person, for the very same purpose, drag his adversaries before Mr. Justice Barnard, on the twelfth, on an order, granted or not granted, "at the court-house in New York City" or elsewhere, by Mr. Justice Barnard, on the tenth, the day of his mother's funeral in Poughkeepsie.

But for the purposes of this paper the election proceedings have the most interest.

On the evening of the sixth of September, the day before the election, there was a meeting at the Delavan House. There were present, with others, Mr. James Fisk, Jr., Mr. Thomas G. Shearman, and Mr. David Dudley Field. The whole plan of operations for the election was there discussed and arranged. The enjoining of the inspectors was mentioned. The injunction was already there, with the printed copies ready for service. It was then also mentioned that the officers were to be arrested. The order of arrest was then on its way to Albany, and had on that day been obtained in New York on papers drawn days before in the office of Messrs. Field and Shearman. It was, on this evening, too, arranged that a meeting was to be organized at a quarter before twelve, twelve being the hour regularly appointed. "It was part of the programme," says Mr. Shearman. It was also mentioned that "persons" were coming from New York to vote. The first set of resolutions, reciting that the inspectors "have been enjoined," were drawn long before the injunction was served, and copied by Mr. Samuel North, who it was arranged should offer them; and that there might be no mistake, this first set of resolutions was indorsed "immediate," signifying that they were to be offered "immediately" after the meeting was organized. The draft of these resolutions Mr. North swears he received from the hands of Mr. David Dudley Field. The resolutions to the effect that the meeting proceed with the election were drawn hours before the meeting was organized, and copied by the same Mr. North, and he received them at the same place and at the same time. It was arranged who should be nominated for new inspectors at the early meeting. Mr. Hamilton Harris was one of these proposed inspectors. And he testifies that he was asked to be such candidate, "beforehand," by Mr. David Dudley Field. This elaborate mechanism, this "programme" for carrying an election, this enjoining of inspectors, this arresting of officers and counsel, this filling the room where the meeting was to be held with "rough, rude, and dangerous persons," this device of what the court calls a "sham" meeting before the hour, this preparation of resolutions, this selection of officers,—in whose brain was it begotten, that of client or counsel? And in the brain of which counsel?

And the manner in which this cunningly devised plan was carried out deserves admiration. These "persons" left New York together the day before, and reached Albany in the morning; they breakfasted together, received their proxies together; they were kept together until about half-past eleven o'clock, when they marched together to the Susquehanna offices, and together followed Mr. Fisk and Mr. David Dudley Field to the directors' room, which they filled. They voted together at that so-called stockholders' meeting, under Mr. Field's eyes; they voted together in the treasurer's room for directors, by Mr. Fisk's direction, under Mr. Field's eyes. They had been brought from New York that they might so vote, as Mr. Field very well knew.

And as to the arrest suit, the facts are peculiar. Mr. Dudley Field, the son, testified as follows, when examined as to the authority of his firm to bring this action:—

I have in my possession a resolution of the executive committee of this company requesting our firm to bring this action. I don't know of anything else except a letter received from Mr. Hamilton Harris, which accompanied this resolution, which referred to the bringing of the suit, the contents of which I do not further recollect.

Question. Was the receiving this resolution and letter of Mr. Harris the first information you had of the bringing of the suit?

Answer. No; I had discussed it repeatedly with my father, who is my senior partner, for days before that time, and the bringing the suit was only delayed until we received a formal authorization from the company.

Q. Will you give a copy of Mr. Harris's letter, or that portion relating to this suit, and the resolution?

A. I will give you a copy of that portion; it is dated September 3, 1869, and is addressed to Field and Shearman, and commences with the following words: "Gentlemen,—Enclosed I send you the resolution of the executive committee of the Albany & Susquehanna Railroad Company, directing proceedings to be instituted for the recovery of the books of the company." I think that is the letter referred to, but if not, the letter is not in my possession. I will annex to my affidavit a copy of the resolution referred to.

The portion of the resolution referred to reads:—

Resolved, That Field and Shearman be employed to take all legal means for the recovery and restoration of the said books, and for the *arrest* and punishment of the persons abstracting them.

Mr. Hamilton Harris, who is thus stated to have sent this resolution to Messrs. Field and Shearman, authorizing this arrest, testified in relation to the same matter as follows:—

Question. When did you first know of the order of arrest which was issued against Joseph H. Ramsey, William L. M. Phelps, Robert H. Pruyn, and Henry Smith, or either of them?
Answer. Soon after the poll was closed I heard that Mr. Ramsey and Mr. Smith had been arrested under some process, which I afterwards learned from Mr. Smith himself was an order of arrest. That is all I know about it.
Q. Was that the first knowledge or information you had of such an order, *or that such an one was to be applied for?*
A. It was.

The defendants against whom this order of arrest was obtained were all well-known citizens of Albany, who had lived there for years. Mr. Henry Smith is one of the first advocates in the state of New York, and one of the leaders of the Albany bar. These defendants were the president, secretary, receiver, and the counsel of a railroad company, which held its annual election at twelve o'clock, noon, on the seventh of September, and these four defendants were the head and front of the opposition to the election of the Church or Fisk board, for whom Messrs. Field and Shearman had been counsel through this whole contest. The papers on which this order was obtained were completely ready in Messrs. Field and Shearman's office before the second of September. Mr. David Dudley Field had already "discussed it repeatedly" with his son and partner. Messrs. Field and Shearman "delayed" bringing the suit until the resolu-

tion of the third. Messrs. Field and Shearman ''delayed'' obtaining the order of arrest until the sixth. Someone or other
''delayed'' arresting these gentlemen until after the coveted
books had actually been returned to the company's office, and
until precisely twelve o'clock on the seventh of September, when
the loss of one single minute might ruin the labors of a lifetime.
Mr. Henry Smith, in his closing argument in the case already
mentioned, said, speaking of Mr. Ramsey's arrest, ''I saw this
man in charge of the sheriff, and held there as a prisoner, just
as this election was to be proceeded with, and at the same time
saw David Dudley Field coming in and standing in the doorway,
with his fingers in his vest, tauntingly laughing and sneering at
him.'' Mr. David Dudley Field, in his closing argument in this
same case, speaking of the same arrest, says, ''It is clear that
nobody in the Church party had anything to do with that arrest
at that particular time.''

This arrest suit was afterward dismissed by the court, after
hearing Mr. David Dudley Field in opposition thereto, and after
reading his partner's affidavit, on the ground that it had been
brought without any authority.

And this is, according to Mr. David Dudley Field, practice of
the law. Is there not danger lest, if such practice obtain, the
delicate courtesies and gentle sentiments of the profession be
lost?

Mr. David Dudley Field has seen the palmy days of the New
York bar. What are to the younger men of the profession merely
dim traditions of a past age, are to him the fresh memories of a
present life. Mr. Field is a legacy to the present generation at
the bar from the golden age when, as we are told, counsel showed
one another the knightly courtesy of a Bayard. He was taught
in the days of Chancellor Kent. He is one of the most eloquent
apostles of legal reform. He is, even now, urging an amendment
to the New York Code, providing that no receiverships shall be
granted on the *ex parte* order of a judge. To him, probably more
than to any other one man, the people of New York are indebted

for the Code of Procedure. To him, of course, one of the oldest, ablest, and most cultivated members of the bar, the younger men are to look for an example of professional conduct. And they are to look for this example, doubtless, in Mr. Field's management of these Fisk litigations. For it is of them that Mr. Field says: "Nothing but a profound conviction that I could not with honor retire from these suits has kept me in them. Being in them, I shall do my whole duty to my clients." And this "whole duty to the clients" consists, we are to infer, in the devising and carrying out of a transaction like the following.

Mr. James Fisk and his associates, all of them, in this matter, clients of Mr. David Dudley Field, acting under his advice, endeavored to get control of a railroad and elect its Board of Directors. As the court has decided, they own not more than a fifth of its stock. This is their procedure. They suspend the president, who is opposed to them, by an order of Mr. Justice Barnard, granted, as they themselves show, without a hearing, on not one word of evidence. They tie their opponents hand and foot with injunctions restraining any application for relief, "except to this court in this action," "this court" being Mr. Justice Barnard. They pack a "sham" meeting with "rough" men from New York, Mr. David Dudley Field himself being at their head, to hinder the stockholders of the company from meeting in their own office to protect their own property. To bar the possibility of these stockholders meeting anywhere else, Messrs. Field and Shearman, at the very moment of the election, when an hour's delay costs millions of property, have the sheriff arrest the officers and counsel of this company, in a suit commenced, without authority, under the advice and direction of Mr. David Dudley Field; and the arrest is made under his eyes to his complete satisfaction. They pretend to elect a Board of Directors by votes cast on stolen stock, in defiance of an injunction of the Supreme Court. And, after all, they commit the unpardonable sin of failure.

All this is done in pursuance of a cunningly devised plan. The court called it a "fraudulent conspiracy." Mr. Shearman calls it a "programme." Mr. Fisk calls it a "raid."

In "conspiracies" there are no accessories. All are principals. This particular "conspiracy" did not spring, Minerva-like, from the brain of Mr. James Fisk. Mr. David Dudley Field, for one, helped devise it. Mr. David Dudley Field, for one, did execute it. Other lights of the bar, doubtless, had their share in it. Do they wish to claim it?

And this is, it is to be presumed, the "whole duty to clients." These are, it is to be presumed, the proceedings in which Mr. David Dudley Field is kept by "nothing but a profound conviction that he cannot with honor retire" from them. This is, it is to be presumed, Mr. Field's lesson to us from the days of Chancellor Kent.

And is the order of arrest henceforth to be one page of the advocate's brief?

It may be said, perhaps, that, after all, this decision of Mr. Justice Smith is merely the decision of a single judge; that it may be all wrong, may be reversed on appeal; that it is, as yet, too early to judge Mr. Field. The matters here stated in relation to Mr. Field do not in the least degree depend on the correctness or incorrectness of the decision of Mr. Justice Smith. To be sure, the language of that decision has been here sometimes borrowed, but merely for the purpose of showing that very respectable authority has already given a name to some of these proceedings taken on the part of Mr. Field's office. But the point of that decision is, Which board of directors was or was not legally elected? With that point we have here nothing whatever to do. It has been attempted here to make clear the character of some of those legal proceedings, by statements which are true, and which remain true whether Mr. Justice Smith's decision be reversed or not. And as to the direct share of Mr. David Dudley Field in these proceedings, no word of comment is here given, nor do any of the statements here made in relation thereto depend in any degree upon the decision of Mr. Justice Smith. These statements are made solely on the sworn testimony of Mr. Field's clients and his associate counsel. Mr. Field, assuredly, will not question the veracity of these witnesses.

Nor has Mr. Field been unheard in these matters. If guilty of anything, he is guilty of the same charges on which judgment has already gone against his clients in the case already mentioned. In that case Mr. Field and his associate counsel, with consummate ability, produced their witnesses, and argued the law and the facts before an able and impartial judge. He did his utmost there to clear his clients and failed. The issues and evidence here are precisely the same as in that case.

No one can ask of Mr. Field a higher standard of professional conduct than he himself lays down in this correspondence with Mr. Bowles. He says, ''The lawyer is responsible, not for his clients, nor for their causes, but for the manner in which he conducts their causes.'' ''I do not assent to the theory of Brougham, that the lawyer should know nobody but his client. I insist that he should defend his client *per fas* and not *per nefas*. By this rule I am willing to be judged.''

And Mr. Field says: ''I have never been consulted beforehand . . . about any transaction whatever of this company or these gentlemen, to which, so far as I now recollect, any exception has been taken.''

Does Mr. Field ''recollect'' this Susquehanna litigation?

And Mr. Bowles admits that Mr. Field ''believes himself right''; that Mr. Field has ''sinned against no statute,'' and has not ''violated any prescript of the code professional.''

In the *New York Revised Statutes*, II, 691, are certain definitions and certain penalties of certain conspiracies. A portion of the statute reads as follows:

If two or more persons conspire . . . falsely and maliciously to indict another for any offence, or to procure another to be charged or arrested for any such offence, or falsely to move or maintain any suit, or for the perversion or obstruction of justice, or the due administration of the laws, they shall be deemed guilty of a misdemeanor.

Whether or not any of the matters here related fall within the definitions here cited, or either of them, need not here be discussed.

Mr. Warren, in his work on Law Studies (Vol. I, p. 423), after relating a case of professional misconduct on the part of a member of the English bar, adds: ''This case has been presented to the reader because of the singularity of its circumstances. It appears to be the only instance recorded in the books of misconduct by a member of the bar, judicially cognizable, and punished, because of his being such.''

V

AN INQUIRY INTO THE ALBANY & SUSQUEHANNA RAILROAD LITIGATIONS OF 1869, AND MR. DAVID DUDLEY FIELD'S CONNECTION THEREWITH*

BY

GEORGE TICKNOR CURTIS

Opinion.

IN order to a right understanding of the history of these litigations, it is necessary to state the position and relations of the Albany & Susquehanna Railroad. This road commences at Albany and terminates at Binghamton, a distance of about 140 miles. It lies wholly in the state of New York, and is a New York corporation, subject, of course, to the courts of New York in relation to all its corporate rights and duties. The corporation was organized in 1852, and the construction of the road was begun in 1853; it was completed and opened for traffic in January, 1869. Albany is the eastern terminus of the great trunk line known as the New York Central Railroad. Binghamton, in the southeastern part of the state of New York, lies on the Erie Railway, which is another great trunk line extending from a point in Jersey City opposite to the city of New York, through the northern part of New Jersey, and above the northern boundary of Pennsylvania to Dunkirk and Buffalo on Lake Erie. It has access to and connections with the great anthracite coal fields of Pennsylvania.

In 1869, at the time of the opening of the Albany & Susque-

* Reprinted from the second edition, published by D. Appleton & Co., 1871. The affidavits on pages 105–124 of the pamphlet, referred to, *post*, p. 315, are omitted.

JAMES FISK

hanna Railroad, the Erie Railway was under the management of a Board of Directors, consisting of Jay Gould, A. S. Diven, James Fisk, Jr., Frederick A. Lane, J. C. B. Davis, William M. Tweed, Peter B. Sweeny, Daniel S. Miller, Jr., Homer Ramsdell, John Hilton, George M. Groves, John Ganson, Charles G. Sisson, O. W. Chapman, Henry Thompson, and George M. Diven. The Albany & Susquehanna Railroad was under the management of Joseph H. Ramsey, Jacob Leonard, Jeremiah J. Austin, William A. Rice, Jonathan R. Herrick, Charles Courter, John Westover, John Cook, Azro Chase, David Wilber, Eliakim R. Ford, Samuel North, Ira E. Sherman, and Alonzo Everts.

The Albany & Susquehanna Railroad, from its position, was, when completed, capable of being made a connecting link between the Erie Railway and the city of Albany, and from thence with the lines extending from Albany, north and east, into New England; or it might, by being kept from close business relations with the Erie Railway, be kept as a mere line of communication between the cities of Binghamton and Albany, and the towns and regions lying between those places. This capacity of the Albany & Susquehanna Railroad to become an important link by which the coal of Pennsylvania might be made to reach Albany, and thence be distributed to the New England states, by means of a close business relation with the Erie Railway, is an important fact to be stated here; because that relation is and has been regarded as one of the main motives which are said to have actuated the managers of the Erie Railway in their efforts to assist those who wished to retain the control of the Albany & Susquehanna Railroad. So far as this motive is an element in forming a correct opinion as to the conduct of any person who may have been concerned as a lawyer in any of the matters involved in the contest for the majority of the direction in the last-mentioned corporation, it ought to be distinctly stated that it was desirable to the Erie Railway Company to have the Albany & Susquehanna Railroad become a connecting link by which the anthracite coal from the great coal beds of Pennsylvania could be made to reach the coal consumers of New England more directly and cheaply than it otherwise could reach them.*

But there is another fact which, with equal fairness, ought also to be stated. Before the Albany & Susquehanna Railroad was finished, and, therefore, before it was capable of becoming practically connected with the Erie Railway, there was a condition of dissatisfaction among its stockholders and directors, who were to some extent scattered along its line, concerning its financial management. At the election of its directors in 1868, by the choice of the stockholders, a majority of directors, representing a decided opposition to Mr. Ramsey, were chosen; so that when the election of 1869 was approaching, there was an open contest between two parties in this corporation to obtain a majority of the new Board of Directors, wholly independent of any question of connection with the Erie Railway, and growing out of differences that had sprung up within the corporation itself as to the financial policy which had been pursued by Mr. Ramsey in building and managing the road. Mr. Ramsey and his friends were at this time a minority of the board; his opponents were the majority; and each party was anxious at the approaching election to secure the control of the new board.

The condition of the stock of the Albany & Susquehanna Railroad Company at this time was as follows: Its authorized capital was $4,000,000 (40,000 shares). There had been issued $1,723,800 (17,238 shares), which were undisputed. Of the original subscriptions, a considerable amount had been forfeited to the company for nonpayment of assessments;† and of this amount there were at least $300,000 (3,000 shares) which were alleged to have been reissued to parties who had not paid more than 25 per cent of the par, and which were therefore disputed. Assuming that no greater amount of the forfeited stock had been reissued, there remained in the hands of the company 19,762 shares.

---

* In 1869 the coal traffic of the Erie Railway was 1,038,000 tons.

† The original subscribers of this forfeited stock had paid, as required by law, 10 per cent.

The party desiring to oust Mr. Ramsey from the management (which for convenience may be called the Church party),* were obliged to rely upon what they held or could obtain of the portion of the stock (17,238 shares) that had been previously issued, and about the issue of which there could be no question. In such a situation, the attitude of the two parties within this corporation would inevitably lead to efforts on the side of the Church party to obtain the right of voting on so much of the 17,238 shares of undisputed stock as they could command, and to watch and control any proceedings of the Ramsey party to make an improper use of portions of the forfeited stock or of the stock that had not up to this time been subscribed for. On the other hand, the effort of the Ramsey party would be to increase their ownership or control of so much of the 17,238 shares of undisputed stock as they could command, to add from the forfeited stock (if it was rightfully reissued) and from stock not as yet subscribed for, so much as might be needful to secure a majority of the voting power, and to watch and control any attempts of the Church party to vote upon stock not entitled to be represented in the vote for directors, or not entitled to be voted upon by the persons who should undertake to claim that right. I state these as the objects at which the two parties might be expected respectively to aim, because they were on the one side and the other lawful and proper objects in themselves. They could be pursued by lawful, proper, and fair means; they might possibly be sought to be accomplished by unlawful, improper, and unfair means. Whatever was the danger arising from a temptation to use means that might be either illegal or improper, any fair investigation into the conduct of either of these parties must assume that there was a lawful and proper object which each could seek to accomplish by lawful and proper means. The object of each party was to elect a majority of the Board of Directors at the election

* Mr. Walter S. Church was the leading candidate on the ticket for directors in opposition to Mr. Ramsey, voted for in 1869, and was chosen president by that board.

which was to take place on the seventh of September (1869);
and this could only be done by each party voting on all the stock
on which it could lawfully obtain the right to vote, and by each
preventing its adversary from voting on stock not entitled to be
voted on, or not entitled to be voted on by the persons who
might undertake to use it. Moreover, in such an investigation as
I design to make into the proceedings of these parties, I shall
assume that each of them is entitled to the presumption, at the
outset, that none but lawful and proper means would be used to
accomplish their objects.

Beginning then with the Church party, it is proper to state
here that at an early period in the preparation for this contest,
some of the leading persons among them, under the circumstances
hereinafter stated, sought the aid of Messrs. Fisk and Gould,
officers of the Erie Railway, to assist them in acquiring the right
to vote on so much of the 17,238 shares of stock, then in the hands
of *bona fide* holders, as could be commanded. This required a
large amount of money. Was it a lawful and proper thing to be
done? On this point no doubt whatever can be entertained, if it
was lawful and proper for the Ramsey party to obtain the control of any portion of the same stock, or of any portion of the
stock remaining in the hands of the company. It was furthermore perfectly natural and right for the Church party (if they
considered it to be for the interest of the Albany & Susquehanna Railroad, of which they then were a majority of the directors, to bring about a close business connection with the Erie
Railway) to seek the assistance of the leading managers of that
road in accomplishing the object which they had in view; just as
it was, on the other hand, perfectly natural and right for the
Ramsey party, if they deprecated any connection with the Erie
Railway, or for any other reason wished to prevent the Church
party from continuing to be a majority of the Board of Directors
of the Susquehanna road, to use all lawful and proper means to
accomplish *their* objects.

In pursuance, then, of what must be regarded as in itself a

lawful and proper object, the Church party proceeded, with the
aid of Fisk and Gould, to purchase stock of the Susquehanna
Road then in the stock market, and to obtain from individuals
and towns on the line of the road the right to vote on stock held
by such individuals or towns, by obtaining either transfers or
proxies or pledges of votes. Among the directors who represented
the dissatisfaction with Mr. Ramsey's management of the road,
were Mr. Leonard, who lived at Albany, Mr. Wilber, who lived at
Milford, but whose place of business was in the adjoining town
of Oneonta, and Mr. North, who lived at Unadilla. These two
towns, Oneonta and Unadilla, were on the line of the road, and
both of them held stock in the company. In the month of July,
Messrs. Leonard, Wilber, and North, in preparation for the election, applied to Messrs. Gould and Fisk for assistance in purchasing stock of the company. They represented that with the
stock they already had, and the stock of such towns as they knew
to be favorable to their views, they already had a majority of
the stock, but to guard against Mr. Ramsey's proceedings they
considered it desirable to purchase more. They stated to Mr.
Gould that they could pledge the stock of Cobleskill, Milford,
and Unadilla, to vote for the Church ticket of directors. Mr. Wilber was one of the town commissioners for holding the stock of
Milford, Mr. C. Courter, another of the directors in the same
interest, was one of the commissioners for Cobleskill, and Mr.
Chase was one of the commissioners for Maryland. Mr. North
could command the vote on the stock of Unadilla. They considered, therefore, that the four towns of Cobleskill, Unadilla,
Maryland, and Milford, were sure to vote against the Ramsey
ticket, as the taxpayers of those towns had been opposed all
along to Mr. Ramsey's management, and were anxious, moreover, to avail themselves of the first opportunity to have the
stock of their towns sold at par. Messrs. Leonard, Wilber, and
North, represented to Mr. Gould that although they believed that
a decided majority of the stockholders were opposed to Mr. Ramsey, they desired to place the election beyond peradventure by

purchasing stock which they did not then control. Mr. Gould concluded, after deliberation, to assist them, and authorized them to
buy stock in the market for him, but not in his name. This was
done to some extent. As the controversy became warmer, and
there was reason to doubt how the commissioners of some of the
towns would act, these directors urged Mr. Gould to furnish the
funds necessary to buy the stock of some of the other towns. This
was done with the stock of several towns, and the stock was transferred on the books, but when the stock of the town of Oneonta,
purchased by Wilber, was presented for transfer, the town commissioners being present, the treasurer refused to transfer it. On
the next day an injunction, obtained from Judge J. M. Parker,
against its transfer was served, and before this injunction could
be removed the books were clandestinely removed from the office
of the company;—they were hidden for a time in a tomb in a
graveyard in Albany, and were afterward carried from place to
place, remaining concealed for a whole month. Agreements were
then made by which the stock of Oneonta and Colesville was contracted to the Church party, to be paid for when transfers could
be made. The stock of Davenport was purchased, and the full
amount paid for it, but the transfer was refused. When the election came on, the stock of Davenport was voted on by Mr. Harris
under proxies from Mr. Gould and from the town commissioners.
He also voted on the stock of Oneonta (purchased by Wilber)
under proxies from Wilber and from the town commissioners.
He also voted on the stock of Colesville purchased by North, but
without any proxy from the commissioners. The stock of other
towns, Seward, Summit, and Westford, was purchased, and
transfers made to the Church party before the books were taken
away. The towns of Cobleskill, Unadilla, Maryland, and Milford,
through their commissioners, gave proxies to the Church party,
and Mr. Harris voted on them, the commissioners being present.
Besides holding the proxies, Mr. Harris also voted under an assignment of the stock of these four towns embraced in their
agreement to vote for the Church directors.

It is now necessary to describe a movement made by the Ramsey party. That movement consisted in a resort by Mr. Ramsey and his friends, to the shares still remaining unissued and unsubscribed for in the hands of the company. On the evening of the fifth of August, Mr. Ramsey assembled the minority of the then directors, at his house, having an old stock subscription book of the company with him. They subscribed among them for 9,500 shares, on the understanding that the subscribers individually were to make no present payments, but that 10 per cent should be paid in immediately, for which Mr. Ramsey was to provide; *the remainder to be called in when and as the board of directors expected to be chosen by the aid of this stock might direct*. It was further agreed, that if any of the subscribers did not wish to keep their stock, Mr. Ramsey should take it off their hands after the election. Mr. Ramsey, therefore, had to raise immediately $95,000, to pay in the 10 per cent on these subscriptions for 9,500 shares. To accomplish this, he drew a draft for $100,000 on David Groesbeck, who cashed it; and to secure Groesbeck, Mr. Ramsey deposited with him as collateral security $150,000 *of the equipment bonds of the company, belonging to the company, and which Mr. Ramsey obtained from the treasurer for this purpose*. The 10 per cent being thus paid in, the 9,500 shares were credited on the books of the company to the supposed subscribers, and they gave their proxies to Mr. Ramsey to vote at the coming election.

It has been said of this transaction, that while "its legality is open to criticism," and "its good faith even might well have been suspected," it was "justifiable" under the circumstances.* The circumstances alleged in its justification are, that Mr. Ramsey "was fighting men who had set the most infamous precedents ever known for transactions of a not dissimilar character"; that the "positions" of "these men in the community, their standing in the courts, their financial and fiduciary relations, were notorious." The amount of these excuses is that Messrs. Fisk and

* *North American Review* for April, 1871, Article "An Erie Raid."

Gould were men whose reputations for fair dealing were bad; not that they had thus far done anything in regard to this particular corporation that could be regarded as fraudulent, but that they had set "infamous precedents" in other affairs, that they might therefore be expected to act like knaves in this contest, and hence that it was necessary to fight them with weapons of the kind which it was said they were accustomed to use. I presume it must be unnecessary for me to say to any class of readers, whose opinion is of the slightest consequence, that the alleged bad reputation of the men Mr. Ramsey was "fighting," can afford neither legal nor moral justification for any act of his, that was either illegal or wrong in itself; and that it is by its own intrinsic character, that both the legality and the morality of this transaction must be judged. If the kind of justification or apology which has been set up for this transaction, is to be admitted as a test of its legality or morality, then the same rule must be applied to any subsequent act done by the opposite party, who must be acquitted of wrong by the "precedents" afforded by their opponents. No such rule will be followed in the present examination of these occurrences.

Up to this point, namely, the fifth of August, there had been sundry suits commenced. The first that was commenced by the Ramsey party was a suit in the name of the town of Oneonta, against the company and David Wilber, commenced August 2, in Otsego County, in the interest of the Ramsey party, to restrain the transfer of seven hundred shares of stock purchased of the town commissioners by Wilber, who was in the interest of the Church party.* An *ex parte* injunction was granted by Judge J. M. Parker of the Supreme Court. It was promptly dissolved, on the fifth of August, on proof that Wilber had purchased the stock in good faith and for full par value.†

On the fourth of August two suits were commenced by David

---

* A suit instituted by Bush on the same day, will be described hereafter.

† I understand that no service of any injunction or other papers in this case has been made upon anyone excepting Phelps, the treasurer of the company.

Wilber in the Supreme Court for the City and County of New York. The first was a suit against the Albany & Susquehanna Railroad Company, Ramsey, its president, and Phelps, its treasurer, to compel the transfer to Wilber on the books of the company of the stock which he had bought of the town of Oneonta (seven hundred shares) and certain other stock which he had bought of the town of Worcester. The plaintiff alleged in his complaint that he had presented the certificates to Phelps, the treasurer, for transfer, and that the transfer had been refused, on the pretense that the plaintiff had not paid par to the towns for the stock, *"which pretense"* the plaintiff alleged *"was untrue."* This allegation the plaintiff supported by his own oath, and of course the fact was within his own knowledge. He also alleged, on his information and belief, that Phelps, in refusing to transfer his stock, acted in the interest of Ramsey to prevent the plaintiff from voting on the stock at the approaching election. Whether this was true or not was not material to the plaintiff's right to have his stock transferred. What it was material for the judge to know was, whether the objection to the plaintiff's title made by the treasurer, was true or untrue; and he was informed that it was untrue, by the oath of the plaintiff. Judge Barnard granted an order (on the same day, August 4) directing the defendants to refrain from their refusal to transfer the stock, and to refrain from their refusal to issue certificates to the plaintiff, until the further order of the court.

Was this a proper order to be granted? I can see no reason to question it. It was, undoubtedly, an *ex parte* order; but the relief which it gave, was a relief to which the plaintiff was instantly entitled, if the judge believed that par value had been paid for the stock, and this he was bound to believe on the oath of the plaintiff that the treasurer's assigned reason for refusing to transfer was untrue, for all the purposes of the order which the order was made to embrace. By reserving to the defendants an opportunity to come in and ask for a "further order," the judge protected them in the right to contest the plaintiff's title to the stock if they should choose to contest it. What he protected the plaintiff in, was the right to vote on the stock, on the title which he had shown, provided that the defendants should not controvert that title.

The other suit by Wilber was a suit commenced in the Supreme Court, in the county of New York, on the fourth of August, in his capacity as a director of the company, making the company, Ramsey, the president, and all the other directors codefendants. The complaint alleged that Ramsey, the president, had at various previous times issued three thousand shares of the stock of the company to various persons as full-paid stock, when none of such persons had paid more than 25 per cent of the par value; that he had ordered the treasurer not to transfer other stock to persons who had bought it; that he had caused collusive suits to be brought for the purpose of preventing *bona fide* owners of a majority of the stock from voting at the coming election of directors; that the transfer books would be closed on the seventh of August, and that Ramsey was seeking to prevent a fair election; that forty-four shares of stock had been issued to one Goodyear without payment of the par value by him to the company, and solely on the false pretense that the company owed Goodyear a debt : and that this issue of stock was in fact made to Goodyear for the purpose of creating votes in favor of Ramsey as a director. This complaint was supported by the positive oath of the plaintiff in respect to the election, the closing of the books, and the wrongful issue of stock to Goodyear, all of which allegations were stated by the plaintiff as within his personal knowledge. In other respects, the complaint rested on information and belief. The complaint prayed for the removal of Ramsey from the offices of president and director; that he be suspended from exercising those offices; that all the defendants be restrained from issuing any stock of the company, except upon subscriptions made in pursuance of a resolution of the Board of Directors, and after public notice of the time and place for making subscriptions, and on cash payments of the par value or upward. Judge Barnard on the same day (August 4) made an order covering but a part of the relief sought. The order recited that it appeared satisfactorily to the judge, on the complaint duly verified by the plaintiff, that sufficient grounds for an injunction existed; it directed that the defendants, and each of them, and their agents, refrain from creating or issuing stock except upon subscriptions made after public notice, and at or over the par value paid in cash; and that Ramsey *refrain from exercising* the offices of president and director, and from issuing any stock, or in any way interfering in the affairs of the company, *until the further order of the court*. This order was served on Mr. Ramsey on the fourth or the fifth of August.

Was this a proper order to be granted on this complaint and its verification? The order had two branches. In one part of it, it restrained every officer of the company from issuing any stock, excepting in a mode of proceeding which would in no way cripple the company in its efforts to realize money on any of its stock yet unsubscribed for, and at the same time it protected the company and the *bona fide* stockholders from just such issues as those which were arranged by Mr. Ramsey on the fifth of August, the very next day after this order was made, and after it had been served upon him. It is true that this occurrence had not happened when the order was made; but its happening within a little more than twenty-four hours is a good illustration of the bearing of the order on the interests of the company. It is true, also, that the complaint gave the court no information that those issues arranged for on the fifth of August were contemplated or threatened; but it did allege positively as to a part, and as to the rest on the plaintiff's information and belief, that wrongful issues of large amounts of stock had theretofore been made, and the plaintiff thus attesting his information and belief of this fact was himself a director. Considering that a contested election of directors was approaching, I think that a judge exercising the powers of a court of equity, when he went no further in ordering a mode of proceeding in the sale and issue of stock, than the protection of the company and the law itself required, acted wisely, especially as he reserved to the directors a power to come before the court, which was always open, and have the order modified, if it should work any inconvenience. As to that part of the order which *suspended* Mr. Ramsey from the present exercise of the offices of president and director until the further order of the court, it is to be remembered that this corporation had thirteen other directors, among them a vice-president, who could attend to all the business of the election, and all other affairs of the company; that the order in no way interfered with Mr. Ramsey's candidacy for a reëlection as director; and that it simply created a practical vacancy in the office of president, until Mr. Ramsey should choose to ask to be restored to the exercise of his office. If it is said that the judge should have required more positive evidence of Mr. Ramsey's alleged previous misconduct in his office, and that it was improvident or improper to suspend him from it on an allegation of facts supported only by the information and belief of the plaintiff, I think that the facts that the plaintiff was himself a director, that all the other directors were made defendants, that Ramsey and the other directors, or any of them, could immediately have had this order rescinded if the plaintiff's allegations were not true, that there was a positive averment of a wrongful issue of stock to Goodyear, and that the reëlection of the new board was not to happen for more than a month, brought the application within the discretion which a judge may exercise in granting injunctions, when he is not required by statute to issue a notice to show cause before taking any action. In this case, the discretionary power does not appear to have been exercised in a manner to do any injury to the interests of the company.

But it has been objected to this order that it was granted without proper evidence of Ramsey's alleged misconduct in his office, because the sole evidence in support of the complaint was, as it is said, the oath of Wilber, the plaintiff, to his "information and belief" of the facts of that misconduct. A proper analysis of the complaint and the *jurat* shows that a material part of the facts alleged were sworn to be within the knowledge of the plaintiff. As to the matters stated, and sworn to be stated, upon information and belief, I am not prepared to admit that it was not proper for the judge to regard at all what was stated on the plaintiff's information and belief. If we concede the general principle that an injunction is not to be granted on mere information and belief, there was yet enough averred in this complaint, on the plaintiff's own knowledge, to support the injunction. Thus, the facts that the plaintiff was a director, that Ramsey was president, that Phelps was treasurer, that there was to be an election on the seventh of September, that the transfer books were to be closed on the seventh of August, that forty-four shares had been issued to Goodyear without payment of the par value, and that no debt from the company to Goodyear had been audited by the board or their committee, having the sole power to audit claims, were all averred positively in the complaint, and were all within the general rule which makes the plaintiff's verification of facts so averred by his oath to the complaint, sufficient evidence. Will it be said that it was improper in the judge to connect these facts with the facts averred and verified on the plaintiff's information and belief, respecting Ramsey's complicity with this wrongful issue of stock to Goodyear, and with his alleged wrongful issue of stock to other parties? That depends upon the proper application of the general rule which declares that mere information and belief is not evidence. Although as a general rule, information and belief is not legal evidence, it may, *under certain circumstances,* furnish sufficient ground for granting a motion. Thus, if the party against whom a fact is sworn on information and belief must know whether the allegation is true or false, and he is silent, there is reasonable ground for presuming existence of the fact.* In like manner, where the question was whether the defendant had purchased certain stock with the money of an intestate estate of which he was administrator, and the plaintiff, on a motion for an injunction, made affidavit that, from his ac-

* *Oakley* v. *Aspinwall,* 3 New York R. 559, per Bronson, Chief Justice.

quaintance with the defendant's insolvent circumstances, he *believed* that he could not have purchased the stock excepting with money of the estate, *and that he had applied to the defendant's stockbrokers to inform him of the truth of the fact, and the information was refused,* the Court of Exchequer held that the evidence was sufficient to grant the injunction, because the party whom the statement was meant to affect had had an opportunity to deny it and had not done so.* Let this decision be compared with one of the allegations of this complaint, positively sworn to by the plaintiff, who averred that he had been informed by the clerk in charge of the transfer book that the issue of stock was made to Goodyear by the order of Ramsey, under pretense that some indefinite amount of money was due from the company to Goodyear.

The general rule that a bill of complaint, in order to afford foundation for an *ex parte* injunction, must be supported in its averments by something more than the plaintiff's information and belief, relates to cases where the bill or complaint, in respect to all its allegations of fact, rests on information and belief alone. Yet, in such a case, there may be a temporary injunction, with an order to show cause. In *Campbell* v. *Morrison,* 7 Paige, 157, 161, Chancellor Walworth said: "In cases of emergency, where serious injury would probably be done to the complainant before a reasonable time to show cause would expire, the master, upon a bill thus framed [on information and belief *alone*], may allow a temporary injunction in the meantime; which fails, of course, when the time for showing cause arrives, if not continued by the court." This was precisely the character of the injunction by which Judge Barnard suspended Ramsey from the office of president, and, moreover, the complaint was not founded on information and belief alone. Indeed, it is the general practice to grant such injunctions on information and belief. It will be seen hereafter that several such injunctions were granted by Judge Peckham to the Ramsey party on *mere* information and belief. I

* *Scott* v. *Becher,* 4 Price, 346–352; 2 Exchequer R., 137, 139.

have not heard that the counsel who advised, or the attorneys
who procured them have been censured; and yet, Field & Shearman have been denounced as guilty of the grossest impropriety
of professional conduct for doing what the critics have overlooked in their adversaries. I do not cite what was done by their
adversaries as a justification, if it was illegally done. But I cite
it as proof of a general and prevalent practice of the courts to
receive statements sworn to be made on information and belief
as evidence to be regarded in granting injunctions; and I must
add that, in the Albany proceedings in these litigations, the practice was carried to a very great length, for none of the *jurats* in
any of the Ramsey suits (I believe I have examined them all)
made the allegations of the complaints to rest upon anything
more than information and belief.

It may be proper to state here, for the information of those
who are not familiar with the statute law of New York, that this
suspension of Mr. Ramsey from the exercise of the office of president of this corporation, was the exercise of a power vested in the
court from which the injunction emanated. By the Revised
Statutes, Part III, chap. viii, Art. 2, § 33, it was declared: ''The
chancellor shall have jurisdiction over directors, managers, and
other trustees and officers of corporations, . . . 3, to *suspend* any
such trustee or officer from exercising his office, whenever it
shall *appear* that he has *abused his trust:* 4, to *remove* any such
trustee or officer from his office, upon *proof* or *conviction* of
gross misconduct.'' § 35. ''The jurisdiction conferred by the preceding thirty-third section, shall be exercised *as in ordinary cases,
on bill or petition,* as the case may require, or, the chancellor may
direct, at the instance of the Attorney-General, prosecuting in
behalf of the people of this state, or at the instance of any
creditor of such corporation, *or at the instance of any director*,
trustee, or other officer of such corporation having a general
superintendence of its concerns.'' This ample jurisdiction passed
by the Constitution of 1847 to the Supreme Court.

It is to be observed here that the orders hitherto made by

Judge Barnard, two only, afforded to Wilber, the plaintiff, the provisional relief to which he was entitled, and, at the same time, afforded to the defendants power to have them rescinded or modified, whenever they should appear before the court and offer proofs that Wilber was not entitled to the relief which the orders had given him. If the allegations of his complaints were not true, the defendants could at any moment have shown that the orders ought to be rescinded or changed; and, whether it can or cannot be said that the order suspending Ramsey from acting as president was improvidently granted, there can be no pretense that it was void. It was therefore entitled to be obeyed. But if I read the history of Mr. Ramsey's proceedings rightly, this order was not obeyed, although no attempt was made to have it set aside or modified, nor was that part of the order obeyed which restrained the issue of new stock excepting upon certain terms and in a certain mode, nor was any application made to the court to vacate or change it. On the contrary, Mr. Ramsey proceeded on that day, August 5 (no doubt under advice of counsel, but nevertheless as it seems to me under a mistaken idea of what he could lawfully do), to do acts which violated both branches of Judge Barnard's order of August 4. These acts were official acts as president, and the order had suspended him from the exercise of that office. One of them consisted in taking the subscriptions for 9,500 shares of stock, as above described, on the evening of August 5, and constituting the alleged subscribers stockholders of the company. The other consisted in instituting a suit in the Supreme Court in Albany County of a retaliatory nature, *in the name of the corporation,* against four of the directors, Leonard, Herrick, North, and Wilber, and making Phelps, the treasurer, a codefendant. This complaint alleged, on information and belief, *inter alia,* that the four directors named defendants had entered into a wicked and corrupt conspiracy and combination with Jay Gould and others, managers of the Erie Railway, to transfer the corporate property and franchises of the plaintiff, and its whole control and management, to the corpora-

tion known as the Erie Railway Company, which last-mentioned
company it averred was managed and controlled by Jay Gould
and others for their own selfish purposes of stock speculation and
other private ends, and not in the true interests of the said Erie
Railway Company, and that the success of the conspirators in
transferring the plaintiff's company to the same control and
management would ruin it. The complaint further alleged as acts
of the conspirators, in pursuance of their corrupt and wicked
purpose, the commencement of suits by Wilber, one of the defendants, on false allegations, and the obtaining of an injunction issued by Judge Barnard, *ex parte,* in the city of New York,
where none of the parties resided, suspending Ramsey, president
of the plaintiff corporation, from acting in that office, with the
purpose of preventing him from so acting at a meeting of the
directors to be held on the same day when the injunction was
served, and to get the aid of Herrick as vice-president, acting as
president, in furtherance of the general object of the conspiracy;
that the injunction was obtained by fraud and falsehood; that the
three thousand shares alleged in Wilber's complaint to have
been wrongfully issued by Ramsey were lawfully and rightfully
issued; that the other allegations of Wilber in his said complaint
were untrue; and that the Wilber suit was instituted and the injunction suspending Ramsey from acting as president was obtained in pursuance of the conspiracy to transfer the plaintiff's
property and the management of its road to Jay Gould and
others, etc. That Phelps, the treasurer, might, if not restrained,
transfer stock in plaintiff's corporation under the order and
direction of the four directors named defendants. The complaint
thereupon prayed that the four directors be restrained and enjoined from taking any further steps in pursuance of the conspiracy, and be removed from their positions, and in the meantime be restrained and enjoined from acting as directors, and
that Herrick be restrained from acting as vice-president, and
that Phelps, the treasurer, be restrained from transferring any
stock by order of these four directors, or by any resolution of the

board carried by their votes, or either of them, and for further relief, etc.

This complaint was sworn to by Mr. Ramsey, *as president*, on the fifth of August, before the Albany County Judge; the affidavit being, that the complaint "is true of his own knowledge, excepting as to those matters therein stated on information and belief, and as to those matters he believes it to be true." As the corporation was the plaintiff, there could be no allegation of knowledge made by the plaintiff. Mr. Ramsey's oath to the complaint, which asserted nothing but that the whole complaint was on information and belief, was made in the capacity of president. The Albany County judge, acting in the Supreme Court, granted the injunction prayed for on the same day, restraining the four directors named defendants from acting as directors, and from voting at any meeting of the board, until the further order of the court; and restraining Herrick from acting as vice-president (without saying until further order), and also restraining the treasurer, Phelps, from complying with any direction or demand of the other defendants with reference to the disposition or custody of the books and papers of the company, or with any resolution of the board carried by their votes, until the further order of the court.

Whether such a suit as this could be instituted in the name of a corporation without a vote of the Board of Directors or of its Executive Committee expressly authorizing it, admits, of course, of the gravest doubt.* Whether the president could have instituted it in his own private name, although he was under an injunction suspending him from the exercise of his office, is another matter; but, instituted in the name of the corporation, it was one of the highest corporate acts that could be performed, and in so instituting it Mr. Ramsey necessarily acted as president, and he so described himself in the *jurat*. He could not have determined to take this step without having determined to disobey the injunction of Judge Barnard, which had suspended him from the

---

* It was not authorized by statute.

exercise of his office; and it is a remarkable proof of such a determination, that all the facts of conspiracy, etc., alleged in this suit could, if true, have been presented on affidavits to Judge Barnard, on an application to vacate his order suspending Mr. Ramsey from acting as president, and (if the order had been vacated) he would then have been free to effect the removal of his four codirectors from office, in his capacity of president, if there were facts and law to warrant it.

The reader, therefore, who has thus far followed the history of the two parties within this corporation, must now observe that he has arrived at a period when the leading person at the head of one of them has determined that he will not obey an injunction issued by a judge of the Supreme Court, although he has an opportunity to apply to have it vacated. Am I to discuss the question whether this determination was made in reference to the orders of the particular judge, and to enter into conjectures whether it was due to a belief that Judge Barnard himself was a party to the alleged conspiracy? Until I hear of an impeachment of a judge and his removal from office, I will not so disgrace the judiciary of the state as to inquire for any man's reason for disobeying his official orders, or seek to know whether they are founded in scandal more or less in general circulation. I know of nothing that can justify any breach of a judicial order made by a judge in office; and I beg to say to the public who may read these observations, that when once it is supposed, for any cause, that the orders of one judge are entitled to less respect than the orders of any other judge, the orders of all judges may be set at defiance by any party who does not choose to obey them. But it is the less necessary to inquire whether Mr. Ramsay thought that *Judge Barnard's* orders could be disobeyed with impunity, because he averred in this complaint that Judge Barnard's orders were obtained from him by fraud and falsehood; not that they were made corruptly. If the orders were obtained by a fraud upon the judge, they could have been vacated on showing to him, or any other judge of the Supreme Court in New York

County, that fraud. To disobey and violate the orders of a judge, on the ground that he was imposed on when he issued them, without *asking him*, or any competent authority, to rescind them, is an act without any excuse.

The reader has also now to notice the situation of this corporation on the close of that day, the fifth of August. Ramsey, the president, was restrained from acting in that capacity or as a director. Leonard, Herrick, North, and Wilber, four of the (Church) directors, were suspended from their offices; and Herrick, the vice-president, was in like manner prohibited from exercising in any way the duties of his office. Out of fourteen directors, therefore, there remained eight having at that time a legal competency to act. But neither the charter nor the by-laws made any provision for appointing an acting president in the absence or incapacity of both the president and vice-president. Moreover, the management of all the business of the road was in the hands of an Executive Committee of five directors; and a majority of this committee were made incapable of acting by the operation of Judge Clute's injunction. Without violating an injunction of the Supreme Court, the business of the company could not be carried on in the manner prescribed by its charter and by-laws. Payments could only be made by a warrant or check signed by a majority of the Executive Committee; and, besides all its employees and servants, who were to be paid monthly, the company had other large obligations falling due within sixty days.

The only alternative was to place the road in the hands of a receiver or receivers. It could not be run for a week without being so placed. Accordingly, on the sixth of August, a suit was instituted in the Supreme Court in the City and County of New York by Azro Chase, a stockholder and a director, against the corporation and all the other directors as codefendants. The complaint contained two classes of allegations as the grounds on which the interposition of the court was asked. One class of facts, averred on the information and belief of the plaintiff, related to Ramsey the president's alleged misconduct in issuing stock unlawfully for the purpose of creating votes for himself at the approaching election, and in obstructing the transfer of stock on the books for the purpose of preventing a fair election. The other class of facts, averred positively and supported by the plaintiff's oath as within his own knowledge, related to the present situation of the company under the injunction which had suspended four of its directors, and that suspending Ramsey its president; its incapacity to make an acting president; the fact that the Executive Committee were incapable of acting, and that the business of the company could not be carried on according to its charter and by-laws without violating one or more injunctions of the Supreme Court, and the pressing nature of its business engagements. The complaint prayed for the suspension or removal of Ramsey from the offices of president and director, and for a receiver of all the property of the company, to administer the same under the direction of the court, with the usual powers, until a full and legal meeting of the directors could act on the appointment of a new president without violating any injunction. Under this complaint Judge Barnard, on the sixth of August, made the following order, the original of which is now before me:

SUPREME COURT

Azro Chase

against

The Albany & Susquehanna Railroad Company, Joseph H. Ramsey, Jeremiah J. Austin, Jacob Leonard, William A. Rice, Charles Courter, John Westover, John Cook, David Wilber, Eliakim R. Ford, Samuel North, Ira E. Sherman, Alonzo Everts, and Jonathan R. Herrick.

On the complaint in this action and the affidavits hereto annexed, and the consent of sundry defendants, I do order that Charles Courter and

James Fisk, Jr., be and they are hereby appointed receivers of all the property, franchises and effects of the Albany & Susquehanna Railroad Company, with all the powers and authority of receivers in like cases; that the said receivers file with the clerk of this court, or deposit with a judge thereof, to be afterward filed, a bond with two sufficient sureties, in the penalty of one hundred thousand dollars, for the faithful performance of their duties; that they take immediate possession of the said property, receive all moneys and make all payments necessary or proper for the due operation of the road; that they have power to employ counsel and such assistants as they may require; that they pay for the legal expenses attending their appointment, and that they be empowered to do all things which any or all of the existing officers, agents and servants might lawfully do. That said receivers shall not be personally liable, except for their wilful wrongs or gross personal negligence.

And let the defendants show cause before me, at a Special Term of this Court, at the Court-House in New York City, on the sixteenth day of August, 1869, at noon, why this order should not stand, and a further order be made in the premises.

    NEW YORK, *August* 6, 1869.

                                        GEORGE G. BARNARD, J.S.C.

We consent to the making of the annexed order:

    NEW YORK, *August* 6, 1869.

                                        SAMUEL NORTH,
                                        AZRO CHASE,
                                        ALONZO EVERTS,
                                        J. R. HERRICK,
                                        DAVID WILBER,
                                        JACOB LEONARD,
                                        C. COURTER,
                        The Albany & Susquehanna R. R. Co.
                                        J. R. HERRICK, V.P.

That this was an order proper to be made, under the circumstances set forth in the complaint and verified by the oath of a director and his knowledge of the facts, seems to me entirely clear. It will be observed that the order took no action in regard to the averments made on information and belief, as grounds for the removal or suspension of Ramsey, but that it acted only on the receivership, the grounds for which were duly verified. Those grounds being duly verified, the receivership seems to have been a necessity, pressing and immediate; and as the order directed notice to the defendants to show cause at a Special Term in the city of New York, on the sixteenth day of August, before the judge who issued it, why it should not stand, and a further order be made, there can be no just pretense to say, as has been said, that this receivership was obtained in order that by having the control of the road and its property the receivers might by means of that control fraudulently or unfairly carry an election of directors that was not to be held until the seventh of September. In fact, a similar charge is just as applicable to a receivership obtained in Albany on the same day and about the same hour by the Ramsey party, which will be described hereafter, as it is to the receivership obtained in the city of New York.

But there are circumstances said to have been connected with the granting of this receivership by Judge Barnard, which it has been a part of my duty to investigate, and to which I now invite the reader's attention. Many things have been said or insinuated about this matter which are entirely unfounded. The charge that has been made is virtually, that Judge Barnard was acting collusively with the parties who obtained this order, to assist them in carrying out their unlawful conspiracy for obtaining the means of effecting a fraudulent or unfair election of directors. He has been called "the favorite judge of these litigants,"* and it has been said that Field & Shearman, their attorneys, must have known that he was so. In proof of this telegrams have been hunted up and most improperly given up by some telegraph office or operator, in shameful violation of the clear duty of the telegraph, which have been published as proofs that Judge Barnard was resorted to to grant this receivership, because he was "the favorite judge of these litigants," and that as such he was very willing to aid them. This whole matter is capable of a simple and natural explanation.

* General Barlow's letter.

On the sixth of August, Judge Barnard was necessarily absent from his official duties in Special Term at chambers, attending the bedside of a very near relative (his mother), in Poughkeepsie, who was dangerously ill. In the early part of that day, it appears from the published telegrams, a dispatch signed by James H. Coleman* was sent to Judge Barnard from the city of New York, informing him that certain matters of business in which the city corporation counsel was concerned, had been postponed to the following Monday, and ending with the inquiry, "How is your mother?" About the hour of five thirty that afternoon, Judge Barnard answered this dispatch with the information that his mother was "very low." At a later period in that evening it appears from a dispatch that has been published as "No. 3," that the following was sent to Judge Barnard:

[No. 3.] Hon. G. G. Barnard, Poughkeepsie. Come to New York without fail to-night. Answer care 359 West Twenty-third Street. 1. 15 D. H. Fisk's pass 550.   JAMES H. COLEMAN.

The obvious construction of this dispatch, as Judge Barnard must have read it, was, that his friend Mr. Coleman meant to inform him that there was urgent judicial business requiring his presence in this city that night, and as he was the judge assigned to hold the Special Term during that month, and, as he understood that all the other judges were absent from the city, he felt bound to comply with the summons.† But comment has been made on the fact that this dispatch went under Mr. Fisk's pass, and that No. 359 West Twenty-third Street was "the house of Mrs. Mansfield, where Mr. Fisk was a frequent visitor."‡ I do not perceive that the fact that Mr. Fisk paid or franked the dispatch, is in any degree material, or that it should have attracted

---

* Coleman was an intimate personal friend of Judge Barnard, in no way connected with these litigations.

† It is the practice in this judicial district, when a particular litigation has been commenced before one judge, for the other judges to refer all subsequent applications to him.

‡ General Barlow's letter.

Judge Barnard's attention, if it had been on the copy that was delivered to him. But it was not on that copy. If it had been, it could not have affected his construction of the dispatch; and as to the house to which he was requested to send his *answer*, it will be seen presently what that has to do with the matter. Judge Barnard's answer, published as No. 4, was the following:

Poughkeepsie, *August* 6.

To James H. Coleman, care No. 359 West Twenty-third Street. I will be there, if sent by you.

Answer.

9. Col. 30.   G. G. BARNARD.

The meaning of this answer was, "If you, *Coleman*, have sent for me, I will be *there;*" not at 359 West Twenty-third Street, but in the city of New York. Whether any more dispatches passed, the telegraph office has not enabled the searchers to state; but the fact is, Judge Barnard came to the city that evening at a late hour, and the order was signed as he was on his way from the Hudson River railroad station, which is in Twenty-ninth Street, to his own house, which is in Twenty-first Street between the Sixth and Fifth Avenues.

But it has been insinuated that Judge Barnard signed the order appointing Fisk and Courter receivers, at the house of Mrs. Mansfield, where it is argued or surmised he was found by Mr. Sterling, a partner of Field & Shearman, who proceeded with the papers of the application from Mr. Shearman, who had prepared them at a room in the Opera House, on the corner of Twenty-third Street and Eighth Avenue, between the hours of 10.20 and 10.35 P.M., to find Judge Barnard. But the fact is that Judge Barnard did *not* sign the order at Mrs. Mansfield's house, or at any place where it was improper for him to transact such business; but he was met in the street by Mr. Sterling, went into the nearest place then open, which appeared to him to be a real-estate office, there examined the papers of the application, heard Mr. Sterling's statements, and signed the order where he happened to have stopped on his way to his own house, after leaving the railroad station. What is stated about it here is stated upon the authority of Judge Barnard himself, of whom I thought it my duty to make inquiry.

It is shameful to be obliged to discuss such details, but the reader will perceive that the discussion has been made necessary by the charges, insinuations, and surmises that have been made respecting this order. To be sure, the insinuations have not been very consistent. It has been suggested that the order was signed at a certain house, in order to give color to the charge that Judge Barnard was "the favorite judge of these litigants." Again, it has been darkly insinuated that there is a mystery about this order; that it never was signed at all; in order to give color to the charge that the attorneys falsely pretended that a receivership had been granted. Having seen the original order, and knowing Judge Barnard's signature, I may expect at least to be considered as having put an end to *this* part of the insinuations; and having been informed by Judge Barnard that it was signed in no improper place, and was not signed at the house supposed, I may be thought to have disposed of another part of these imputations.*

It has also been said that four of the directors who signed the consent to this order—North, Herrick, Wilber, and Leonard— violated the injunction of Judge Clute, which had restrained them from acting as directors. This is true. But it in no way affects the validity of the order—first, because an act done in violation of an injunction, if otherwise valid or material, is not void or immaterial because the party doing it has exposed himself to be punished for a contempt; second, because the recital of the order that it was granted on "the consent of sundry defendants," even if the consent of North, Herrick, Wilber, and Leon-

---

* For the benefit of readers not familiar with the practice in this city, it may be stated here that the judges of the Supreme Court in this county are by law empowered to perform such judicial acts as signing injunctions and orders wherever they are and at all hours.

ard, had not been given, was supported by the consent of Chase, Everts, and Courter, who were under no injunction. Moreover, the order was also granted on the facts alleged in the complaint and verified by the oath of Chase, the plaintiff, respecting the situation of the company. It was upon the same situation of the company that the Albany receivership was appointed on the next day, but with, perhaps, less propriety.

It is now necessary to follow this order to Albany, where it was taken by Mr. Sterling on that night, accompanied by the receivers, Fisk and Courter, for the purpose of demanding pos-- session of the office, books, and other property of the company in that city. On the morning of the seventh of August, Mr. Sterling learned in Albany that at some time on the previous night, Judge Peckham, of the Albany Supreme Court, had signed an order making Robert H. Pruyn receiver of the road, on a complaint made by John W. Van Valkenburg, *general superintendent of the road*, against the corporation; and that the possession of Fisk and Courter, as receivers, who had already taken possession of the office of the company, would be resisted by force. This information was promptly communicated by Mr. Sterling to Mr. Shearman by telegraph. Rival receivers being thus appointed by the action of the Supreme Court in different counties, it necessarily became a question to be fought out by further proceedings, as to which of the opposing receivers should be first put in possession of the whole property by the process of the law. The collision of authorities was direct. There could be no solution of the difficulty, if the contending parties did not agree to put an end to it themselves, excepting that one of the courts should yield to the other, on the ground of priority of jurisdiction attached; and even this question could not be raised and solved, excepting by putting in motion, on the one side or the other, the appropriate process for enforcing the order that one or the other of the courts had made. When such process had issued to enforce either order, a proceeding in the other court to control the execution of that process, on suggested grounds of superior equity or legal right, would raise the question of priority of jurisdiction or superior right or equity, and present the propriety of vacating the receivership granted on the side of those who might seek to control the process. In no other way could the deadlock be dissolved.*

Accordingly, Mr. Shearman proceeded, on the seventh of August, to make and file a supplemental complaint, in the Supreme Court in the county of New York, in the name of Chase, on whose original complaint Fisk and Courter had been appointed receivers. This supplemental complaint set forth, among other things, the superior equities and rights which the plaintiff claimed for the New York receivership over the Albany receivership. It claimed, as was strictly true, that Fisk and Courter had been appointed receivers on the sixth, and that Pruyn had been appointed on the seventh. [That readers not familiar with the law of this state may understand this matter, it is proper to explain that a judge's order takes effect *instanter,* on its being signed, when signed out of court; that in the county of New York a judge out of court has power to appoint a receiver, and his order takes effect the instant that it is signed, and does not need to be filed, while in every other county a receiver cannot be appointed otherwise than by an order *in court,* which takes no effect until it is filed in the clerk's office, and this can only be done between 9.00 A.M. and 5.00 P.M. Judge Barnard's order making Fisk and Courter receivers was signed in the evening of August 6. Judge Peckham's order making Pruyn receiver was signed on the same evening, but it was not and could not be filed in the clerk's office until 9.00 A.M. on the seventh.] Chase's supplemental complaint set forth the grounds on which resistance to the New York receivers by force was anticipated, and was then actually going on. It demanded judgment as prayed for in the original complaint, and further that the defendants and all other persons be enjoined from obstructing Fisk and Courter

---

* All applications by either party were required by law to be made in the district where the original order obtained by such party had been made.

in the discharge of their duties as receivers, and that Pruyn be enjoined from acting as receiver or claiming to act, and from making any application respecting his alleged receivership, excepting to the Supreme Court in the present action; and that all the defendants be enjoined from prosecuting their actions against the company, or the plaintiff, or the New York receivers, and from commencing or prosecuting any action for the appointment of a receiver, and from making any application therefor except in the present action, and that they be required to submit all claims and alleged rights to a receivership to the Supreme Court in the present action. The verification of this supplemental complaint was made by Mr. Shearman by an affirmation of his information and belief of what had taken place at Albany, and in a separate affidavit he gave the sources of his information respecting the organized opposition to the possession of the New York receivers, and the necessity for writs of assistance. Judge Barnard thereupon, on the seventh of August, sitting in Special Term, made an order, embracing the several injunctions as prayed for, and requiring the defendants to prosecute their claims to the receivership in the Supreme Court in the present action, and directing writs of assistance to issue forthwith to the sheriffs of the counties where the company had any property, in order to put the New York receivers in possession, and authorizing those receivers to employ any necessary force to resist all attempts to oust them from possession.

It has been said of this proceeding, *first,* that, "instead of applying to the judges in Albany, all men of high character, to control their own receiver, and to protect Fisk and Courter, if they had any legal rights in the premises, these injunctions and writs of assistance must be telegraphed for and obtained from *Judge Barnard.*"* The insinuation couched in this remark proceeds upon an entire mistake as to what the parties to either side of this controversy about the receivership could do. Neither of them could by law apply anywhere for support of the receiver-

* General Barlow's letter.

ship that had been granted to either side, or for control of the opposite receivership, *excepting* in the court which had made the appointment; and General Barlow's observation, *mutatis mutandis*, is just as applicable to the parties proceeding in the court at Albany as it is to the party proceeding in the court at New York. It will be seen presently that the Albany parties and their counsel understood this point perfectly.

Secondly, it has been said that Mr. Shearman had nothing but information conveyed to him by telegraph on which to apply for these injunctions and writs of assistance, and that he could only give to Judge Barnard his belief that this information was true. I am not prepared to admit that, when a court has appointed receivers of such a property as a railroad, by an order which took effect as soon as it was signed, and is subsequently informed by an affidavit of the plaintiff's attorney that intelligence of resistance and of an adverse claim of title has been received by telegraph or otherwise by that attorney, and the supplemental matter is duly brought forward by a supplemental bill or complaint, it is not proper for the court to act and to act promptly upon such a state of things. Open and forcible resistance to the orders of a court, whether carried on with or without the aid of another court, is a serious matter; and the only way in which the claim of the legality of such resistance could be brought to a test in this instance was to enjoin the parties offering it to submit their claims to the court whose order they were resisting, and in the meantime to support that order with the proper process of the law. That this could be done, and ought to have been done, on the information that was laid before Judge Barnard, I think most lawyers will agree; for the rule that information and belief is strictly not evidence, does not extend and ought not to extend to the issuing of process to enforce an order previously made in a cause.

On the same day, August 7, a corresponding proceeding took place in Albany, at the instance of the Ramsey party and in support of Pruyn's receivership. This proceeding, which has been called an *omnibus* suit, was instituted by a complaint made in the names of the company and William A. Rice, a director and stockholder, as plaintiffs, against all the other directors, together with Samuel Sloan, Ossian D. Ashley, Samuel C. Thompson, David Groesbeck, Joseph Bush, C. H. Dabney, J. P. Morgan, G. H. Morgan, J. J. Goodwin, W. H. Burns (holders of controverted stock), Van Valkenburg (the applicant for the Albany receivership), Pruyn (the Albany receiver), Fisk, Gould, and Courter (alleged conspirators against the rights and interests of the company), Phelps, the treasurer, and Herrick, vice-president, as codefendants. The purpose of this action was twofold: *first,* to draw into the exclusive adjudication of the Supreme Court in Albany County all the matters in controversy in all the other pending suits; *secondly,* to obtain immediate injunctions against the further prosecution of those suits, and against all proceedings and processes to put Fisk and Courter in possession as receivers. It is remarkable, considering how much has been said concerning injunctions granted on "information and belief," that every allegation in this complaint (excepting, perhaps, that Rice was a stockholder) was stated therein on information and belief alone; nor did the *jurat* of Rice, annexed to the complaint, give it any other force as evidence than hearsay. It is remarkable also that the charge of conspiracy, made against certain of the defendants, as a principal ground for invoking the control by the court in Albany of suits pending in New York and processes issued in those suits, was unsupported by a single affidavit.

The complaint in this Rice suit, which, for convenience, may be called the *omnibus* suit, after describing the internal organization of the corporation, proceeded to charge Gould, Fisk, Leonard, Courter, Herrick, Wilber, and Chase, as the principal instigators and plotters in a corrupt conspiracy to obtain the control and possession of the property of the plaintiff corporation in order to subserve their speculations in its stock and the stock of other railroads, and to transfer its franchises and other property to the Erie Railway Company, then wholly under the control and management of Fisk and Gould, to the great detriment and certain ruin of the plaintiff corporation and its property; that there was to be an annual election of directors on the seventh of September, and that in the event of the said conspirators not being able to secure a majority of the stock before the election, in order to carry out their design, they threatened to prevent an election by the illegal and fraudulent use of the process of the court. In support of this charge, the complaint then set out in detail the various suits that had been commenced; viz.: by Bush and Wilber (of the Church party), the Ramsey suit in the name of the corporation against the four conspiring directors and Phelps, Van Valkenburg's suit to obtain the appointment of Pruyn as receiver, the suit of Chase to obtain the appointment of Fisk and Courter as receivers, and the various orders and injunctions that had been respectively granted therein, all of which, on the Church side, were alleged to have been for the wrongful and fraudulent purposes of the conspiracy charged, and not for any real interest or advantage of the company or its stockholders. In respect to the Albany receivership, this complaint alleged that Pruyn was appointed by the Albany Supreme Court, *at a Special Term,* on the sixth of August, and that he "immediately took actual possession" of the office and property of the company in Albany; that Chase's action to get receivers appointed was commenced "thereafter" in pursuance of the conspiracy, and that under a paper "purporting to be an order granted at chambers in the city of New York by a justice of the Supreme Court," and "under color thereof," Fisk and Courter came to Albany on the seventh of August and attempted to take possession of the property and effects of the company forcibly, and fraudulently.* The complaint further set

---

* Whatever may be said of this charge as a *pleading,* it was wholly incapable of being sustained in respect to the priority of the Albany receivership, either *de jure,* or *de facto;* for the Albany appointment did not take effect until the order was filed in the clerk's office, at nine o'clock, on the morn-

forth the necessity for an adjudication of all these matters and controversies *in the present action,* in order to prevent the inconvenience and mischief of a multiplicity of suits; and it further averred that Herrick, who had represented the city of Albany in the Board of Directors, was no longer a director, as he had been removed by a vote of the Common Council of that city on the seventh of August.

The complaint then prayed an adjudication of all these matters and controversies so described, in the Supreme Court in Albany County, in the present action, a removal from office of the directors who were parties to the alleged conspiracy, a stay of all the other proceedings, an adjudication of the titles of the claiming receivers, injunctions against Fisk and Gould to restrain them from acting or claiming to act as receivers, a confirmation of Pruyn as receiver, and injunctions against the alleged conspirators to restrain them from all further acts in the premises and the prosecution of all suits, and to require them to submit all their claims to the court in the present action, and for further relief.

On the same day, August seventh, Judge Peckham signed an

ing of the seventh, and if Pruyn had, in fact, taken any possession of the office of the company before that time, such possession could not avail anything against the order of Judge Barnard, appointing Fisk and Courter receivers, which took effect on the evening of the sixth, when it was signed, and was actually in Albany and possession demanded under it before nine o'clock on the morning of the seventh. With respect to the allegation that Judge Peckham's order, making Pruyn receiver, was made *at a Special Term,* I understand that in point of law, even if Judge Peckham did adjourn his Special Term, on the sixth, to the place and time when and where he signed the order on the evening of that day, or to any place and time at which he might be, his order could not take effect until filed in the clerk's office. In this respect, I understand there is an important difference between the powers of the judges in the county of New York and the powers of the judges in all the other counties, as above explained. Judge Barnard's order was not filed in the clerk's office, and did not need to be. Judge Peckham's order was so filed, and did need to be. No adjournment of Judge Peckham's Special Term on the sixth to the time and place where he signed the order, or to any other time or place, had been made, as I am informed.

order to show cause on the thirteenth of August, at a Special Term, why all the respective prayers of the complaint should not be granted, and in the meantime, and until the decision thereon, enjoining and restraining Fisk and Courter from acting or claiming to act as receivers, and enjoining and restraining the alleged conspirators and all other persons from prosecuting any of the suits described in this complaint, and from prosecuting any other suits to effect a removal of any of the directors of the corporation, or for the procurement of a receiver, and staying all such proceedings.*

This injunction also contained an extraordinary prohibition, addressed to all other persons who might act in concert with the defendants, or might bring actions or institute proceedings of a like nature, or intended to accomplish the objects sought to be obtained by the actions already brought by the defendants, from advising, commencing, or carrying on, or assisting to commence or carry on, any suit, petition, or proceeding, having for its object, in whole or in part, the removal or suspension of any of the directors of the company, or the procurement of a receiver of its property, and from continuing, or helping to continue, any such proceeding already commenced. Much comment has been made upon the fact that the injunction in Chase's suit, granted on the same day, had restrained the defendants in that suit from taking any proceedings for the appointment of a receiver excepting in that action; but the injunction granted at Albany by Judge Peckham went much further than this, and forbade any application anywhere.

At the time of the service of this order, on the seventh of August, Harris Parr, sheriff of the county of Albany, had in his hands a copy of the writ of assistance granted by Judge Barnard on that day, which copy had been telegraphed by Mr. Shearman from the city of New York. Much comment has been

---

* With respect to the powers of the judges in the county of New York as compared with the powers of the judges in the other counties, see Section 24 and 401 of the Code of Procedure.

made upon the fact that this writ of assistance was *telegraphed* to Albany. I can perceive no impropriety in sending to a sheriff or other executive officer a telegraphic copy of legal process, in order that he may be prepared to execute the precept as soon as the original is received. Indeed, it is not an uncommon practice for officers to execute telegraphic copies of process. Of course, in so doing, they take the risks of acting before they receive the original, and the practice is liable to abuses. But it is not necessary to justify Mr. Shearman on any such ground. In fact, what he did was to telegraph to his associate counsel that a writ of assistance had been granted, and that the original was on the way. Upon their request he telegraphed to them a copy of the writ, giving no directions for its use. The sheriff, in fact, did nothing more with the telegraphic copy than to inform the opposite party that he had received it. But when the original came, he prepared to execute it. In the meantime, Pruyn, the Albany receiver, commenced a suit in the Supreme Court in Albany County, against the sheriff and his deputies, to restrain them from executing this copy, and from executing the original when it should be received. In the complaint it was expressly alleged that the sheriff had not executed the copy, but it was averred that the original would be furnished to him in a short time, and that he might undertake to execute *that*. As the ground for restraining the execution of the original, it was averred that no writ of assistance could be lawfully issued before judgment in the action, and therefore that this original, if it had been issued, was "utterly void." On this ground, expressly recited in the injunction, the recorder of the city of Albany, exercising the powers of a judge of the Supreme Court at chambers, signed an order on the ninth of August, which enjoined the sheriff, etc., from executing this writ, copy, or original, or any other writ issued before judgment in the action of which it might be entitled.

The eagerness and celerity evinced in these proceedings suggest an amusing inquiry, why the mistakes of the Albany gentlemen of the profession should not be visited with the reproach that has been so lavishly bestowed upon some of their brethren in this city. Their attitude in regard to the validity and authority of this writ of assistance was clearly wrong, if I read the code rightly, which expressly authorizes a court, *whenever* it has ordered the delivery of property, and the order is disobeyed, to make an order *requiring* the sheriff to take the property and *deliver* it in conformity with the previous order.* This provision is contained in the very section in which the courts are authorized to appoint receivers *before judgment*. And the same power belongs to any court of equity, when it has made an interlocutory order which is resisted. But what would the gentlemen of my profession in Albany think of me, if, because they had made an allegation in a pleading which seems to me to have been untenable in point of law, and had obtained an injunction according to it, I should charge them with gross professional misconduct?

It is time now to state with precision what, if anything, Mr. David Dudley Field had to do personally with any of these proceedings up to the time at which we are now arrived; not that I propose to separate his vindication from that of his partners or his colleagues, none of whom, in my opinion, need any other vindication than a clear statement of their acts, but because an exact history of this matter is important. Mr. Field was at his country place in Stockbridge, Mass., 150 miles away from New York, from the thirtieth of July to the ninth of August. He knew nothing whatever about any of these proceedings, and had not been consulted about them. On the ninth, Monday, he was telegraphed to and requested to go to Albany. He arrived there on the evening of that day, and then for the first time learned the state of things in regard to the two receiverships. He found his partner, Mr. Sterling, acting as attorney, and Judge Amasa J. Parker and Mr. John Ganson acting as counsel for the New York receivers, and he immediately joined them.

On his arrival at Albany, Mr. Field learned that all parties on

* Code of Practice, § 244.

all sides were now effectually restrained, by the injunctions and
counter-injunctions issued, from further prosecution of the
claims of their respective receivers in the courts, and that the
sheriff of Albany County was restrained from executing the
writ of assistance which he had received. But he also learned
that the New York receivers were in actual possession of the
Binghamton end of the road, that the Albany receiver was in
actual possession of the Albany end, that the two parties had
been for some time approaching each other on the line of the
road, and that Judge Barnard's writs of assistance were in the
hands of the sheriffs of some of the counties on the line. It is
unnecessary to recount here what had taken place on the line of
the road. The danger of collision was imminent, and the population along the road were in some degree involved in the excitement. Moreover, in the city of Albany itself, there was danger
that the peace would be broken, for Courter had been forcibly
ejected from the office of the company that evening. It would
be nearly a week before even the Albany court, under the order
made in the *omnibus* suit, could adjudicate the title of the rival
receivers, or even hear an argument upon it. Mr. Field saw that
a step must be taken at once, to secure the intervention of the
Governor for the preservation of the peace. Instead of promoting
any action under the writ of assistance, which so far as Albany
County was concerned was already stayed, and instead of doing
or advising any forcible step whatever in assertion of the claims
of Fisk and Courter, Mr. Field immediately desired one of the
Governor's clerks to communicate with the Governor who was
absent from the city of Albany, and at or near West Point, and
request him to intervene for the preservation of the peace. This
was done, and Governor Hoffman reached Albany the next evening, the tenth. On the eleventh, early in the morning, in the
Executive Chamber, the respective receivers, attended by their
counsel, signed a letter addressed to the Governor, informing
him that in consequence of certain judicial proceedings and
conflict of jurisdictions, it had become impracticable to run and

operate this road, either under the management of its directors, or the control of the persons claiming to be receivers; and as contending claimants to the possession of the road, they requested the Governor to appoint some suitable person as superintendent, to operate the road under the Governor's directions and during his pleasure, or until the necessity should cease; this appointment and possession not to affect the legal rights or present actual possession of the parties respectively to any part of the road, its offices or property. The Governor was also requested to employ such financial or other agents as he might require, and to fix their compensation.

Mr. Field informs me that his idea in advising this arrangement was, that the Governor should exercise a civil power in taking and holding this temporary possession; but in consequence of the disturbances and excitements on the line of the road, the Governor deemed it necessary to take a *quasi* military possession, by appointing a member of his military staff, Colonel Banks, executive financial agent to run and operate the road. Colonel Banks thereupon took charge of the road; but the books of the company had been previously removed from its office in Albany to some place of secrecy, where Phelps, the treasurer, had access to them, and continued to make entries in them. This removal took place on the night of August 5. The books were not returned to the office of the company until the night of the sixth of September.

Mr. Field remained in Albany until the evening of the eleventh of August, when he came down to New York, where he stayed until the evening of the twelfth, when he returned to Albany. On the thirteenth he went to West Point, at the request of Governor Hoffman, to confer with the latter on the subject of funds to be supplied to Colonel Banks as financial agent of the road. He met the Governor at West Point on the evening of the thirteenth, and then went back to Hudson; and from thence, on the morning of the fourteenth, he reached his home in Stockbridge, where he remained during the greater part of the month.

He was in New York only three days and a half during the whole month, viz., the twentieth, part of the twenty-first, the twenty-fourth, and the twenty-fifth.

But there was an occurrence on the fourteenth of August which has formed one of the principal topics in the charges that have been made against Mr. Field. He has been charged with complicity in a fraudulent scheme to wrest from some of the holders of stock of this company, by the abuse of legal process, a large number of shares, with intent to have them used at the election in casting votes for the Church ticket of directors. I do not forget that a judge of the Supreme Court, in Monroe County, sitting at Special Term (Judge E. Darwin Smith), has declared himself satisfied that such a wrongful scheme existed, although he has in no way implicated Mr. Field in a conscious purpose to promote it. It is proper, however, to say, that an appeal from Judge Smith's decision in *The People* vs. *The Albany & Susquehanna Railroad Company,* and others, is now pending, which involves all his findings of fact and conclusions of law. For this reason I should refrain from expressing any opinion on the question whether there was any such fraudulent purpose on the part of anybody in the transaction about to be described, if it had not been charged publicly that Mr. Field consciously promoted that purpose, in such a way as to make it necessary for me to examine and weigh the facts in reference to its probable existence. It has been observed in a somewhat triumphant, and, as it seems to me, hasty manner, and very erroneously, that Mr. Field, in his published explanation of this matter, has "perverted the truth."* I shall endeavor not to "pervert the truth," either of fact or of law; nor shall I impute any such *intentional* perversion to others. But I cannot help observing that in this, as in every other inquiry into men's motives or purposes, a full and correct statement of the facts is essential; that I have not seen a full and correct statement in any of the publications which have imputed impropriety to Mr. Field, nor do I find it in Judge Smith's

* General Barlow's letter.

opinion, which has imputed a fraudulent purpose to some of those for whom Mr. Field is said to have acted. I have been obliged, therefore, to examine all the material facts for myself, and to present to the consideration of the reader what seem to me to be the true aspects of both the legal and the moral questions arising upon this transaction. In this examination I have had before me all the legal proceedings that took place, all the evidence that has been taken under oath in regard to this transaction, together with information not embraced in those sources, but which I have endeavored carefully to verify. I have also attentively perused the opinion of Judge Smith, which, so far as a judicial finding ought to influence one, might be expected to produce a bias toward his conclusions on the collateral topic of the existence of a wrongful intent to obtain possession of this stock for the purpose of voting upon it at the election.

But before I enter upon this examination, it is proper to repeat that Mr. Field was not in New York at the time, and that he knew nothing of any purpose to have a receivership of the stock in question obtained. Whatever blame should rest upon any lawyer, rests upon his partner, Mr. Shearman, though none in my opinion belongs to anybody.

I now come, therefore, to this topic about which there has been a great deal of comment; namely, the FULLER RECEIVERSHIP of the stock claimed by Groesbeck and others. On the second of August, Joseph Bush had instituted a suit in the Supreme Court in the county of New York against the company and the directors, in which an injunction had been granted on Saturday, the thirty-first of July, after business hours, but which was not served until Monday, August second. In the complaint, the plaintiff described himself as a stockholder bringing the suit in his own behalf, and in behalf of all the other stockholders, to obtain certain relief. The part of the relief sought which it is necessary to notice here, is the relief which was granted, on the fourteenth of August, by the appointment of a receiver, and which was obtained by the receiver's demand and possession of certificates. The complaint alleged that certain of the defendants, Groesbeck and others, held a large amount of the stock of the company, which had been issued to them by Ramsey, the president, as full-paid stock, at some time in 1868–69; that the company had never received therefor more than 25 per cent of the par value, and that the issue was therefore unlawful and void. In point of fact, a portion of this stock of which the receiver demanded and obtained possession of the certificates, and *on which he afterward voted at the election of directors* (three thousand shares), was forfeited stock belonging to the company, but which had been reissued to the parties who held it at the time this suit was brought by Bush. Among other prayers, the complaint prayed that the *issue* of this stock be declared unauthorized and void, and set aside, and that the stock be given up to be canceled, and for a receiver. On the fourteenth of August, at a Special Term, Judge Barnard granted a provisional order, appointing W. J. A. Fuller receiver of three thousand shares of the stock thus held by the several defendants, and authorizing him to take immediate possession thereof, and directing the present holders of these shares to show cause before him, at a Special Term to be held in the city of New York on the nineteenth of August, why this order should not stand and such further order be made in the premises as might be just, and in the meantime that all proceedings on the part of the defendants be stayed.*

Was this an order proper to be made? There are two provisions of the Code of Practice which are applicable to this order. By section 244, subdivision 1, ''a receiver may be appointed, on the application of either party, when he establishes an apparent right to property which is the subject of the action, and which is in the possession of the adverse party, and the property, or its rents and profits, are in danger of being lost, or materially

---

* For their appearance, see *post*. It has been stated that Mr. Fuller was a former clerk of Mr. Field. He left Mr. Field's office twelve years before this occurrence, and has been largely engaged in practice since as a well-known member of the bar. I am informed that during twelve years he had had no business connection with Mr. Field's office.

injured or impaired." I take it to be clear that this provision is not confined to cases where a legal title to property is established or shown. The term "apparent right to property" must be held to include all equitable interests as well as legal titles. The "property," in this case, consisted of the legal title and all the equitable interests in certain shares of the capital stock of a corporation. The plaintiff, acting for himself as a stockholder and for all the other stockholders, "established," by his sworn complaint, an "apparent right" of the corporation to three-quarters of this "property," by showing that the holders of the shares to whom they had been issued had not paid to the corporation more than 25 per cent of the par value, and that, without payment in full of the par value, the corporation was entitled to have the stock delivered up and canceled, as an illegal and void issue. Now the question whether the *certificates* were *void*, or whether the *issue* was *void*, would be for trial after an answer; and the judgment to be rendered would be, whether the certificates should be given up to be canceled, and on what terms, or be retained by the defendants, and on what terms. But before judgment on this question, it was clear, if the allegations of the complaint were believed by the judge, that the corporation or whole body of the stockholders, who in contemplation of law were the plaintiffs, had an "apparent right" in these shares, namely, an equitable title to receive three-fourths of their par value, if the final judgment should leave them in the hands of the defendants. The question whether the issue of this stock should finally be declared unlawful and void, should not be confounded with the question whether the plaintiff Bush had established for himself and the other stockholders an "apparent right" in these shares. The first was a question to be determined on the final judgment in the suit. The last was a fact to be shown before judgment, as a foundation for the provisional remedy of a receiver. That it was shown, appears to me not to admit of any doubt. The next inquiry is, whether this "apparent right" of the stockholders in this property was in such danger of being lost or materially injured or impaired as to make the appointment of a receiver necessary to protect it. For, I take it to be the clear meaning of the Code, that a receiver is to be appointed, *when* the party asking for a receiver has shown that his *interest* in the property is in danger of being lost, or materially injured or impaired, *unless* a receiver is appointed. The *interest* of the whole body of stockholders in this case, to be regarded before final judgment, was the right of the corporation to receive three-fourths of the par value of the stock. It was manifest on the face of the facts averred in the complaint, that this stock could be transferred by the defendants to parties who would become *bona fide* holders of it for value, and who might take it purged of any infirmity in its title; so that while the corporation might have, as against the present holders, a right to demand their 75 per cent on the stock, they could not have that right against a *bona fide* purchaser for value, who might have taken it without notice that its original issue was unlawful.* If it is said that the simple injunction already issued not to transfer the stock would have protected the corporation, or the whole body of stockholders, the answer is, that the Code manifestly intended that in such a case there should be another protection by the appointment of a receiver. A simple injunction not to part with the stock could be disobeyed; if it was placed in the hands of a receiver, the corporation would be fully protected in the "apparent right" which it was the purpose of the Code to protect, by the provisional remedy of a receiver before judgment on the main issue in the case.

The other provision in the Code is subdivision 5 of section 244, which declares that a receiver may be appointed before judgment, "in such other cases as are now provided by law, or may be in accordance with the existing practice, except as otherwise provided in this act." Assuming, for the purpose of argument only, that the case now under consideration did not fall within

* *New York and New Haven R. R. Co.* v. *Schuyler and others,* 34 *N. Y.,* 39.

subdivision 1 of section 244, can there be any doubt that under the chancery practice existing when the Code took effect the appointment of a receiver in this case would have been proper? That practice required that a receiver should be prayed for in the bill. This was done in this complaint. The existing practice allowed of a receiver, without notice to the opposite party, under peculiar circumstances demanding immediate action, to be made to appear upon the papers on which the application was made. The peculiar circumstances demanding immediate action in this case were, that without a receiver the interest of the corporation in this stock could be destroyed by those who held it, before judgment could be had; and this was apparent on the facts averred in the complaint. By the former practice, the receiver was appointed for the protection of property *pendente lite,* and the order did not assume to make a final disposition of the property without a hearing of the parties. This was exactly what was done, and all that was done, by Judge Barnard's order appointing this receiver. By the former practice, on a motion for a receiver the merits were not inquired into; the motion related only to the preservation of the property. So in this case, everything in relation to the merits was reserved by the terms of the order, and what was done was to protect the plaintiff's interest in the property *pendente lite.**

Mr. Shearman, who acted as the plaintiff's attorney in this application for a receiver, informs me that he relied on the two provisions of the Code on which I have commented above. I think that either of them authorized the appointment of a receiver; and that the question whether the issue of the stock was unlawful and void, which constituted the chief merits of the action, had nothing to do with the question whether the plaintiff had established an apparent right in the property, as it then stood, to be protected by a receiver *pendente lite.* The issue of the stock might have been unlawful and void; but until that was

---

* See the authorities on the existing practice collected in Note A, on section 244 of the Code, Voorhis' edition.

determined, the corporation, or whole body of stockholders, had
an interest in it, and the final judgment might be that defendants
keep the stock and pay 75 per cent on it to the company, or that
it be surrendered to the company on their paying the holders 25
per cent, or whatever the company had already received.

It is now to be considered whether the main allegations of this
complaint respecting the apparent interest of the company in
this stock, by reason of its having been reissued for a payment
of not more than 25 per cent of its par value, were duly verified for the support of the order that was made. That the
plaintiff was himself a stockholder was averred positively in the
complaint, and his *jurat* made this averment to be on his own
knowledge. The other main allegations were averred on information and belief, and the *jurat* was made in the proper form, necessary to show that the plaintiff had sworn to his information and
belief of the facts so stated. Whether it was judicially proper
for the judge to regard these statements, so verified, as ground
for the provisional remedy of a receivership, depends upon the
principles and authorities to which I have referred in a previous
discussion, and which need not be repeated here. It is to be remembered that this order appointing a receiver of the contested
stock reserved to the defendants an opportunity to show cause
against it on the nineteenth of August; that the possession obtained by the receiver was therefore provisional until after the
expiration of that time, and that when that day had expired
without any cause being shown why the order should not stand,
the possession of the receiver became confirmed by operation of
law, *pendente lite,* and until final judgment upon an answer.

Now, undoubtedly, if we assume that there was a conspiracy
to get possession of this stock wrongfully for the purpose of voting upon it in the interest of the conspirators, and if we assume
further that the attorneys who procured this order, and the receiver himself, were parties to or cognizant of that conspiracy,
it is very easy to censure them. Whether those assumptions
ought to be made depends upon the force of the evidence which

is relied upon to show a purpose to obtain a wrongful possession of the stock, in order to vote upon it at the coming election. That evidence relates to acts and occurrences three weeks subsequent to the appointment of the receiver, with the single exception of what he is said to have done at the time he obtained some of the certificates from Groesbeck. It is said that he threatened Groesbeck with a writ of assistance if he did not deliver the certificates. This might have been done by any receiver making a demand for property of which a court had ordered him to take immediate possession, without any improper purpose, if anything occurred which seemed to him to render it necessary to refer to the ultimate process of the law. The true question to ask, in reference to this matter, is, had such a thing occurred? Mr. Fuller has testified under oath that when he went to demand the stock of Groesbeck he took a deputy sheriff with him; that he thinks he did not say that he had a writ of assistance, but that he told Groesbeck that if he refused to deliver the stock he would have him punished for a contempt. Had anything occurred to render this necessary or natural? It appears from Mr. Fuller's testimony that Groesbeck hesitated about delivering the stock, for he testified that Groesbeck placed the scrip in his (Fuller's) hands three times, on a pledge that he (Fuller) would return it. This, which must have occurred, if Mr. Fuller is to be believed, before Groesbeck finally gave up the scrip, is sufficient evidence that all the threat which Mr. Fuller used was deemed by him to be necessary; and considering that Mr. Fuller was a lawyer who could inform Mr. Groesbeck of the consequences of refusal, *and that Mr. Groesbeck's counsel was present,* this occurrence does not seem of itself to indicate any improper purpose on his part. Whether Mr. Fuller's subsequent act of voting on the stock has any tendency to show that the suit in which he was appointed receiver was instituted for a wrongful purpose, I shall consider hereafter. All that I am to be understood as saying now is, that on the face of the suit itself, the complaint and its verification and the nature of the claim asserted on behalf of all the stockholders of the company to have this stock secured in the hands of a receiver, I can see no evidence of any improper purpose, or complicity in an improper purpose, on the part of the plaintiff's attorneys. What was done was exactly what would have been by any lawyer with the most honest and upright purpose of enforcing a legal right; and I suppose it can scarcely be necessary for me to say that the presumption of a rightful purpose on the part of the attorneys and counsel ought to be carried through this whole investigation, until something arises to control and overthrow it. No amount of popular prejudice or opinion that may exist concerning some of the clients for whom they are supposed to have acted, ought to be regarded for one moment as depriving these members of the bar, in the judgment of their fellows or the public, of the benefit of that presumption. If we assume that the supposed character of a client is to be regarded as proof that what a lawyer does in his behalf was done with a wrongful intent, when the professional acts done were consistent with a rightful intent, the capacity of the bar to fulfil its appropriate functions is at an end, and men who are reputed to be bad will be found to have no rights which any lawyer can enforce or defend.

It is now necessary to describe the material facts attending the organization of the stockholders' meeting on the seventh of September, and the results of the election, which ended in the choice of two boards of directors. I shall express no opinion upon the question as to which of those two boards was entitled to be considered as the lawfully elected board or whether there was any valid election at all, because these questions are still *sub judice,* in the appeal that has been taken to the General Term from Judge Smith's decision in the case of *The People* v. *The Albany & Susquehanna Railroad,* and because that case may possibly be carried to the Court of Appeals. But in respect to all the charges that have been made against Mr. Field in public prints, of complicity in a scheme to carry that election by fraud or violence, I deem myself at liberty to describe what occurred.

A very thorough judicial investigation has shown that the relative strength of the two parties among the stockholders, when they assembled, was as follows:

		Shares.
Whole number of shares then out, including the stock disputed and undisputed..............		29,738
Deduct Groesbeck's stock held by the receiver....	3,000	
Deduct stock claimed to have been subscribed for by Ramsey and others, August 5	9,500	12,500
Leaving of undisputed stock..............		17,238
The Church party held in certificates of clear undisputed stock, and proxies, not including the stock held by the receiver, and certain other parcels..		9,964
Assuming that the Ramsey party held the balance of the undisputed stock, which is not probable as to the whole of it, viz....................		7,274
Minority of the Ramsey party on undisputed stock........................		2,690

These figures show that without voting on some part of the whole of the 9,500 shares of Ramsey disputed stock, that party could not carry the election, whether the receiver voted or not on the 3,000 shares of Groesbeck stock. As the Groesbeck stock held by the receiver was supposed by the Church party to be neutralized, and not likely to be voted upon,* they knew that they could elect their ticket without the aid of the Fuller stock, unless the 9,500 shares of Ramsey disputed stock should be voted on and counted.

It became therefore important to the Church party to have the election presided over by inspectors who would properly discharge their duties, and on whose firmness they could rely. The inspectors who had been chosen in the previous year (1868) to act at this election of 1869, Hand, Lathrop, and Haskell, were not stockholders, as the by-laws required them to be. For this reason they were enjoined from acting by an injunction granted

---

* For reasons stated *post*.

by Judge Clerke, of the Supreme Court in New York, at the suit of Stanton Courter, a stockholder, which injunction was served on them on the morning of the seventh, before the hour fixed for the election. Whether their displacement from office and the subsequent choice of other inspectors in their place were valid or not, in reference to the election of directors, I express no opinion, for reasons already given. But the question of a fraudulent intent on the part of those who obtained and served the injunction forbidding them to act, is involved in the charges that have been made in the public prints. The reader is now in a situation to judge of this charge, because he can see that the Ramsey party, holding a minority of the undisputed stock, held 9,500 shares of stock on which only 10 per cent had been paid, and which had been clearly issued in order to make votes at the election. If the legal advisers of the Church party saw a legal disqualification of those inspectors to act, they could advise their clients to have them enjoined, without any unfair purpose of any kind; and their purpose must be judged by the situation of the two parties to this contest, and by the steps that were taken to supply the places of the inspectors whom they caused to be removed. After having read and weighed all that has been said on this subject, and after a careful examination of the evidence that has been taken upon it, I do not see any ground for imputing any wrongful purpose to those who advised this injunction. It appears to have been signed in New York by Judge Clerke on the sixth, and like other processes used by both parties, and granted on that day, it could not be served in Albany sooner than the morning of the seventh. The charge that it was kept back until that morning, is far more applicable to the Groesbeck injunction, which was obtained in Albany, but was not served until the Harris poll was opened at twelve o'clock; whereas the Courter injunction, removing the old inspectors, was served at twenty minutes past eleven o'clock. I cannot see that the latter operated as a surprise upon the Ramsey party, and prevented them from assembling promptly, because, as will hereafter appear, the Ramsey actual stockholders were all present in person or by proxy before twelve o'clock, and because they came attended by a large number of persons who were not stockholders, and who are proved to have actually voted *viva voce*, when the meeting was first called to order, either with or without proxies.* In like manner the Church actual stockholders were present in person or by proxy before twelve o'clock, and they came attended by persons who were not stockholders, but each of whom held a proxy before he entered the building.

On the evening of the sixth, in preparation for the meeting, the Church party had certain resolutions drawn, to be introduced at the meeting, reciting the removal of the old inspectors, and providing for the immediate choice of new ones. This step has been considered one of the proofs of a scheme for carrying the election by surprise and fraud, because, as has been said, it presupposed the service of the injunction at the proper time to effect a surprise. It seems to me to have been a natural step, on the part of those who knew that the injunction would be served on the next day before twelve o'clock, to make preparation for supplying the expected vacancies in a regular and orderly manner, so that proper minutes of the new appointment could be preserved, if a trial of its legality should afterward become necessary; and as I cannot see any proofs that any stockholder in the Ramsey interest was kept away by the supposition that the old inspectors were to act, I do not see any reason for imputing to the Church party a fraudulent intent, because they prepared resolutions in advance for the purpose of giving all the legal certainty they could give to the new appointment.

On the same evening, the sixth, it became apparent, inasmuch as a new appointment of inspectors would become necessary,

---

* Mr. Ramsey was aware of the purpose of the Church party to enjoin the old inspectors as early as ten o'clock on that morning, and then conversed with his counsel on the necessity for having a stockholders' meeting to appoint new inspectors, in case the old ones should be enjoined. See his testimony, pages 202, 203, folios 909, 910, in the case of *The People* v. *The Albany & Susquehanna Railroad Company.*

that, at the preliminary organization of the meeting, votes would
have to be taken without a stock list, *viva voce,* and to be decided according to the numbers of persons present and voting on
each side. All the stock held by the Church party was known to
them, and was held in certificates or proxies. The same was the
case with the Ramsey party. If, in a *viva voce* vote taken in the
preliminary organization, persons should vote on either side
without being holders of either certificates or proxies, the
other side would be outnumbered by mere intruders. To prevent
this effect on the Church stockholders, the Church party were
advised that proxies should be given to a sufficient number of
persons to make the proportions of numbers correspond to the
proportions of stock on the two sides, and they were particularly
cautioned against giving a proxy to any but a perfectly unex-
ceptionable person. It has been said that the men whom Mr. Fisk
brought there were "roughs," which I understand to mean, in
common parlance, fighting men, whose vocation it is to put their
physical force at the disposal of any man who wants such
services; that they were brought there to overawe the meeting,
and that by their presence they excluded a large portion of the
stockholders from access to the room, and precluded them from
an open, free, and fair participation in the proceedings. The
numbers of these persons will be stated hereafter. At present, it
seems proper to say that I think the fair result of the sworn
testimony is, that some of them were conductors and other agents
of the Erie Railway, and that some of them were laboring men
in the employment of that company; that although some of them
did not wear good coats, and some were in their shirt sleeves (it
was very hot weather), none of them were men who could be
justly classed as "roughs," if I understand rightly the meaning
of that term; that their conduct in the room was decent and
orderly, and that no stockholder, and no person representing a
stockholder, was excluded by their presence or prevented from a
full, free, and open participation in the proceedings. The instructions were to have each of the persons furnished with a

genuine proxy before he should enter the building; the proxies were distributed to them on each block of the stock represented, so that no one of them, in giving a *viva voce* vote, would represent less or more than the stock owned by the person whom he represented; and I am informed that these instructions were fully carried out.

The rooms in which the meeting took place were on the second floor of the building, the hall being in the center, and the rooms being on three sides of the hall. The rooms on that floor were respectively the superintendent's room, the library, the directors' room, the president's room, and the treasurer's room. Commencing in the southwest corner (the superintendent's room) and passing round, the different rooms were connected together, in the order above named, by doors, and each had a door opening into the hall. The president's room was between the directors' room and the treasurer's room. In these three last-mentioned rooms, and the hall, all the business of both meetings was transacted. The persons who came to take part in the election, or to be present at it, first assembled in the directors' room. I have found no difficulty in ascertaining from the evidence, with approximate certainty, the number of persons present in this room at fifteen minutes before twelve, when the first meeting was called to order, and a chairman and secretary were chosen, and I think the evidence shows of which party these persons were adherents. The room was *capable* of holding from 103 to 150 persons; I assume the largest number as the *capacity* of the room.* Of the Church party there were present Leonard, Chase, Wilber, C. Courter, North, Everts, Fisk, Church, Stanton Courter, Harris, Bush, and Oliver, holding among them certificates or proxies for 9,964 undisputed shares. Besides these twelve

* Mr. Herrick, the vice-president, computed the superficial area of the room at 309 square feet. Allow 3 square feet to a person, this would give a capacity of 103 persons but Van Valkenburg, the superintendent, estimated the capacity of the room to be from 125 to 150 persons. I therefore assume the larger number. The door of the library, which could hold 44 persons, was open, and, if there was any crowding, the crowd could overflow into that

persons, there were present as counsel Messrs. Field, Parker, Shearman, and Redfield, advisers of the Church party.

Of the Ramsey party there were present Ramsey, Hendrick, Rice, Perry, Dawson, Blackall, McCormick, Clark, Harder, and Westover, holding among them certificates or proxies for 7,274 shares of undisputed stock and 9,500 shares of the Ramsey disputed stock. Besides these ten persons, there were present on their side as counsel, Messrs. W. F. Allen, Porter, Vanderpoel, Charles Tracy, Hand, Smith, Peckham, Jr., Hale, MacFarland, Moak, and Swartz. Mr. Fuller, the receiver of the 3,000 shares of Groesbeck stock, and Mr. Groesbeck, claimant of that stock, were also present.

Including Fuller and Groesbeck, the whole number of persons present, whose names were afterward proved, was forty; seventeen being on the Church side and twenty-one being on the Ramsey, if we exclude from either side Fuller and Groesbeck.

It has been asserted that the Church party also brought in from fifty to sixty unknown men. If we assume that they brought fifty-five, there would be only seventy-two persons present in the Church interest, which would leave space for one hundred and twenty-two on the Ramsey side, supposing that both the directors' room and the library were filled. But the evidence does not warrant the belief that the Church party had more than twenty-five to thirty persons present beyond those named. Assuming the largest number which the evidence shows, there were forty-seven in all present on the Church side, and all holding proxies or certificates. If, then, there was a crowded state of the room, occasioned by the presence of a large number of persons not being either stockholders or holders of proxies, that crowd was not caused by the Church party, and was not there in their interest. If we assume that the crowd filled both rooms to their

room. Colonel Banks, the Governor's agent, then managing the road, gave special directions and notice that the stockholders were to assemble in the directors' room, and that the voting for directors should take place in the treasurer's room. At the suggestion of Mr. Field, a strong body of the Albany police were present to preserve order.

greatest capacity, then there were present about one hundred and twenty-four unnamed persons not in the interest of the Church party. If we assume that only the directors' room was fully occupied, there were present about eighty unnamed persons not in the interest of the Church party.

These results, which I find on examination of the evidence, have satisfied me—first, that no stockholder was excluded from the room by reason of its preoccupation by the Church party with persons who had no right to be there, or by a crowd occasioned by the Church party; second, that the crowded state of the room, if it was crowded, must have been produced far more by the presence of men brought there in the Ramsey interest. I think, also, that the evidence clearly shows that the unnamed persons who attended in the Church interest occupied the eastern end of the room, and that the unnamed persons who attended in the Ramsey interest occupied the western end; that, so far as there was any disorder or improper language of any kind, it was in the western end of the room; that the unnamed persons who stood at that end were mostly working men, employees of the Albany & Susquehanna Railroad, with a sprinkling among them of men of Albany of the lowest class, some of whom were recognized; and that there were men in the hall armed with clubs, who were known to be in the employment of the road. Outside of the building stood a large crowd of similar persons from the neighborhood, who were certainly not brought there by any sympathy with the Church party.

There is another test that may be applied by figures to ascertain the relative *numerical* strength or *physical* force of the two parties. At both polls, seventy-four persons voted, thirty-five at the Harris poll, thirty-nine at the other poll; sixty ballots were cast for the Church ticket, one hundred and ninety for the Ramsey ticket. So that when the voting took place, the numbers of persons voting on the Ramsey side, not in their own right but under proxies, must have greatly exceeded those so voting on the Church side at the Harris poll.

To return to the time at which the assembly in the directors'
room was first called to order. This was at ten or fifteen minutes
before twelve; at that time Colonel North called the meeting to
order as a stockholders' meeting, nominated Mr. Church as
chairman, and he was elected by a *viva voce* vote, without any
negatives. In like manner, Mr. Herrick was chosen secretary.
Colonel North then moved resolutions, the first of them declaring
the offices of inspectors vacant. When the vote on this resolution
was taken, there was a heavy negative vote given at the western
end of the room; but the resolution was declared to be carried.
A resolution was then moved, appointing Mr. Harris, Mr. Bush,
and Mr. Oliver inspectors, and was declared to be carried by the
ayes. Harris, Bush, and Oliver then proceeded through the
president's room to the door of the treasurer's room which was
closed. It was opened by a policeman; who, on an explanation
that they came to open a poll as inspectors, was directed by Mr.
Banks or Mr. McQuade (agents of Governor Hoffman in the
management of the road) to admit them. They proceeded to make
preparations to open the poll. They were followed into the room
by several of the gentlemen in the Ramsey interest, including
some of the counsel on that side, Mr. Groesbeck and Mr. Ramsey
himself. Either at four minutes before twelve, or precisely at
twelve (watches differed), the Groesbeck injunction was served on
them.* A copy of it was handed by Mr. Harris to Mr. Shearman.
Mr. Shearman went back into the directors' room, found Mr.
Fuller, explained to him that this injunction had been served,
and told him that he had better vote.† Mr. Fuller came into the
directors' room, and approached the polling place, just after
Mr. Harris had proclaimed that as inspectors appointed at a
stockholders' meeting in the directors' room, he and Bush and
Oliver now formally opened a poll for the choice of directors.
Mr. Fuller then took out the papers showing his appointment as

* For an account of this injunction, see *post*.
† For a precise account of what Mr. Shearman said to the receiver, see
post.

receiver of the Groesbeck stock and the certificates which he held, and handed them to Mr. Harris. At this moment Judge Allen came up to the polling place, *and protested against proceeding with the election, because the hour of twelve had not arrived,* pointing to the clock in the room. The clock in the room showed two minutes before twelve; Mr. Harris's watch showed two minutes after twelve. Mr. Harris then told Judge Allen that the inspectors would not receive any ballots until the hands of the clock indicated twelve precisely.* The remaining two minutes were occupied by Mr. Harris in examining Mr. Fuller's papers. When the hand of the clock had arrived at twelve precisely, Mr. Harris received Mr. Fuller's votes on the three thousand shares held by him, and then proceeded to vote himself on nine thousand shares for which he held proxies. After this the voting at the Harris poll went on briskly, until about fifteen minutes past twelve, when Mr. Vanderpoel, one of the counsel in the Ramsey interest, came up to the desk, and read aloud an injunction, issued from the Supreme Court by the Albany County judge on that day, on the complaint of Minard Harder, forbidding Hand, Lathrop, and Haskell, inspectors of election, and "John Doe, Richard Roe, and James Jackson," *or any other persons, that might be appointed inspectors,* from holding any election of directors or receiving any votes that might be cast at any attempted election. Mr. Vanderpoel explained that Mr. Harris was the "John Doe" of this injunction, Mr. Bush was the "Richard Roe," and Mr. Oliver was the "James Jackson." Thereupon voting at the Harris poll ceased for the space of ten or fifteen minutes.

In the meantime another stockholders' meeting had been organized in the Ramsey interest *in the hall.* Mr. Smith, who called this meeting to order, has made an affidavit that he did so at precisely twelve o'clock; and it is also in evidence that he said

---

* The clock was said to have been regulated by the time at the Albany Observatory; but as I am not considering the question whether these proceedings were strictly regular, I attach no importance to the precise moment of these various occurrences. The order in which they occurred, and what occurred, are alone material here.

at the time, in the hall: "The hour for which this meeting was called having arrived, I now call this meeting to order."

At this meeting Messrs. Snow, Eddy, and Harder were appointed inspectors of the election. They proceeded into the treasurer's room, passed inside the railing within which the other inspectors, Harris, Bush, and Oliver, were holding a poll, and at twenty-three minutes past twelve, announced that they then opened a poll for the choice of directors of the Albany & Susquehanna Railroad. It does not appear, from anything that I have seen, whether these gentlemen did or did not regard themselves as the John Doe, Richard Roe, and James Jackson, of Judge Clute's injunction, which had forbidden any persons that might be appointed inspectors from acting as such until the further order of the court, although one of them, Harder, was the injunction plaintiff. They proceeded to receive votes, and voting then went on at both polls with the following result:

At the Harris poll, the Church ticket received 13,400 votes.

At the Snow poll, the Ramsey ticket received 10,742 votes.

Two other injunctions need to be mentioned, which had relation to the 9,500 shares of stock that had been issued by Mr. Ramsey on the fifth of August, and on which votes were cast at the Snow poll. By an injunction issued by Judge Barnard, at the instance of Jay Gould, on the third of September, upon a complaint, sufficiently verified for this purpose, the holders of those 9,500 shares were prohibited from voting upon them at the election of directors. Judge Clerke had also granted an injunction in Courter's suit making the same prohibition. By a counter-injunction issued by Judge Clute, the Albany County judge, on the sixth of September, at the instance of John Eddy, on a complaint not sufficiently verified for this purpose, the inspectors were prohibited from receiving any votes from the whole Church party of stockholders, *unless* the holders of those 9,500 shares should first have had an opportunity to vote upon them.

There were also three suits instituted in the Ramsey interest, having relation to the votes expected to be given for the Church side on the town stock of the towns of Oneonta, Milford, Maryland, Cobleskill, and Unadilla, in which injunctions were obtained to prevent the stock of these towns from being voted on. There was also another suit, being the sixth injunction served at the election in the Ramsey interest, to prevent any election.

No other facts attending the election need to be mentioned here, excepting those relating to Mr. Fuller's voting on the Groesbeck stock, and the arrest of Ramsey, Phelps, and Smith, which I have reserved for special consideration.

It will be remembered that on the seventh of August Judge Peckham had granted an injunction which effectually restrained all the Church directors, Fisk and Courter, claimants of a receivership, and all other parties in the same interest, from taking any steps or doing any acts in relation to the affairs of this corporation, excepting in the suit in which the injunction was granted, which was pending in the Supreme Court in Albany County, and which has been called the *omnibus* suit. When this injunction was issued, the books of the corporation had been clandestinely removed from its office in Albany, and the Church directors, a majority of the whole board, were, by the effect of the injunction, absolutely inhibited from taking any legal measures to reach them. The impropriety of this state of things was so manifest that, on the thirty-first of August, Judge Hogeboom, on a motion argued by Mr. Field and Judge Amasa J. Parker for the defendants, modified Judge Peckham's injunction so far as to allow the injunction defendants to institute a suit to compel the production of the books and their restoration to the office of the company. Without them, the Church directors and the stockholders, who concurred in their views and measures, could have no means of knowing what stock had been issued, and no means of protecting themselves against votes on stock that might have been wrongfully issued, or against votes cast by unauthorized persons. They appear to have been in the position of parties who had to carry on a defensive contest against adversaries who had every means in their hands for active aggression, by the creation of votes which would be of doubtful legality or of clear illegality. But when Judge Peckham's injunction had been modified, the Church directors were free to protect themselves, so far as they could do so by obtaining access to the books. They endeavored to trace them, and did trace them to the house of Mr. Henry Smith, where they remained for several days, and then were taken away. They supposed at one time that they had been removed to Pittsfield in Massachusetts, and, following there the clew which they had discovered, their agents endeavored to reach the books by a writ of replevin, but without any success. Baffled in all directions in this search, the Executive Committee had to consider whether there was any legal proceeding which they could institute against the persons who were believed to have the books under their control, that would compel their production or restoration to the office of the company. The election .was now less than a week distant. The person who went to Pittsfield in pursuit of the books, and who found evidence that they then were or had been there, and that they had probably been brought there by Van Valkenburg, the superintendent, for Pruyn, who had left the state, returned to Albany on the second of September. Further fruitless search was made in Albany, which consumed a part of the time remaining between that date and the day of the election. It appears to me that great diligence was used, and that it was not until the sixth of September that any legal proceedings could be taken. On that day, by authority of the Executive Committee of the directors, and of Herrick the vice-president,* a suit was commenced in the Supreme Court in

* The authority to commence the suit was embraced in the following resolutions, which are here taken from the minutes of the Executive Committee:

"At a meeting of the Executive Committee of the Board of Directors of the Albany & Susquehanna Railroad Company, held at the city of Albany on the 3d day of September, 1869.

"Present, Azro Chase, David Wilber, and Jacob Leonard.

"*Whereas,* certain books of this company, two stock-ledgers, two transfer-books, book of stock certificates, cash-book, book of minutes, and two subscription-books, have been abstracted from the office of this company by Joseph H. Ramsey, William L. M. Phelps, Robert H. Pruyn, and Henry

New York, in the name of the corporation, against Ramsey, Phelps, Pruyn, and Smith (the latter being one of the counsel of Pruyn, the Albany receiver), charging them with the abstraction and concealment of the books, and withholding them from the inspection of stockholders, and laying the damages at $50,000. This action was commenced under section 179 of the Code of Procedure, which authorizes a personal arrest in such cases. On the same day Judge Barnard granted an order authorizing the arrest of the several defendants, and requiring the sheriff of Albany County to hold each of them to bail in the sum of $25,000. This order of arrest was placed in the hands of the sheriff of Albany on the morning of the seventh of September. On the night of the sixth the books were secretly returned to the office of the company, being drawn up in a basket to a window in the rear of the building by Phelps and Mr. Ramsey's son. But their return was unknown to any of the Church directors or their counsel or attorneys, either in Albany or New York.

It has been charged that this order of arrest was obtained for the purpose of preventing Ramsey and the other defendants from participating in the election, by seizing their persons; and among other proofs of this purpose, the alleged exorbitant amount of bail required has been pointed to. The amount of bail, considering the wrongful acts charged in the complaint, does not appear

Smith, acting in concert with others, and it is important that said books should be recovered and restored to the office of the company: therefore

"*Resolved*, That Field & Shearman be employed as counsel to take all legal means for the recovery and restoration of the said books, and for the arrest and punishment of the persons abstracting them, with liberty to employ associate counsel as they may find it expedient; and further

"*Resolved*, That the books, as soon as recovered, be deposited in the office of this company, to be there kept with the other books of the company.

(ENDORSED.)

"The within resolution was this day passed at a meeting of the Executive Committee, all being present excepting Messrs. Ramsey and Rice.

"Dated September 3, 1869.

"AZRO CHASE,
"DAVID WILBER,
"JACOB LEONARD."

to have been excessive in itself; and it is only by applying it to the hypothesis of an oppressive and fraudulent purpose in making any arrest, that it can be regarded as excessive. It was an amount of bail which men in the positions of the defendants could and did easily procure as soon as they were required to do so. With respect to the time and other circumstances of the actual arrest, I shall consider hereafter what tendency they have to establish the charge of a fraudulent intent. At present, it is enough to say that all correct reasoning on such a subject must involve the inquiry whether there was not, on the part of the Executive Committee who authorized and the counsel and attorneys who conducted this proceeding, another purpose, of an entirely legitimate and proper character, with which all their acts in regard to it are more consistent than they are with a wrongful purpose.

I am informed that the expectation with which this order of arrest was obtained, was that it would compel the production of the books; and that no other use was ever intended to be made of it. Is this a rational supposition? To those who are predisposed to look upon every step that was taken by one of the parties to this excited contest as so many proofs of a base conspiracy to obtain the control of a railroad by fraud and against the wishes of a majority of its stockholders, nothing will seem rational that conflicts with that view of their conduct. But to those who reflect that this suit was instituted under the advice of men of mature years, great experience, and hitherto unblemished integrity—I refer to the counsel who procured a modification of Judge Peckham's injunction—who recollect that the production of those books was essential to a fair election of directors, and that the process resorted to was one expressly authorized by law, it will not seem an irrational supposition that such men relied upon it as an effectual means of compelling the production of the books, and of securing to their clients the inspection and use of the books to which they were unquestionably entitled. There are few lawyers, I apprehend, who are accustomed to advise on such affairs, who would not regard an arrest of parties unlawfully and clandestinely concealing property to the possession of which their clients were entitled, as a legitimate and proper weapon of the law to compel the wrongdoers to make restitution, when the law itself expressly authorizes an arrest in such cases. What was and is the whole object of an arrest for debt on mesne process, when it was or now is authorized? Was it and is it not to compel payment of the debt? It surely never was, in any true theory of the law, to incarcerate the defendant as a punishment for not paying. The legitimate and proper purpose is to compel payment. In like manner, the proper purpose of an arrest on mesne process of one who is charged with a wrongful embezzlement or concealment of personal property, is not that the arrest may operate as a punishment, but it is that it may operate to compel the production of the property. In any inquiry, therefore, of an ethical nature into the motives or purposes of a lawyer who has advised such an arrest, this legitimate and proper use of legal process is not to be overlooked. A lawyer, like all other men, when a moral judgment is to be passed upon his professional acts, is entitled to demand that his acts shall be judged by applying them to the proper motive with which they might have been performed, and with which they are clearly consistent. It is as great a wrong to assume an improper motive in forming our opinions of a man's conduct, and to array the evidence only in reference to that hypothesis, as it is to pervert the evidence or to misrepresent the facts. He who would judge truly must embrace the whole circle of rational motives, and especially he must not exclude a motive which is commonly acted upon in doing that about which he is inquiring.

Furthermore, it is worthy of consideration here, whether the wrongful purpose which has been imputed to these gentlemen is a rational supposition. How could they imagine it possible for them to arrest those parties on the eve of that election, *for the sake of preventing them from acting at the election,* without incurring a liability of a most serious character? The reader must remember that, in this investigation, we are not dealing with the characters of men who are either tyros or fools; but with men of large experience in affairs, of acknowledged forecast, of extensive professional knowledge, and of undisputed ability to discern the limits of legal and moral rectitude. To whatever extent they may be supposed to have been zealous for the interests of their clients, I am quite free to say that, according to my observation, men of their years and abilities do not commonly allow zeal for their clients to carry them into acts, and to pursue objects, which would be irrational because they could not possibly be successful, even if there were no higher restraint operating to prevent them. The election of the Church ticket of directors at that corporate meeting, could no more have been carried, so as to be valid, by arresting Mr. Ramsey and lodging him in jail until after the election had been held, with a purpose to prevent his acting, than it could have been carried and be made valid by placing a file of soldiers at the polls, with orders to shoot every man offering to vote the Ramsey ticket. And I presume that this was just as well known to the counsel who advised the bringing of the suit, as it is known now to me, and every other lawyer in the land.

With respect to any improper purpose in arresting Mr. Phelps, he was not, I understand, a stockholder, had no special duty to perform at the election, and the Church party could therefore have had no motive in preventing him from being present. As to Mr. Smith, although he was one of numerous counsel acting in the Ramsey interest, it would be difficult to find a reason for preventing *him* from being present at the election, and at the same time leaving Judge Allen, Judge Porter, and all the other counsel who were present, to render their valuable and important services to their clients. So that, as it appears to me, the reader must commence his inquiry into the facts and circumstances attending that arrest, with an irrational hypothesis on the one side to which to apply them, and with an entirely rational hypothesis on the other side, with which the actual occurrences are perfectly consistent throughout.

The facts attending the arrest were these: The papers author-

izing the suit to be brought arrived at the office of Field &
Shearman, in New York, on Saturday the fourth of September,
between one and two o'clock. Mr. D. D. Field had then left his
office to take the train for Stockbridge. Mr. Dudley Field, his
son, proceeded to draw the complaint with all dispatch, but the
whole of the necessary papers could not be prepared until Monday the sixth. On that day, Mr. Morgan, of the law firm of
Lowe, Clarke & Morgan was employed as counsel to obtain the
order of arrest and take it to Albany. Judge Barnard was then
holding the court at chambers. Mr. Morgan proceeded to chambers, found that Judge Barnard had left for the day, followed
him to his house, and there obtained the order of arrest. He then
took the first train to Albany, where he arrived at about midnight. At Albany he delivered the papers for the arrest to Conway, a clerk of Mr. Hamilton Harris, with directions to deliver
them to the sheriff at the earliest possible moment that morning,
the seventh. Before the sheriff's office was open that morning,
Conway handed the papers to the sheriff in person, at his house.
The time at which the sheriff's office was opened was nine o'clock.
No orders were given as to the time or place of service; but
when Conway placed the papers in the hands of the sheriff, the
latter asked if there were any instructions, to which Conway
answered, "Only to do your duty." At the same time there was
placed in the sheriff's hands a *pluries* non-bailable attachment,
issued by Judge Barnard, directing him to arrest Pruyn for an
alleged contempt of one of Judge Barnard's previous orders.
Pruyn was at this time out of the state, and the sheriff had
heretofore been unable to find him. Without any further communication with anyone concerning the service of any of these
papers, the sheriff went to consult his own counsel, William J.
Hadley, who was in no way connected with either of the parties
to these controversies, and to obtain his advice concerning the
time and mode of serving the papers that had been placed in his
hands.* Hadley advised the sheriff to look for Pruyn at the office

* It has been stated with absolute incorrectness, in the *North American*

of the Albany & Susquehanna Railroad, as he would be likely to go there if he had returned to Albany, and that it was his (the sheriff's) duty to look for Pruyn at that place. In regard to the arrest of Ramsey, Phelps, and Smith, Mr. Hadley told the sheriff that if he should meet Ramsey and Phelps when searching for Pruyn, it would be his duty to serve the process of arrest, otherwise he would be liable for an escape, but that he should take care to have bail bonds with him, and give them as little inconvenience as possible, *in order not to interfere with the election, or to prevent their participation in it.* The sheriff thereupon went to his office to procure bail bonds, leaving the papers in the hands of his counsel, for further examination. Having procured the necessary blanks for taking bail, the sheriff returned to Mr. Hadley's office, and Mr. Hadley repeated to him the instructions and advice he had already given respecting the arrest of the several parties named. Some other necessary business which the sheriff had to transact that morning, and the preparations and consultations with his counsel in regard to these arrests, had occupied so much time, that it was about *half-past eleven o'clock* when the sheriff left Mr. Hadley's office to go to the office of the railroad. He was accompanied by his undersheriff. When they arrived at the office of the company, Pruyn was not there, but Ramsey, Phelps, and Smith were. The sheriff informed each of them of the process which he held; stated to them that he wished to cause them no inconvenience, and requested them to procure bail. While the bonds were preparing, they passed in and out of the room in which the sheriff met them, into the adjoining room, the sheriff using no other restraint than to desire them not to leave the building.* Bail was at once procured and offered. The sheriff himself had some doubt about the sureties, but Mr. Shearman,

Review, that the sheriff consulted a lawyer who was ''one of Mr. Fisk's numerous counsel.'' Mr. Hadley has made oath that he was not counsel for any of the parties, and that he had no interest or motive in advising the sheriff excepting to aid him in the discharge of his official duty.

* Mr. Ramsey testified on the trial of the case of *The People v. The Albany & Susquehanna Railroad Company* and others, that the sheriff would

who knew their standing, requested the sheriff to accept them, in order to have them released from all restraint as speedily as possible. The bail bond was executed for all three before the voting began.

Any extended comments on these facts seem to me wholly unnecessary. They are not reconcilable with an attempt to arrest these men and remove them from that building, in order to prevent them from taking part in the election, or to restrain them within the building until the meeting should be organized and the voting should have taken place. It has been said that "the whole proceeding certainly spoke volumes for the ingenuity and resource of those who engineered it. In its style it could not have been improved."* There is no ingenuity in engineering an occurrence which transpires by mere accident, as did the sheriff's first meeting with these gentlemen at the time and place where he did; but there may be a great deal of a certain kind of ingenuity displayed in misstating and suppressing facts, as has been done to an extraordinary extent in the article in the *North American Review,* entitled "An Erie Raid." It is twice stated in that article that the sheriff's legal adviser was one of Mr. Fisk's counsel. The sheriff's legal adviser has sworn that he was disinterested. It is stated in the article that "the officials of the road were arrested just when they should have been organizing their meeting." None of them had any special duty to perform in or-

not allow him to leave the room. But the sheriff, on the same trial, gave a very different account of this matter, when cross-examined as follows:

Q. Do you remember the circumstances of your refusal to allow Mr. Ramsey to go out of the room while the bonds were being prepared?

A. No, sir; he went just where he had a mind to. . . .

Q. Will you take your oath that you did not tell him not to leave the room?

A. I don't remember. I was very kind to him. I did not want to give him any inconvenience. They went about the room, in and out. Mr. Smith was the last one, and I waited at the corner of the desk, and I think that I sent away to ask if he was at leisure. . . .

Q. When you went down to the Susquehanna offices on the day of the election, had you any intention to interfere with the election?

A. No, sir.

* *North American Review.*

ganizing the stockholders' meeting; but Ramsey, who was the only stockholder among the three, had a right to be present and to vote. His presence was never for an instant interrupted. Even if no bail bond had been signed and accepted, it is impossible, if the sheriff and his counsel are to be believed on their oaths, to imagine that Mr. Ramsey would have been prevented from voting, either in the organization of the meeting, or in the choice of directors.

From a full and careful collation of all the evidence that has been given on this subject, I am satisfied that the Reviewer has not correctly stated the facts respecting the time of the arrest; that his representations that "half an hour" was occupied in arranging the bail bonds, that thus Mr. Shearman's *"coup* had been completely successful," because Mr. Ramsey had been kept under restraint until the polls of the Church organization "had been long open;" that Mr. Smith, in consequence of the arrest, was unable to attend to the organization of another stockholders' meeting until after "the Erie party" had so matured their plans as to feel sure that they were "in possession of the Albany and Susquehanna Railroad beyond peradventure," have given an entirely false coloring to this occurrence. A fair examination of the evidence shows, in my opinion, that the sheriff made known to Mr. Ramsey and the other defendants in the process of arrest, that he had such a process, at *ten or fifteen minutes before twelve o'clock,* which was the hour fixed for the election; that very little time was consumed in arranging the bail bonds, in consequence of Mr. Shearman's promptness in accepting the sureties offered; that none of the parties subjected to the technical arrest were in any way restrained in their movements through the different rooms; and that the bail bonds were executed and the parties released from the arrest before twelve o'clock and before the voting at the "Harris poll" began. If Mr. Shearman had any "coup" to effect, by causing Mr. Ramsey, Mr. Phelps, and Mr. Smith, to be *arrested in those rooms, at the moment when their presence was most necessary*—a supposition that is entirely irrec-

oncilable with the sworn statements of the sheriff and his counsel in their affidavits—then Mr. Shearman took the very course
most likely to defeat his own object. A lawyer, who had the
alleged purpose to effect, would not have promptly come forward
to advise the sheriff to accept the bail offered. In my opinion,
the time and place of the arrest were pure accidents, over which
Mr. Shearman had no control, and for which he is under no moral
responsibility; nor do I think that Mr. Field, Judge Parker, or
Mr. Harris, knew, or could have known beforehand, of the
sheriff's movements during that forenoon, or that any arrest was
likely to be made at the time and place where it was made. In
fact, among all the judicial orders that were served at that meeting, on the one side and the other, this arrest, accidentally made
there by the sheriff, appears to have caused less real embarrass-
ment to anybody than any other order or process that was brought
there. As soon as it had been served, the defendants made known,
and then for the first time, that the books were in the company's
safe, to which they had been returned, secretly, on the previous
night.

Again: the Reviewer has torn from its context a sentence of
Mr. Shearman's testimony, and perverted it to a bearing on this
arrest, to which it had no relation, in the following manner:

> The thing [the arrest] could not have been better timed. To under-
> stand the full possible effect of this move, and the spirit in which it
> was made, it is necessary to bear in mind a remark of Mr. Shearman
> in his subsequent testimony: "I didn't want to lose a second's time,
> because I knew the value of time in this case, and I knew that the whole
> question would have to depend upon the question of which meeting
> was organized first." The officials of the road were, *therefore,* arrested
> just when they should have been organizing their meeting.

I know not whether the reader will entertain the same opinion
that I do respecting such gross perversions of testimony. When
they occur before a court or jury, they commonly receive the
castigation they deserve. Are they less worthy of rebuke, when
they are made in print for the purpose of influencing public
opinion? At all events, whatever may be the disadvantages with

which Truth has to "draw on his boots" in order to pursue what has gone before him, the reader will now learn that Mr. Shearman's remark had no reference whatever to this arrest, and, moreover, that his testimony has been garbled as well as misapplied. Mr. Shearman, on the trial from which this extract was taken by the Reviewer, was subjected to a severe cross-examination respecting his motives and movements on that day, in the course of which the following occurred:

Q. Did you go beforehand to see Mr. Banks, and inquire which was the room where the stockholders' meeting was to be held, so that you could find it on election day? *A.* For that and other purposes.

Q. Didn't you go to him to find out which room they were going to occupy, so that it could be preoccupied by those in your interest? *A.* No, sir.

Q. Then tell me what motive you had? *A.* I wanted to know when I went down there which room to enter.

Q. Was you afraid you could not find it? *A.* I didn't want to lose any time; I wanted to be there at the minute exactly.

Q. Do you mean to say that you went there and made inquiries of Mr. Banks in reference to those rooms, for fear you wouldn't be able to find the proper rooms when you went there to the election? *A.* Yes, sir, that's it exactly.

Q. And that was your only reason? *A.* Yes, sir, and for the purpose of giving information to the gentleman that was with me, and I didn't want to lose a second's time, because I knew the value of time in this case, and I knew that the whole question would have to depend upon the question of which meeting was organized first.

But it is needless to follow further in detail the misrepresentations that have been made concerning the circumstances and the purposes of this arrest. The reader will find the material facts fully set forth, in a series of affidavits annexed to this opinion, which were read by the counsel for the Church party on the hearing of a motion made in the interest of the Ramsey party in May, 1870, in the Supreme Court, in Albany County, for a discontinuance of the suit in which the arrest was ordered, *upon the ground that it was brought without due authority, and also on the ground that the Ramsey Board of Directors, after they had been put in possession, had directed its discontinuance.* The judge who heard this motion (Judge Ingalls), after the reading of affidavits on both sides, inquired whether the suit had not answered its main purpose, the books having been restored to the office of the company before the election; and upon the counsel for the plaintiffs answering in the affirmative, he ordered a discontinuance, *without any costs.* It is not true, therefore, as has been asserted, that this suit was discontinued because it had been brought without authority. The motion was made to effect not only a discontinuance, but also to compel the payment of the defendants' costs by the plaintiff's attorneys, or the Executive Committee. This the judge denied.

Among the other incidents of the election it is now necessary to examine the act of Mr. Fuller in voting on the shares which he held as receiver, and the connection of Mr. Field or Mr. Shearman with that act. It will be remembered that the charge is, that this receivership was obtained on the fourteenth of August, for the fraudulent purpose of voting on these shares in the interest of the Church party, at the election on the seventh of September, against the wishes of the alleged owners of the shares; and that the act of voting by the receiver, coupled with the circumstances under which he gave his vote, *proves* the original purpose of obtaining the receivership to have been fraudulent. It is, perhaps, needless to remark that the receiver's act of voting may or may not have some tendency to establish the conspiracy charged, according to the circumstances under which the vote was given. If those circumstances make the act of voting just as consistent with a rightful as with a wrongful purpose, I suppose that very few readers will expect me to arrive at the conclusion that this receivership was part of a plot to carry the election by fraud. I take it to be as sound a rule in forming the moral judgments of everyday life, as it is in courts of law, that a base fraud is not to be imputed to any man, unless upon very clear evidence; and that when the evidence is circumstantial, it ought to have a very strong tendency to exclude the possibility of an honest purpose, before it is allowed to convict any man of a dishonest one.

The reader has seen all the material facts connected with the appointment of the receiver. He has now to follow the receiver to Albany.

Mr. Fuller has testified under oath that he went to Albany to attend the election, *at the request of no one,* although he had previously conversed with Mr. Shearman, and possibly with Mr. Field, but of that he was not clear; that neither of these gentlemen requested him to go to Albany and vote on this stock; that when he went he was undecided in his own mind about voting, but that he meant to watch the proceedings and be governed by circumstances; that his general purpose was not to vote, unless some emergency should render it necessary; that on the morning of the election in Albany he had some conversation with Mr. Shearman, and went with him to the place where the election was to be held; that he was not acting in concert with Mr. Field and Mr. Shearman; that before going to the room Mr. Shearman gave him a ticket having the names of the Church directors; and that he voted that ticket after Mr. Groesbeck's injunction had been served on the inspectors at the Harris poll, and after Mr. Shearman had advised him to vote, first exhibiting to the inspectors the papers of his appointment as receiver of the stock referred to in the injunction, together with the scrip. He testified, further, that he did not consider it his duty in voting to consult the wishes of those who claimed to own the stock, i.e., Groesbeck and others.

The poll at which Mr. Fuller voted was what was called the "Harris poll." The facts attending the organization of the meeting have been already detailed. The facts show that the Groesbeck injunction, served on the inspectors at the "Harris poll," just as they had opened their poll, forbade the receiving of any votes of the Church party, unless the "holders" of the Groesbeck stock should first have been allowed to vote on that stock. One of the copies of that injunction, which was one of the copies served, is now before me. It is a printed copy; which fact shows that previous preparation for its service at the polls had been made in advance. By its date, it purports that the original was signed on the sixth of September. At the foot it has the words and figures "Dated September 6, 1869," all of which are in print excepting the figure "6," which was inserted with a pen in a blank left for the purpose. It is morally certain, therefore, that this injunction, prepared for in advance, was not obtained until the sixth; that it was intended to be served on the seventh at the election; and it is a fact that no intimation of it was given to the Church party until the moment when it was served on the inspectors at the Harris poll. It thus created suddenly an unexpected situation, which the Church party could not have foreseen. They supposed, as I infer from the injunction which had been obtained by Bush on the thirty-first of July, and from the receivership which had been ordered on the fourteenth of August, that the Groesbeck stock (three thousand shares) was neutralized; and it was clearly unnecessary for *them* to use those shares in voting, *because* they had a majority of all the outstanding undisputed stock. It was not, therefore, until Groesbeck's injunction had been served, that it became of any importance to the Church party to have this Groesbeck stock voted on by anybody. But when that injunction had been served, a new and unexpected necessity arose for receiving votes on that stock from somebody. The votes on it were cast by the receiver.

It will thus be seen that two questions arise in regard to the act of the receiver in voting on this stock. One is, whether he could lawfully cast a vote which ought to be counted in the election, supposing that what was called the "Harris poll" was duly and properly held. The other question is, whether Mr. Shearman, or any other lawyer, could on the spot have honestly advised Mr. Fuller to vote. The first is purely a question of law. The second is a question of professional ethics, depending, for the true elements of a moral judgment, on the inquiry whether it was so clearly illegal and improper for the receiver to vote, that no lawyer could have advised him to vote without acting from an improper motive and with an improper intent. For, I presume all impartial and intelligent lawyers and laymen will agree, that unless Mr. Shearman was bound to have seen that it was clearly unlawful for this receiver to vote, his advice to the receiver to give his vote is no evidence that Mr. Shearman was acting in pursuance of a corrupt conspiracy to carry the election fraudulently, as it is also no evidence that such an conspiracy existed.

Now I shall endeavor to state the argument both *for* and *against* the lawfulness and propriety of this receiver's voting on this stock, with equal fairness; and I begin with the reasons that may be assigned against his voting:

In the first place, it may be said that the purpose of the action in which the receiver was appointed was professedly to have the issue of the stock declared void, and the scrip delivered up to be canceled. In the next place, it may be said that a receiver is a mere officer of the court, holding the possession of property as a trustee for a temporary purpose, and that if there are to be any acts done with or concerning the property which are to be done by virtue of the legal title, it belongs to the owner of the legal title to do those acts, rather than to a trustee who has the mere possession for a temporary and judicial purpose. In the third place, it may be said that a receiver of stock in a corporation, the lawfulness of whose issue is in contestation in a suit, cannot vote at an election of directors along with holders of stock whose right to vote is not contested, because stock so held by a receiver ought not to be considered as held for the purpose of voting, since it may be used against the wishes of those in whose names it stands registered. Finally, it may be said that it is the duty of a receiver holding stock in a corporation situated as this stock was by the pendency of the action in which he was appointed, to apply to the court which appointed him for directions, and not to assume to vote upon the stock without an express authority from the court; and that if this receiver had so applied, there is ground for saying that no such authority would have been rightfully given, because the court does not vote at corporate meetings.

On the other hand, it must be remembered that when property is placed in the hands of a receiver by a court of equity, the party who held the legal estate at the time the possession was so transferred, is not necessarily the sole *cestui que trust*. Receivers hold in trust for all the parties having any beneficial interest in the property, while their official possession continues, and for whomsoever the final judgment shall be when their official title and possession terminate. There may be, therefore, various *cestuis que trust*, all of whose rights and equities are for the time being held by the same trustee; and I have already suggested the grounds, which seem to me very plain, on which it is to be held that the plaintiff in the suit had established for himself and all the other *bona fide* stockholders an apparent right of equitable interest in the property, according to the meaning and purpose of the Code, for the purposes of a receivership, which right or interest must be regarded as existing until final judgment on the merits of the action, *notwithstanding* the allegation of the complaint, that the issue of the stock to the defendants was unlawful and void. In regard to the question of allowing a trustee of stock to vote, instead of one or more of the *cestuis que trust*, I know of but one case that can be cited against the right of the trustee to cast the vote. It is the case of *ex parte* Holmes, 5 *Cowen*, 426, where the Supreme Court set aside an election of directors that had been carried by the vote of a trustee. But a proper examination of that case and of the view of it taken by Savage, Chief Justice, in the later case *in re* Jacob Barker, 6 *Wendell*, 509, will show that neither of those cases touches the right of a receiver to vote, who holds stock situated as this stock was at the time of Mr. Fuller's voting. In *ex parte* Holmes, the stock belonged to the company, but was registered in the name of a trustee who held it for the company; and it was held that the trustee could not vote, not because the *cestui que trust* was the proper party to vote, but because the whole beneficial property in the stock belonged to the company, and could be controlled by its officers the directors, who might use it to perpetuate themselves in office by requiring the trustees to vote for themselves. "All that was said in that case," said Savage, Chief Justice, "in relation to the rights of a trustee of *cestui que trust* to vote on stock standing in the name of the trustee, either generally or specially, in his representative character, was said in reference to the peculiar circumstances of that case. The court never could have doubted the right of a person to vote upon stock standing in his name, although held by him in trust for another," etc. (*In re* Jacob Barker, *ut supr.*) The stock held by Mr. Fuller, and on which he voted, was not registered in his name, but is a peculiar case. It stands, therefore, unaffected by *ex parte* Holmes, unless the reasons assigned in that case for not allowing the trustee to vote are also applicable to the case of this receiver. In *ex parte* Holmes the legal title was in the trustee, but the *whole* beneficial interest was in the company; and because the directors could, therefore, dictate his vote to the trustee, it was held that stock so situated must be considered as not held for the purpose of voting. But how was it with the stock held by this receiver? The *whole* beneficial interest was not in the company, and the stock stood registered in the names of Groesbeck and others, who had 25 per cent of the beneficial interest in it, as the receiver was bound to assume on the papers in the action, and who, moreover, claimed the whole interest. How, then, could the directors of this company dictate a vote to the receiver? They could not remove him, or control him, as it was said in *ex parte* Holmes the directors could have done with the trustee in that case. As representatives or officers of the whole body of stockholders, the directors of this company could only leave the receiver to act on his own judgment of what was required by the interests of all the *cestuis que trust*, of whom he was the representative in a much more direct and specific sense than the directors, for the plaintiff and the other stockholders were acting in reference to this stock not through the directors, but by the intervention of the court. The mischiefs, therefore, on which *ex parte* Holmes was decided, do not affect this case. The directors could not control the receiver, and no evidence exists that any party among them attempted to do so.

In regard to the supposed rule that a court of equity does not vote at corporate meetings, it obviously will not do to say that a receiver of stock is not to vote under any circumstances. Under such a rule, if the receivership happened to comprehend ninety-nine hundredths of the whole stock, there would be an election of directors by the remaining one-hundredth, and the ninety-nine hundredths would not be represented at all. No court of equity would allow of this, but it would allow and direct its receiver to vote for the protection of the interests of all whom he represents. And in regard to the necessity of an application to the court for directions to the receiver, while such is undoubtedly the general rule, may there not be circumstances in which the receiver may be obliged to act on his own discretion, before he can ask for directions, in order that there may be an election at all, or that there may be a fair election? In this case I conceive that there were such circumstances. For, the service of the injunction obtained by Groesbeck, as above stated, forbidding the inspectors to receive the votes of the whole Church party among the stockholders, unless Groesbeck and others, claimants of the three thousand shares in controversy, and all the "holders thereof," should "*first* have had an opportunity to vote upon all the shares by *them held respectively,*" placed the receiver under a species of moral duress to decide instantly two questions: *first,* whether he had a general power to vote; and *secondly,* whether he was not to be regarded, within the terms of this injunction, as the holder of the stock, whose previous vote was the key that was to unlock the prohibition and permit the votes of the Church party to be received. A fair construction of the injunction certainly raised the question whether it was not the duty of the receiver to vote as "holder" of the three thousand shares. Groesbeck and the other plaintiffs in the injunction were not the holders of the stock or of any part of it; for they had surrendered the scrip to a receiver, who was for all purposes the "holder" of the shares while his receivership continued. Groesbeck and the other claimants of the shares could not cast the vote upon them merely because they were a branch of the *cestuis que trust*. If they were to be voted upon at all, the vote must be cast by the receiver; and it was the clear meaning of the injunction that somebody should vote upon them, otherwise the votes of the whole Church party among the stockholders, representing 10,400 shares, would be excluded. Moreover, Mr. Groesbeck was in the room when his injunction was served at the "Harris poll." He did not claim the right to vote on the stock himself, nor did he ask the receiver to vote according to his (Groesbeck's) wishes, nor did he or anyone else challenge the receiver's vote. As soon as Mr. Shearman had an opportunity to read Groesbeck's injunction, he saw the necessity for someone's voting on this stock, and acting upon a construction of the injunction of which it was certainly capable when applied to the situation of things at that moment, he said to the receiver, "An injunction has been served restraining this election from going on unless the votes upon the 2,400 shares which you hold are first received, and you had better vote." Mr. Field gave no advice to the receiver about voting, one way or the other.

It seems to me that these facts need only to be stated to relieve Mr. Shearman from all imputation of a wrongful intent. He was obliged to construe that injunction. Will it be said that he did not construe it rightly, and that it meant by "holders" of the stock no one but Groesbeck and others, the injunction plaintiffs? If this *was* its sole meaning, which under the actual situation of things in my opinion it was not, is Mr. Shearman to be charged with an intent to carry that election by a *fraud*, because he *misconstrued* an injunction? Then why not charge Groesbeck and others with an intent to *prevent* an election by fraudulent *use* of an injunction, which they obtained without reference to the fact that the stock was in the hands of a receiver, and which they served at a moment when it would have excluded the whole of the Church votes if the receiver had not come forward and voted? The answer is, that in neither case are these charges of fraud to be lightly made, by him who would do equal and exact justice in his judgments upon the acts of these parties. But Mr. Shearman not only had to construe that injunction, he had also to apply it to the real situation, so that the clients for whom he was acting could have their votes received. There was but one way in which their votes could be received, namely, by first allowing someone to vote on the three thousand shares held by the receiver. That the receiver was in contemplation of law the "holder" seems to be quite clear.

It has struck me very forcibly that in the long complaint of Groesbeck and others on which the Albany County judge granted this injunction, the fact that the stock claimed was in the hands of a receiver was not stated. While this complaint dealt very minutely in charges of a conspiracy, and while it informed the Supreme Court in Albany County that Bush had *prayed* for a receiver, it did not inform the court that a receiver had been appointed; and the sole information it gave was that at the instance of Bush an injunction had been granted restraining them (Groesbeck and others) from parting with the stock. But Mr. Shearman did not and could not know that Judge Clute's injunction requiring a vote to be first received on these three thousand shares had been granted in ignorance of the fact that they were then "held" by a receiver. If he was bound to presume anything about it, he was bound to presume that Judge Clute knew the precise situation of the stock, and to construe and apply his injunction accordingly. It was certainly no unfair construction of that injunction, under the circumstances, to regard it as a direction to the receiver to vote.

But it has been said (erroneously) that Groesbeck's suit in which he obtained this injunction, "set forth the circumstances *under which the receiver had been appointed,* and showing the

illegality of the proceeding."* There was not a word in Groesbeck's complaint, from which the judge who granted the injunction could infer that this stock had been ordered into the hands
of a receiver, nor was the receiver made a defendant in Groesbeck's suit, as he must have been if the injunction obtained was
intended to affect *him*. But if he had been made a party to the
suit, or the Albany court had been informed of his receivership,
and the injunction about voting had been issued just as it was,
then the true legal construction of that injunction would have
been that Fuller was the "holder" of the stock. As it was, in
point of fact, the injunction not being specially directed *against*
the receiver and there being nothing to inform Mr. Shearman
that the judge who granted it did not know of the receivership,
Mr. Shearman was obliged to assume that the injunction meant
by "holders" of the stock the person who was then the "holder"
in contemplation of law. It has been said that this view of Mr.
Shearman's course is a "pretense" resting "on an intrinsic
absurdity," and that when Mr. Field explained Mr. Fuller's
voting, in one of his published letters, by reference to the operation of this injunction in creating a necessity for his voting, he
"misstated the facts." I have only to submit to the candid judgment of the bar, whether there is any "pretense" or "intrinsic
absurdity" in the view which I have taken of the operation of
that injunction, and of the necessity for giving it a construction
under which it was proper for the receiver to vote. That there
is any "intrinsic absurdity" in this view, I think few sound
lawyers will affirm, even if they think the injunction should not
have been so construed; and that Mr. Shearman could honestly
construe it as he did, will be thought by most impartial persons
to be a very clear proposition of morals, even if they do not
concur in his law.

In the foregoing discussion I have considered only the question of whether Mr. Shearman, in construing the injunction as
he did, acted fairly and honestly. This is all that is necessary to

* General Barlow's letter.

his vindication. I ought to add, however, that in my opinion, after the service of this injunction on the inspectors, it became the duty of the receiver to vote, and that Mr. Shearman's construction of the injunction was under the circumstances correct. I do not think that this question depends upon the intention with which Groesbeck and others obtained the injunction. It depends upon the true legal construction of the injunction. It could not be construed to mean an absolute prohibition against receiving the votes of the parties who held 10,400 shares of stock. It was a conditional order, meaning that when votes had been received on the 3,000 shares of (so-called) Groesbeck stock, the parties who held the 10,400 shares might be allowed to vote; and there was no mode in which that condition could be complied with excepting by allowing the receiver to vote.

And this seems to be the proper place in which to state that this receivership still continues. It will be remembered that the original order appointing the receiver required the defendants Groesbeck and others to show cause before Judge Barnard on the nineteenth of August (1869) why it should not be confirmed. It has been represented that Groesbeck and the other claimants never appeared. General Barlow, in his letter to the *Tribune,* in rejoinder to Mr. Field, said: ''Groesbeck's counsel were too familiar with the performances of Fisk, Gould, Field, Shearman, and Barnard, to waste their time in arguing against the order before the judge who granted it. They did not propose to go through any such farce. They waited until the matter could be heard before an impartial judge (Smith), and the receivership was then pronounced to be illegal. Their omission to show cause against it before Judge Barnard, merely showed their entire distrust of him as a judge, and their knowledge of the relations existing between the judge, parties, and counsel.''

There is no foundation for these statements. On the contrary, I have personally inspected a long series of orders made in the case, extending from August 19, 1869 to May 1, 1871, showing the appearance of the defendants, and the repeated confirmation of the receivership from time to time, until cause should be shown against it. On the nineteenth of August, 1869, the defendants, Groesbeck and others, appeared by a highly respectable firm of lawyers, and the hearing was by consent adjourned to August 24, on which day an order was made, reciting that a motion for continuing the appointment of the receiver coming on for argument and parties on both sides appearing by counsel, it was ordered that the motion stand over to the fifteenth of September, and that in the meantime, and until the hearing and decision of the motion, the appointment of a receiver theretofore made be confirmed and continued, and that the injunctions issued therein be also continued and confirmed. This order was made by consent of the defendants' counsel; so that when the election of directors came on at Albany, the provisional possession of the receiver had been confirmed with the assent of the very parties who are said to have known too well the relations between the judge, the other parties, and their counsel, to make any appearance in the case. By a series of similar orders, all regularly made by consent, the motion has been adjourned, and the receivership has been continued, down to May 1, 1871, at which time I am writing.

It remains for me to examine briefly the complaints that have been made against Mr. Field on account of what he did or is supposed to have done in a suit brought by Mr. Ramsey against the Erie Railway corporation and certain of its directors. I have found some difficulty in reducing these complaints to a substantive and tangible form. They have been made and discussed in a way that seems to me to be conducive to anything rather than to the promotion of a sound professional morality; for there appears to have been a serious lack of condemnation in regard to the proceedings which it became Mr. Field's duty to oppose. Perhaps this is owing to the fact that he had to act in some degree in defense of interests with which are identified the names of Fisk and Gould; persons whose names it would seem it is only necessary to mention, to call into activity an amount of prejudice before which it is apparently expected that Justice will drop her scales and Reason renounce her office. But as I have never seen either of them, to my knowledge, and do not possess any acquaintance with their general merits or demerits, I may be permitted to observe that if they have never done anything worse than to defend the great corporation whose interests are said to be under their charge as they defended them against Mr. Ramsey's suit, they have not much to answer for.

On the thirteenth of September, 1869, a suit was commenced by the attorney-general of the state in the name of The People against the Albany & Susquehanna Railroad corporation, both of its claiming Boards of Directors, and the contending receivers, to determine whether either and which of those boards and receivers had a good and valid title to the offices which they claimed, and if neither, to order a new election. Prominent among the defendants to this suit were Messrs. Fisk and Gould, officers and principal managers of the Erie Railway Company. This case was to come on for trial in the Supreme Court, Special Term, in Monroe County, at Rochester, on the twenty-ninth day of November, 1869, before Judge E. Darwin Smith.

On the seventeenth of November, 1869, Joseph H. Ramsey made oath in the city of Albany to a complaint made by himself as plaintiff against Jay Gould and James Fisk, Jr., Frederick A. Lane, and others, and the Erie Railway Company as defendants. The attorneys employed by Mr. Ramsey to bring his suit were practitioners in the city of New York. The principal offices of the Erie Railway Company were in this city, and here all its principal officers and all the individual defendants named (except one, who lived at Jersey City) had their residences or places of business. The original complaint, which I have seen, was at first entitled as of "Broome County," but was afterward altered to "Delaware County." "Broome" is the county of which Binghamton is the seat, at which city Judge Balcom, of the Supreme Court, resides. Whether the plaintiff applied to Judge Balcom, or any judge in Broome County to make the orders for which the complaint prayed and which were granted in Delaware County, is perhaps not sufficiently indicated by the fact that the complaint was entitled of Broome County. This fact may afterward have given rise to a suspicion that Judge Balcom had been applied to and had refused to make the orders. If this was so, it was a clear violation of a statute to obtain the same orders from another judge. But when the first knowledge of this suit reached the defendants, their attention was not directed to this inquiry, for they did not know that the complaint had been originally so entitled.

The complaint alleged that the plaintiff Ramsey was a creditor and stockholder of the Erie Railway Company, and that he brought the suit also in behalf of all others in the like situation. The statement that he was a creditor and stockholder was the only averment made in the complaint on personal knowledge. The only cause of action against the defendants, filling more than 330 folios, was averred on information and belief alone, and the *jurat* gave it no greater force.

In regard to the plaintiff's interest as a creditor and stockholder, he represented himself as the owner of several bonds issued by the company, and of certain shares of its stock not registered in his name, but *"entitled* to be standing in his name on the books of the company.'"* (In point of fact, as a subsequent affidavit of Mr. Ramsey shows the plaintiff borrowed some money of David Groesbeck, with which certain bonds and stock of the Erie Railway were purchased, and in some way they were left or pledged in the hands of Groesbeck as security.) The *gravamen* of his complaint was, as stated on his information and belief, that certain funds and property of the company were left by its officers in the hands of one or more of the other defendants or other persons not collected or properly cared for and in peril

---

* The Circuit Court of the United States in this district has recently held that a person whose name is not registered as a stockholder cannot sue as such, although he may have purchased stock.

of being lost; and further, that the company was generally in a
perilous condition in consequence of the neglect of its directors
to meet and give the necessary attention to its affairs for the
protection of its property in the discharge of their functions.
The complaint prayed, *first,* for a special receiver of the funds
and property specially described to be in danger of being lost;
secondly, for a general receiver of all the property and franchises
of the company (except the franchise of being a corporation)
and of all its funds, books, papers, and property, excepting those
to be placed in the hands of the special receiver. On this complaint and certain affidavits accompanying it, Judge Murray,
of Delaware County, at a Special Term of the Supreme Court,
held at Delhi, in that county, on the twenty-third of November,
1869, on motion of Mr. Henry Smith, of counsel for the plaintiff,
granted an order, appointing David Groesbeck special receiver of
the funds and property specially described in the complaint to
be in peril of being lost, with very extensive powers in relation
thereto, and also in relation to an examination of the books and
papers of the company. The order further declared that it appeared to the court that if the unsuspended directors of the company should omit to meet, or neglect to take charge of, and give
necessary attention to its affairs or the protection of its property
and the discharge of their functions, or if a certain number of
the unsuspended directors should resign, or omit, or refuse to
attend meetings of the board, so that no quorum and legal action
could be secured, in either event the public interests would be
seriously prejudiced, and the company and its creditors would
suffer great loss. The order further declared that it appeared to
the court that the company was in a perilous condition, and that
there was imminent danger of some such event; and that upon
the happening thereof, there ought to be a receiver of the court
ready and competent, and whose right and duty it should then
be to enter at once into possession of the property and exercise
the franchises of the company, with the powers provided in the
order on the happening of any such event. The order then pro-

ceeded to appoint David Groesbeck receiver of the company, its property, and franchises, as prayed for, with power to operate the road and all its branches, and with the most extensive and sweeping powers that can be conferred upon a receiver. On the same day, November 23, Mr. Smith, on behalf of the plaintiff Ramsey, obtained from Judge Murray another order suspending Gould, Fisk, Lane, and five other directors of the company, named defendants, from acting either as directors or officers of the company, or acting about its affairs in any capacity whatever till the further order of the court in that case, and appointing a referee to take evidence to be used on the final exercise of the powers of the court in reference to their suspension or removal from office. Mr. Smith also obtained, on the same day, November 23, a third order from Judge Murray, restraining all creditors of the company from instituting any suit to collect or secure their debts; restraining all the defendants from instituting any suit to embarrass or delay Mr. Ramsey's present suit; restraining the defendants from accepting or admitting service for the company of any summons, complaint, notice, or other paper, either in Mr. Ramsey's present suit or in any other suit involving their official conduct, and restraining them from authorizing any appearance in any such suit, and directing the company and the directors not suspended to take promptly proper action for causing the company to be faithfully and adequately represented in this (Mr. Ramsey's) present suit, and restraining them, the unsuspended directors, from resigning without three days' written notice to his (Mr. Ramsey's) attorneys, stating when such proposed resignation was intended to take effect.

It is not my purpose to characterize these proceedings and occurrences (the original suit, the strange appearance of Mr. Runkle as attorney for the company mentioned hereafter, and the orders obtained), further than to say that they were calculated to arouse the utmost suspicion on the part of the legal advisers of the Erie Railway Company, and to call for the most vigorous measures of defense. It has been said that, if the order providing for a receiver had been carried out, the company would have failed the same day; and I cannot but think that the remark was well founded. The case bore no comparison whatever to the appointment of a receiver of the Albany & Susquehanna Railroad. In that case, as I have shown, a receivership was a measure of immediate and pressing practical necessity. In this case a receivership was necessary only in a theoretical and fictitious sense. In the one case, those who had the official charge of the road under its ordinary organization could not act. In the case of the Erie Railway, at the time Mr. Ramsey brought his suit, every officer of the company was in the actual discharge of his functions, and, but for the contingency created by the three orders obtained by Mr. Ramsey, must have remained competent to the discharge of his duties. Yet the orders were so framed as to make it possible, by their combined operation, if withheld from the knowledge of the officers of the company for a certain period of time, to have the whole property, franchises, and management of this great corporation swept into the hands of Mr. Groesbeck, as receiver, Mr. Groesbeck being the person who had advanced money to Mr. Ramsey to enable him to purchase, or having purchased for him, the bonds and stock on which Mr. Ramsey founded his claim to take these proceedings against the company as a creditor and stockholder.

I do not think it can be claimed that Mr. Ramsey had shown in this complaint that he was such a creditor or stockholder of the company as could demand the appointment of a receiver of even the special funds which he sought to reach by the special receivership. But if this point were conceded, it is clear, in my opinion, that the Code has not authorized the appointment of a general receiver of all the property and franchises of a corporation, to take effect on the happening of a future contingent event, which may or may not happen, and which must happen before any necessity for a receiver can be said to exist. If the Code had made any such provision, then it would be in the power of a plaintiff to exercise some control, or lay some plan for the hap-

pening of that event, and by his own act bring about the event
on which the appointment of the receiver would take effect. But
such as this singular order was, it came into operation with the
two other orders, because they were signed by a judge of the
court.

On the twenty-fourth of November the secretary of the company was served with the summons, complaint, and injunction
in this suit (but not with the order for a receiver), the place of
trial being fixed at Delhi. This village, one of the most inac-
cessible in the state from the city of New York, was then over
twenty miles from any railroad, and must be reached by a drive
of that distance over a mountainous region. On the same day,
the twenty-fourth, the plaintiff's attorneys in New York arranged with Mr. Runkle, an attorney in this city, to appear for
the corporation, and received from him a notice of his appearance as attorney for the corporation in the suit. The reason
afterward given by Mr. Ramsey's attorneys for making this
arrangement with Mr. Runkle was that they supposed themselves to have been authorized to accept Mr. Runkle's appearance by Mr. Diven, one of the directors; but this turned out not
to be correct. The secretary of the company immediately took
the papers which had been served upon him to the office of the
company, and thereupon the Executive Committee of the directors immediately authorized Field & Shearman to appear for the
corporation. These gentlemen, on the same evening, sent a notice
of appearance to Mr. Ramsey's attorneys in the suit, who refused to receive it, stating that another attorney had already
appeared, whose name they declined to give. Prompt and energetic action on the part of the defendants became thus necessary.

The situation appears to me to have been most extraordinary,
embarrassing, and perilous. That the unprofessional reader may
properly appreciate it, some explanation in detail is necessary.

An attorney who appears in a suit is an officer of the court,
and is presumed to do his duty. His appearance is conclusive
upon the party whom he undertakes to represent, until it is set

aside by an order of the court. If he assents to any order or proceeding in the cause, although it may have been entirely unauthorized by his client, it will not, as a general rule, be afterward set aside, until the client who is injured has shown affirma-
tively that the attorney is not of sufficient pecuniary ability to
respond in damages for the wrong occasioned by his unauthorized
act.

It must have been obvious, then, to Field & Shearman (who,
with their clients, were kept in ignorance of the name of the
receiver until December 2) that after the appearance of an
attorney for the company defendant, whose name the plaintiff's
attorneys refused to disclose, the rights and interests of the
company were exposed to a very uncommon peril; that to change
this state of things and to be admitted themselves to appear for
the company was a step of the first necessity and their manifest
duty; and to this end they must ascertain the name of the unknown attorney. There was but one mode of proceeding in the
cause itself, by which they could compel the plaintiff's attorneys
to disclose the name of the unknown attorney who had appeared
for the company, and by which, after they had ascertained his
name, to cause themselves to be substituted in his place. If they
were to attempt to make any motion whatever in the cause, before
they had been substituted as attorneys for the company defendant, they were liable to be turned out of court because
another attorney had appeared for the company. Now, a motion
to compel the plaintiff's attorneys to disclose the name of the
unknown attorney who had appeared for the company, would
have to be made in the Sixth Judicial District, in which Delaware County is embraced. A motion for this purpose, upon notice
of at least eight days to the plaintiff's attorneys, would have to
be made to some judge in that district. If such a motion were
made and granted, the plaintiff's attorneys could cause further
indefinite delay by an appeal from the order, or by other means.
When the name of the unknown attorney had been at length
obtained, another motion would have to be made in the Sixth

District, upon a like notice of at least eight days to that attorney himself, who could appear and oppose the motion, for his removal and the substitution of Field & Shearman as the properly authorized attorneys for the company. If the motion were granted, compliance with this order might, in turn, be greatly delayed; and yet until all these preliminary steps had been taken and fully accomplished, Field & Shearman, the only authorized attorneys for the company in this suit, could not do one act in the suit itself for the protection of the company against the combined operation of the three orders which had been obtained from Judge Murray by the plaintiff. There was, however, one alternative. They could bring a cross suit against Mr. Ramsey, his attorneys, the unknown attorney who had appeared, and the unknown receiver, and enjoin them all from proceeding to enforce the three orders until the further order of the court. No one, I think, can justly say that such an injunction was either unnecessary or oppressive. Nor does it appear to me that there is any ground whatever for the imputation that its purpose was to put Mr. Ramsey's original suit within the control of *Judge Barnard*. He happened to be the only judge holding a Special Term in this county, who was in town on the evening when the injunction was for the first time found to be necessary.

The papers in the cross suit were prepared on the evening of November 24, and were immediately presented by Mr. Aaron J. Vanderpoel* to Judge Barnard, who signed an injunction the next morning, with an order to show cause on the thirtieth why it should not be continued. This was served on Mr. Ramsey's New York attorneys on that day, and on him at Albany on the next day. After the service of this injunction, Mr. Ramsey's New York attorneys arranged with Mr. Runkle to withdraw his appearance for the corporation, and informed Field & Shearman that he had done so; but they did not recognize the appearance of Field & Shearman. Mr. Ramsey's attorneys in New York then caused the substitution of Peckham & Tremaine, of Albany, in

* A counselor of well-known standing in this city.

their place, as attorneys for the plaintiff, and informed Field & Shearman that they had ceased to be attorneys for the plaintiff, but would not give the names of the attorneys substituted. Peckham & Tremaine, however, notified Field & Shearman, on the twenty-ninth, of their substitution, and Field & Shearman obtained from Judge Balcom, on the twenty-first of December an order that their appearance for the company be accepted, and that any notice of appearance from other attorneys be disregarded. On the twenty-first of December, Judge Balcom, on a motion made by Field & Shearman, at Binghamton, set aside Judge Murray's three orders made in Mr. Ramsey's original suit. From this order of Judge Balcom's Mr. Ramsey appealed, but the appeal was withdrawn in September, 1870. Pending the appeal, Judge Murray's orders remained without operation until the case should be finally heard.

In May, 1870, as soon as Mr. Ramsey's original suit was at issue, Field & Shearman made an application to the Supreme Court at Delhi, to change the place of trial to the county of New York, on account of the convenience of witnesses.* This was opposed at first by Mr. Ramsey, on an affidavit stating that he was under an injunction in the cross suit, and could not therefore take such measures as were necessary to oppose the motion. This objection was answered by Judge Gray, of Elmira, now a member of the commission of appeals, then acting as counsel for the company, and was overruled by the court. Mr. Ramsey then asked for an adjournment. This was granted for two weeks, the motion for changing the place of trial to be heard at Binghamton on the thirty-first of May. Mr. Ramsey appealed from this order, and then got a stay of the proceedings from Judge Clute, in Albany, but did not serve it until the thirtieth of May, in order, as it appears from an affidavit that his counsel avowed in court, to prevent Field & Shearman from having the stay set aside. When this stay was served on Field & Shearman in New York, they obtained an order from Judge Cardozo to show cause

* This application was made under a statutory provision.

the next day at Binghamton why the stay should not be set aside. The next day was the day for hearing the motion at Binghamton to change the place of trial. Judge Cardozo's order to show cause was served at Albany on Mr. Ramsey's attorneys in 'the afternoon of the thirtieth. At 9.00 P.M. that evening, a train left Albany for Binghamton. Field & Shearman's messenger carried Judge Cardozo's order and an affidavit of service to Binghamton by that train. Mr. Ramsey's attorneys, in Albany, on the same day, obtained from Judge Peckham a counter-stay of Judge Cardozo's order, and sent it down to New York and had it served on Field & Shearman at ten minutes before ten A.M. on the thirty-first, when the motion to change the place of trial of Mr. Ramsey's original suit, and the motion to vacate Judge Clute's stay, were to be made at Binghamton at ten o'clock that day. Mr. Shearman, who was then at Binghamton, brought on both motions in ignorance, of course, of this last stay granted by Judge Peckham, and both were granted. Mr. Ramsey's counsel then moved, at Binghamton, before Judge Murray, to vacate Judge Balcom's order changing the place of trial; but Judge Murray held that the motion must be made in New York. Mr. Ramsey's attorneys then gave notice of motion before Judge Barnard, in New York, to vacate Judge Balcom's order. This motion came on to be argued in August, and was denied; and Ramsey's attorneys thereupon appealed from this denial to the General Term, by which the denial was afterward affirmed.

After Mr. Ramsey's original suit had been transferred to the county of New York, his attorneys noticed the cross suit for trial at a Special Term to be held by Judge Barnard, in October. Field & Shearman then noticed the original suit for trial at the same term. Both cases were called in the order of the calendar on the fifth of October. Mr. Ramsey's counsel moved to postpone both for the term. The court refused this motion, and the cases were set down for trial on the twentieth of October. Mr. Ramsey's counsel again moved to postpone for the term, on his own affidavit. Mr. Field, appearing as counsel for the company and the first seven individual defendants, together with counsel appearing for the other defendants, opposed this motion. The principal grounds on which the motion to postpone was urged were, that Mr. Ramsey had made no preparation for trial, because he was under an injunction in the cross suit, and that his preparation required an extended examination of the books of the company, and conferences with numerous witnesses; also that in a proceeding against him for a contempt of the injunction he had appealed to the General Term, and that if their decision should be against him, he should appeal to the Court of Appeals, and that, with this matter pending, the trial of the cases should not go on. On the other hand, it was answered that the witnesses were in New York, which was now the place of trial, that both suits had been on the calendar from the beginning of the term, that no application had been made by Mr. Ramsey for a discovery or inspection of the books, that the nature of Mr. Ramsey's suit and the three orders which he had obtained, had placed the company in a position in which it was absolutely necessary to hold the plaintiff now to proof of his case, which could be proved, if true, as well now as at any future time. It was further answered, that he had not brought himself within the rule respecting motions for postponement, because his affidavit did not aver the existence of any facts or suggest the name of a witness not known to him when he made the allegations of his complaint; and that he had not shown by his affidavit that the books contained evidence in his favor. It was further answered that, as to the injunction in the cross suit, the judge who granted it had set the case down for trial on the twentieth, and that it was not to be supposed that Ramsey would be punished for a contempt in violating that injunction by making preparation in a case the trial for which had been so appointed; that he might have applied on the fifth of October for a preliminary examination of witnesses or of the books, and that he had made no such application. It was also answered, that he had already disobeyed the injunction on several occasions which were detailed and described by the counsel for the company and his associate.

As a matter of law and practice, I take it for granted that, by noticing the case for trial, the counsel for the company had waived the injunction to this extent that they could not proceed for a violation of it after that notice; that inasmuch as the court, on the fifth of October, had set the cause down for trial on the twentieth, it was not to be presumed that the court would entertain any application to punish Mr. Ramsey for a contempt in making preparation for a trial which the court had ordered, and that as Mr. Ramsey had shown that he could previously disregard the injunction, it ought not to have been considered now as an obstacle to a trial. But it appears, on the proceedings, that in order to obviate all objection on account of the injunction, Mr. Field offered in court a stipulation that the injunction in the cross suit should not be held to interfere with the trial or Mr. Ramsey's preparation for it. Thereupon the court refused the postponement, and the cause was set down for trial peremptorily on the twenty-fifth. Mr. Ramsey subpoenaed several of the directors and officers of the company for that day, and they were in attendance. When the case was called, his counsel again moved to postpone. After argument on both sides, embracing the entire history of both cases, the court denied the motion to postpone, and ordered the trial to proceed. Mr. Ramsey's counsel then asked leave to withdraw for consultation, which was granted. In about half an hour they returned into court, and objected to trying the case before the judge then holding the court, because he was prejudiced. Thereupon the court, on motion of the defendants' counsel, ordered the complaint to be dismissed with costs, with an extra allowance to be fixed by the court before the entry of judgment, the extra allowance to be fixed on the fourteenth of November and the judgment to be thereafter entered, but with leave to the plaintiff then to come in and try the cause. The order was, in fact, not entered, but was noted on the clerk's minutes. The defendants' attorneys were about to enter an order and to give notice that the extra allowance would be fixed on the fourteenth of November, but with leave to the plaintiff then to come in and try the cause; but the plaintiff anticipated this by a notice of motion, accompanied by an order staying all proceedings. On the twenty-third of November the plaintiff obtained an order at chambers, setting aside the incomplete proceeding of October twenty-fifth. From this order the defendants appealed to the General Term, which has the matter still under advisement.

The mere statement of these proceedings in the order in which they occurred seems to me sufficient to dispose of the charges that Mr. Field brought the cross suit against Mr. Ramsey for the purpose of oppressing him; and that he forced Mr. Ramsey to trial of his original suit with his hands tied. In regard to the cross suit, it certainly cannot be said to be settled law in this state, that an injunction may not, in any case, be granted in one judicial district of the Supreme Court, to restrain the proceedings in another suit instituted in another judicial district. And as to the general principles and practice which regulate the exercise of equitable jurisdiction by judges of coördinate authority, it is well settled that there are two classes of cases in regard to which a discrimination is to be made. In all ordinary cases where a Court of Equity is invoked to act upon proceedings in another court of coördinate jurisdiction, I understand it to be the practice of judges to give effect to the comity that is due to each other. But there may be cases in which mere comity would defeat the ends of justice. Where there is reason to believe that a suit is fraudulent, where great mischief would ensue from a forbearance to use the restraining powers of a Court of Equity, and where the wrong that is threatened would inevitably result from an abuse of the process of another court, I understand that an injunction may issue, not to act upon the other court, but to act upon the party who is misusing its process.

In regard to "forcing a party to trial with his hands tied," I confess that I do not appreciate the doctrine which would oblige counsel to refrain from using all available and legitimate weapons of the law to defeat a suit which he had reason to be-

lieve, and did believe, was of a character to which no indulgence
should be extended. But it is not necessary to enlarge upon this
topic, because I do not think that Mr. Ramsey had any just
reason to complain of Mr. Field, when the latter finally insisted
that the case should be either tried or dismissed. And as to the
charge that has been made against Mr. Field, of having for a
wrongful purpose procured a transfer of this case into this
county, in order to get it under the control of Judge Barnard,
it is like most of the other charges which I have had occasion to
examine. It begins by assuming the corruption of the judge, and
the willingness of the counsel to avail himself of that corruption,
and then proceeds to the conclusion that, although there existed
a statute provision authorizing the place of trial to be changed,
the counsel could not have made an honest use of that provision.
I do not think I ought to occupy more of the reader's time in discussing such a proposition.

In reviewing these proceedings and what has been said about
them, I have been much impressed by the fact that this community is now brought face to face with direct imputations of corruption made in the public prints against one of its judges, over
the signatures of known members of the bar. I have had to deal,
however, with the alleged existence and character of that corruption, only by reason of what is complained of in Mr. Field,
namely, that he ought to have refrained from applying to the
particular judge who has been named, to obtain orders and injunctions in the interest of persons with whom it is alleged that
this judge has relations that are tantamount to a corrupt connection, because, as is alleged, he knew of that connection. If the
judge in question is a man who is capable of using his office
contrary to law and to what is right, to promote the interests of
anybody, which I for one do not believe, it is wrong for the other
judges who sit with him on the bench to transact judicial business with him. It was wrong for the Governor to assign him as
one of the judges in General Term for five years—a most responsible and important position. Nay, it was doubly wrong for

the people to elect him to the bench, as they have done twice by majorities that have shown that he is not indebted for his position solely to a party. If he is a corrupt judge, the people, their Executive, and his associate judges, are all engaged in a general conspiracy against the public virtue and honor. In the name of all that is pure and sacred, let us have an end of these imputations, or else let them be proved to be true by some other form of proceeding than by attacking a leading member of the bar for appearing before the judge who is the subject of such suspicions. Instead of having gone out of his way to seek a judge said to be notoriously favorable to his clients, I should infer from the proceedings that I have had occasion to examine, that Mr. Field has paid no attention to the inquiry whether the judge in question was on the bench, that he has acted just as he must have acted if he had applied to any other judge, and that there is no ground whatever for charging him with a conscious purpose to avail himself of a supposed willingness of Judge Barnard to fulfil the function of "the favorite judge" of his clients. I think this was the proper course to pursue; for I cannot concur in the opinion that he should have avoided Judge Barnard, because of any prevalent scandal. I do not see how the judicial business of this community is to be transacted, if censure of Mr. Field on this ground is to prevail.

The following is a summary of the conclusions at which I have arrived:

1. That the contest to obtain a majority of the Board of Directors of the Albany & Susquehanna Railroad, in the summer of 1869, originated between two parties among its stockholders and directors, and not with any person connected with the Erie Railway Company; but that one of those parties, after the contest had commenced, sought the aid of Messrs. Fisk & Gould, officers of the Erie Railroad, in the purchase of stock preparatory to the election, which aid was afforded in a lawful and unobjectionable manner.

2. That the several orders granted by Judge Barnard, direct-

ing the transfer of certain stock to Wilber, directing the suspension of Ramsey from the offices of president and director, appointing Fisk & Courter receivers of the road and its property, and issuing writs of assistance to enforce their title, and also the several orders made by Judge Clerke, removing the inspectors of election chosen in 1868, and conditionally restraining votes on 9,500 shares of stock claimed to have been subscribed for on the fifth of August, were all duly and properly made and granted, and were made necessary by incidents successively arising in the progress of the contest.

3. That the appointment of Mr. Fuller as receiver of certain stock claimed by Groesbeck and others, was obtained by Field & Shearman, and was duly and properly made by Judge Barnard, for the protection of important interests of the company, and not for the purpose of putting the votes on that stock within the control of one of the parties to the contest, to be voted upon by them or in their interest at the election of directors.

4. That the act of Mr. Fuller in voting at the election on the stock held by him as receiver, was made necessary by an unexpected and unforeseen occurrence, and was under the circumstances correct.

5. That the suit instituted by Field & Shearman, for the purpose of compelling a restoration of the books and papers of the company to its office, from which they had been clandestinely removed, was instituted by the express and formal authority of the executive committee of the Board of Directors, and of the vice-president acting as president; that the order of arrest issued therein was duly and properly issued, in order to compel the production of the books and papers; that the arrest of Messrs. Ramsey, Phelps, and Smith, at the rooms where the election was to be held, and just as the first stockholders' meeting was about to be organized, was accidental and unpremeditated; that the sheriff alone was responsible for it, and that none of the counsel or attorneys of the Church party directed it or knew that it was likely to happen; that bail was procured and accepted on the

spot; that no material restraint was exercised beyond the sheriff's request to the parties arrested not to leave the building until bail bonds had been executed; and that the arrest prevented none of the parties from participating in the election.

6. That both parties were attended at the election by a considerable number of persons who were not stockholders; that those who so came in the interest of the Church party, not exceeding thirty in number, were not brought there for the purpose of overawing the meeting, and did not in fact by their presence exclude any stockholder in the Ramsey interest from the room; that each of them held a genuine proxy for some stockholder in voting at the preliminary organization; that their conduct was not disorderly; and that the evidence that has been taken on this subject does not warrant the belief that the room was preoccupied by a crowd of "roughs," in the interest of the Church party, for the purpose of carrying the election by violence or fraud.

7. That whatever may be the true legal conclusions respecting any question of law or practice involved in any of the acts done or advice given by Mr. D. D. Field, or any member of the firm of Field & Shearman, in any of these proceedings, no just imputation of professional impropriety rests upon them or either of them on account of any such act or advice, either in respect to the proceedings connected with the contest for the election of directors of the Albany and Susquehanna Railroad Company, or in respect to any act done or advice given by them or either of them, in defending the Erie Railway Company and certain of its directors against the suit brought by Joseph H. Ramsey, in 1869, or in the cross suit against him.

I cannot dismiss this subject—to which I do not mean hereafter to revert, unless some statement that I have made shall be called in question—without expressing my opinion that such discussions, charges, and imputations as those which I have been obliged to examine, have no tendency to promote professional integrity and honor. The surest way to do that, is to recognize and maintain the distinction between counsel and client, and not to identify them; for while, on the one hand, it is of the utmost importance to a sound administration of justice that a lawyer should be allowed to do everything for his client that he can honestly do, it is on the other hand perfectly clear that no lawyer can act freely and fearlessly within the limits of that principle, if he is to be subjected to a criticism which seeks for bad motives to the exclusion of the common presumption of good ones; which refuses to regard his conduct by the light of the law itself, and seeks to explain it by the suggestion that he acted for parties whose objects and methods are supposed to be subjects of general suspicion. There can be no safer rule for a lawyer to follow, than to assume it to be right to do for any man what the law allows to be done. In his efforts to reach what is lawful, and to apply it to the interests of his clients, he must undoubtedly not divest himself of a sound conscience; and he is in truth in the less danger of doing so, in proportion to the extent of his learning and his ability to discover and apply the law, for the law, it must not be forgotten, is the measure of the rights of all men in civil society. Nor is it just or rational to hold a lawyer to a moral responsibility for acting on what may afterward prove to be the wrong side of a legal question, or the failing side of a legal controversy. He is not responsible for the correctness of what he urges as law, because it is the function of a court to declare the law, and the function of the advocate to help the court to discover it, by presenting one side of the question, while precisely the same function is performed by another advocate on the opposite side. Neither is a lawyer morally responsible, in the use of legal process, for anything but a conscious, fraudulent abuse of such process, by employing it and perverting it to accomplish a purpose other than that for which the law has provided it. For this he certainly is responsible; just as one is, who uses a weapon maliciously to kill or wound another, which the law allowed to be created for the lawful purpose of self-defense. But in neither case is the unlawful and malicious abuse of a thing to be confounded with its lawful and proper use.

In submitting to the reader the results of my investigation into the complaints that have been made against Mr. Field, it is perhaps proper for me to say that, when I began them, I had know him for many years, as one lawyer knows another, but that we had never been intimate. Our relations were mutually respectful, and nothing more. In the prosecution of my inquiries into the numerous and involved controversies which I have had to examine, I have found him constantly ready to afford me any information that I required; and I hope it is scarcely necessary for me to say that, I have *endeavored* to make my inquiries as searching as the subject demanded that they should be. With regard to the three gentlemen who stand before the public as his prominent accusers, I can conscientiously say that I have sought to impugn the motives of none of them; and that I have therefore not sought to inquire for, or cared to know, whether there are or are not any relations which have caused them to view Mr. Field's conduct unfavorably, or to make the strictures which they have made. But as they are all by a good many years my juniors at the bar, I may perhaps suggest that, if their experience has not already taught them, further experience will teach them, that to the merits of most legal controversies there are two sides; and that, when a question is made concerning the professional conduct of those employed upon one of those two sides, there are important rules of judgment which in this instance they may have possibly failed to apply in making their strictures. And I may add, that those rules are to be derived not only from the law of the land, but also from a moral code that has a higher than any mere human sanction. For I do not understand the command, "Judge not that ye be not judged; for with what judgment ye judge, ye shall be judged, and with what measure ye mete it shall be measured to you again," to have been intended to prevent us from forming and expressing opinions on the conduct of our fellow men. He who gave that command, was well aware that judgment is at once a human function and a human duty, without which civil society cannot be carried on, whether that judgment is by a public official appointed to pass upon a charge of a formal nature, or whether it is by the private voice of individuals passing upon a less formal accusation. But I do understand that this great precept was intended to embody a rule which is alike to govern the judge on the bench, and the citizen who contributes in his degree to the formation of public opinion. I understand that this golden rule appeals not to charity, but to righteousness; not to mercy, but to a definite law and standard of determination. It is as if it had been said: Judge not unrighteously, lest ye be judged yourselves unfairly. Put away prejudice and sophistry and passion; form your conclusions by the proper laws of a rational belief; exclude no proper motives when they are consistent with the acts on which you are called to pronounce; believe in human integrity and virtue, until you are compelled by the immutable laws of right and wrong to believe that they have been overborne by temptation or swept away by the eagerness with which a rightful object may be pursued. Mete to others the same measure which ye demand for yourselves, for it is not lawful to judge of others as ye would not yourselves be judged.

Supplement

A SECOND edition of this opinion having been called for, the writer avails himself of it to add a letter which was printed in *The World* and the *New York Evening Express*, about ten days ago. The occasion for writing it appears in its context.

New York, June 15, 1871.

New York, June 4.

To the Editor of The World.

SIR: I have been asked by a layman of high intelligence whether the opinion lately given by me to a friend of Mr. D. D. Field, concerning the connection of the latter gentleman with the Albany & Susquehanna Railroad litigations, is to be regarded merely as an argument or as a paper expressing my personal convictions. The inquiry seemed to me, as I suppose it would seem to most lawyers, a singular one. In the course of a practice of five-and-thirty years I have never given a written opinion to a client on any subject that did not express my personal convictions, so far as it expressed any decided conclusions at all, and I suppose that this is the rule with most lawyers. In this respect the function of a counsel in giving an opinion to a client differs from the function of an advocate in arguing a cause in court. In the latter function the advocate usually argues from his convictions; but he is not bound to do so, and it is not material whether he does so or not. But in giving an opinion to a client, whether the matter is or is not likely to come before a court, or before a tribunal of any kind, a lawyer, as I think, is bound to say what he believes to be true, and to affirm nothing that he does not believe. If he entertains doubts, he should say so; if he has no doubt, he should say what he believes. I suppose this is the general rule; it is certainly my own. Having great respect, however, for the gentleman who asked me the question above stated, and who at the same time expressed a wish to read my opinion on the complaints that have been made against Mr. Field, I answered him frankly that the opinion was undoubtedly argumentative because it was necessary in it to *reason* on the subject, but that it contained throughout my sincere personal convictions, arrived at in the course of a month exclusively devoted to an examination of the subject.

In a prefatory note to the published copies of the opinion, I gave the reader to understand as explicitly as I could that I rendered this service to the friends of Mr. Field on the ordinary professional footing. I did so because I chose to have it known that I was not a volunteer in this controversy, and because I considered it proper that the reader should know my precise relation to it. In view of the attacks that have been made upon me since the publication of the opinion—made in the spirit and with the kind of weapons with which Mr. Field himself has been assailed—notwithstanding my avoidance of all discussion of the motives of those who had publicly charged him with professional improprieties—I shall now add a word in regard to my relation to this matter. It is a mistake to suppose that a lawyer who is applied to for an opinion is necessarily or usually biassed toward the side of those who apply to him by reason of the fact that he receives a compensation for his labor, any more than a judge is necessarily or usually biassed toward the government because it pays him a salary for his official services. We often say of judges that from habit of mind, from peculiar temperament, or from party feeling, they uphold and enforce the prerogatives and interests of government more than they should; but in all my experience I never heard this tendency imputed to a judge because the government pays him for trying the causes in which it is interested as well as those in which it is not. It is true that the judge takes an oath of office which binds him to administer justice impartially, and this is relied on as the safeguard against any supposed influence of his pecuniary compensation. It is also true that a counsellor-at-law takes an oath of office which is as binding upon the conscience as the oath of a judge is. A lawyer's oath of office binds him to serve his client with all *due fidelity;* and my interpretation of that obligation, in giving a client an opinion on any question, is that one is bound to use all the means within one's reach by which to form correct opinions, and when any opinions are expressed to take care that they are honestly entertained. So that those who differ from me on any of the questions concerning Mr. Field's professional conduct on which I have given an opinion, and those who assail me for having given that opinion, must understand once for all that my conclusions were formed upon a very full and careful investigation, under a sense of the obligation above stated, that they express my sincere convictions, and that I do not believe I was influenced at all by the compensation that was very properly paid to me for my labor by the gentleman who asked for the service. On this latter point, however, others can judge, and to enable them to do so my precise relation to the controversy was stated.

I claim for that opinion no other weight than would belong to the opinion of any lawyer of my age who had examined the subject with the same care and fidelity, with the same means of investigation, and under the same circumstances. If the opinion is incorrect in any of its statements of fact, or unsound in its reasoning, legally or morally, it can be shown to be so. It is proper for me to say, however, that in forming my conclusions I read the whole of General Barlow's letters, the articles in the *North American Review* and the Boston *Law Review,* with great attention; and I analyzed and digested the charges which these publications had made against Mr. Field, and examined the proofs which they adduced or referred to in support of those charges; that I read the opinion of Judge E. Darwin Smith, and went step by step through the evidence taken in the case in which his opinion was pronounced, examined every record used as an exhibit in that case, and when it became necessary to go out of these exhibits I called for and received original documents; that I took nothing for granted that was stated to me because it was so stated, but that in every instance in which I made a statement of a fact that appeared to me to be important, unless it was expressly put as information derived from Mr. Field or his partners, or from Judge Barnard, I inspected the proper record evidence, or derived my statement from some third person who knew personally what he affirmed. I also carefully investigated every question of law arising in the course of my inquiries. The result of all this patient labor has been that I have reached conclusions that are manifestly distasteful to those who have accused Mr. Field of wrong-doing. I shall quarrel with nobody who differs from me in courteous language, but I shall certainly stand by every word that I have said. I have lived through a good many clamors more or less noisy and violent, and have never yet found myself unable to withstand one when it came within the line of any duty to do so.

I remain, Mr. Editor, with much regard, yours,

GEO. TICKNOR CURTIS.

VI

A GREAT LAWSUIT AND A FIELD FIGHT*

BY

JEREMIAH S. BLACK

IN the years 1869 and 1870 there occurred a contest for the control of the Albany & Susquehanna Railroad which, in some of its features, is among the most remarkable that this generation has known. It concerned vast material interests, and, from peculiar circumstances, engaged an amount of public attention not often bestowed on such subjects. It produced a long series of litigations, angry, complicated, and multifarious. The judicial authorities were wholly unequal to the task of settling the dispute; for, instead of composing the strife, their intervention only intensified it, until at last the parties, mutually scared by the cross fire of conflicting injunctions which the courts were launching at all alike, sought relief in the more peaceful arbitration of pike and gun. When this was stopped by the Executive, the newspapers took up the war, and, going over the whole ground again, they not only canvassed the rights and wrongs of the parties, but assailed counsel and judges with most unlimited censure. The character of one gentleman in particular (Mr. David Dudley Field), noted hitherto and honored not less for high integrity than for profound learning, was traduced with a license which knew no bounds.

The two books whose titles stand at the head of this article† are chiefly interesting because they contain the opposing views of two very able men upon the whole of this controversy; and the

---

* *The Galaxy*, XIII (March, 1872), 376–392.

† The titles were *Chapters of Erie and Other Essays*, and *An Inquiry into the Albany and Susquehanna Railroad Litigations of 1869.*

recent republication of both, with notes and other addenda, is a new appeal to the great tribunal of public opinion. Before final judgment we propose to say a few words more, but, being nobody's attorney, and representing no personal interest, we must be considered as speaking in the character of *amicus curiae*.

Mr. Curtis' great advantage over Mr. Adams, and indeed over everyone else who has discussed this subject, consists in the high tone of his essay and the spirit of perfect fairness which pervades it from beginning to end. Though a great master of rhetoric (as the biographer of Webster ought to be), no provocation tempts him to any display of it here; his style is eminently judicial; his statements are severely accurate, and for all his averments he quotes chapter and verse in a way which makes contradiction hopeless. His only apparent ambition is to build up a solid wall of argument; he constantly tests its perpendicular with the plummet, and strikes every stone with the edge of his trowel to make sure that it lies firm in its place.

Mr. Adams is a hereditary bondsman to the truth; by his blood and birth he owes service to the right, and if he flies from it we have a warrant to reclaim him as a fugitive. We do not believe that he would lend the authority of his great historical name to a wilful misstatement, or that he would even take up an evil report against his neighbor and help to propagate it for the mere purpose of gratifying anybody's malevolence. But his intense dislike of James Fisk, Jr., seems to have unbalanced his judgment upon every subject with which Fisk has the remotest connection. This is the one masterless passion which sways him in all the moods and tenses of his thought. Fisk is his *bête noire*. His enmity to Fisk is extended not merely to Jay Gould, Fisk's partner in business, but it embraces all Fisk's associates in the management of the Erie Railroad, and takes in every lawyer who has ever defended his rights and every judge who has ever allowed him to use the legal process of his court. The moral sense of Mr. Adams has been offended, perhaps very justly, by something he has seen in Fisk's conduct or character; and his indig-

DAVID DUDLEY FIELD

nation has become so preternaturally excited that he likes or loathes all other men as they happen to be for Fisk or against him in any of his contests, whether right or wrong. Inasmuch as Mr. Adams must necessarily be, and is without doubt, a man of sound moral principles, we give this as the only rational explanation we can furnish of his attack upon Mr. Field, and of what needs explanation quite as much, his idolatrous veneration of Ramsey and his pronounced admiration of Judge Darwin Smith's decision at Rochester.

It was not necessary for Mr. Curtis to tell us that he had no personal knowledge of or association with Mr. James Fisk, Jr., or his partner Jay Gould. Nobody would have suspected that grave and learned gentleman of any close companionship with a man so *outré*, irregular, and eccentric in his tastes and habits as Mr. Fisk. If ignorance of Fisk and all that Fisk inherits be a virtue, then we can claim to be as virtuous as anybody. But we make no pretensions whatever to that outrageous and extravagant righteousness which prompts Mr. Adams not only to denounce Fisk himself, but to assail every man that does him justice and heap laudations without measure on all who try to swindle him or his associates.

Most of our readers will altogether fail to understand the merits of the controversy or the incidents which attended it unless they make themselves acquainted, at least to some little extent, with the singularities of New York jurisprudence, produced partly by what is called a reform in the Code of Procedure, and partly by a most anomalous and extraordinary organization of the judicial system. A moment's attention to this will explain our meaning, and show that the confusion, misapprehension, and total failure of justice which took place in these cases, while they could not possibly have happened in any other country, could scarcely have been avoided in New York.

It was in 1830 that Lord Brougham—that many-sided man, who spoke and wrote continually on every conceivable subject in literature, science, and art, but who knew less and cared less

about the science of his own profession than about anything else
—of whom Sugden said that it was "a pity the honorable gentleman did not know a little law, for he would then know a little of
everything"—extended his notoriety by an elaborate and plausible speech on law reform. It was easy to point out defects in any
system, and that of England, though expansive in its nature, had
not grown with the growth of the nation. Some of its excres-
cences needed to be rubbed off; some of its forms were effete; a
part of its process was costly and useless; its machinery was
clogged with the quantity of business which the increased commerce of the country had thrown upon it. Brougham's eloquence
had the effect to stir up the leading minds of Parliament and call
their attention to the necessity of some changes. But they went
about it cautiously. They cheapened the law to the suitor by
establishing new tribunals, they swept away impediments that
stood in the path of justice, and they abolished many offices
which merely encumbered the courts. But with reverend care
they preserved the exquisite logic which for ages has been crys-
tallizing into the forms of pleading. Instead of throwing it loose
and lawless to the mercy of ignorant pretenders, it was made
more exacting and precise than before; the declaration must give
perfectly accurate notice of the demand; a plea must disclose the
very defense to be proved; the general issue in most cases was
abolished, and special pleading was made more special than ever.
Nor did they for a moment think of dispensing with those rules
of evidence which the experience of mankind had shown to be
necessary to the successful investigation of truth.

But Brougham's speeches, together with the maledictions of
Bentham, created a far profounder sensation in America than in
England. Here they produced among many influential men a
passionate appetite for radical revolution. Everything that was
old or English began to be looked on with contempt; whatever
had been held in reverence by our fathers, on this or on the other
side of the water, was set down as worthless; even the writ of
habeas corpus and trial by jury were strongly suspected of

being obsolete humbugs, and the public mind was preparing itself to see them trampled under foot without an effort to save them. Good and great men, as well as the weak and the wicked, were subjected (of course for opposite reasons) to these malign influences, and both classes were in equal haste to bury the old system out of sight.

In New York, where this feeling was strongest, the revolutionary party did itself honor by accepting the leadership of the ablest and most distinguished jurists of the state. A full Code, as comprehensive as that of Napoleon and as minute in its details as that of Livingston, was the work of their hands. They laid it at the feet of the Legislature, and that body adopted the Code of Procedure, but rejected all else that was proposed. They put into operation just enough of it to abolish the distinction between law and equity, without preventing the possible abuses of either; to confound all remedies by mixing them together and making one form of action serve against every species of wrong; and to banish every trace of science from pleading. What might have been the success of this empirical raid on the Common Law if the whole Code had been adopted, it is impossible to say; but the experiment as actually made is not merely a failure—it is a disastrous visitation upon the people of the state. Instead of the cheapness, certainty, and promptness which the reformers no doubt intended to promote, the unlucky suitor is vexed with endless delay, impoverished by enormous costs, and at every turn is liable to be tricked and deluded to his ruin. The new Code encourages ignorance, rapacity, and fraud, by inviting everybody to practice it who cannot live at any other trade, and gives a large share in the administration of justice to a class of men for whom the English language had no name until a new epithet of contempt was added to the vocabulary.

The separate administration of law and equity used to be a standing subject of invective with the reformers. A court of law could not refuse judgment in favor of a plaintiff who claimed a legal right; but if the defendant had an answer founded on a paramount equity, a chancellor might enjoin his adversary not to take advantage of his mere legal superiority. It was thought extremely absurd that the authority of two tribunals should be invoked to do justice in the same case between the same parties, and that what was called right in one court should be pronounced wrong in another. We do not stop now to defend, as we might, the wisdom of circumscribing the power of judges and assigning different functions to different classes of them. But under the Code, the wall of partition between law and equity is completely broken down; the law judges are all chancellors, and, *vice versa*, all chancellors are law judges, and they administer both equity and law in forms so exactly alike that the judges themselves do not know, and are not bound to know, which is which. There is, therefore, no possible excuse for employing more than one tribunal in the same cause. Nevertheless, the frequent and allowed practice is for the defendant, instead of answering a complaint, to file a counter complaint against his adversary. An injunction is the favorite weapon in all contests. Its simplicity commends it to the professional mind, as the simplicity of the knout and the bastinado makes them dear to the heart of the Muscovite and the Turk. It can always be got for the asking, if the request be accompanied with an affidavit that somebody wants it "to the best of his information and belief." It is granted of course, *ex debito justitiae*, without examination and without notice to the opposite party; it is granted privately; it is not put on record; it is not placed in the hands of a public officer to be served or executed, but the judge gives it to the complainant himself or his attorney, who keeps it a secret if he pleases until he catches his victim at a disadvantage, and then springs it upon him from his pocket. Unfortunately, however, this is a game that two or a dozen can play at as well as one. The party enjoined by one judge can go to another judge equally facile, and get an injunction against his adversary, commanding that the order of the first shall be disobeyed. Or a third person may seek a third judge, who will readily throw his force against either or both. There are thirty-three judges in the state, of equal grade and coördinate power, elected in eight districts, and residing in different regions, to whose jurisdiction there are no territorial limits except the lines of the state. Each one of these claims the right, and exercises it, of enjoining whom he pleases, without regard to the cognizance which may have been previously taken of the subject or the parties by one or more of his brethren; and his process, orders, or decrees are equally potential in every part of the state. A man enjoined by a judge in New York City to do a thing may be ordered by a Buffalo judge *not to do it;* and a Brooklyn judge who has commanded one of his constituents to refrain from a particular act may be met the next day by a counter order from Rochester in which the same party is solemnly directed to *refrain from refraining.* These injunctions are not mere *brutum fulmen;* the judicial guns on either side are loaded to the muzzle with the heaviest metal they can ram down. Each judge demands implicit obedience to his own order, and the penalty of disobedience cannot be escaped by showing that the parties are under conflicting orders from another quarter; for the learned magistrates who administer the Code act on the principle of that ultra-democracy which insists that one man is not only as good as another, but a great deal better. It happens thus that, in a case involving numerous and complicated interests of great value, all persons concerned get hemmed in with injunctions from various parts of the state, commanding them by authority which they dare not question to do everything, and at the same time to do nothing. They can neither move nor stand still without incurring a penalty somewhat like that of outlawry in feudal times. Their cause may be pending in a score of courts at once; a party who prosecutes or defends in any one of them is guilty of contempt, and if he fails, a decree is pronounced against him by default. His condition is like that ascribed by Lorenzo Dow to a predestined reprobate under the creed of Calvin:

> You shall and you shan't—you will and you won't;
> You're condemned if you do, and you're curs'd if you don't.

When all the parties are bound hand and foot so that justice or even an investigation in the courts has become a thing of impossible attainment, the case is considered about ready for trial in the newspapers, where the suitors, the counsel, and the judges are plastered with praise or covered with odious imputations, according to the various interests and tastes of those who engage in the discussion. We venture, though with some diffidence, to pronounce this rather a poor substitute for the trial by battle which would have been accorded in the Middle Ages. So thought the parties in the Albany & Susquehanna suits; for they actually loosened the deadlock of the courts by physical force. It is true that the champions did not go out on the open plain, and, after taking an oath against witchcraft, beat each other with sandbags to show whose cause was holiest in the sight of God; but they did try whose judges had made the most righteous injunctions by rushing against one another with colliding locomotives.

It is due to the framers and original supporters of the Code to say that they never contemplated the frightful perversions which it has been made to undergo, nor are they at all responsible for the absurd arrangement of the judicial department which causes these scandalous conflicts of jurisdiction.

We devoutly believe that a fair consideration of the Albany & Susquehanna litigations will throw the blame of them on shoulders which have heretofore not borne their proper share. We will briefly present the most important of the facts pertaining to this *cause célèbre,* and leave the public to judge whether the attacks on the long-established fame of Mr. Field and his partners have any foundation in truth. The same public may determine, if it can, "by what conjuration and most mighty magic" the Ramsey party have managed to invest their leader with the reputation of a persecuted saint. If we happen to have any readers who feel an interest in the most important of all worldly concerns—the distribution of justice among the people of a great state—some of them may be led to inquire if the system of judicial procedure which produces such intolerable evils cannot be

amended, or if change be impossible, what amount of passive
fortitude is required to bear it as it is;

> How end this dire calamity;
> What reinforcement may be gained from hope;
> If not, what resolution from despair.

The Albany & Susquehanna Railway Company was incorporated in 1852, and began work in 1853, but the line was not
opened for traffic until January, 1869. It stretches a distance of
140 miles from Binghamton, where it connects with the Erie, to
Albany, whence its freights may be carried by direct routes to
divers parts of New England. The Erie had previously sent
its branches into the anthracite deposits of Pennsylvania, and
needed the use of the Albany & Susquehanna as a means of
getting the coal it brought to Binghamton as far as Albany on its
way to the New England market; and it was of course the interest of the new road to take all the business it could get in that
way. Its track had been laid on the exceptional broad gauge of
the Erie, which shows that its projectors had from the beginning
contemplated that it would support and be supported by that
line. It would undoubtedly have been improper for the great
company to take control of the smaller one, or to appropriate
its earnings; but their geographical relations, the similarity of
their structure, their duty to the public, and the mutual interests
of their proprietors, all required a cordial coöperation in business. Nevertheless, there was no special arrangement to that end,
and no proposition to make one, until the stockholders of the
Albany & Susquehanna solicited the aid of the Erie to rid them
of the dangerous dishonesty which had crept into the management of their own internal affairs.

It was the great misfortune of the Albany & Susquehanna corporation to have trusted one Joseph H. Ramsey as its president
and financial manager. He did not prove himself faithful. The
bargains by which he raised money at usurious rates were not
only disapproved by his constituents, they were indefensible on
the score of common prudence. When his own interests were in

conflict with the duties of his trust, he showed a lack of qualities even more important than sound judgment. He paid himself on one occasion $16,000 for services which he alleged he had rendered the company as its attorney. He made the bill and settled it, absolutely refusing to let the Finance Committee pass upon it. He made a contract on behalf of his corporation with an express company, in which he ruinously sacrificed the interests of the party he professed to represent; it turned out afterward that he was a partner in the express company. Mr. Adams has proudly claimed for him, as a great merit, that he went to the Legislature "in behalf of the enterprise." Of such are the Albany rings. He ran for Congress once, and while he was a candidate he issued three thousand free passes over the road to as many electors, whose favor he sought to win at the expense of the company. At the time of his suspension from office he owed the company $20,000, which he had taken from its funds for his own purposes, on his own terms, and by his own leave. Whether he subsequently disgorged this money does not appear.

It was manifest to the stockholders that these practices could not be continued without ruin to their prosperity and infamy to the character of their corporation; and they determined to stop them. But, like many other reformers, they committed the fatal mistake of adopting half-way measures. Instead of turning Ramsey out neck and heels, they reëlected him, but by a very decided vote chose a majority of directors strong enough, as they thought, and true enough, to control his action and compel him to be honest. Seeing their forbearance, and probably mistaking it for timidity, he was hardy enough to tell them to their faces that he would permit no such oversight of his conduct as they proposed; that he would not belong to a divided direction; that at the next election either he or his opponents must go out. The stockholders accepted the issue thus tendered to them, and to maintain that issue was the object of all their subsequent struggles. Thus the corporators were hopelessly divided into two hostile factions. One of them, known through the legal proceedings as the Church party, and holding a large majority of the stock, was bent on having officers whose fidelity they could trust; and the other, led by Ramsey, wished to subordinate all the interests of the company severely and constantly to his own.

The next election was to take place in September, 1869, and the parties began without delay to look around them for the material of the contest. The authorized capital of the company was $4,000,000, divided into 40,000 shares of $100 each. Of these 40,000 shares 17,238 were outstanding in the hands of *bona fide* holders, who had paid full price for them, and whose right to vote them could not be disputed. The Church party were thoroughly satisfied that they and others opposed to the existing management held a clear majority of the legal and honest shares. On the other hand, Ramsey was not without expedients by which he hoped to win. About 2,400 shares had been forfeited by the failure of the original subscribers to pay for them. These were reissued by Ramsey to one David Groesbeck for twenty-five cents on the dollar, in direct violation of a general law which forbade any railroad company to sell its stock for less than par. Groesbeck was not only unscrupulous enough to become a party to this fraudulent overissue, by which the honest stock would be watered, but he was entirely willing to vote it as Ramsey, his partner in the fraud, might desire. When the latter gentleman discovered that he could not balance the real stockholders in that way, he resorted to another trick, which was, if possible, baser as well as bolder. He got together certain of his confederates secretly at his own house, and distributed among them certificates for 9,500 shares of stock, for which they had not paid, and did not mean to pay, a single cent. It was necessary that something should appear to have been paid, but the recipients of the shares could not or would not furnish any money for that purpose. Ramsey himself had no cash of his own to advance, but he went to the company's safe, of which he had the key, took out bonds, the property of the company, amounting to $150,000, pawned them to the same Groesbeck who had taken his former overissue, and thus raised enough to pay 10 per cent on the 9,500 shares. It is not easy to conceive a transaction more thoroughly iniquitous than this. It was a double fraud; it was intended to stuff the ballot box with bogus votes, and make the stockholders pay the expenses of the cheat upon themselves out of their own funds. That it might want no aggravating circumstance, it was planned and executed by a trustee whose solemn duty it was in law and conscience to protect and defend the rights of the injured parties against the knavery of others—not make them the victims of his own.

In the meantime the Church party, not knowing of these things, and unable to foresee what Ramsey might do, thought it prudent to reinforce themselves by getting as many of the *bona fide* shares into their hands as possible, and thus make their majority large enough to balance any fraud which he could carry out. A considerable amount of the stock was held by towns along the line of the road, and it could not be got for less than par. In these circumstances they applied to the Erie managers for assistance in money to buy the shares which might be needed. The request was acceded to. There was no lawless intrusion of Erie, or of Fisk and Gould, into the affairs of the Albany & Susquehanna; no volunteering in the dispute between Ramsey and his constituents; no compact for any undue share in the control of the road. The men of the Church party desired to save their corporation alive out of the hands of Ramsey, and the Erie managers knew that by assisting them they would promote the true interests of every honest stockholder in both companies. Where motives so fair and wise and obvious exist for one party to make, and the other to accept, a business proposition, it is not necessary, but it is shameful, to allege corruptions which there is nothing to prove or even to suggest.

When the assistance of the Erie men was assured to them, David Wilber and others of the Church party proceeded by the authority of Mr. Gould, and with money furnished by him, to buy Albany & Susquehanna stock wherever they could get it;

and they secured a considerable number of shares, mainly from the towns, paying full price for them. By the third of August the Church party, and the friends of the company who acted with them, had 11,400 shares of the undisputed stock, leaving only 6,139 in other hands. Assuming that Ramsey might get all these he must be beaten nearly two to one. Even if his friend and fellow sinner Groesbeck should vote the 2,400 fraudulent shares held by him, the Church men would still have a majority of 2,864. Judge Barnard, at the instance of Mr. Bush, a member of the Church party, put Groesbeck *hors de combat* by an injunction which commanded him to deliver up his stock into the hands of Mr. W. J. A. Fuller, who was appointed to hold it as receiver, so that Groesbeck could not vote it unless he would come forward and show that he had a title, which of course he did not attempt to do, knowing very well that he could not. The 9,500 false shares mentioned above had not yet been fabricated, nor had the corporation safe been robbed to pay for them at the time we now speak of.

Ramsey did not confine his operations to mere aggressive frauds upon his constituents; he was a master of defense as well as offense. "Fitz James's blade was sword and shield." When he saw the heavy purchases his opponents were making, he instantly directed the treasurer to make no more transfers upon the books of the company to the Church party. Accordingly Phelps, the treasurer, refused to make official note of the transfer from the town of Oneonta, although there was no appearance of illegality about the sale, and the commissioners were personally present to affirm its perfect regularity.

To strengthen himself in his false position, he got an Albany judge to make an injunction forbidding the transfer. This was and could be nothing but a mere sham. It was in effect, though not in form, a suit by himself against himself, to restrain himself from performing a duty which he had predetermined not to do anyhow. The Church party not only got his Albany injunction dissolved, but fulminated another upon him from New York, which commanded him to refrain from his refusal to make the transfer.

But Ramsey defeated the object of this last injunction by an outrage which has no parallel even in the history of his own iniquities. He furtively took the books of the company, carried them away, and hid them part of the time in a tomb in the Albany graveyard, and part of the time in other lonely places where they were beyond the reach of judicial process, out of the stockholders' sight or knowledge, and accessible only to himself and a few of his trusted accomplices. By this *conveyance,* as Pistol would call it, of the record, he not only prevented all transfers to *bona fide* purchasers, but put it into his power to fabricate without detection as much bogus stock as he might need for his own purposes. In point of fact, it was on the same night signalized by the disappearance of the books that he manufactured the 9,500 shares which he pretended to pay for with the proceeds of the company's bonds.

It was very plain by this time that the stockholders needed the help of judicial authority to save their rights from the most atrocious violation; and it will be seen hereafter that judicial authority, as administered in New York, was very far from being effective to that end. However, the war of injunctions had already commenced. The next gun was a heavy one. It was an order obtained *ex parte* from Judge Barnard in New York City, suspending Ramsey from office, and restraining the issue of any more stock unless under a resolution of the directors, after public notice, and upon payment of its par value. This order was made at the instance of David Wilber, a stockholder, a director, and an active supporter of the Church party. The complaint charged Ramsey (and no doubt charged him truly) with divers misdemeanors, which showed that he was wholly unfit for his trust, or indeed for any other. The proceeding was justifiable in this particular case, not only because the law allowed it and the court awarded it, but because the special end it aimed at was right and proper.

But it is not easy to defend on general principles the wisdom of the law which permits even a guilty man to be scourged before he is condemned. It is true that Ramsey was offered a chance of being heard in his own defense *after* he was deposed; but this reverses the inflexible rule of the Common Law, which in all cases and under all circumstances requires the hearing to *precede* the punishment. Indeed, the New York Code has in this respect but one example to keep it in countenance, and that is found in the hard ruling (according to Virgil's report) of the judge who presided in what may literally be called "the court below":

> Gnosius hic Rhadamanthus habet durissima regna,
> Castigatque, auditque dolos, subigitque fateri.

Sir Edward Coke, quoting these lines, says: "The philosophic poet doth notably describe the damnable and damned proceedings of the Judge of Hell. First he punisheth, and then he heareth, and lastly he compelleth to confess. But good judges and justices abhor these courses."

Ramsey and his advisers not only learned the lesson their opponents taught them, but they bettered the instructions. They were quick enough to see that, under a law which struck without hearing, a false accusation was just as good as a true one. Ramsey, therefore, did not close his eyes to sleep before he trumped up a series of charges against Mr. Herrick, the vice-president, and four of the directors, that they were in a conspiracy with the managers of Erie for a surrender of their line to that corporation, which was corruptly managed by Gould, Fisk, and others, for their private ends. On this complaint a judge of the Supreme Court at Albany promptly, and without the least hesitation or demur, granted an injunction to restrain the vice-president and directors from exercising their functions. This swept the board clean, and left the Albany & Susquehanna Railway Company with millions of dollars' worth of property in a most critical situation, and without a soul who could legally take charge of it.

The judges of New York were as rapid in their movements as the old courts of Pie Poudre. Ramsey got his injunction to stop transfers on the second of August. On the third he was enjoined to make the transfers. On the fourth Wilber's injunction deposed him; he was notified of it on the morning of the fifth, and on that same day he made his counter complaint; in the course of the night he carried off the books and fabricated the false stock; on the next morning he served his order upon the vice-president, and the corporation was broken to fragments.

Thus far Ramsey was the winner. With the records of the corporation in his exclusive possession, a treasurer at his elbow to whom his word was law, and numerous active confederates to do his bidding, he was master of the situation. To be sure, his enemies had deposed him, but he had also deposed *them*, and put their property in peril of extreme and ruinous loss; "which, if not victory, was at least revenge."

Things had come to a crisis in the affairs of the company where the stockholders could do but one thing, and that was to have receivers appointed who would keep the road running until its regular management could somehow be restored. The Church party, who owned by far the larger part of the stock, and who had paid not only fair but high prices for it, could not look upon their condition with calm indifference. They were constrained to act promptly. Accordingly, on the evening of the sixth of August, they applied to Judge Barnard, and got him to appoint two receivers, Charles Courter and James Fisk, Jr. The appointment of Mr. Fisk provoked a torrent of vituperation. It has been considered a sufficient reason for charging the judge, the counsel, and all others concerned in it, with gross corruption. Without stopping to inquire whether Mr. Fisk was or was not as proper a person as any other for such a trust, we note two facts which should stop this outburst of calumnious accusation. In the first place, the authority given the receivers was joint, and Fisk could do no act, good, bad, or indifferent, without the approbation of his colleague, who was and is a gentleman not only of a very large estate, but of most unblemished character; and secondly, the appointment was made with the consent, expressed in writing, of seven directors representing an undoubted majority of the stockholders. The order was privately signed by the judge, after the manner of New York judges; but if this was law and custom in all cases, as it undoubtedly was, why should there be an outcry about the observance of it on this occasion? It becomes especially absurd when we find that another judge, acting in Ramsey's interest and at his request, was doing the very same thing at Albany on the same night and at about the same hour.

Yes, Ramsey had countermined the Church party again. Before Messrs. Courter and Fisk could reach Albany with Judge Barnard's warrant to take possession of the trust, Judge Peckham had privately, in the office of his son, invested a Mr. Pruyn with the same powers, and Mr. Pruyn had possession of the company's office and the road at that end of it. Messrs. Courter and Fisk, by their agents, got hold of the Binghamton end, and that was all they could do. This brought the parties to close quarters. The conflict between opposing receivers, holding their authority from courts of equal jurisdiction, and acting under irreconcilable orders which each party claimed to be of superior obligation, presented in a practical shape the ancient problem of an immovable body encountered by an irresistible force. Judge Peckham's receiver determined to hold fast, and the magistrate who made him did not suffer him to languish for lack of helpful process and reinforcing decrees. Judge Barnard, not to be behind his brother Peckham in pluck and energy, provided *his* receivers with writs of assistance and all the other weapons they asked for out of his judicial arsenal. Everybody was in contempt, and everybody was in default. The sheriff, whose duty it was to execute the conflicting orders, was utterly bewildered. He was required to call out the *posse comitatus* to support each party against the other. He could not perform the functions of his office unless he would "divide himself and go to buffets with the pieces." A great battle was impending, and as the sheriff with his *power of the county* was to be on both sides, the result could not possibly be foretold. Hostile bodies of workmen were drawn out, armed with pistols and bludgeons, and locomotives got up steam and ran into one another. The scene would be an odd one in any civilized country outside of the state where it occurred; for all parties were fighting under the ensign of public authority. It was judicial power subverting order and breaking the peace; it was law on a rampage; it was justice bedeviled; in one word, it was the New York Code in full operation.

The Governor, it seems, had been watching the current of this heady fight; he thought it might be his duty to interpose the militia between the combatants, and conquer a peace by making a war upon both of them. The opposing receivers, to "stop the effusion of blood," were persuaded to unite in a petition to the Governor to take possession of the road and operate it by a superintendent of his own choosing. The Governor thereupon appointed Colonel Banks, stipulating that his custody should end as soon as the rights of the contesting parties could be ascertained and settled. This peaceable adjustment was effected by the exertions of Mr. D. Dudley Field, who, though his partners had previously been concerned for the Church party, now first appeared as an active participant in the controversy. His wisdom, good temper, and sound sense discerned what was not seen by others—the incapacity of the judicial department to manage such a business, and the necessity of putting it under executive arbitration.

The property of the company being now safe from destruction, the stockholders had nothing to do but watch and pray that Ramsey might not by any stratagem defeat their right to choose an honest Board of Directors. The election day came round in the fulness of time; the majority proceeded to business and cast their votes; but Ramsey pronounced their organization illegal, retired with his confederates to an adjoining room, opened a poll, and declared himself and others in his interest duly elected. He did not vote the 3,000 shares sold to Groesbeck, nor the 9,500 fabricated on the night of the fifth of August; but he and his friends held some undisputed shares which they did vote at their own poll, and by ignoring the majority he was able to count himself in without difficulty. Both boards claimed to be duly elected, and they organized by choosing Messrs. Church and Ramsey their respective presidents. Both demanded the surrender of the corporate franchises into their hands, but the Governor did not think himself authorized to decide between them.

Two or three circumstances connected with the election, though unimportant in themselves, require to be noticed here, because they have been much commented on elsewhere.

The fraudulent asportation of the records was accomplished on the fifth of August. The election was on the seventh of September. On the night of the sixth, Phelps and a son of Ramsey secretly carried the books to the rear of the building and hoisted them up to the window of the treasurer's room in a basket, with a rope tied to its handle. Nobody but Ramsey and his little band of confederates knew of this midnight restitution of the books until they were produced at the stockholders' meeting next day. In the meantime the Church party, seeing the election approach and feeling the necessity of having the ledgers and stock lists for inspection, and having failed in various efforts to get even a sight of them, resolved upon taking a legal remedy. They brought suit in the Supreme Court for the city of New York against Ramsey, Phelps, Pruyn, and Smith, charging them with carrying away the books and concealing them from the stockholders. By the Code the defendants in such a case are liable to personal arrest, and bail was accordingly demanded in $25,000. The process was issued on the sixth of September, and the parties were arrested (and bail taken immediately) on the morning of the seventh (the election day), the sheriff having chosen his own time to execute the process. We have entirely failed to comprehend what the meaning of the men can be who vilify Messrs. Field and Shearman and their clients for bringing this suit. Of all the measures taken by either of the parties against the other, throughout the contest, this seems to us the most unquestionably just and popular. It is mere nonsense to call it harsh or oppressive. It was meant to redress a most atrocious wrong, for which the perpetrators, by the law of any other Christian country, would have been condemned as criminals to heavy fines and long imprisonment, without bail or mainprise. Even the legislation of New York does not overlook the necessity of punishing an outrage like this, just as it might have been punished in a civil action before reform was thought of. It is some honor to the Code that, for once, it spoke out in the well-measured and majestic tones of the Common Law.

The presence of what has been called "a congregation of roughs" in the room was subsequently talked of very freely. It is doubtless true that on both sides of the apartment there crowded a considerable number of men not clothed in purple and fine linen, nor having much the appearance of heavy capitalists. It happened thus: The inspectors under whose auspices Ramsey designed to hold the election were disqualified for their office by reason of not being stockholders. To restrain them from acting, the Church party of course betook themselves to the everlasting injunction, and on the morning of the election got out one of those convenient engines to neutralize the illegal authority which Ramsey wished to bestow and probably to abuse. This would leave the inspectors to be chosen *viva voce*, and the impressiveness of assent or dissent might depend on the number of throats and strength of lungs employed in expressing it. Probably both parties anticipated this or something like it. It is certain that both improvised a force of courageous and muscular gentlemen, and, by putting a proxy in the hands of each one, they gave them all a technical right to be present and to swell the volume of the *ayes* and *noes* with their "most sweet voices." But there was no actual disorder, no intimidation, no violence or threat of violence.

Another thing: Groesbeck had been enjoined, and his 2,400

fraudulent shares had been put into the hands of a receiver to be held so that Groesbeck could not vote them. The Ramsey men, on the morning of the election, undertook to trump this injunction by getting from Judge Clute, of the Albany County court another injunction which forbade the inspectors to receive *any votes of the Church party* unless the *holders* of the fraudulent stock should first vote on that. Fuller, the receiver, happened to be present. No doubt he was puzzled. He *held* the stock, and, by legal intendment, Judge Clute's order applied to him if it applied to anybody. He could not give it back to Groesbeck without defeating the purpose for which he held it and exposing himself to the danger of being laid by the heels. If he refused to vote it or let it be voted, a large majority of *bona fide* stockholders, with rights to vote otherwise undisputed, would be totally disfranchised. He took the advice of counsel and untied the knot by literally obeying the Clute injunction and voting himself. Ramsey and his men were fairly infuriated by the failure of their shallow and impudent trick. He and his counsel and his judge had made the blunder of supposing that Groesbeck was in law the holder, and they got an injunction which they fancied would reinstate his fraudulent possession or else defeat the clear right of all their opponents. But they got one which in fact and in law defeated themselves. Mr. Ramsey is not the first engineer that was hoist by his own petard.

The Governor naturally desired to get rid of the perplexing and anomalous trust imposed upon him by the agreement of the parties. Perceiving that the election was an abortion, and seeing that the judiciary had completely failed to settle anything in any of the numerous suits pending between the parties, he directed the attorney-general to commence another in the name of the people *against both parties together*. This was not a *quo warranto*, nor a *mandamus*, nor a *bill in equity*, nor an action in *case* or *trespass;* these terms belong to "the jargon of the Common Law," and the Code does not condescend even to pronounce them. It was a proceeding against the corporation itself which the Governor had under his care, and against forty-nine individuals, of two fierce parties, contending against one another for its management. The complaint does not charge them with any offense against the plaintiff, but with mutual injuries committed by one set of the defendants against the others; and these wrongs consisted mainly in bringing suits for what they respectively averred to be their rights, a course of conduct which the Governor (truly enough, perhaps) thought would result in no good to anybody.

Of course the defendants could not make up an issue either of law or fact between themselves, no matter how they might sever in their answers to the plaintiff. In the dark days of Kent and Livingston and Spencer it was thought morally impossible to introduce evidence until there was an issue to which it might have some kind of application. But here the defendants were called in and permitted to fight one another to their hearts' content without pleadings or proofs, and the judge was wholly emancipated from that barbarous bondage which in past times would have compelled him to pronounce his decree *secundum allegata et probata*. The proceeding seemed sufficiently free from "technicalities." It was apparently not fashioned, like the injunction, on the principle of the bastinado, but rather modeled after that other form of Turkish justice in which the Sultan, when he finds a cause too difficult to be otherwise dealt with, sews up the stubborn disputants in the same sack and casts them into the Bosphorus to go down the tide together—which they generally do with a most edifying disregard for the rules of navigation.

This curious cause came on for hearing (which, in the nomenclature of the Code, is called a *trial*) at Rochester before Judge E. Darwin Smith, without a jury. It was argued by Mr. D. Dudley Field for one portion of the defendants and by Mr. Henry Smith for the other, the plaintiff apparently taking no part whatever; and it was decided in December, 1869. Probably nothing more severe has been said, or could be conceived, of Mr.

Justice Smith's judgment than the laudatory words bestowed upon it by Mr. Adams. We quote them:

There are cases where a judge upon the bench is called upon to vindicate in no doubtful way the purity as well as the majesty of the law; cases in which the parties before the court should be made to feel that they are not equal, that fraud is fraud even in a court of law—that cavilling and technicalities and special pleading cannot blind the clear eye of equity. It is possible that even a judical tone may be overdone or be out of place. There are occasions when the scales of justice become almost an encumbrance, and both hands clutch at the sword alone. Whether the magistrate upon whom the decision of this cause devolved was right in holding this to be such an occasion is not now to be discussed; it is enough to say that his decision sustained at every point the Ramsey board, and crushed in succession all the schemes of the Erie ring. The opinion was most noticeable in that it approached the inquiry in a large spirit. Its conclusion was not made to turn on the question of a second of time, or a rigid adherence to the letter of the law, or any other technicality of the pettifogger; it swept all these aside, and spoke firmly and clearly to the question of fraud and fraudulent conspiracy. All the elaborate comparisons of watches, and noting of fractional parts of a minute, which marked the organization of the Erie meeting, were treated with contempt, but the meeting itself was pronounced to be organized in pursuance of a previous conspiracy, and the election held by it was "irregular, fraudulent, and void." The scandals of the law—the strange processes, injunctions, orders, and conflicts of jurisdiction—were disposed of with the same grasp, whenever they came in the path of the decision. The appointment of Fuller as receiver was declared to have been made in a "suit instituted for a fraudulent purpose," and it was pronounced in such "clear conflict with the law and settled practice of the court" as to be explicable only on a supposition that the order was "granted incautiously, and upon some mistaken oral representation or statement of the facts of the case." The order removing the regular inspectors of election was "improvidently granted" and was "entirely void"; and the keeping it back by counsel, and serving it only at the moment of the election, was "an obvious and designed surprise on the great body of stockholders." The suit under which the Barnard order of arrest was issued against Ramsey and Phelps was instituted without right; the order of arrest was unauthorized; the order to hold to bail was "most extraordinary and exorbitant," and procured "in aid of fraudulent purposes." The injunction forbidding Ramsey to act as president of the company was "entirely void." The 3,000 shares of forfeited stock reissued to Mr. Groesbeck were pronounced "valid stock," and numerous precedents were cited in which the principle had been sustained. Even the injudicious subscription for the 9,500 new shares of stock by Ramsey and his friends, on which they had not attempted to vote at the election, was declared in point of law regular, valid, and binding. Upon the facts of the case the decision was equally outspoken; it was fraud and conspiracy everywhere. "The importation and crowding into a small room" of a large number of "rude, rough, and dangerous persons," and furnishing them with proxies that they might participate in the proceedings of the meeting, "was a gross perversion and abuse of the right to vote by proxy, and a clear infringement of the rights of stockholders, tending, if such proceedings are countenanced by the courts, to convert corporation meetings into places of disorder, lawlessness, and riot." Finally, costs were decreed to the Ramsey Board of Directors, and a reference was made to Samuel L. Selden, late a judge of the Court of Appeals, to ascertain and report a proper extra allowance in the case, and to which of the defendants it was to be paid.

It is not likely that Judge Smith will complain of this notice of his judicial merits, from the pen of a rapturous admirer. And yet, when we consider their import, how damning are these words of praise! "There are occasions," says Mr. Adams, "when the scales of justice become almost an encumbrance, and both hands clutch the sword alone." So there are indeed. Jeffreys thought so when into the west of England he carried terror and death among the unhappy peasantry who had followed Monmouth, and came back to his master red with the gore of the Bloody Assizes. Ananias the high priest *approached the inquiry in a large spirit of disregard* for what Mr. Adams calls *technicalities* when he commanded them that stood by Paul to smite him on the mouth; but we must not forget the indignant rebuke administered by the great apostle of the Gentiles: "God shall smite thee, thou whited wall; for sittest thou to judge me according to the law, and commandest me to be smitten contrary to the law?" When Saunders was asked to pronounce an impartial judgment in the *quo warranto* against the corporation of London, *he* thought a *judicial tone might be overdone or out of place.* A military commission, organized to please the powerful and false accuser by hanging the weak and innocent victim of his malice, will admire the virtue of a civil magistrate who *made the parties feel that they were not equal.* "Judge Smith," says his eulogist, "did not make his decision turn on the letter of the law, or on any other technicality of the pettifogger." True enough; but is it not just possible that even a pettifogger, whose worst vice is adherence to the law, may be a safer sort of person in the land than one whose great glory is to trample it under foot? The fame of judges who throw away the scales, clutch at the sword alone, and smite contrary to the law, is not a possession generally coveted by men in ermine; but Mr. Adams' compliments apply not less to Jeffreys and Scroggs and Saunders, to Herod and Ananias, to Fouquier Tinville and Hunter and Holt, than to the man whom he describes as a judicial gladiator, fighting against legal justice on the side of Ramsey.

Mr. Adams' summary of Judge Smith's decision could have been much abridged if he had stated simply that this remarkable arbiter of men's rights pronounced everything that Ramsey had done to be valid and admirable, and everything done by those opposed to him dishonest, unlawful, and worthy of unmitigated reprobation. So far, indeed, did the largeness of his spirit carry him, that, to borrow the language of Mr. Adams, *"Even* the injudicious subscription for the 9,500 shares of stock by Ramsey and his friends, on which they had not attempted to vote at the election, was declared in point of law regular, valid, and binding." There is a significance in the word *"even"* at the beginning of this sentence which implies very strongly that Mr. Adams had not expected so much as this from anybody on the bench. Ramsey, reckless as he was, feared to tread where the headlong Smith rushed in. He was bold enough to fabricate the fraudulent stock, but he did not vote it, as he might have done had he dreamed that there was on the face of the earth a judge prepared to pronounce his fraud "regular, valid, and binding." It is not strange, observing the temper of Judge Smith's opinion, that, on the morning after it was published, he was secretly

closeted with Ramsey's attorneys, and engaged, as he himself
stated, "in looking over the findings of fact and comparing and
adjusting them with his opinion." A single circumstance will
show that this labor was not in vain. In the body of the opinion
the judge declared, referring to Ramsey's secret issue of stock:
"The subscription for the 9,500 shares by Hendrick, Hunt, and
others, I think made them stockholders upon such stock of said
corporation. They paid the 10 per cent upon it, and *cannot avoid
the payment of the balance due upon such subscription.* The
company has had the 10 per cent, and the subscription was made
in the regular subscription-book in the hands of the officers of
the company, and created an absolute legal obligation to take the
stock and PAY for the same." And in framing his conclusions of
law, there was one inserted, as the original paper on file in his
court shows, to correspond with this paragraph of his opinion:

That the 9,500 shares of stock subscribed for in the books of said
company, by Jared Goodyear, Robert H. Pruyn, John Eddy, William A. Rice, Eliakim R. Ford, John Cook, Joseph H. Ramsey, James
Hendricks, Minard Harder, and Harvey Hunt, whereon 10 per cent
was paid in money on the fifth day of August, 1869, thereupon became,
and were, and still are, lawful and valid shares of the capital stock of
said company.

It is needless to say that his Honor Judge Smith, when he
wrote this "conclusion," and the passage in his opinion with
which it was made to correspond, meant to do a very kind thing
for the men of Ramsey's faction. Indeed, as we have seen, he was
out-Ramseying Ramsey. The stock which he had pronounced
"valid" was never intended to be taken or kept; the 10 per
cent paid on it had actually been "lifted" out of the treasury
of the company; not a penny had been advanced by the nominal
holders, and it was expressly understood that they were not to
concern themselves about any future payments. Moreover, the
stock had been created merely to serve an emergency which was
now past. Nothing, therefore, could have been of more startling
or disastrous import to Ramsey and his confederates than a judi-

cial conclusion of law to the effect that they actually owned the shares for which they had subscribed, and were bound to pay the balance due upon them into the treasury of the company, to wit, the sum of $855,000.

No wonder that when Ramsey's attorneys were employed "in looking over the findings of fact, and comparing and adjusting them with the opinion," they made haste to correct this shocking blunder and to rid their clients of the liability it would impose on them. It was too late to tinker the opinion, which was already in print, but the damaging "conclusion" was stricken out, and the judge, by this last and efficient bit of service, added nearly a million dollars' worth of thanks to the heavy debt of gratitude which the Ramsey people owed him already.

Everything being decided in favor of Ramsey, the judgment of course included a decree that he and his board were lawfully elected, although they had received a very small minority of the votes. The scales being discarded, the majority weighed no more than the minority.* An order was accordingly made that Ramsey and his board "be immediately let into possession." The first thing they did was to put the property forever out of the owners' reach by a perpetual lease to the Hudson and Delaware Canal Company. This was not all or nearly all. Within one

---

* The statements both of Mr. Adams and Mr. Curtis are obscure concerning the votes given by the respective parties at the election. The important and leading fact, however, is well established, and not denied, that the Church party owned, and held, and voted nearly two-thirds of the *bona fide* stock; and the Groesbeck stock was voted for them besides under an injunction of their opponents. Mr. Adams informs us that Ramsey did not attempt to vote any part of the 9,500 shares. If he voted only those *bona fide* shares which he held and had a right to vote, his own return must have shown him in a very meager minority. But the court declared him elected. Whether this was done by throwing out of the count *all* votes of the Church party, or by throwing out *only enough* to put them in a minority, or by *adding* to Ramsey's vote others which were *not cast at all* by either party, or by transferring votes *actually* cast for Church to Ramsey, for whom they were *not* cast, we have no information. All these modes of electing a defeated candidate are adopted when occasion requires by Philadelphia return judges, and sometimes they are very ingeniously compounded together.

month after Ramsey and his board got possession, they voted to
him, at his own request and on his own dictation, two sums of
money, amounting in the aggregate to $62,802.25, and 1,330
shares of stock, worth at par $133,000. If this was not a mere
gratuity—a naked robbery of the stockholders—it was based on
some transaction grossly corrupt; for Ramsey refused to explain
the ground of it, and the board has ever since steadily resisted
all efforts to investigate it.

This cause it took but little time to dispose of. In two months
from the day when the stockholders were called into court—
"two little months or ere those shoes were old"—they were
turned out, despoiled of their property, and branded as fraudulent conspirators for trying to hold it. We would suppose that
this could not be a very expensive operation. On a road at once
so short and so rough the tolls should not be heavy. The justice
which the Church party got in Judge Smith's court ought to
be a cheap article, since it has no other quality to make it desirable. But costs were awarded—extra costs—not in favor of the
plaintiffs, nor against the defendants in a body, but against
some of the defendants in favor of other some. A former judge of
the Court of Appeals was appointed assessor to aid in fixing the
amount, and it was fixed at *ninety-two thousand dollars!* An economical nation might carry on a small war without spending
more than it costs a private citizen to defend his plainest right
in a Rochester court.

The Church party appealed to the General Term, where all the
rulings of Judge Smith were reversed, through and through,
except upon the validity of the election. That was affirmed on
the ground that he was *competent* to pass upon it; that is to say,
he had legal authority which made his determination upon the
point conclusive. How he got power to decide that or anything
else between parties who were on the same side and not at issue
we do not pretend to conjecture. But the Code especially delights
in jurisdictional absurdities. This, however, has gone up to the
Court of Appeals, *et adhuc sub judice lis est.*

If a dispute like this had occurred in a country where the principles and the rules of the Common Law* prevail, it would have been determined easily and satisfactorily, without parade or trouble. An action at law would have brought the defaulting agent of the corporation to justice very soon; or a bill in equity would have called everybody interested into court at once, given them all a full hearing, and made a clean settlement of the whole matter. But here was a petty offender, strong only in the weakness of the law, who was able to defy justice and to triumph over it. The men whom he had wronged took after him with the Code; twenty-eight injunctions were exploded from different and distant parts of the state; the attack and the defense raised such an uproar that the framework of society was in danger of being broken; actual violence was commenced and extensive bloodshed was imminent; yet he retained his possession of all he took, and took as much more as he wanted. To drive this nibbling rat from the corporation cupboard, they gave chase with force and noise and numbers enough to hunt down a Bengal tiger, and the vermin was not dislodged after all. The Code is not a "terror to evil-doers," nor "a praise unto them that do well."

It is a rule of epic poetry that the story stops when the hero has reached the zenith of his fortunes. As the Iliad closes when the wrath of Achilles is appeased by dragging the body of Hector around the walls of Troy, and as the Æneid concludes abruptly when the death of Turnus makes Æneas master of Italy, so Mr. Adams closes his account of Ramsey's high career at the point of time when his cheat upon the owners of the Albany & Susquehanna Railroad was completely successful. But Mr. Curtis, in his matter-of-fact production, carried the narrative a little further on.

Ramsey, being elated with his conquest of the Albany and

* It can hardly be worth while to say, that by Common Law we do not mean merely the ancient laws and customs of England, but those rules and principles which the first colonists transplanted here for the protection of life, liberty, and property, and which have since been modified from time to time as experience has proved to be necessary.

Susquehanna, determined to invade the Erie, in hopes of subjugating that also. He was not a creditor nor a stockholder; but to give him nominal status, Groesbeck—the same Groesbeck—bought for him thirteen shares of stock and six bonds. With these he went to Delhi, the most secluded county town in the state, situated twenty miles from any railway line, and accessible only by mountain roads. There he found Judge Murray, one of the thirty-three, and to him he complained that he was in danger of losing the money he had invested in these bonds and this stock, by reason of certain mismanagement of its officers and directors, the recital of which covered 340 folios. On this complaint the judge gave him, not merely an injunction, but a great quantity of injunctions; suspended a majority of the directors, appointed a receiver, restrained the suspended directors from making defense in this or any other suit involving their official conduct, commanded the unsuspended directors to see that the company was promptly represented by such counsel as they should select, ordered that no creditor but Ramsey should institute any suit to collect or secure his debt, and directed the defendants, under penalty of contempt, to bring no cross suit which might embarrass the plaintiff in his prosecution of this one. Under these orders Ramsey managed to have the defendants *promptly* represented by a family connection of his own. When this destructive missile burst on the men of Erie at their New York office, it no doubt produced some terror. They immediately sought the ablest counsel they could find, and directed Messrs. Field and Shearman to adopt energetic measures of defense. But those gentlemen were informed that they could not appear, their clients being already represented by an attorney who had been selected for them, whom they did not know, and whose name even they were not permitted to learn. Nor could they discover who was the person appointed to take charge of their client's property, and exercise over it the unlimited control of a receiver. The alarm of the parties was greatly increased when they learned that their rights were to be in the keeping of David Groesbeck, the man

who had aided Ramsey in all his previous frauds, and whose
sense of moral and legal obligation may be learned from a fact
stated by Mr. Adams; namely, that he defended Ramsey's fab-
rication of fraudulent stock and his appropriation of the Albany
& Susquehanna Company's bonds, and "declared that under
the same circumstances and fighting the same men he himself
would have gone as far, and further too if necessary."

Here was such a case as no community living under any kind
of a code had ever seen before. All the property of a corporation
worth sixty millions of dollars, and employing in its service the
daily labor of twenty-five thousand hands, was snatched from
the owners in the twinkling of an eye by an order made behind
their backs, and all their rights and the rights of their employees
and creditors were put at the mercy of a man who, speaking of
these very owners, had openly avowed that in dealing with them
he would be restrained by no moral principle; that fighting the
same men he would betray the most sacred trust, clandestinely
appropriate their property, make false papers to cheat them, and
injure them otherwise by going still further if necessary. All
these perilous notions of right and wrong were fully shared by
the plaintiff, who had secured an attorney for the defense, and
so made himself *dominus litis* on both sides. *Ex parte* injunctions
had often before this torn men's property out of their possession
without a hearing, but the Rhadamanthian justice of a subsequent trial was always conceded. Here the right to make even an
ex post facto defense was taken out of their hands.

We see no reason to suppose that Judge Murray was not both
a competent and an honest man. He acted according to the Code,
which never refuses to do any amount of wrong if it can be put
into the form of an injunction. But the Code itself could not
endure such a pressure as this. Messrs. Field and Shearman,
after much difficulty and delay, got on the track of the unknown
person who was representing their clients, wrung the case out
of his hands, and gained a position where the plaintiff was compelled to face them with his proofs. He broke down utterly, and

his complaint was dismissed. Afterward he and his backers raised a clamor that he had been forced to trial with his hands tied. In truth his hands were as loose as need be, but they were not clean enough to be shown.

The general question of *ethics,* which Mr. Adams raises, would tempt us to an extended discussion if we had unlimited space for it. As it is, we cannot let the subject pass without saying that Brougham is not a leader fit to be followed, even in a matter so simple as every moral question must necessarily be to a man who believes in the New Testament. Brougham was nothing if not sensational, and before such an audience as he addressed in the Queen's case the impulse to be extravagant was more than he could resist. We prefer the higher and more ancient authority of Roger l'Estrange, whose "Character of an Honest Lawyer," written in the English of the seventeenth century, is at once accurate and epigrammatic. Supposing a candid seeker for truth to be still unsatisfied, let him read Sharswood's admirable book entitled *Legal Ethics,* supplemented, if need be, with Redfield's article in the July number of the *American Law Register.* The lego-theological side of the subject is presented by Judge Agnew, in his address to a western college on the "Philosophy and Poetry of the Law"; and the theologico-legal aspect is displayed by Sidney Smith, in his sermon on "The Lawyer that tempted Christ." That member of the profession who receives the spirit of these teachings into his heart, and acts accordingly, will be worthy of his high vocation while he lives, and, to use the words of old Roger, "When Death calls him to the *Bar of Heaven* by a *Habeas Corpus cum Causa* he will find his *Judge* his *Advocate, nonsuit* the Devil, obtain a *Liberate* from all his infirmities, and continue still one of the *Long Robe* in Glory."

Disdaining the advantage of Brougham's eccentric theory, and trying Messrs. Field and Shearman by the severer standard of the better men whose works we have cited, what have they done to merit reproach? or wherein have they come short of their duty in all this difficult business? The only semblance of a specific accusation is, not that they took up an unjust cause, but that they were retained by a bad client. Mr. Adams thinks it very sensible and proper to make a grave exhibition of this charge, and to circulate it far and wide over the world; therefore (and only therefore) we are not permitted to say in plain terms that it is most absurd and wicked.

If no counselor can be concerned for Fisk and Gould in any case whatever without becoming infamous, it follows that no court can, without incurring a similar penalty, extend the protection of the law to their plainest rights. They are mere outlaws; they may be slandered, swindled, robbed with impunity, "and it shall come to pass that whosoever findeth them shall slay them."* If this be consistent with the genius of our institutions, we have misapprehended those provisions of the fundamental law which declare that the courts are open to *all* men, and that *all* shall have a fair trial with counsel to assist them in getting justice.

This style of attack upon Mr. Field looks to us like a very unmistakable tribute to his good fame. The character of a lawyer must be more than commonly spotless when his enemies have no material for defaming him except what they get by raking about among the faults and follies of his clients. But that society is a very unsafe one to live in whose sense of justice will permit one man to be hunted down merely because the wolf's head has been placed on another. The reputation of lawyers—which is the life of their lives—will be extremely precarious, however virtuous their own acts may have been, if the concentrated odium of all their clients' sins can be cast upon themselves.

The Church party—that is to say, the proprietors of the Albany & Susquehanna Railroad—had a cause as just, legal, and fair as any court ever saw. They had been remorselessly plundered by a gang of reckless knaves, who made no secret of their

---

* This was written and in the hands of the printers before the assassination of Colonel Fisk.

intentions to repeat the robbery in the same as well as in other forms. Messrs. Field and Shearman accepted the retainer of these injured parties, and gave them the promise of such redress and protection as they could legally obtain for them. Now it is charged that this engagement to procure justice by legal means, in a perfectly upright case, was a prostitution by Messrs. Field and Shearman of their talents and influence, because one or two of the parties thus injured are supposed to have been previously engaged in other transactions in which they were themselves to blame. Whether this be true or false, it furnished no reason to Messrs. Field and Shearman for rejecting the case on moral grounds. If the cause, though just, was likely to become unpopular because Fisk and Gould were in it, that was an additional reason for taking it. Mere public clamor will not deter any honorable man from the performance of a duty; on the contrary, he is excited to higher efforts when "the heathen rage and the people imagine a vain thing."

That they behaved with scrupulous uprightness in the progress of the cause, and used no unfair means to reach the ends of justice, is a proposition which will not be denied unless by some who think that it is wrong in all circumstances to take out an *ex parte* injunction. Certainly the law which allows this mode of proceeding is entitled to no commendation. But while it is in full force it may be used for a proper purpose with a safe conscience. Every man is justified in defending the right against the wrong with such weapons as the law puts into his hands. Even L'Estrange's "Honest Lawyer," rigid as he is, "uses the nice snapperadoes of practice, in a defensive way, to countermine the plots of knavery, though he had rather be dumb than suffer his tongue to pimp for injustice, or club his parts to bolster up a cheat with the legerdemain of law craft."

But then it may be said that Mr. Field, being the author of the Code, is responsible for the law itself, and for the mischief it produces in other hands as well as his own. The fact may be assumed too hastily. He is not the author, or supporter, or ap-

prover of that system which we have called the Code in this
paper. Whenever we have said "Code," we meant the New York
system of jurisprudence, a very small part of which was furnished by him. A piece of his work was taken and joined on the
half-demolished ruins of the Common Law, and afterward there
were added to both the outrageous provisions which have made
such confusion and conflict in the jurisdiction of the courts. That
he meant well by what he did has never, we believe, been doubted.
If he erred, his error was shared by thousands of the best men
and truest philanthropists in Europe and America; and the faith
of many in "law reform," like that of Joanna Southcote's dis-
ciples in their "Shiloh," is robust enough to live on under all
the discouragement of past failures. Let us hope that the pure
benevolence of their efforts will meet its reward in the higher
success of a far better reform, which may restore us to the golden
age of the law.

The Code actually prepared by Mr. Field and the commission
which he headed has not had a trial in New York. When a portion of it was torn from its context and united with a mutilated
part of the Common Law, the symmetry of both was destroyed,
and confusion became unavoidable. The legislature, when they
abolished the old forms of pleading, rejected the new forms with
which Mr. Field proposed to supply their place; these latter were
scientific and logical, and would have saved much of the evil
which has happened for want of them. It was the experiment,
which has always failed, of putting new wine into old bottles.
In some of the western states they have tried the Code pure and
simple, and very wise men are animated with the hope of its
complete success. Mr. Field has no lack of adherents at home
and abroad, who believe in the Code apparently on the principle
of that Roman citizen who said he would rather be wrong with
Cato than right with all the rest of the world. No doubt Mr.
Field is a better man than Cato ever was; but we are not "rav-
ished with the whistling of a name," and therefore we say to all
Americans who are still permitted to enjoy the blessing of the

Common Law, that they should watch over that inheritance faithfully, and show no quarter to codifiers. Let them lay to their hearts the solemn warning of the Hebrew prophet: ''Walk in the old paths; stand upon the ancient ways; observe them well, and be ye not given unto change.''

VII

THE TRUTH OF A "GREAT LAWSUIT"*

BY

ALBERT STICKNEY

A CHANCE shot of a journalist into a very vulnerable reputation has raised a tornado of letters and counter-letters, "opinions" and reviews, and in the hurly-burly the original point of the matter seems nearly lost, as indeed some of the parties are quite willing it should be. After the dust and splinters of adjectives and reputations have slightly cleared away, it may be well to call to mind where the trouble began, and what, good or bad, has come of it at last.

A stray paragraph in the New York correspondence of the *Springfield Republican* contained the expression of a somewhat unfavorable opinion as to the professional character and action of Mr. David Dudley Field, a member of the New York bar. *Vixere fortes ante Agamemnona.* And before this present time there have been many men who have been abused in print, or have been the victims of a newspaper paragraph, and yet have not greatly troubled themselves on account thereof; and generally their unconcern has been in proportion to their innocence. But, for some reason, ten lines in a New England newspaper were enough to make Mr. David Dudley Field, the author of the New York Code, one of the leaders of the New York bar, rush into a long correspondence to vindicate his character and save his reputation. If the reputation needed saving, it was quite natural for its owner to rush into print, and quite certain that the reputation would come out of the fight no whiter than it

* *The Galaxy,* XIV (October, 1872), 576–582.

went in. Mr. Field did not deny that his clients, the Erie gentlemen, had done things to which "exception had been taken"; nor did he deny that his son's firm of Field & Shearman had done and performed certain very peculiar legal services. Mr. Field carefully, however, cut himself away from the Erie clients and from his son's firm, explained to the public very fully that he had never been consulted "beforehand" about the exceptionable acts, and that he was not responsible for the practices of Field & Shearman. It was surely somewhat ungenerous toward the Erie people and his son. But what would you have? It is better to save one character alone, if you can have only one. Reputations are not lightly to be thrown away. One must sometimes make sacrifices.

But Mr. Field's protestations of professional innocence did not go unnoticed. General Barlow took up some of Mr. Field's litigations, especially the Albany & Susquehanna litigation between the Fisk-Field party on the one side and the Ramsey party on the other, examined it carefully, showed precisely what share Mr. David Dudley Field himself had taken in it, and left a very unpleasant impression on the minds of intelligent men, and especially of lawyers, as to Mr. Field's code of legal morals. Mr. Field replied by calling General Barlow a "person," which statement was undoubtedly true, but hardly relevant to the matter in hand—i.e., Mr. Field's professional character. Mr. Charles Francis Adams, Jr., who had often couched lance against knaves, gave a picture of an "Erie Raid," and the distinguished part in it borne by the author of the New York Code. And to judge by the abuse Mr. Adams has received in certain not very reputable newspapers, his words must have cut. The reputation of Mr. Field certainly suffered in the public mind. It certainly suffered in Mr. Field's own mind. Presently there came to the rescue the somber stateliness of the Honorable George T. Curtis, who delivered his "opinion" that Judge Barnard was an upright judge, and Mr. Field was an upright lawyer. To which may be added the "opinions" of Mr. Field and Judge Barnard, delivered of each other, to the same effect. And it will be remembered that Mr. Fagin had a very deep admiration for Mr. Jack Dawkins.

And at last, as at the gentle tournament of Ashby, when the joyous passage at arms seems wholly done, when the lookers-on are somewhat weary and the gallant knights lie scattered over the field with heads or legs broken, there appears in the lists, no one knows from where, the Black Knight of the Fetterlock, to recue with his mighty arm the hard-pressed champion. The Honorable Jeremiah S. Black, formerly Attorney-General of the United States, has been moved to come forward in what might by some be called a defense of Mr. David Dudley Field. His paper in the March number of *The Galaxy* is certainly very entertaining. No one will deny Mr. Black's very great ability. His story of ''A Great Lawsuit and a Field Fight'' is full of wit and full of facts. The wit is excellent, being Mr. Black's own. The facts are very bad, being taken from a brief of Mr. David Dudley Field.

Now what had Mr. Field done? And what was shown against or for him? The liberty of action rightly allowed to the advocate is very broad; and judgment on his conduct should be very cautious and charitable. He must never knowingly misstate facts. But every man, in the heat of argument, and even in the heat of ordinary professional employment in behalf of his client, often will honestly (if he does it unconsciously) color facts, leave out of view facts which make against him, bring unduly into view facts which make for him. He may make mistaken statements in argument. He may do mistaken things in action. Mr. Field must have, and we think has had, the widest allowances made to him for all the influences to which counsel can be exposed. No one, in the criticisms on his professional conduct, as far as I am aware, has rested on charges of mere undue warmth of advocacy—of his urging before courts doubtful or mistaken views of fact or law.

The charges against Mr. David Dudley Field have been widely

different from these; and in the many papers that have been now written on the matter the points of these charges have been lost sight of.

In all modern times, the raising of grain, the making of boots and shoes, the buying and selling of tea, the everyday practice of medicine and the law, have been occupations, not very romantic, not very full of excitement, but very sure, if followed with ability and honesty, to yield a reasonable income. There have been, however, at times, adventurous spirits, like Mr. Richard Turpin, who have deemed the pursuits of trade and commerce too tame and tedious to satisfy the cravings of their souls. Instead of creating property by toil, they have been willing rather to take it by force, already created, from the industrious plodders who have given it existence. They have, it is true, by so doing taken their chance of the halter; but this, in their eyes, merely lent excitement to the game. Mr. Turpin's imitators, of late years, have given their time and thought to bank vaults, bullion, and railway bonds, rather than to attacks on armed travelers. Said Charles Lamb, when asked how he learned to smoke with such wonderful vehemence, ''Sir, I toiled for it, as for a virtue.'' And there are now, in most large cities, men who use the greatest mechanical skill and the finest appliances of science in opening safes and forging bonds, who with half the labor in an honest walk of life might earn fortunes.

They all, however, honestly take their chance of a term in the state prison. Certain gentlemen in New York City have, in their pursuit of wealth and pleasure, deemed it needful to control the revenues of large railway corporations, and to divert these revenues from their normal use of paying dividends to stockholders into the more pleasing and picturesque, if not more honest, channels of French opera and fast horses. But formerly, at least, the stockholder who did not receive his dividends could go into a court of law and get them. It became necessary, then, if any gentlemen wished to use other men's railway dividends, to secure for their protection a court, or at least a judge; and ''to carry a judge in one's pocket'' became a necessity as well as a pleasure for any set of corporation directors who desired to use the income, without owning the stock, of a large moneyed corporation. And if they own a judge, surely it would be undignified to ask him to draw all the decrees in their suits as well as sign them. There must be then a member of the bar to complete the retinue. And the ''law department'' of a large corporation, arranged on the system stated, contained consequently members, such as they were, of both bench and bar. Now, if Mr. Richard Turpin before mentioned, or any modern professional thief in New York, should go into a banker's office, bind and gag the banker, break open his safe, and take from it two or three thousand shares of stock, men would call it robbery; and if this be all done under circumstances of great danger, you may have a certain kind of admiration for the boldness of the deed. But suppose the case where a dozen men, completely armed, come suddenly on one poor defenceless wretch and snatch from him his watch and purse. The crime is still the same, and we despise the cowardice.

Now a judge of the Supreme Court of the state of New York is a very powerful man, and the writ of the people of the state of New York is a very powerful thing. They both should be, and generally have been, used for the purpose of doing right and justice.

But if a judge of the New York Supreme Court chooses to break open a safe with a sledge hammer, men call it robbery; and if he directs the sheriff to do this under a writ which he has no shadow of right or jurisdiction to grant, the moral offense is much the same, although unfortunately he cannot be sent to the state prison for it, as the decisions now are. If this same judge takes two thousand shares of stock from a banker's safe with his hands, he commits larceny, and he takes his term in the state institution. But if he does it through the hands of a receiver, whom he appoints, and orders to take the stock, without any right or jurisdiction so to appoint or order him, where will you draw the distinction, except in the statutory penalty? And doing these outrages in the circumstances above stated, having been elected to a high office by (it is supposed) the votes of the people, having sworn solemnly to faithfully discharge the duties of his office— being beyond the reach of an indictment, and practically, in most cases, beyond the reach of punishment of any kind—he not only robs, but he violates his trust, breaks his oath, and adds to his other guilt that of the meanest cowardice.

But no decrees or writs are granted until they are asked for by counsel. These counsel are sworn officers of the law. Mr. David Dudley Field is a member of the New York bar of many years' experience and of ability, and knowing well what he can and cannot rightly do. He has always for himself claimed to be a respectable practitioner. And the case shown against Mr. David Dudley Field is this: Certain clients of his, Mr. Jay Gould, Mr. James Fisk, Jr., and others, whose names are now somewhat noted or notorious, have been engaged in large railway and stock operations for several years last past. They have controlled the Erie Railway. They tried to control the Albany & Susquehanna Railway. Mr. Fisk attempted what he truly and humorously called a "raid" on the Union Pacific Railroad Company. It is very seldom, in the financial history of any state or country but New York, that corporate elections have had to be carried, or even decided, by the aid of courts. It has been very seldom in the history of New York that a corporate election has had to be carried or decided by the aid of courts, except in New York City. These cases have almost all happened since the year 1867. In almost every one of these cases James Fisk, Jr., has been a party interested. In almost every one of these cases the application for the aid of a court has been made to the Honorable George G. Barnard, and it has been made by David Dudley Field, or by one of his firm. And in that court apparently these gentlemen have always had on their side law and justice. For is it not law and justice that ensure success in courts? It is not meant indeed that Mr. David Dudley Field in his own proper person has, in all cases, drawn or copied the writ or order needed for the special occasion. This is done by his clerks. And he has indeed, in a somewhat ungenerous manner, of late tried to throw the blame and disgrace of them upon his son and his son's partner. But Mr. David Dudley Field has, whenever these writs or orders were brought into court for consideration, appeared and argued to uphold them. And he has been paid for them. And in behalf of these clients Mr. David Dudley Field and his firm have been engaged in the business of breaking open safes, taking railway-stock certificates from the lawful owners of them, putting presidents of corporations out of their offices. To be sure, it is not here meant that Mr. David Dudley Field has himself wielded the burglar's jimmy that forced open the safe of the Union Pacific Railroad Company. What he did was to procure through his firm a writ directing the sheriff of New York County to break or blow open that safe, Mr. Field all the time knowing that the writ was granted without a shadow of authority in law, by a corrupt judge, for his client, from corrupt motives, Mr. Field himself being paid by his client for his services in that very matter. Nor is it meant that Mr. Field has boldly gone into a railway office and by main force put a railway president out of the room. He has done it by an injunction from a judge of the Supreme Court, knowing all the time, if we use the words of one of his own briefs, that the order was "absolutely void," and, to use the language of the Supreme Court of the state of New York, was "in clear conflict with the law and settled practice of this court." By way of pleasing interludes in these employments, Mr. Field has done for those same clients other professional services, for which he has been paid. He has been a party to what has been called by the Supreme Court of the state of New York "a conspiracy to carry an election by the use and abuse of legal process and proceedings." And as a part of this "conspiracy," Mr. Field was guilty of, or honored by, the arrest of the present speaker of the assembly of the state of New York, a leading member of the Albany bar, and of the president of a large railroad corporation, when the one was trying to save the property of his client, and the other the property of his company, from the benign protective hands of James Fisk, Jr. While Mr. Field had this railroad president under arrest, in the hands of the sheriff, Mr. Field took occasion to address to him the particularly gentle and courteous remark, "How are you now, Ramsey?" Mr. Field then standing very politely with his thumbs in the armholes of his waistcoat. None of these facts has Mr. Field ever ventured to deny. As to the remark to Mr. Ramsey above told, Mr. Field in a recent proceeding has said under oath that he "had no recollection of it." Mr. Shearman, his partner, has testified under oath, in effect, that he did not believe Mr. Field could ever have made the remark, because he knew Mr. Field to be a refined gentleman. But suppose the fact of the remark having been made to be proved beyond question, pray what would be Mr. Shearman's inference?

These are the services of the advocate. But Mr. Field has gone even further in his loyalty to his client. The Supreme Court has decided that "in pursuance of said conspiracy" Mr. James Fisk, Jr., brought from New York a large number of "rough, rude, and dangerous persons," in order to "intimidate and prevent lawful stockholders" from attending their own meeting in their own railway office, to elect the officers of their own company. Mr. David Dudley Field, showing then the versatility of genius he always shows, and in order to insure the full success of this *coup Napoleonien* (Napoleon III, not I), undertook himself to marshal these black-eyed and broken-nosed heroes to victory, and, arm-in-arm with Colonel James Fisk, Jr., shared the dangers of the assault at the head of this forlorn hope.

And, finally, we have Judge Black's "Great Lawsuit and a Field Fight," which, as its author will probably not deny, is meant for a defense of Mr. Field. At least, it is as such a defense alone that it will be here considered. No one will deny its brilliancy, its ingenuity, its strength, in most points. Mr. Black's genius and thorough training in the law could not fail to show

themselves, on this or any subject. We are given a humorous and
true description of the absurd reforms made in practice by what
is called the New York Code of Procedure. But surely this was
slightly unkind, inasmuch as this same New York Code was the
pet creation of Mr. David Dudley Field, who on a late occasion,
under oath, stated that he was, "as you may suppose, a believer
in and a strong partisan of the Code." Mr. Black, indeed, apparently thinks that all the troubles in the Susquehanna litigation
arose from those very absurdities of practice under this dreadful Code. Mr. Curtis, on the late examination into Judge Barnard's official conduct or misconduct, under a charge of a "conspiracy" with James Fisk and others, tried to show that a judge
could not be guilty of such an offense as a "conspiracy" under
the Code; that the Code, in fact, was a great safeguard against
judicial crime. Mr. Curtis asked Mr. Field, on this point, the
following question:

Qu. I want your judgment, as a lawyer, to be given to this committee,
as to whether any such offense as that, under the practice of the Code,
wouldn't be an exceedingly difficult and almost impossible thing to
take place? I want your judgment as a lawyer on the bearings of the
provisions of the Code on the liability or exposure to the happening
of such an offense as that; and when I say "the provisions of the Code,"
I refer to those requirements preceding the issue of process which the
Code demands in comparison with the old common law practice.

To which Mr. Field made answer: "I really don't understand
your question." Nor did anyone else.

Mr. Black, having given his idea of the wrongs for which the
New York Code must be held answerable, goes to a further point.
Mr. Field had, in his conduct of the Susquehanna litigation,
early acted on the hint given by an experienced barrister: "If you
have no case, abuse the plaintiff's attorney." Mr. Field had in
his practice modified the maxim, and having little law in his case,
had taken to abuse of Mr. Ramsey out of the case. And certain
statements about Mr. Ramsey's conduct, made up first by Mr.
Field alone, have been so persistently repeated, that although
they have no foundation in fact, some persons begin to believe

them. This present controversy began on the professional conduct of Mr. David Dudley Field. That was the point of dispute,
though for Mr. Field and his friends a very dangerous one. They
have tried the old game of attacking your enemy by way of defending yourself. It does very well in war, but not in logic. And
it has become advisable to state very briefly a very few of the
points about Mr. Ramsey's connection with the Albany & Susquehanna Railroad and the "Great Lawsuit." And from the
statement of these few points, and a comparison between the
facts and Mr. Black's assertions on these points, we can come to
some idea of his care and accuracy on others.

The statement has been often made on the part of Mr. Field's
advocates, that the Fisk party, or the "Church party," as they
are for an obvious reason eager to call it, were the owners of a
clear majority of the stock of the Albany & Susquehanna Railroad, and that Mr. Ramsey and his friends were trying by unjust
means to hinder these owners of a majority of the lawful stock
from electing in a lawful manner their Board of Directors. It is
a fact full of meaning that Mr. Fisk and his friends, when they
once failed in securing, through Judge Barnard's injunctions
and receiverships, the control of that railroad, never again made
the slightest effort to get that control. No one ever heard of them
at any election prior to the one in 1869, or at any later one. Why
was it so? Where did the stock vanish? Why was such tame
submission rendered to the decision of the Supreme Court given
by Mr. Justice Smith? For lack of a better reason, we may be
permitted to give this one, that the decision was right; and the
decision was, as far as the ownership of the stock is concerned,
that the entire number of shares legally existing when the transfer books were closed in 1869 was about 30,000; and of this number more than 21,000 shares, as was proved on the trial and
decided by the court, were held by the Ramsey party. And throwing entirely out of the question 9,500 newly issued shares, and
2,400 of the Groesbeck shares, so called, which were claimed by
the Fisk party to be illegal, there remained somewhat more than

18,000 shares of undisputed validity, of which, as the Supreme Court decided, the Ramsey party held and voted on 9,342 shares, which was more than a clear majority; and these 9,500 shares and 2,400 have been voted on at every election since, without question or dispute on the part of any person. These points may perhaps be enough to meet Mr. Black's statement that the Fisk party "had been remorselessly plundered," and "had a cause as just, legal, and fair as any court ever saw."

And then comes the charge against Mr. Ramsey and his friends of a midnight subscription to 9,500 shares of stock, which Mr. Black gives us in the following guise:

He got together certain of his confederates secretly at his own house, and distributed among them certificates for 9,500 shares of stock, for which they had not paid, and did not mean to pay, a single cent. It was necessary that something should appear to have been paid, but the recipients of the shares could not or would not furnish any money for that purpose. Ramsey himself had no cash of his own to advance, but he went to the company's safe, of which he had the key, took out bonds, the property of the company, amounting to $150,000, pawned them to the same Groesbeck who had taken his former over-issue, and thus raised enough to pay ten per cent on the 9,500 shares. It is not easy to conceive a transaction more thoroughly iniquitous than this. It was a double fraud; it was intended to stuff the ballot-box with bogus votes, and make the stockholders pay the expenses of the cheat upon themselves out of their own funds.

The facts are these: The stock of the company had not been wholly issued. Mr. Ramsey and his friends feared the plans of the Fisk party to get possession of the road. They immediately, in a perfectly legal way, subscribed for 9,500 shares of stock, in the regular subscription books, which were in the hands of the regular officers of the company, and paid at once, as required by law, 10 per cent of the par value of the stock into the company's treasury, in precisely the same amount, and in precisely the same manner, as such subscriptions and such payments had been made ever since the first share of the stock had been issued. The 10 per cent amounted to $95,000. This amount was paid in cash with money borrowed from Mr. David Groesbeck, and the money was immediately deposited to the credit of the company in bank. To secure Mr. Groesbeck, Mr. Ramsey incautiously pledged to him some securities belonging to the company itself. But these securities were immediately replaced with others, before a word of complaint had been made by any person whatever, on the motion of Mr. Ramsey and Mr. Groesbeck themselves; and the securities of the company, which had first been so pledged did not remain so pledged more than a very few days. The remaining 90 per cent on the par value of the stock was paid in full as soon as it was called in by the company, and every cent of the money used in a lawful manner for the company's expenses; and not a word of complaint on the subject has ever since been heard from any party having any interest in the stock or the money. These points Mr. Black either knew or might have known. These points he has not stated. But he says, Mr. Ramsey "got together certain of his confederates secretly at his own house, and distributed among them certificates for 9,500 shares of stock, for which they had not paid, and did not mean to pay, a single cent." Where does Mr. Black gain this inmost consciousness of other men's intentions? Is he not bound to remember that some men may believe what he says, or writes, to be true, simply from his former official position? Can he presume that most persons will know that his statements on this matter rest only on the assertion of Mr. David Dudley Field? Before he gave the weight of his name to these statements, should he not have found them to be true? Are all things that Mr. Black says equally true with what he has written on this point? If he attacks other men's reputations with this lack of care, will his own reputation suffer nothing thereby? We have been, in this country, in the habit of believing what is said by an attorney-general of the United States.

This perfectly regular subscription to new stock, on which the entire par value was paid as soon as it was called in by the company, has been the heaviest gun in the whole Field armament. In Mr. Field's argument at the Rochester trial, the same points precisely came forward, as we have later heard from Mr. Black

and Mr. Curtis. It was a symphony, with Mr. Ramsey for the
theme ("Ramsey" without "Mr.," Mr. Field used always to
say), in about three movements. There was the midnight subscription, andante; the issue of the Groesbeck stock, allegro; and
the stealing of the books, scherzo; with a grand introductory
overture of praises for the virtuous "Church" party. The matter of the Groesbeck stock, which Mr. Black calls a "fraudulent
over-issue" by Mr. Ramsey, was not the case of an issue by Mr.
Ramsey at all, and was a perfectly fair legal transaction throughout, and was thus:

In the spring of 1868 the Albany & Susquehanna Railroad
was nearly built. There was still needed, to finish the road, a
large amount of money. The first-mortgage bonds of the company had all been placed. The full-paid capital stock of the company was selling in the market at about 20 per cent of its par
value, as the road was still unfinished, and it was entirely uncertain when the whole road could be in running order. At this
time Mr. Ramsey made efforts to get further advances of money
to finish the road. The company had still some second-mortgage
bonds, and some stock which had been issued to the subscribers
but afterward forfeited to the company for nonpayment of assessments, and which consequently was the lawful property of the
company, and could be sold by it. This forfeited stock was not at
this time issued by Mr. Ramsey, or by anyone else, for any price
at all. It was sold. It was not sold by Mr. Ramsey. It was sold by
the company, by a unanimous vote of its Board of Directors. It
was sold at 5 per cent above the then market price of full-paid
stock. And the resolution of the Board of Directors authorizing
this sale, passed at a meeting of the Board, where were present,
among others, Messrs. North, Leonard, and Everts, afterward
members of the "Fisk board," who were so fierce in abusing
Mr. Ramsey for this fraudulent "issue" of stock. It is well, under the circumstances, to give a copy of this resolution. It is as
follows:

Resolved, That the contract with David Groesbeck and others by the

President is hereby approved, providing for a loan of five hundred and sixty thousand dollars, upon eight hundred thousand dollars of the second mortgage bonds of the company, for eighteen months, with privilege or option to said Groesbeck and others of taking the bonds within fifteen months at eighty per cent, and two hundred and forty thousand dollars stock of the company, at twenty-five per cent, unless better terms can be obtained by the Finance Committee prior to the 10th of June instant.

No "better terms" were obtained by the Finance Committee. At the meeting when this resolution was passed, twelve out of the fourteen directors of the company were present. The resolution was passed unanimously. And Mr. David Groesbeck and others obtained their stock lawfully, by a *sale* from the Albany & Susquehanna Railroad Company, made under this resolution. And this is the sum and substance of the "fraudulent issue by Ramsey" of this fearful "Groesbeck stock." And behold, this is the only ground ever put forth for Mr. Ramsey's removal from his office as president, by the *ex parte* order of the Honorable George G. Barnard, obtained from that upright official by the upright firm of Mr. David Dudley Field. And it is this action of the Board of Directors that Judge Black calls "a fraudulent over-issue" by Mr. Ramsey. Should not country newspapers be called in to supply some epithets for Mr. Black? The eccentric Timothy Dexter wrote a book, with a few pages of commas, semicolons, and other punctuation, printed at the end of it, giving his reader full liberty to use them, as he or she might wish. Could not the same course be taken with a few pages of vituperative adjectives in the case of Mr. Black, and still with no risk of doing him wrong?

And the company's books were removed from the railway office, as everyone now knows, by the regular officers and the counsel of the company, who were the persons bound to protect them, for fear lest they might fall into the hands of James Fisk, Jr. Mr. Ramsey remembered well, as do many other men, former performances of Mr. Fisk and Mr. Field. It was then only two or three months since the Union Pacific Railroad Company had

had their experience of one of Mr. Fisk's "raids," wherein he had let loose his dogs of law on a corporation, and New York City had its first experience in judicial safe breaking. The books of the Susquehanna Company, it was thought, should not be exposed to the Erie manipulations. They were not kept in a tomb at any time. No one has ever been able to show, or has ever seriously, during all the time they were removed from the office, charged the making of a single false entry in those books, or the refusal to make a single entry which should have been made.

These matters thus far mentioned, the subscription to the new stock, the sale of the Groesbeck stock, and the removal of the books, all had something to do with the Susquehanna litigation. There was some reason in Mr. Black's discussing them. They had been previously discussed. But there is something very singular about Mr. Black's article. Mr. Black had never, as far as I am aware, had any quarrel with Mr. Ramsey. Mr. Ramsey has never wronged him in any way. Yet for some reason Mr. Black has gone out of his way to abuse Mr. Ramsey, and make a large number of statements about him which are wholly untrue, and which rest merely on the authority of Mr. David Dudley Field. It is necessary to make a quotation:

It was the great misfortune of the Albany and Susquehanna corporation to have trusted one Joseph H. Ramsey as its President and financial manager. He did not prove himself faithful. The bargains by which he raised money at usurious rates were not only disapproved by his constituents, they were indefensible on the score of common prudence. When his own interests were in conflict with the duties of his trust, he showed a lack of qualities even more important than sound judgment. He paid himself on one occasion $16,000 for services which he alleged he had rendered the company as its attorney. He made the bill and settled it, absolutely refusing to let the Finance Committee pass upon it. He made a contract on behalf of his corporation with an express company, in which he ruinously sacrificed the interests of the party he professed to represent; it turned out afterward that he was a partner in the express company. . . . Of such are the Albany rings. He ran for Congress once, and while he was a candidate he issued three thousand free passes over the road to as many electors, whose favor he sought to win at the expense of the company. At the time of his suspension from office he owed the company $20,000, which he had taken from its funds for his own purposes, on his own terms, and by his own leave. Whether he subsequently disgorged this money does not appear.

During the many years that Mr. Ramsey was connected with the Albany & Susquehanna Railroad, except in the one case when he pledged to Mr. Groesbeck bonds of the company, which were immediately replaced with other securities, and whereby the company suffered not one cent of damage, Mr. Ramsey was never indebted in the sum of one dollar to this railroad company. Not one word of evidence has ever been brought forward by anyone to show that he was. There have been merely irresponsible statements by persons having no knowledge whatever of the company's affairs. The books of the company have for a long time been in such a position that the truth or falsity of any statements as to the indebtedness of Mr. Ramsey could be easily found out. No one has ever yet proved that he owed one cent to the company, unless in the one instance mentioned. Mr. Field had, during the trial at Rochester, the full examination of the company's books for two weeks. He failed to find any evidence of any such indebtedness of Mr. Ramsey, but he did not for that reason cease asserting it. Mr. Ramsey never was a stockholder in any express company with whom he made a contract on behalf of the railroad. Mr. Ramsey never had a bill of sixteen thousand dollars "settled" in any way for his services to the company; and all bills allowed him have been paid in precisely the same way in which all other bills of the company were allowed and settled. Nor has any objection ever been made to any charge of Mr. Ramsey for his services, except by Mr. Fisk's friends and counsel.

And as for the charges of Mr. Ramsey's indebtedness to the Albany & Susquehanna Railroad Company in an amount of $20,000, the charge has been often denied, and in ways that must have been brought to Mr. Black's knowledge. Mr. Ramsey denied it under oath, and his affidavit long ago appeared in a printed pamphlet. No one has ever yet ventured under oath to make this charge. Two members of the Fisk party, who were directors with Mr. Ramsey, have made affidavits in these words: "I was then *informed* and believed, and still believe, that the books showed Joseph H. Ramsey to have overdrawn his account in an amount exceeding $20,000." The gentlemen who made this affidavit did not venture to swear by whom they were informed. It was possibly by Mr. David Dudley Field, as Mr. Black was. These gentlemen who thus made oath, however, had been directors of the company for an entire year, and had unlimited access to the books of the company during that time. Mr. David Dudley Field had his chance to examine the books as fully as he wished at the Rochester trial. He found nothing that he cared to use. He found no false entry or statement in them. Nor did he find any entry or statement of any kind in them that he or any other person has ever used against Mr. Ramsey. And still we find Mr. Black repeating this story, which has no truth in it.

What has been the reason of it? Suppose that Mr. Ramsey had made a contract with an express company, issued passes, allowed a claim of his own, and been in debt to the railroad company, precisely as Mr. Black says he had done? Suppose these things were all true? What had they to do with the "Great Lawsuit"? Suppose them, however, to be false, how is it with Mr. Black? When one charges a gentleman with "fabricating" stock, stealing bonds, and fraudulently issuing passes, mistake is unpardonable and impossible. Mr. Black is a man who knows—none better—the meanings of words. He knew what charges he made. He was bound to know they were true. He did not know that they were true. There had never been a particle of evidence to support any of them. Mr. Black, too, knows what evidence is. He knows, none better, how to test the truth of statements. He has not been deceived in these matters. He is too shrewd. And when charges of this kind are made knowingly, what is to be said of the motive? Nor can such charges be made without placing in great danger a reputation for truthfulness. Has Mr. Black nothing to lose in this respect, or has he no fear?

The Albany & Susquehanna Railroad is said to pass through lovely scenery. A ride over it would perhaps be enjoyable. But the sound "Susquehanna" must bring to many ears a feeling of dread. It is to be hoped that the literature of that railroad will be hereafter confined to stock ledgers and cash books, and not stray into reviews and magazines. But who is to be blamed for it? And surely no one would willingly have missed the "Great Lawsuit and a Field Fight." It is not history, indeed, but a most racy fiction.

BIBLIOGRAPHY

I. BIOGRAPHIES OF MEN WHOSE ARTICLES ARE REPRINTED OR QUOTED

Charles Francis Adams

Charles Francis Adams, 1835–1915; an autobiography. With a memorial address delivered November 17, 1915, by Henry Cabot Lodge. Boston, Houghton Mifflin Co., 1916. lx, 224 pages.

Henry Adams

Education of Henry Adams; an autobiography. Boston, Houghton Mifflin Co., 1918. x, 519 pages.

Francis C. Barlow

In memoriam. Francis Channing Barlow, 1834–1896. Published by the authority of the state of New York under the supervision of the New York Monuments Commission. Albany, J. B. Lyon Co., 1923. 136 pages.

Stickney, Albert
  Memorial of Francis C. Barlow.
  (Association of the Bar of the City of New York. Twenty-seventh annual report [1897], pp. 96–107.)

Jeremiah S. Black

Klingelsmith, Margaret C.
  Jeremiah Sullivan Black, 1810–1883.
  (Lewis, William D. Great American lawyers. Philadelphia, John C. Winston Co., 1909. VI, 3–73.)

Niles, Henry C.
  Jeremiah Sullivan Black and his influence on the law of Pennsylvania. A paper prepared for the meeting of the Pennsylvania Bar Association at Cambridge Springs, Pennsylvania, June 29, 1903. 72 pages.

Samuel Bowles

Merriam, George S.
    The life and times of Samuel Bowles. New York, Century Co., 1885.
    2 vols.

George T. Curtis

George Ticknor Curtis
    (Cyclopaedia of American biographies. II, 286–287.)

Albert Stickney

Wetmore, Edmund
    Memorial of Albert Stickney.
    (Association of the Bar of the City of New York. Year book, 1909,
    pp. 139–142.)

II. ON THE CHIEF ACTORS

George G. Barnard

Charges of the Bar Association of New York against Hon. George G.
    Barnard and Hon. Albert Cardozo, justices of the Supreme Court,
    and Hon. John H. McCunn, a justice of the Superior Court of the
    City of New York, and testimony thereunder taken before the Judi-
    ciary Committee of the Assembly of the State of New York, 1872.
    New York, John Polhemus, printed, 1872.
    3 vols. with separate index (88 pages).
    The Committee sat from February 19 to April 11, 1872.
Proceedings in the Court of Impeachment in the matter of the im-
    peachment of George G. Barnard, a justice of the Supreme Court
    of the State of New York. Albany, Weed, Parsons and Company,
    1874. 3 vols.
    The Court sat from May 13 to August 19, 1872.

Daniel Drew

Minnigerode, Meade
    Daniel Drew, the old man of the Street.
    (Minnigerode, M. Certain rich men. New York, G. P. Putnam's sons,
    1927, pp. 83–100.)
White, Bouck
    The book of Daniel Drew. A glimpse of the Fisk-Gould-Tweed Ré-
    gime from the inside. New York, Doubleday, Page & Co., 1910. x, 423
    pages.

David Dudley Field

Barlow, Francis C.
Facts for Mr. Field. The full story of Erie litigation. (*New York Tribune*, March 7, 8, 9, 1871.)
Three letters to the editor of the *Tribune*, filling eight columns, dated March 1, 2, and 3, respectively.
Field's three-column answer appeared in the issue of March 13, and called out a six-column rejoinder by Barlow in the *Tribune* of March 24.
The Erie litigation; a history of a year's lawsuits.
(*New York Tribune*, January 31, 1871, p. 2.)
Mr. Field's answer, dated January 31, appeared in the issue of February 2, 1871.
Field, Henry M.
The life of David Dudley Field. New York, Charles Scribner's sons, 1898. xvii, 361 pages.
Hoy, Helen K.
David Dudley Field, 1805–1894.
(Lewis, William D. Great American lawyers. Philadelphia, John C. Winston Co., 1908. V, 125–174.)
The Lawyer and his clients. The rights and duties of lawyers; the rights and duties of the press; the opinions of the public. Correspondence of Messrs. David Dudley and Dudley Field, of the New York bar, with Mr. Samuel Bowles, of the *Springfield Republican*. [Springfield, Republican Office, 1871.] 21 pages.
Cover title: David Dudley Field and his clients.
Letters dated December 27, 1870—January 28, 1871.
[Letter of David Dudley Field to the Editor of the *Westminster Review*, dated New York, February 13, 1871.]
(*Westminster Review*, 95: 589–592, April 1, 1871.)
An answer to Henry Adams' "New York Gold Conspiracy."

James Fisk, Jr.

Fuller, Robert H.
Jubilee Jim: The life of Colonel James Fisk, Jr. New York, Macmillan Co., 1928. viii, 566 pages.
McAlpine, R. W.
The life and times of Col. James Fisk, Jr., being a full and impartial account of the remarkable career of a most remarkable man; together with sketches of all the important personages with whom he was thrown in contact, such as Drew, Vanderbilt, Gould, Tweed,

etc., and a financial history of the country for the last three years, embracing, also, the lives of Helen Josephine Mansfield, the enchantress, and Edward S. Stokes, the assassin. New York, New York Book Co. [1872]. 504 pages.

Minnigerode, Meade
Jim Fisk, the mountebank.
(Minnigerode, M. Certain rich men. New York, G. P. Putnam's sons, 1927, pp. 189–210.)

Stafford, Marshall
The life of James Fisk, Jr., a full and accurate narrative of his career, his great enterprises, and his assassination. New York [for the author], Polhemus & Pearson, printers, 1872. 326, xvi pages.

Jay Gould

The busy life of Mr. Jay Gould, as related by himself to a committee of the United States Senate. New York, American News Company [1883]. 30 pages.
> Preface dated, New York, September, 1883. Mr. Gould testified before the Senatorial Committee on Education and Labor, in New York, on September 5, 1883.

Halstead, Murat, and Beale, J. Frank, Jr.
Life of Jay Gould. How he made his millions. The marvellous career of the man who, in thirty years, accumulated the colossal fortune of $100,000,000; by far exceeding in rapidity and volume that of any other man in the history of the world . . . to which are added sketches of the great money kings of the present day more or less associated with him, by W. Fletcher Johnson. Philadelphia, Edgewood Publishing Co., 1892. 490 pages.

Minnigerode, Meade
Jay Gould, the wizard of Wall Street.
(Minnigerode, M. Certain rich men. New York, G. P. Putnam's sons, 1927, pp. 135–187.)

Myers, Gustavus
[The Gould fortune.]
(Myers, G. History of the great American fortunes. Chicago, C. H. Kerr & Co., 1910, Vol. II, Chaps. 9–12, pp. 281–368; Vol. III, Chaps. 3–4, pp. 63–101.)

White, Trumbull
The wizard of Wall Street and his wealth, or the life and deeds of Jay Gould. Chicago, Mid-Continent Publishing Co., 1892. 312 pages.

Youngman, Anna
  The fortune of Jay Gould.
  (Youngman, A. The economic causes of great fortunes. Chicago,
  1909, Chap. 3, pp. 55–99.)

Cornelius Vanderbilt

Minnigerode, Meade
  Cornelius Vanderbilt, the Commodore.
  (Minnigerode, M. Certain rich men. New York, G. P. Putnam's sons,
  1927, pp. 101–133.)
Moody, John
  The Commodore and the New York Central.
  (Moody, J. The railroad builders. New Haven, Yale University Press,
  1919, pp. 20–46.)
Myers, Gustavus
  [The Vanderbilt fortune.]
  (Myers, G. History of the great American fortunes. Chicago, C. H.
  Kerr & Co., 1910, Vol. 2, Chaps. 3–8, pp. 95–280.)
Smith, Arthur D. Howden
  Commodore Vanderbilt. An epic of American achievement. New
  York, Robert M. McBride & Co., 1927. 339 pages.

III. ERIE RAILWAY

Adams, Charles Francis, Jr.
  The Erie Railroad row considered as an episode in court. Boston,
  Little, Brown & Co., 1868. 46 pages.
  (Reprinted from *American Law Review*, 3: 41–86, October, 1868.)
Crouch, George
  Another Chapter of Erie. New York, 1869. 48 pages.
Erie campaigns in 1868: or, How they manage things on the New York
  Stock Exchange.
  (*Fraser's Magazine*, 79: 569–584, May, 1869.)
Livingston, John
  The Erie Railway: its history and management from April 24, 1832
  to July 13, 1875, prepared from the undisputed testimony of Legis-
  lative and Judicial records, and official documents which, according
  to familiar and well-known principles of law, prove themselves . . .
  New York, John Polhemus, 1875. 92, xxxvi pages.
Moody, John
  The Erie Railroad.
  (Moody, J. The railroad builders. New Haven, Yale University Press,
  1919, pp. 64–94.)

Mott, Edward Harold

Between the ocean and the lakes; the story of Erie. New York, Ticker Publishing Co., 1908. ix, 524 pages.

Report of the select committee of the Senate, appointed April 10, 1868, in relation to members receiving money from railway companies. 155 pages.

(New York. Senate Documents, 92d Session, 1869. Document No. 52.)

Report, pp. 1–13.

Testimony, pp. 15–155.

Testimony taken, April, 1868—February 22, 1869.

Report dated, March 10, 1869.

Committee members: M. Hale, Francis S. Thayer, Asher P. Nichols.

[Stickney, Albert]

The Erie Railway and the English stock.

(*American Law Review*, 6: 230–254, January, 1872.)

IV. THE GOLD CONSPIRACY

Boutwell, George S.

Black Friday, September 24, 1869.

(Boutwell, G. S. Reminiscences of sixty years in public affairs. New York, McClure, Phillips & Co., 1902. II, 164–182.)

Gold panic investigation. Report (of) the Committee on Banking and Currency, having been directed by a resolution of the House of Representatives, passed December 13, 1869, "to investigate the causes that led to the unusual and extraordinary fluctuations of gold in the city of New York, from the 21st to the 27th of September, 1869." 483 pages.

(U. S. House of Representatives. Forty-first Congress, 2d Session. Report No. 31.)

Report, pp. 1–23.

Testimony, pp. 25–459.

Views of the Minority, pp. 461–479.

Index, pp. 481–483.

James A. Garfield, Chairman of Committee.

Testimony taken in Washington, D.C., January 15–February 15, 1870. Views of minority, dated February 28, 1870.

Report ordered printed, March 1, 1870.